TEAC

GW00384411

COMPAR... LINGUISTICS

Comparative linguistics adopts an historical approach to the study of languages. It traces the evolution of languages and, by comparing one with another, establishes relationships between them. This book is intended as an introductory survey of comparative linguistics and is designed for language students who do not yet wish to confine their studies to any of the specialist fields of the academic linguist. It covers historical linguistics as well as comparative linguistics proper, and also outlines some aspects of general linguistics that are important to the historical and comparative study of language and languages. The text is divided into four parts: Part I introduces the study of language, Part II deals with sounds, Part III with grammar and Part IV with meaning. Keyed exercises are provided in several of the chapters, and a comprehensive bibliography is included as an appendix for those who wish to study linguistics in greater depth.

This is a lively, witty and remarkably comprehensive introduction to linguistics, phonology, accidence, sentence structure and semantics, providing also (with the aid of maps and tables) an excellent account of the distribution of the great languages of the world.

Times Literary Supplement

TEACH YOURSELF BOOKS

COMPARATIVE LINGUISTICS

Robert Lord

ST. PAUL'S HOUSE   WARWICK LANE
LONDON EC4P 4AH

First printed 1966
Second edition 1974

ISBN 0 340 15152 8

Printed and bound in Great Britain
for The English Universities Press Ltd
by Richard Clay (The Chaucer Press) Ltd, Bungay, Suffolk

Contents

Preface to the Second Edition   9

Part I: Introduction

1 The Nature of Language   15
2 Language, Community and Dialect   25
3 The Diversity of Language: A Geographical Survey
   of the World's Languages   41
4 Language in Time   61
5 Writing   90
6 The Comparative Method and the Scope of
   Comparative Linguistics   106

Part II: Sounds

7 Sounds in Language   127
8 Sound Change   137
9 Historical Phonology   152
10 Further Notes on Historical Phonology   164

Part III: Grammar

11 Grammatical Analysis   195
12 Grammatical Structure in Evolution   221
13 Grammar in Comparative Linguistics   236

Part IV: Meaning

14 The Study of Meaning   277
15 Words   288
16 Semantic Structure   299
17 Semantic Change   313

Appendices

Suggestions for Further Reading   347
Key to the Exercises   352

Index   359

**To My Students,
Past and Present**

Preface to the Second Edition

This book was begun at a time when no 'work on historical or comparative linguistics, either sufficiently introductory in nature or comprehensive enough in scope, was available in English. Since the early 1960s things have changed, and there are now several introductory surveys in existence. In preparing this second edition I have attempted neither to emulate them nor to do something entirely different. Instead, I have retained the general structure and style of the earlier edition, though not without taking steps to remedy some of the more serious omissions and shortcomings. I have, of course, to thank my publishers for granting me the margin of extra space in which to do this.

My reasons for retaining my earlier approach are various. The book has proved useful in its earlier form as a 'textbook'; and it is for this reason that I have retained without cuts the more routine technicalities of Chapters 10 and 13. Furthermore, the book has been found entertaining as well as informative by a very wide range of readers, many of whom were interested in language in general. This new edition is, I suppose, more sober in style, but I have made not too many concessions to the current taste for the impersonal and the heavygoing.

My title *Comparative Linguistics*, as before, embraces *historical* as well as *comparative* linguistics proper. The book does nevertheless attempt to provide an outline survey of at least a selection of the many aspects of *general* linguistics, which have had increasing relevance to the historical and comparative study of language and languages. These outlines can be supplemented without too much difficulty by reference to the titles given in the 'Suggestions for Further Reading' at the end of the book.

I wish to record my debt to all those readers from every corner of the world who have taken the trouble to write to me with all kinds of suggestions, queries, questions, comments and corrections. I hope that they will come by this second edition, which is sufficiently different in content to justify a fresh reading.

Acknowledgments

Thanks are due to the following publishers who have very kindly allowed me to use various passages and quotations: Faber & Faber Ltd., W. D. Elcock's *The Romance Languages*, T. Burrow's *The Sanskrit Language*, Owen Barfield's *Poetic Diction*, and Andre Martinet's *Elements of General Linguistics* (trans. E. Palmer); Methuen & Co. Ltd., Owen Barfield's *History in English Words*; Basil Blackwell Ltd., Professor Ullmann's *Semantics: An Introduction to the Science of Meaning*, and Otto Jespersen's *Growth and Structure of the English Language*; Oxford University Press, Joseph Wright's *Old English Grammar*, the same author's *Grammar of the Gothic Language*, E. V. Gordon's *An Introduction to Old Norse*, J. R. Firth's *Tongues of Men* and *Speech*, and the same author's *Papers in Linguistics*; W. Heffer & Sons Ltd., Daniel Jones' *An Outline of English Phonetics*; Rupert Hart-Davis Ltd., Edward Sapir's *Language*; Yale University Press, E. H. Sturtevant's *An Introduction to Linguistic Science*; Peter Owen Ltd., Ferdinand de Saussure's *Course in General Linguistics*; Allen & Unwin Ltd., Otto Jespersen's *Language: Its Nature, Development and Origins*, the same author's *Mankind, Nation and Individual*, Mario A. Pei's *The World's Chief Languages*, and Leonard Bloomfield's *Language*; John Wiley & Sons Inc. and the M.I.T. Press, B. L. Whorf's *Language, Thought and Reality*; the M.I.T. Press, Noam Chomsky's *Aspects of the Theory of Syntax*, and L. S. Vygotsky's *Thought and Language* (trans. E. Hanfmann and G. Vakar); Grune & Stratton Inc., Kurt Goldstein's *Language and Language Disturbances*; Penguin Books Ltd., James Thurber's collection *Alarms and Diversions*, and H. Frankfort and others' *Before Philosophy*; Longman Group Ltd., A. McIntosh and M. A. K. Halliday's *Patterns of Language*; Holt, Rinehart & Winston Inc., H. A. Gleason's *Introduction to Descriptive Linguistics*; Hutchinson Publishing Group, David Diringer's *The Alphabet*; University of Texas Press, W. P. Lehmann and

Y. Malkiel's *Directions for Historical Linguistics: A Symposium*;
Harper & Row, D. Hymes (ed.) *Language in Culture and Society*;
The Bodley Head Ltd., James Joyces' *Ulysses*; Chatto & Windus
Ltd., William Faulkner's *Intruder in the Dust*; University of
Chicago Press, Zelling Harris' *Structural Linguistics*; Edinburgh
University Press, K. H. Jackson's *Language and History in Early
Britain*; McGraw-Hill Book Company, Clyde Kluckhohn's
Mirror for Man; Routledge & Kegan Paul Ltd., Karl Popper's
Conjectures and Refutations: Growth of Scientific Knowledge;
University of Wisconsin Press, L. Hjelmslev's *Prolegomena to a
Theory of Language*.

My indebtedness to the labours of others will I hope be apparent
throughout. I have endeavoured to acknowledge all such debts
in passing.

Part I

INTRODUCTION

1 The Nature of Language

How odd it is that for most people 'language' is scarcely a concept at all, let alone a familiar object. And yet—there is no one who is not aware that he speaks a particular language, be it English or Bantu, Welsh or Afghan, or one of the many thousands of other alternatives. We all *use* language all day and every day, and, as we all know, there are those millions of foreigners who will persist in speaking languages that no one (i.e. you or I) can understand. How peculiar that so many individuals, often well-informed in other respects, have only the haziest notion of what language might be and are reduced to mental incoherence when asked to consider what language means for *them*.

My own limited experiments have told me that only the most extraneous notions arise in people's minds when confronted with the question: 'What is language?' Uppermost for many is a *particular* language, usually a foreign language, French, German or Italian, perhaps; frequently, I might add, not unmixed with unpleasant associations of the school elementary textbook grammar —irregular verbs, declensions and the rest. Urged to probe a little deeper, the subjects of my experiments would more often begin to hedge and exhibit the usual signs of discomfort, covering their retreat with a variety of platitudes: 'Language? I've never really thought about it, but I suppose it's basically speech, talking.' 'And what about writing then?' (Momentary confusion.) 'Writing, I suppose "writing" is speech when it's written down.' 'Language? Language is communication.' 'All I know about language is that it's made up of all those pronouns, verbs, clauses and so on that we had to learn at school, but goodness only knows what *they* are.' 'Language is something you learn as a child,' and so on and so forth.

In case anyone suspects that I am making fun of the layman, let me immediately leap to his defence and admit at once that of all concepts there is none more slippery and elusive than language. There is simply no pinning it down. Language undoubtedly exists, but what this word represents is by no means easy to say.

To *define* language is not necessarily the best approach. Strangely, the only definition that stands up is one that is both negative as well as general enough to accommodate all but the most extreme dissent. I am referring to the one put forward by the

American linguist and anthropologist Edward Sapir over fifty years ago. Sapir modestly suggested what he called a 'serviceable definition': 'Language is a purely human and non-instinctive method of communicating ideas, emotions and desires by means of a system of voluntarily produced symbols.'[1] The key words in this definition are: *human*, *non-instinctive*, *communicating*, *system* and *symbols*.

Despite the work of Von Frisch on communication among bees and numerous investigations since, there is still no real evidence to challenge Sapir's contention that language is restricted to human beings. And few linguists would dispute his claim that language does not arise from instinct, even though there is accumulating evidence that language, if not instinctive, is at any rate *innate* in human beings. The other key words I shall be touching upon shortly.

The various and surprisingly diverse ways of describing and defining language usually leave the beginner bewildered.

To begin with, the newcomer is sometimes disconcerted by his discovery that language is different from what he had supposed. He has usually believed, for example, that the most important feature of language is *vocal sound*. He can readily be forgiven for making this assumption since language, after all, is pre-eminently *spoken* language, people actually *speaking* to one another. But the more deeply he goes into the question of the nature of language, the more he finds that the vocal, acoustic—physical—aspects of language are of peripheral interest to the linguist.

Something our newcomer may not have thought about at all, on the other hand, is the *biological* aspect of language. This aspect is one that has become increasingly important, especially in America. But as long ago as the 1930s the British linguist J. R. Firth was urging that speech be regarded as 'a grouped pattern of *bodily* movements which can be *heard*' (my italics). Firth was firmly wedded to the view of man as a linguistic animal. In his famous *Adam the speaking animal*[2] there is a passage which runs: 'Let us begin by regarding man as inseparable from the world in which he lives. He is just a part of it . . . This applies to man's most important social action, the disturbance of air and other people's ears by means of bodily utterance . . . In dealing

---

[1] Sapir, E., *Language* (New York, 1921), p. 8.
[2] Firth, J. R., *The Tongues of Men* (London, 1937), pp. 19–23.

with the voice of man we must not fall into the prevalent habit of separating it from the whole bodily behaviour of man and regarding it merely as a sort of outward symbol of inward private thoughts.' Since Firth's time the boundary between linguistics and biology has been growing less and less obvious.

One point on which nearly all linguists agree is that language is a function of our social relationships, a function of the way we live. Like social etiquette, public ceremonies, marriage rituals, language is a system of arbitrary social *conventions* and social *symbols*. It is by convention that a European wears black at a funeral, or raises his right hand in military salute; it is equally by convention that I call the piece of furniture I am writing or typing at a *desk* rather than, say, a *bench* or *writing furniture*. It is by a similar kind of common agreement that the London 'city gent' wears a bowler hat and a certain kind of suit, and carries a tightly rolled umbrella. Again, it is by just this kind of common agreement that the very same Englishman says *They like pickled cucumbers* rather than *Cucumbers pickled like they*.

Every community, however insignificant, however 'primitive', has its own fully-fledged set of language conventions (along with its own peculiar social conventions). The Swiss linguist Ferdinand de Saussure was so impressed by this fact that he was convinced that language itself (like Rousseau's body-politic) had come into existence 'by virtue of a contract signed by the members of a community'. Moreover, a speaker of a language deviates from the social linguistic norm only at his peril. The penalties for habitual deviation are as evident as they are severe. It is possible that the people I happen to know will tolerate the use of *stuffed intestine* in place of *sausage* (after all, why not call a stuffed intestine a stuffed intestine?), but if I go into a shop and ask for a pound of stuffed intestines I will either get a black look, or a laugh, or quite possibly snubbed.

To come into being, a language, any language, requires a 'transmitter' (most usually a speaker) and a 'receiver' (in most cases a listener), whose roles are reversible. The transmitter–receiver circuit is the basis of all linguistic communication. This applies even if someone is talking to himself, in which case the circuit is 'internalised'. This communication circuit is part of the set of social conventions known as language.

Like clothes, taste, beliefs, mores, music and fashion, language

varies from region to region—a further corroboration of its
social basis. The folk music and folk dress of Eastern Europe
(and many other parts of the world) show the same variation
from place to place as dialect. The differences are spontaneous
and unconscious. Origins are lost in tradition. 'Speech is a human
activity that varies without assignable limit as we pass from social
group to social group, because it is a purely historical heritage of
the group, the product of long-continued social usage. It varies as
all creative effort varies—not as consciously, perhaps, but nonetheless as truly as do the religions, the beliefs, the customs, and
the acts of different peoples . . . Speech is a non-instinctive,
acquired, "cultural" function.'[1] The term generally used to
embrace the total group of speakers subscribing to a particular set
of linguistic conventions at any one time is *speech community*.
The American linguist Leonard Bloomfield defined speech community with sublime simplicity as 'a group of people who interact
by means of speech'. I shall have more to say about speech
communities in later chapters.

Now let us switch to a completely different angle, and talk
about *signs*. We all know perfectly well how to recognise a sign.
There are thousands of them all around us: traffic signs, shop
signs, direction signs, mathematical signs, and so forth. What
perhaps not everyone knows is that there are also *linguistic signs*.
In actual fact, language may be thought of as a *system* of linguistic
signs. Many linguists have laid great stress on this; and Saussure
made it the basis for his proposed *semiology*, which was to be a
'science of signs' with language but part of it.

Let us begin by taking an example of a *non*-linguistic sign: an
ordinary international road sign (in diagram above). Like any other

[1] Sapir, *op. cit.* p. 4.

sign, this particular road sign has two aspects. The first of these aspects arises directly from the visual symbol itself. Let us call this aspect the *signifier*. The second aspect is what the sign *means*, its *signification*. The visual symbol (signifier) conveys the meaning or message being signalled, in this instance NO LEFT TURN.

Traffic signs, in common with other signs, are conventional and arbitrary. Although the signal in this case is clear enough visually, it has its precise meaning only for someone familiar with the highway code. The simple fact is that alternatives could have been chosen by international agreement; hence the use of the term 'arbitrary'. Has the reader ever asked himself, I wonder, why a traffic light at RED should signal STOP rather than GO?

Linguistic signs resemble traffic and other non-linguistic signs to the extent that they (i) combine the twin aspects *signifier* and *signification*, and (ii) are arbitrary and conventional.

In linguistic signs the signifier is represented by the vocal or by the graphic component: for example, the graphic expression W-O-O-D or T-A-B-L-E. The signification, on the other hand, is what the 'signifier signifies'; in these instances, usually a substance or an article of furniture. We can call this signification the *semantic content*.

It is at this point that the linguistic sign starts to look rather complicated. Non-linguistic signs are generally unambiguous. A NO LEFT TURN sign can *only* mean 'Don't turn left'. But such absence of ambiguity is *rarely* the case with linguistic signs. Take, for example, W-O-O-D. This can mean in English at least two completely different things: (i) timber and (ii) a tract of land occupied by trees. The arbitrariness of these meanings can easily be shown by looking at the (signifier) equivalents in other languages. A glance at the table below will show the reader how arbitrary the relation between signifier and signification can be:

Signifi-cation :	TIMBER	FIBROUS SUBSTANCE	TREE	TRACT OF LAND etc.	
				(small)	(large)
(English)	timber	wood	tree	wood	forest
(German)	Bauholz	Holz	Baum	Wald	Wald
(French)	bois	bois	arbre	bois	forêt
(Russian)	les	derevo	derevo	les	les
(Turkish)	kereste	ahsab/agac	ahsab/agac	orman	orman

Comparative linguistics would be much less of a problematic science than it is if this kind of arbitrariness did not occur. But, as I have already said, arbitrariness is the rule, not the exception. There is, however, one very important compensation. It is just because of their arbitrariness that linguistic signs can tell us a great deal about the cultures of the various speech communities. 'Every language is a special way of looking at the world and interpreting experience. Concealed in the structure of each different language are a whole set of unconscious assumptions about the world and life in it.'[1]

There are some striking differences between linguistic and non-linguistic signs that I ought perhaps to draw the reader's attention to. In the first place, linguistic signs are often *complex*. To take just one example, the English linguistic sign *disc-jockey* has a rather particular meaning. It looks at first to be composed of the two signs *disc* and *jockey*. But when we add these together we find that the total meaning 'a man who broadcasts and hence promotes sales of pop records' is not closely related either to *disc* (which in British English at any rate does not usually mean 'gramophone record') or to *jockey*, where the connection is even more remote. Language is always practising this kind of alchemy. Sometimes (as in semaphore) the meaning of composite signs is dependent on the order in which the components are arranged. *Age-old* does not have anything like the same meaning as *old age*; and an *off day* suggests something quite contrary to *day off*. A second point that should be made is that linguistic signs depend for their efficacy on *context*. Without context a linguistic sign cannot mean anything for certain. W-O-O-D alone cannot tell us *which* meaning is indicated. We need contexts such as *This house is made of wood* or *Babes in the Wood*; only then will the meaning come across unambiguously. The exclamation *Fire!* can mean different things according to whether we are in the vicinity of a rifle range or in a block of offices. In these cases, the ambiguity is limited by a non-linguistic context, or environment. A third and crucial difference, to my mind, is that linguistic signs are *creative*, *flexible* and *adaptable*. If I am travelling on horseback across a stretch of the Australian bush and come upon our NO LEFT TURN sign, miles from the nearest road, I will not take it to mean 'No

[1] Kluckhohn, C., *Mirror for Man* (New York, 1949), p. 159.

boomerangs may be thrown here'; instead I will suppose that someone has been playing a silly joke. The linguistic sign by contrast shows a mercurial mobility. A poet or a commercial advertiser depends very largely on this. But I do not need to be either of these. A friend enters my house and finds me sitting cross-legged in the middle of the floor beating away at the typewriter. My friend asks: 'Why don't you use your desk?' I reply: 'But this is my desk. I don't have any other.' No amount of argument can upset the correctness of my use of the word 'desk' in this context. What has happened is that the sign D-E-S-K, which usually denotes a piece of furniture for writing on or reading at, has been applied with the greatest of ease to an area of floor. Only our linguistic signs are capable of such breathtaking adaptability. And, what is more, language would die if this process were interfered with.

At this point a certain amount of recapitulation is called for. But I shall take a slightly different route this time, using an example from Edward Sapir. To illustrate the complexity of language Sapir takes the word *house*: 'The word *house*,' he says, 'is not a linguistic fact if by it is meant merely the acoustic effect produced on the ear by its constituent consonants and vowels, pronounced in a certain order; nor the motor processes and tactile feelings which make up the articulation of the word; nor the visual perception on the part of the hearer of this articulation; nor the visual perception of the word "house" on the written or printed page; nor the motor processes and tactile feelings which enter into the writing of the word; nor the memory of any or all of these experiences. It is only when these, and possibly still other, associated experiences are automatically associated with the image of a house that they begin to take on the nature of a symbol, a word, an element of language.'[1]

There are still more rivers to cross; for the word 'house' may not be abandoned as a complex symbol, shelved, and left at that. If we look a little closer we discover that such a symbol, if it were no more than a symbol, would be of use to describe a particular house only. Further consideration reveals that 'house' may be used in a universal sense to cover a range of houses, or any house, or all houses. For philosophers no less than linguists, this is a

[1] Sapir, *op. cit.* pp. 11–12.

thorny problem. 'The world of our experiences must be enormously *simplified* and *generalised* before it is possible to make a symbolic inventory of all our experiences of things and relations and this inventory is imperative before we can convey ideas. The elements of language, the symbols that ticket off experience, must therefore be associated with whole groups, delimited classes, of experience rather than with the single experiences themselves.' (My italics.)

This introduces a long-established but often neglected set of facts about language. For it is language indeed that classifies our experience of the real world, as well as our potentialities for coping with it. Any 'language' that fails to attain this level is hardly worth the name. A language with no inventory of 'experiences of things and relations' is not really a language at all. Indian smoke signals, West African drum beats, various gesticulations might be said to provide ingredients for or to supplement language, but they do not in themselves constitute a language.

But language is no mere inventory. Inventory contains the assumption that the world of our experience is somehow already given to us as a set of discrete parts, ready only to be labelled. The notion of language as a catalogue is based on the naïve idea that the world is ordered, prior to perception by man, into perfectly distinct categories of objects, each of which necessarily receives its appropriate designation in each language. Language is very far from being a carbon copy of reality. It is itself a *basic mode of classification*.

The capacity for abstraction immanent in all natural languages makes possible the most breathtaking cognitive 'leaps'. *Blonde* as often as not signifies a particular colour of hair, or even a particular type of woman; but equally the term *blonde* can with supreme effortlessness refer to the entire species of blonde women, to all blondes that have ever lived, real or imaginary. The far-reaching implications of such linguistically innocuous statements as *Gentlemen prefer blondes* are not always apparent. The point of such statements, of course, is that they are meant to be witty, or funny, or entertaining in some way. They are not meant to predict with even the slightest degree of certainty *which* gentleman prefers *which* blonde. It is seldom realised, though, to what an extent language in everyday usage relies on generalisation and every kind of conceptual *tour de force*. Language makes it only too easy for us to refer to remote past or future; to places near or far away; to worlds of fantasy inhabited by creatures sometimes more real than real; to inconceivable scientific abstractions; to an infinite variety of situations mostly outside our range of experience. Language enables us not only to perpetrate hosts of harmless generalisations like *Gentlemen prefer blondes* but also totally gratuitous and pointless assertions of the kind: *There are no blondes on the planet Jupiter*. A statement such as the latter is so unobjectionable or so pointless that most people would simply ignore it, not because it is unverifiable but because it is a sample of the kind of things only silly people say.

A function of language that is sometimes underrated is its power to transmit, geographically and historically, moral values, beliefs, prejudices, customs, skills and so on. Language is not only the cement, ballast—and poison—between nations; it is also the living link between the generations. Learning to talk is also to bring into play a whole gamut of social usage. Every word I use, every idiom, the deadest cliché, is impregnated with history. In a very real sense we are all trapped within the cultural mesh of our own language. An Englishman of an older generation may have reached the melancholy conclusion that there are no gentlemen outside his own country, without being at all aware that the semantic associations belonging to *gentleman* and *gentlemanly* are peculiar to the English language, with no exact counterparts to form a single concept elsewhere. All languages condition, and are in turn conditioned by, every imaginable thing that goes on or has gone on in the community that uses it. To find out how a nation ticks we need to learn a very great deal about its language or languages. Its laws, ways, institutions, economy, outlook, foibles and delusions can only be understood through the prism of language.

The end of the problem we started out with—that of describing language—is even now not in sight. The English language, as indeed any other of the world's great languages, is far more than the language of a particular community. It is an all-embracing thing with a very capacious as well as capricious life of its own; the accumulated wealth created by individuals of all kinds and forged out of imagination, experience, character and humour. At the one extreme stands a Shakespeare; at the other countless anonymous individuals throughout all the ages stretching back into the remotest past. It is this very quality of language that renders it very much more than a function of society and tradition. For language is a great living work of art in whose fibres and veins we live whenever we speak, think or write.

2 Language, Community and Dialect

We now turn to what promises to be a far less thorny problem.

So far, we have been considering language *per se*; now we are going to turn our attention to *languages*. Even if the reader had no idea about language, and had never really thought about it until now, he has probably never been in doubt about what a language is, even if he speaks only one. He knows perfectly well that English, French, Italian, Greek, Hungarian, Japanese, for example, are all *languages*. Each of them is *a language*. To prove it you have only to drop into almost any bookshop or record store. On sale you may find *Portuguese the With-it Way, Brush Up Your Icelandic, Don't Be Beaten by Cantonese, Hindi in 40 Painless Doses* and scores of equally enticing—or daunting—titles.

As if to demonstrate once and for all the tautological pointlessness of this whole discussion, let us begin by taking two fairly ordinary specimens of English:[1]

(1) Hin sed den, 'Ma, a we in lib?' Him sie, 'Mi no nuo, mi pikini, bot duon luk fi hin niem hahd, or eni wie in a di wohld an yu kal di niem, hin hie unu.' Him sed, 'Wel Ma, mi want im hie mi an nuo mi.' 'Lahd nuo, masa! Duo no kal di niem, hin wi kom kil yu!' Him sie, 'Wel Ma, hin wi haf fi kil mi.'

(2) Nah Juabz midlin thik layk, bur iyd a ad ta by a diyal thika nat ta noh at tha wa sumat rang tweh at shu wa prehchin on, an soh i lat pehpa tuml ontat flua an i sat thiyr an gehpt wol shu stopt fa briyath, an then i sez, 'Wot tha hek az ta ageht on, las? Iz that sumat up a sumat?'

Has something gone wrong with my typewriter? Has the typesetter had a brainstorm? I expect you are wondering ... No. Both these passages are indeed English. It is just that they are not *standard* English. The first is Creole English from Jamaica, a distinct and recognised dialect, not a 'debased' English. The second is English from Yorkshire. (In case the reader cannot

[1] I have taken the examples from Randolph Quirk's *The English Language and Images of Matter* (London, 1972), p. 48.

decipher them, a 'translation' is given at the foot of page 29.)
They are, as I said earlier, not particularly outlandish, and are
representative samples of an extraordinary variety of different
speech norms and dialects of English. They are scattered not only
over the ex-British colonial areas of the globe, or missionised
areas of the Pacific and South-east Asia, but are also to be found
only a few dozen miles from London, the town in which standard
English originated, and even inside that metropolis itself.

It transpires, then, that *a language* is no more straightforward a
matter than *language* itself. The difference is that the question of
determining when a language is or is not a language raises a quite
distinct and separate set of problems. I quote from H. A.
Gleason:[1] 'There is no agreed meaning, except for a general feeling that languages are somehow more distinct than dialects:
languages are different kinds of speech; dialects are mere varieties
of languages. Nothing as vague as this can be useful as the basis of
a scientific enumeration of languages. It would be quite defensible
if linguists would take it upon themselves to redefine the term
with sufficient precision so that later linguists would be able to
understand with some exactness just what is meant. Unfortunately, the problem involves a great deal more than definition of
terms. The very nature of language is such that the problem of
classification into such categories as language and dialect is
intrinsically difficult or impossible.'

The status (or non-status) of a language is often more easily
settled by reference to cultural and social, even to political and
economic, factors than to linguistic ones. The layman's innocuous
questions like: 'Is Walloon[2] really French?' 'Can Catalan[3] be
regarded as a language in its own right, or is it a dialect of
Spanish?' 'Is Ukrainian the language spoken by the inhabitants
of the southern parts of European Russia?' 'Is Chinese really a
single language, or is it a group of dialects?' 'Do black Americans
of the Southern United States really speak English, or should they
be regarded as a separate language minority group?' raise all
kinds of intimidating difficulties. To be sure, the linguist can
proffer opinions, but they are likely to carry less weight than the

---

[1] Gleason, H. A., *An Introduction to Descriptive Linguistics* (New York,
1961), p. 441.
[2] The major French dialect of Belgium.
[3] Spoken in Catalonia in North-eastern Spain.

opinions of politicians and policy-makers. Moreover, they are frequently more satisfactorily answered by sociologists and anthropologists.

It is not surprising, then, that *comparing* languages is a somewhat hazardous undertaking. Too often, comparatists have worked on the tacit assumption that languages can be identified and listed; and that they can hence be described and compared.

Even if we temporarily put these difficulties aside, we are sometimes making meaningless comparisons. If I compare English with French, or Arabic, or Chinese, that is perfectly valid; for all these languages are associated with distinct and well-established cultures, with developed and long-standing literatures, with extensive cultural and political influence over large areas of the globe. But to compare a heterogeneous and culturally complex language like English, or any of the three languages just listed, with a restricted and relatively homogeneous dialect such as Hopi or Eskimo is like comparing a city such as New York to a Dahomey village. But an even more disturbing question poses itself: Which *variety* of English—since there are so many—should the comparatist take as one of the 'terms' of his comparison? In their investigation carried out at University College, London, Quirk and Svartik[1] found not only a wide tolerance of deviations from standard among the students they tested but even managed to get them to produce deviations. The following sentences were rated acceptable or unacceptable in about equal proportions:

(a) *They aren't, but they claim so.*
(b) *Food was lacked by the children.*
(c) *The old man chose his son a wife.*
(d) *He isn't much loved.*

Surprisingly, the greatest number of 'don't knows' was registered by (d). And Archibald Hill[2] informs us that three of his subjects who had earlier rejected as ungrammatical the sentence *I never heard a green horse smoke a dozen oranges* changed their minds when they were told that the statement was strictly true.

[1] Quirk, R. and Svartik, J., *Investigating Linguistic Acceptability* (The Hague, 1966), passim.
[2] Hill, A., 'Grammaticality' in *Word*, 17 (1961), p. 2.

What *can* the linguist, then, tell us about languages?

Let us try him. I bring along to him a speaker of a certain language unknown to me and ask him if he can determine what language it is. The reaction of the linguist will probably be: 'Have you asked *him*?' If I reply: 'No, because we don't understand one another,' he will probably advise me to find an informant who does speak his language and to ask him. This is usually the quickest and very often the most reliable method because all but the mentally sub-normal *know* what language or dialect, languages or dialects, they speak. *Objective* evidence is generally laboriously come by and is frequently riddled with pitfalls. When there is disagreement with the opinion of a speaker it is sometimes like playing the historical referee. A group of speakers in the Southern Alps supposed they spoke 'Latin' but had to be told they spoke a dialect of Romansch (a descendant of the Rhaeto-Roman dialects of the Roman Empire), and for obvious reasons. For equally obvious reasons, a large body of speakers in Transylvania and the Danubian plain who once believed they spoke 'Roman' (which they originally did) came to accept that they spoke 'Romanian', not 'Roman'.

Occasionally a linguist may try to avoid the term language altogether and to use instead terms like *standard, dialect, speech community* or *mother-tongue group*.

Let us consider *standard* for a moment. Standard languages are regarded as imitation-worthy, and therefore carry prestige. Antoine Meillet described the standard languages of Europe as 'languages created for an élite'. Political as well as linguistic nationalism has reinforced the prestige of the various European standards in modern times. 'Nationalism has welded together the people of many primary speech communities into secondary speech communities, and thereby counteracted the parochialism and narrowness of the former. The function of the national standard is one reason for its value as a symbol of the nation. It forms an instrument of communication, not only by rulers to subjects or citizens, but also among the citizens themselves. They become part of a larger network, even if they also yield some portion of their linguistic distinctiveness.'[1] Separate or common *literary* standards often mean a separate or common *language*

[1] Haugen, E., 'Linguistics and Language Planning' in Bright, W. (ed.), *Sociolinguistics* (The Hague, 1966), p. 63.

standard. Danish and Norwegian (although not so much New Norwegian) are mutually comprehensible, but they have separate literary standards and are separate languages. The Chinese dialects, which are *not* mutually comprehensible at the level of speech, share a common literary standard, and thus are all regarded by their speakers as Chinese. English and Scottish lost their separate literary traditions (although the latter has been revived in modern times) in the sixteenth century largely for political reasons.

A survey of the origins of a few of the great national languages of Europe shows that in more than one case the influence of a single poet has been critical. Dante created Italian out of the Tuscan dialect, in his own lifetime moulding this dialect and enriching it with the heritage of the classical and mediaeval past and present until it became the glorious vessel capable of containing the *Divine Comedy*. Pushkin, of like stature, at the beginning of the last century fashioned the language which is now the language taught in schools throughout the U.S.S.R.—Russian. He welded together three important strands: the Slavonic of the Orthodox Church, the rich folk language and the conceptual vocabulary of Western Europe. A cultivated Russian will still regard Pushkin's poetry, prose, drama and correspondence as the model of his own usage. It would be easy to continue with examples.

The following are 'translations' of the samples quoted on p. 25:

(1) He said then, 'And where does he live, mother?' 'I don't know, my child,' she said, 'but don't look hard for his name, or anywhere in all the world that you call the name, he will hear you.' 'Well, mother,' he said, 'I want him to hear me and know me.' 'Heavens, no, sir! Don't call the name: he'll come and kill you.' 'Well, mother,' he said, 'he'll have to kill me.'

(2) Now Job is pretty stupid, but he'd have had to be a good deal stupider not to know there was something wrong, because of how she was ranting on. So he let the paper tumble on to the floor and he sat there staring till she stopped for breath. Then he said, 'What on earth is the matter with you, girl? Is there something wrong or something?'

Not all literary standards are generically related to the collo-quial standard. English in India continues to be used as the liter-ary standard (as well as the lingua franca). At one time French was the literary model of cultivated Europeans. Arabic and Sanskrit are used in areas where the colloquial language belongs to a different family of languages. But when there is generic as well as cultural affinity, the spoken and written languages are seen as one entity. This situation, however, is far from common outside Europe, and even where it does occur the identity can be more imaginary than real (only think back to the two samples of English we looked at earlier). Outside Europe it is more likely than not that people making their first attempts to write usually do so in a foreign language. As Martinet says: 'It may happen that the situation becomes stabilised so that educated people, who con-tinue to speak in their vernacular to the exclusion of any other idiom, can write only in a foreign language.'[1]

So far, our linguist does not seem to have been a great deal of help. Let us try him again, this time with a different question. Let us ask him the following: 'Putting aside for the present the difficul-ty of determining when a language is or is not a language, and admitting that there are entities on the continent of Europe known as French, German, Italian, Spanish, etc., how can we locate the *boundaries* of these languages; or, to put the question in a slightly different way, how can we tell, when moving from point A in one language area to point B in a second language area, at what point geographically we pass from the first language (say, French) to the second (say, German)?' Well, our linguist has to disappoint us yet again, because he cannot give us a clear or simple answer. For a number of reasons: (i) the political boundary does not coincide with any language boundary; (ii) the language boundary is not geographical but cultural and social rather; (iii) there will be considerable numbers of the population towards the frontiers who are bilingual, or who at least understand both languages. Moreover, (iv) there will often be a degree of linguistic con-tinuity as one moves from one language area to a neighbouring language area. This is particularly true when moving from the French-speaking area to the Italian- or Spanish-speaking areas, or vice versa.

[1] Martinet, A., *Elements of General Linguistics* (London, 1962), p. 150.

It is now time to look into an even more complex and elusive phenomenon—*dialect*.

Anyone who has observed under a microscope an ordinary pencil line drawn on white paper must have been just a little surprised at the closely packed mottled arrangement of blackish dots not in the least reminiscent of what one was *supposed* to be looking at. Language is rather similar. Take any language and observe it areawise 'under the microscope', and one finds a mass of sub-languages, or dialects, completely heterogeneous and none of them bearing a close resemblance to the standard or official language. The 'wood' has, as so often happens in linguistics, disappeared in the individual 'trees'.

All languages have at least as their basis a geographical pattern of dialects, often of staggering complexity. The regional dialects of English in the British Isles present the usual intricate tapestry, among which standard or R.P. English is nowhere to be found. But our analogy of the pencilled line takes us only a little way. Dialects cannot really be compared to the magnified graphite blobs, nor for that matter to the trees in a wood; for, in effect, dialects are more distinct, separate units, and are very different things even from language. Dialects oddly remind us of the model of the electron sometimes served up for the layman's consumption: of an entity locatable within limits, but never precisely, and behaving like waves rippling over the surface of a pond, without definite boundaries but undulating indefinitely in ever-expanding circles. I shall come back to this point later.

In other ways dialects are analogous to the patterns of the kind, described by ethnographers, observable in the distribution of local customs, folk art, crafts, dress, music, dance and so forth. It may be that dialect is indeed an object of ethnography and arises in ways connected with the latter 'cultural' facets.

Among the first linguists to take a scientific interest in dialect was Henry Sweet, the genial Henry Higgins of Shaw's *Pygmalion*. Sweet, with his uncommonly sensitive ear, was fascinated by the *phonetic*, easily the most complex, aspect of dialect. He was forced to devise a phonetic symbolism of his own since none of the conventional systems could begin to do justice to the remarkable variety of nuance available to speech sound. A legend grew up that Henry Sweet could detect, in certain parts of the metropolis, phonetic changes in dialect from one street to the next. Incredible, but not impossible, if theories of dialect distribution carry any weight.

This brings us to yet another peculiar characteristic of dialect. (I use the foregoing as an analogy, but I believe there to be actually some interconnection between the circumstances.) If I have grown up with identical twins or triplets I have no difficulty in distinguishing between them. But if I am *suddenly* confronted with them I have indeed the greatest difficulty in telling one from the other. Similarly, if I have been living abroad for some time, I find on my return that the English are very much of a muchness, an impression which quickly disappears after a few weeks or even days. On an even larger scale, it is well known that a European is at first bewildered by the similarity of Far-eastern Asiatics, and, of course, vice versa. All this is true of dialect. I do not become familiar with dialect differences of a particular region unless I have lived in that region. Thus the speech of Northern England is of a sameness to the southerner, and again vice versa. I have heard Yorkshiremen and Lancashiremen lump the speech of Southern England indiscriminately together as 'London'. Distance lends homogeneity.

None of this is fanciful; for if one asks what are the criteria for demarcating one dialect from another, and for deciding whether one is dealing with one, two or more dialects, one is presented with the reply that *the local inhabitants are the only criteria*. If someone who lives in village A believes that he speaks differently from the people in village B, then two dialects, A and B, may be posited. The locals are 'the court of last resort, from which there is no appeal'.

In his study of dialects, Sweet found no natural division between one dialect and another. 'There will be no lines of division; the dialects will shade insensibly into one another.' Not only this, but each dialect shares the characteristics of its neighbours, even quite distant neighbours. Any dialect will reveal a mixture of elements in no particular order, and may be analysed into components of other dialects. It is only when these components are assembled in a particular way that one obtains a given dialect, rather like a crossword puzzle. This is not surprising if we recall the wave-like nature of dialect distribution.

Just like waves, which become weaker and weaker the farther they travel from their centre, so we should expect that any given dialect will resemble its near neighbours more than its distant ones. If, for example, you take four villages roughly in line from, say, west to east the following distances apart:

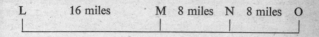

village M will partake roughly equally in the characteristics of villages L and O since, as you will see, M is halfway between L and O. The same thing will apply to village N, which will contain a roughly equal number of elements from the dialects of villages M and O. But, you may ask, what about the relationship of village N to village L or O? Well, if your mathematics is adequate to the task, you will be able to work out that village N will contain characteristics of L and O in the ratio of 1:4; or, in other words, for every element of dialect L it will contain four elements of dialect O.

Needless to say, in practice, distribution of dialects hardly ever occurs with such mathematical precision. Every kind of natural obstacle—forest, marsh, river, mountain—serves to obscure this regularity. More important, cultural influences have distorted this uniformity out of all recognition. Yet, broadly and approximately speaking, our mathematics is correct. The distortions are indicated by *isoglosses* (by analogy with isotherm, isobar, etc.), which are the contours of dialect feature distribution. Isoglosses form very much more complicated patterns than their climatological counterparts. Maps of isoglosses often resemble oblique cross-sections of knots occurring in a piece of wood, with 'bundles' of them traversing a diagram in every direction. Bloomfield, the American linguist, gives an excellent account of these in his *Language* (pp. 325 ff.). Isogloss patterns show that dialect distribution is not simply a matter of geography but also one of history, of language history; just as a cross-section of a piece of wood tells its own story. 'Dialect thus gives evidence as to the former extension of linguistic features that now persist only as relic forms. Especially when a feature appears in detached districts that are separated by a compact area in which a competing feature is spoken, the map can usually be interpreted to mean that the detached districts were once part of a solid area. In this way, dialect geography may show us the stratification of linguistic features . . . Since an isogloss presumably marks a line of weakness in the density of communication, we may expect the dialect map to show us the communicative conditions of successive times . . . France is divided by a great bundle of isoglosses running east and west across the area. The division reflects the mediaeval division of France into the two cultural and linguistic domains of French and Provençal.'

To illustrate an isogloss pattern I have made use of Eduard Kolb's *Phonological Atlas of the Northern Region* (*Linguistic Atlas of England*) (Bern, 1966). I have selected information set out in the chart opposite based on a group of small towns in Lancashire and the West Riding of Yorkshire. I have arbitrarily taken the town of Read (in Lancashire) as the reference point and have compared the data for this town with that of a group of others radiating in various directions from it. The number in the left-hand column refers to the number of the isogloss drawn on the accompanying diagram (Figure 1, p. 36). All entries after the first column of words are in phonetic script; and an entry is included only when it differs from the reference point. Isoglosses can be observed running in every direction, and this pattern is not untypical of dialect atlases. The pattern north–south in this particular instance is rather more marked than that from west to east; the *bundles* of north–south isoglosses are more dense. This no doubt reflects the topography of the region, the north–south isoglosses coinciding with the Pennine moorlands, which have tended to reduce east–west communication in this area. However, there are sufficient isoglosses running from east to west to counter any claim that Lancashire and Yorkshire (Wars of the Roses, and all that) have not communed.

In the hands of the 'dialectologist' the isogloss is a powerful tool indeed, and it becomes in turn a useful adjunct to the linguist. The density of isogloss patterning has been of considerable interest. Bloomfield reckoned that density is in inverse proportion to the *density of communication*. The thicker the bundles of isoglosses, the more certain we are that we are dealing with a geographical break in communication. A density of thousands per unit area will indicate the boundary of a major dialect, or a 'language'. Dialectology has seemed so eminently successful to

Isogloss no.		READ	RIB-CHESTER	ECCLES-TON	HOR-WOOD	GAR-GRAVE	HEPTON-STALL	PILLING	DOLPHIN-HOLME
1a 1b	(April)	ɛːprəl					əprəl	əɛprəl	əprəl
2	(gate)	geɪt				geɪt	jeɪt		geɪt
3	(tea)	teː				tɪə	tɪə		
4	(right)	rɪit		riɪt	riɪt	rɪit		riɪt	riɪt
5	(snow)	snoː			snoʊ				
6	(died)	diːd					daɪd		
7a 7b	(squirrel)	skwɛɜ̃rəl	skwiɪrəl	skwiɪrəl	skwɛrəl	skwɛ̃rəl		skwiɪrəl	skwɛ̃rəl
8	(herrings)	zɪnrɛ̃			jɛrinz		jɛrinz		
9	(any)	ɒni	ani	ani					
10	(hammer)	amə̃(r)				amã	amã		

some that it has been suggested[1] that 'we do not need the term
language at all, because dialect serves all necessary functions—
with the exception of the collective one, the one which says that
"language has, or consists of" dialects.' But for others this is rank
optimism. Doubting the reality even of dialect, Pavel Ivić writes:

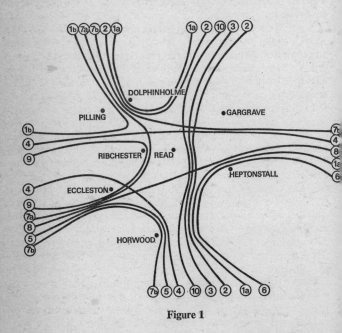

Figure 1

'Upon closer inspection, considering the multitude of isoglosses
crossing one another in all possible directions, territorial dialects
have often proved to be fictitious entities, established on the basis
of arbitrarily chosen features, or on the basis of extralinguistic
criteria. This fact led either to the negation of the very existence of
territorial dialects or to the opinion that this concept has a relative character, and that the central concept of dialectology should

[1] Pulgram, E., 'Structural Comparison: Diasystems and Dialectology',
in *Linguistics*, 4 (1964).

be that of the isogloss.'[1] If Ivić is right, the wood really has disappeared behind the trees, and our graphite blobs are the only real things, not the pencil line drawn on the paper.

The problem of knowing when a language is or is not a language, now compounded by the added difficulty of deciding when a dialect is a dialect, is still further complicated by the existence of *bilingualism.*

Many people, perhaps most people, are bilingual; bilingualism being defined as the fact of belonging to two distinct speech communities. (Please note that by this definition bilinguals are not only those who speak two fully-fledged languages but also those who speak, or understand (passive bilinguals), a language standard and one of its dialects. As you will already have guessed, quite a fair number of people are by this definition *multilingual.*) In some countries there are speakers who may belong to a considerable number of speech communities. Take, for instance, a Swiss graduate living in the German-speaking part of Switzerland. He will *read* and *understand* High German but *speak* Swiss German, a totally distinct dialect of German, not at all readily understood by German speakers. If he hails from the countryside he will almost certainly know besides a *local* dialect, which not all Swiss German speakers will understand. Moreover, he will use this dialect quite often, not only in the home but also among friends, and elsewhere. The same man will, in addition, probably speak good French and fair Italian, and quite possibly fluent English as well. The Swiss are expected to be polyglots. Finally, our already linguistically overloaded Swiss may also be an airline pilot, or a brain surgeon, a musician or an archaeologist, in which case he will be affiliated to a 'professional' speech community (speech communities being not only geographically but also *socially* distributed).

There are literally millions of human beings who belong to two or more speech communities. Most frequently, they use their two or more languages or dialects in a co-ordinate manner; that is, they employ one 'language' in one situation and another 'language' in a different situation. The 1951 census in India revealed an astonishingly high incidence of reported bilingualism of an active kind (in other words, those who said they were bilinguals also said they spoke more than one 'language'), ranging in one

[1] Ivić, P., 'On the Structure of Dialectal Differentiation' in *Word*, 18 (1) (1962).

state alone (Madhya Pradesh) from 87% to 2%. Bilingualism tends to be more frequent when the mother-tongue group is small, and this feature has been observed in many parts of the world.

It is very common indeed for the monolingual speaker (a speaker of only one language) to understand several dialects or 'languages'. Mother-tongue speakers of English are constantly encountering types of spoken English they have never met before; and, more often than not, communication is achieved. As long as I know that the language I am listening to is *supposed* to be English, I will bring to bear on the situation my full range of adaptability and will understand most, or at least some, of what I hear.

The most important implication of all this for comparative linguistics is that bilingualism is only rarely pure. It is even doubtful if pure bilingualism exists outside the U.N.O. interpreters' cubicles. The usual situation is that the two 'languages' used by the bilingual *interfere* with one another. *Interference* is an exceedingly fascinating as well as a complicated phenomenon. We shall discuss later its role in language change and language stabilisation. The factors causing or inhibiting interference are many and varied, the most important ones being social or extralinguistic.

More recently, it has been established[1] that even within a single speech norm (language or dialect) there exists a considerable repertoire of choice. 'Role-relationships' of a seemingly delicately categorisable kind determine our choice of language in a particular situation. Whether we happen to be reading, writing or speaking also counts a great deal. If this new approach is pushed to its logical conclusion, we may be compelled eventually to recognise that the use of stylistic levels or 'registers' within a single standard are extensions of the better-known phenomenon of bilingualism. It is not at all fanciful to suppose that eventually 'bilingualism' will be superseded by the more comprehensive term 'domains of language choice'. To make my point clearer, let us compare the various possible ways of asking a person to go: *Get out!; Would you mind leaving (me), please; Leave, please; Be gone!; Buzz off!; Be off with you!; That's all for now.* The only features that these phrases really have in common are: (i) if they

---

[1] Fishman, J., 'Who Speaks What Language, to Whom, and When?' in *Linguistique*, 2 (1965); and *Language Loyalty in the U.S.A.* (The Hague, 1966).

are spoken by the same person they will be pronounced with a uniform pronunciation, and (ii) they employ a single set of writing conventions. Otherwise, they have precious little in common. Grammatically, they are far from being identical; they do not have the same meaning, and their use is called for in vastly different situations.

But, you might argue, we can all recognise English words when we see them. Then what about *feme sole*, *cestui que trust*, *joie de vivre* and *coup d'état*? If you know your legal terms you will be aware that the first two came into English with the Norman Conquest. But you will be wrong if you pronounce them in a French way. Lawyers don't; and they will be amused if you do. The second two are definitely French you say? I wonder if they really are. *Coup d'état* has been in English for well over a century; and we have the authority of the Oxford Dictionary behind it. *Joie de vivre* is not in the dictionary; but many English speakers use it, and my 1962 edition of *Roget's Thesaurus* lists it.

English speakers are using imported words all the time, and they do not often realise it. This is because the imported words have become associated with definite situations. I would not dream of using *feme sole* unless I were a lawyer (if only because I would probably not be absolutely sure how to use it, let alone pronounce it); nor would I describe the French Revolution as a *coup d'état*. My usage is just as fixed by the situation that calls for it as is the bilingual's usage. The Franco-English bilingual living in England with his French family says *bonjour* at home but *good morning* at the office. His English friends after an evening in a pub with him will probably use neither French nor English but will very likely use the Italian *ciao* to each other. Similarly, the British-as-British Pennine shepherd who does not 'go in for foreign lingos' can nevertheless, when counting his sheep, still be heard using a set of numerals from a pre-English dialect (not unlike Welsh). He is not aware of this, simply because he uses the familiar English numerals in all other situations. If you told him he was bilingual he might even take offence; at the very least, he would know you were pulling his leg.

Whenever there are large numbers of (active) bilinguals—and we are all now suspected of being bilinguals—in any speech community, some rather extraordinary and unpredictable things can happen. What linguist in the 1870s could have foreseen that *cab* 'a public carriage pulled by one horse' (a shortened form of *cabriolet*) would only a few decades later have come to mean 'a public vehicle propelled by several mechanical horses'; that the weird compound *taxicab* would in turn have been shortened to either *taxi* or *cab*; or that in British English a snobbish distinction would have crept in between these two words; but that even those who appreciated the snob value of *cab* would on occasion use *taxi*, especially when they are not in England, and also when they are in the counties more remote from London? What a curious, but after all perfectly ordinary, prostitution of 'bilingualism'!

We have seen, then, that not only a term like 'language' but even a more definite one like 'dialect' is fraught with problems. And just as a language may, geographically speaking, be doomed ultimately to unravel itself into strings of isoglosses, so, from a socio-cultural point of view, a language no longer presents the integral organic unity that layman and linguist alike have supposed it to present. A cultural article of faith, it seems, does not always make for a scientifically consistent model. But not only this; the objective probings of the linguistic scientist could in the fullness of time help to break down the now artificial barriers between 'languages'. This would be particularly so in the case of languages that are culturally closely related, like the Western European group. Many years have passed since John Orr argued that French and English were really dialects of a common language; and no one needed to argue that, until the sixteenth century, Latin was the common written language of Europe and, among certain sections of the community, the common vernacular as well. While economists are exercised in creating a Eurodollar, why should we not try for a Eurolanguage too? The major obstacles are not linguistic but are created by the Mandarins, culture salesmen, grass-root politicians, tradition-conscious educators and, last but not least, by you and me.

3 The Diversity of Language: A Geographical Survey of the World's Languages

It is difficult to account for the immense number and variety of languages and separate dialects scattered throughout the world on any of the current hypotheses. Their exact number is hard to estimate, but the total certainly runs into four figures. Some idea can be gained from the fact that the gospels have been translated into 825 tongues. These are all languages with literary status, and their rules of structure and idiom are known. This figure by no means includes the unrecorded or incompletely recorded languages; for example, those spoken by localised American Indian tribes throughout the Southern American Continent.

Nearly all the recorded languages fall into nine 'families', classified on the basis of various common features and resemblances. A list of these 'families', arranged in order of the size of population speaking them, may prove useful for reference:

	million
Indo-European	1000
Sino-Tibetan	500
African	100
Dravidian	100
Japanese-Korean	100
Malayo-Polynesian	90
Semito-Hamitic	75
Ural-Altaic	60
American Indian	10

The *Indo-European* family has the largest number of speakers by far, and covers the largest geographical area. This can quite easily be explained, for English, French, Russian, Spanish, Portuguese, Afrikaans, Persian and the many languages of the Indian subcontinent are members. Most of these languages have been or still are being disseminated by means of colonial expansion or nowadays less objectionable spheres of influence. English is, of course, spoken throughout North America, the Dominions and the Commonwealth, and is rapidly becoming the international language. English has become the lingua franca of India owing to the large number of mutually incomprehensible languages spoken within that nation. French is spoken widely in North and Central Africa, in French Canada and elsewhere, and is said to be regaining some of its former prestige. Spanish is the first language of all the former Spanish colonies of Central and South America; Portuguese of Brazil and Central Africa. Afrikaans, a language belonging to the same class as Dutch and Flemish, has long-established roots in South Africa. Russian has been widening its sphere of influence for the last 300 years and is still far from the limits of its possible expansion in the Asiatic Republics of the U.S.S.R.

Sino-Tibetan is a loosely knit set of language groups, the relationship between the groups not having been proved in every case. Culturally, Chinese is easily the dominant language of this family and is reckoned as an independent member of it. The Chinese system of writing, the written language in fact, embraces a number of mutually unintelligible dialects. The other members of this family are the Tibeto-Burman group, the Thai languages and certain dialects of lower Burma. All the groups assigned to this family have a tendency to be monosyllabic (although this raises tricky problems as far as Chinese is concerned); they are all tonal and employ classifiers or numeral adjuncts.

The *African* languages contain a vast assortment of dialects grouped into two wide belts. The first of these belts comprises all the West African and Central African dialects as far south roughly as the equatorial region, and is known sometimes as Sudanese-Guinean. Among the better-known dialects are Ewe, Hausa, Yoruba and Ibo (the last three being spoken in the different regions of Nigeria). The *Bantu* belt stretches right down to the southern tip of Africa, including all the African dialects to be found there except the surviving Bushmen and Hottentot dialects.

Japanese and *Korean* appear to be distantly related. Japanese, although it incorporates Chinese characters into its writing system, has no connection with Chinese whatsoever. Its grammar is intriguing and teeming with surprises. The verbs, for instance, are conceived totally differently from European systems. They are all impersonal verbs, there being no real personal pronouns. Instead, notions of familiarity, politeness and extreme politeness are marked in the verb forms.

Dravidian is a class of languages confined to Southern India and

Northern Sri Lanka (Ceylon). The existence of these languages alongside Indo-European has created serious social problems, and in recent times has led to political unrest and civil violence in Sri Lanka, when the question was raised as to which language, Sinhalese (Indo-European) or Tamil (Dravidian), was to become the official language.

Malayo-Polynesian is, as one can see from the map in Figure 2, spread over an astonishing distance, an area consisting largely of vast expanses of sea and comparatively minute islands, from Tahiti in the east to Malagasy in the west, rather in the manner of an elongated ellipse. This distribution has naturally provoked speculations from a generation familiar with Kontiki and Aku-Aku. It is almost inconceivable that the Malayo-Polynesian language of Malagasy has arisen independently and spontaneously, and yet what a distance across the Indian Ocean from Sumatra or Malaya to this African off-shore island. Ethnologists seem to agree that some of the inhabitants of Malagasy must have come from the East Indian islands. It has been suggested[1] that Malagasy was populated as the result of accidental voyages from that direction. The currents from the East Indies to Malagasy are, it seems, among the most constant in the world, and hence favour one-way, though not return, voyages.

Semito-Hamitic falls into two very large sub-groups: Semitic and Hamitic. Semitic, of which Arabic is the most widely diffused group of dialects, is spoken in what are now roughly speaking the Arab countries. Hebrew, the language of Israel, is also Semitic. Hamitic dialects, on the other hand, are spoken in discrete pockets of North Africa and also in the Sudan and Somalia (see Figure 2).

Ural-Altaic, as we shall see below, is a not too satisfactory label under which to group a very large number of probably unrelated (historically) languages and dialects, ranging all the way from Northern and Central Europe to Far-eastern Siberia. They are in the main the dialects of scattered nomadic tribes. In recent times this group of languages and dialects has suffered gravely from the ascendancy of Russian and, earlier still, of Chinese. At its eastern extent Ural-Altaic is spoken in Manchuria and Mongolia, whereas Finnish and Hungarian stand out as surprising islands in an Indo-European sea in Europe. The present location of Hungarian

[1] Sharp, A., *Ancient Voyages in the Pacific Ocean* (London, 1956), pp. 36–7.

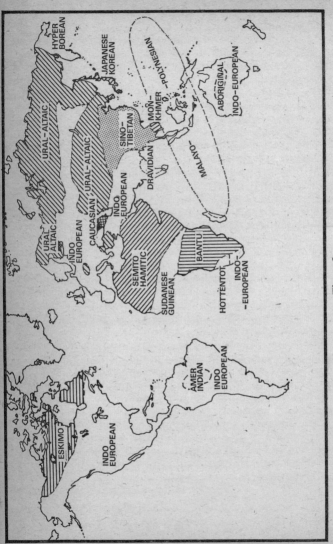

Figure 2

is attributable to historically recorded westward migrations in the ninth and tenth centuries.

The *American Indian* languages might more properly be called a 'clan' rather than a family, a clan that embraces a vast agglomeration of quite distinct and, in most cases, unrelated dialects in North, Central and South America, all the way from Alaska to Tierra del Fuego. In the Central Western United States alone, as many as thirty different families of languages have been recorded in close geographical proximity. Of these languages the Mayan and Aztec had developed writing. A very considerable number of American Indian dialects are known to have become extinct since the white man settled in North America. Nearly all the American Indian languages are either distinctly 'polysynthetic' or have a tendency to be so. At the risk of oversimplification, polysynthetic languages can be thought of as consisting of words that in European languages would occupy entire sentences. The Yana word *yābanaumawildjigummaha'nigi* means 'let us, each one of us, move indeed to the west across the creek'. According to Sapir,[1] this word consists of three types of elements: a nuclear element or stem ('several people move'); a modal and a personal element; and elements of a modifying sort which cannot occur independently but which express ideas that are normally rendered by separate words. However, Yana is an extremely polysynthetic language, and not all the American Indian dialects are clearly polysynthetic.

There remain a few language groups which cannot be fitted into any of the nine classes already mentioned. *Basque*, spoken by as many as a million people in a pocket stretching from Southwest France into Northern Spain, has not the least resemblance to any of its neighbours; indeed, it is unlike any known extant languages. Attempts have been made to link it with North African dialects, and even with the long-extinct Etruscan of Italy and with Sumerian of the Middle East, but without success. Basque is presumed to be a survival from a group of languages spoken throughout the Iberian Peninsula before the Roman colonisation.

A group that has aroused a considerable interest among philologists on account of their extreme grammatical complexity are the

[1] A comprehensive survey of the American Indian languages is to be found in Mandelbaum, D. G. (ed.), *Selected Writings of Edward Sapir* (Berkeley and Los Angeles, 1958), pp. 169–78.

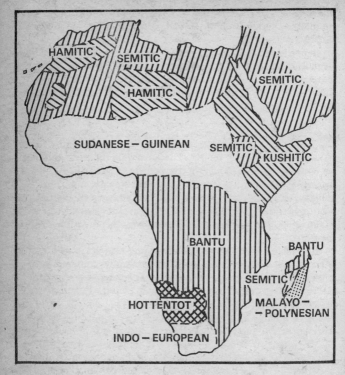

Figure 3

so-called *Caucasian* languages, the most important of which is Georgian with an important literary tradition of its own. These languages are generally regarded as indigenous survivals owing to the mountainous terrain, many parts of which were quite inaccessible before the development of modern transport.

The *Mon-Khmer* family is to be found scattered in patches over South-east Asia and right down the Malay Peninsula. The name Khmer is now better known in the West, as it appears in the new name for what was formerly Cambodia.

Among the remaining isolated families one should mention the

Ainu of the northern island of Japan (Hokkaido); and also the numerous *Australian* and *Papuan* dialects spoken in the main by aboriginal peoples.

It now only remains to take a closer look at some of these language families, and especially at Indo-European, partly because English and all the more familiar European languages belong to it, and partly because the illustrations used in subsequent chapters are drawn almost exclusively from it.

Indo-European

As we have seen, this family of languages is the most significant of the modern world and is the only group that is still to any noticeable extent extending its sphere of influence, mainly through English and Russian. Many are of the opinion that English may one day become the universal language. Apart from anything else, there are important linguistic reasons why this possibility cannot be ruled out.

English and Russian, politically at any rate the unrivalled bigwigs of their ill-assorted Indo-European family, could not provide a greater contrast. The language of the Soviet technocracy exhibits many features of the more archaic state of Indo-European as the latter is known through comparative study. All the early and many of the present-day Indo-European languages, including Russian, German and Modern Greek, are highly 'inflected'; that is, they modify the endings of their nouns, adjectives, pronouns and verbs according to their function in the sentence. English, on the other hand, only exceptionally behaves in this manner.

As already suggested, Indo-European is the most well-documented and thoroughly investigated 'family' of languages. Its earliest known representative is Hittite, a language spoken in Asia-Minor in the second millenium B.C. and extinct almost before recorded history began. Indo-European languages have been discovered in locations as far flung as Chinese Turkestan, there having been much speculation as to how they came to be spoken there. Comparative linguists refer to these Asiatic branches as Tokharian.

The contemporary Indo-European languages may be grouped in the following way:

Germanic (see Figure 4)

This comprises a number of important languages, including English. They all had a common source of origin in pre-historic times but had not shown very much divergence at the time when they were first recorded in second-century Roman.

They are usually divided into two main classes:

(1) *Northern:* Swedish, Norwegian, Danish and Icelandic.
(2) *Western:* English, High and Low German, Swiss-German, Dutch and Flemish (with Afrikaans).

Of the Northern group, Icelandic is by far the most conservative, having preserved its more ancient Norse characteristics, whereas Swedish, and particularly Danish and Norwegian, have undergone simplification and reduction of inflected forms. In Danish and Norwegian this process has been a deliberate one.

In the Western group, High and Low German refer to what are in fact quite separate languages, without, however, any inferiority or superiority being indicated. High German is the official and literary language of Germany and Austria, whereas Low German is confined to the Rhineland and to North and North-west Germany and has only dialect status. Flemish is spoken in northern and western areas of Belgium.

All the Northern Germanic languages share the unusual characteristic of a suffixed definite article. Thus Swedish *bord* 'table' appears as *bordet* 'the table' and *sten* 'stone' as *stenen* 'the stone'.

All the Germanic languages, Northern and Western alike, exhibit common features in the treatment of verbs. All have a simple past tense (Eng. *I did*) and a composite perfect (*I have done*), and they all form their future tenses by the use of modal auxiliary verbs (*I will do, we shall go, she would look*, etc.). In addition, they all preserve a single archaic Indo-European feature—the tendency to alter the root vowel in their so-called 'strong' verbs. Examples in English are *sink, sank, sunk*; *give, gave, given*, etc.

Romance

This is a term derived etymologically from the word 'Roman', covering all those languages and dialects which have originated

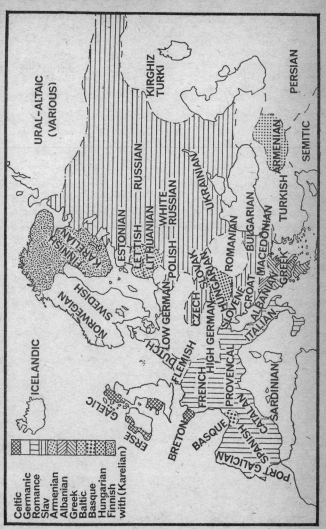

Figure 4

in the language spoken eighteen centuries ago by the ordinary citizens of the Roman Empire. This language is referred to as 'Vulgar Latin' and was no doubt a common language which grew up among diversified populations whose native language was of a non-Latin kind, much as English performs a similar function in modern India and parts of Africa.

The modern boundaries of the Romance languages correspond remarkably closely to the ancient boundaries of the continental Roman Empire.

The Romance languages fall into four groups:

(1) Spanish, Portuguese, Catalan.
(2) French and Provençal.
(3) Italian.
(4) Romanian.

All these languages retain the fundamental structure of Vulgar Latin and have diverged only in the earlier part of the Middle Ages. These languages have two genders, masculine and feminine, and none of them retains the intricate case system of Classical or literary Latin. Romanian differs to some extent in having a suffixed article. Compare:

	'dog'	'of the father'
Vulgar Latin (accusative)	*cane* (*m*)	*patris*
French	*le chien*	*du père*
Italian	*il cane*	*del padre*
Spanish	*el* [*perro*]	*del padre*
Romanian	*câin-el*	[*tata*]-*lui*

Balto-Slavonic
This group falls into two subdivisions, Baltic and Slavonic, as follows:

(1) *Baltic:*   Lithuanian, Lettish.
(2) *Slavonic:* Eastern: Russian, White Russian, Ukrainian.
             Western: Polish, Czech, Slovak.
             Southern: Serbian, Croatian, Slovene, Macedon-
                 ian, Bulgarian.

All these languages share a relatively archaic flexional system. Bulgarian is the only language that does not preserve the six cases: nominative, accusative, genitive, dative, instrumental, locative. All preserve three genders. Polish has in addition a special gender declension for certain classes of masculine persons, and hence possesses really two masculine forms.

The verbal system of Slavonic has distinctive characteristics. Verbs do not accord with our familiar tense patterns (e.g. future, present, perfect, pluperfect) but instead fall into two *aspect* groups. The 'imperfective' aspect is used whenever the action of the verb is self-contained or descriptive; the 'perfective' when some purpose or result *beyond* the verb is envisaged (compare: *he is always trying to come to a decision but never reaches any*).

Indo-Iranian

This comprises many separate languages and dialects, the principal ones of which are as follows:

(1) *Iranian:* Persian, Kurdish, Balochi, Afghan.
(2) *Indic:* Hindi, Urdu, Bengali, Panjabi, Marathi, Rajasthani, Sinhalese, Gujarati.

These languages show considerable variation. A number of them use an adaptation of Arabic script, and Persian has many words of Arabic origin. The ancient languages of this group, Sanskrit and Old Persian (owing to their great antiquity), are of great importance to comparative linguists.

Celtic

'Celtic Fringe' describes the location of the surviving Celtic tongues, which are now confined to the western extremities of the British Isles and Brittany. In Roman times, Celtic languages must have been spoken over large areas of Europe, including Gaul, parts of the Alps and Northern Italy. The name Galicia crops up in Poland and in North-west Spain. Ethnographers have found Celtic influence as far east as the Carpathians. It is likely that at one time, when Rome was still in its infancy, Gallic influence extended far into Asia-Minor (Galatia).

The extant Celtic languages fall into two groups:

(1) Scots Gaelic, Irish Gaelic or Erse, Manx.
(2) Welsh, Breton, Cornish.

Breton is not a remnant of continental Gallic but a transplantation from South-west England during the period of Saxon encroachments. Breton is identical with Cornish, last spoken in the eighteenth century but in recent times revived by enthusiasts. Breton and Welsh are the remnants of languages spoken throughout Britain before it became part of the Roman Empire. Many English rivers still bear Celtic names, e.g. Avon, Ouse, Exe, Usk, Don, Wye, etc., and the occasional hill or mountain, e.g. Pen-y-Ghent, Helvellyn.

Gaelic is much more complicated in structure than either Welsh or Breton, possessing four cases as compared with Welsh which has none. The verbal systems are highly complex with a multiplicity of tenses and moods.

The Celtic languages are somewhat of a challenge, having much less in common with English than with many other European tongues. Perhaps the greatest obstacle is that the student has to familiarise himself with a series of phonetic rules affecting the initial consonants of words in a variety of ways, thereby precluding a ready use of a dictionary or glossary in the earlier stages. For example:

Irish: *Bo* 'cow' becomes *mbo* in the combination *ar mbo* 'our cow'.
Welsh: *Caernarvon* is written *Nghaernarvon* in the combination *yng Nghaernarvon* 'in Caernarvon'.

Greek

Modern Greek is derived from the Greek spoken in Byzantium and differs in a number of ways from the Classical Greek. The area in which Greek is spoken takes in a number of separate dialects. Greek is the only Indo-European language whose present area is not substantially different from what it was in the pre-Christian era.

As far as the West is concerned, Greek has had a greater influence than any other language. Rome early came under its influence; early Christianity was mainly propagated through it; and the Renaissance was in many respects a Hellenic revival. All the major European languages of today are teeming with words of Greek origin—not least the English language. Greek is a kind of joint fund which can be drawn upon by any European language as and when the need arises.

Albanian

This is a modern survival of what is supposed to have been Illyrian, a language presumably spoken widely throughout the Balkans and possibly beyond. Modern Albanian contains, as one might expect, many Turkish words inherited from the time of the Ottoman occupation.

Armenian

Once an important language but now confined almost exclusively to the regions of Soviet and Turkish Armenia, and hence subject to constant pressure from Russian and other languages, Armenian is of immense value to comparative linguists owing to certain distinctive Indo-European characteristics inherited and preserved by it.

Semito-Hamitic

The extant subdivisions of this scattered group are as follows:

(1) *Semitic:* Northern: Hebrew.
  Southern: Arabic, Ethiopian.
(2) *Hamitic:* Libyco-Berber, Kushitic, Coptic.

There was in ancient times an eastern branch, containing the two historically important languages of Babylonia and Assyria, known to us from cuneiform inscriptions on stone and clay, dating from as early as 2500 B.C.

Semitic

The languages of this group consist of words composed of a di-syllabic root. In writing only the consonants are printed; vowels are either not indicated at all or represented by diacritic marks.

Thus in Arabic: كَسَرَ *Kasara* 'he broke', the three dashes re-present the vowels whilst the squiggles denote the consonants (written, incidentally, from right to left).

Hebrew was superseded by Aramaic in the second century B.C. but was retained as a written language through the Middle Ages. In modern times Hebrew has been artificially but successfully revived as a spoken language and is now the language of Israel. Edmund Wilson described Hebrew as 'a system of 22 integers, a set of unsupplantable blocks . . . each Hebrew word makes a shell into which a varying content of vowel sounds may be poured . . . What impresses us is the hardness of this shell.'

From the Arabic consonant 'block' *k-t-b*, a large number of nouns and verb forms and tenses can be derived by what at first glance appears to be little more than a permutation of the three available vowels, thus:

kataba	'he has written'
kutiba	'it has been written'
yaktubu	'he will write'
'aktib	'I wrote'
kitabun	'writing, book'
katibun	'a writer'

Semitic is expressive in ways completely beyond the powers of Indo-European. Hebrew, for example, teems with emphatic and intensive forms. The language has verb pairs such as: 'to grow'—'to grow luxuriantly'; 'to kill'—'to kill brutally'; 'to walk'—'to walk with God'; all forming a normal and natural part of the language structure. Some forms of verbs would appear to be capable of becoming suddenly 'highly charged' by a simple inflexion.

Hamitic

Spread out across North Africa are the Hamitic languages. Their present-day lack of prestige contrasts markedly with one of their distant forebears, Ancient Egyptian. The language of Ancient Egypt is the first known language to have developed writing, recorded in hieroglyphic inscriptions dating back to 4000 B.C.

Ural-Altaic

This language family is made up from a multiplicity of widely scattered languages and dialects often declining in importance. The several branches may be grouped as follows:

(1) *Uralic* (more usually termed *Finno-Ugrian*):
        Finnish (including Estonian and Karelian)
        Hungarian
        Lapp (including Cheremiss, Votyak)
        Ostyak
        Samoyed
(2) *Altaic:* Turkish (including Tatar, Turcoman, Kirghiz)
        Mongolian (Kalmuk, Buryat, etc.)
        Tungus (Manchurian)

Only the languages of the Uralic group have been shown to be historically related; and they display only typological similarities with the Altaic group. No genealogical connection has been established either between the separate members of the Altaic group or between any of them and the languages of the Uralic group. The two features these languages have are a phonetic feature known as *vowel harmony* and a morphological structure known as *agglutination*.

Agglutination means that all particles and modifiers are tacked onto an initial stem to form a single word. Take, for instance, the Turkish word *kirilmadilarmi*. This consists of six syllables. The first (*kir*) contains the meaning 'break'. The remaining syllables *-il-ma-di-lar-mi* represent the passive voice, the negative, the past tense, the third person plural and the interrogative respectively. Thus the word literally translated into English means 'break-en-not-were-they?' = 'Were they not broken?'

Vowel harmony

A phonetic principle whereby if the vowel of the root noun happens to be a 'frontal' vowel (e.g. *e, i, ö*) the vowels of the remainder of the word will also be frontalised; conversely for 'back' vowels (*a, o, u*). For example:

	ház + ban = hazban	'in the house'
but	kéz + ban = kézben	'in the hand'

Hungarian offers perhaps fewer difficulties to the student than Finnish, which has no less than fifteen case endings making a total of thirty separate endings (singular and plural) for each noun. As someone wryly put it, asking for an ice cream in Finnish is a major linguistic exercise!

Hungarian offers a curious variety of verbal aspects and moods. The verb 'to write' gives, for example:

ir	'he writes'
irat	'he causes to write'
irogat	'he writes repeatedly'
irhat	'he may write'
irkát	'he scribbles'

Turkish goes even further with an aspect of 'impossibility', e.g. *sevememek* 'to be unable to love'.

Sino-Tibetan

The Sino-Tibetan 'family' of languages is spoken in one form or another by a very large proportion of the world's population. It comprises several hundreds of languages or distinct dialects. Chinese stands out from all these—indeed, from all the rest of the world's languages—as a unique linguistic as well as a cultural phenomenon. Although Chinese can be said to share certain formal features with the Tibetan, Burman, Thai and other languages—the use of tones, the monosyllabic structure—it forms a quite separate entity, with an independent and rich historical development stretching back more than four millenia. Moreover, Chinese has culturally dominated East Asia and large parts of South-east Asia for a very long time, and has influenced many neighbouring and unrelated languages and cultures, not always in known ways.

Chinese consists of several groups of dialects or languages, linked together by a common writing system. Seven groups have been recognised:

(1) *North Chinese* or *Mandarin* (387 million speakers): a group of dialects spoken in China north of the Yangtse River and in the south-west of China.

Figure 5 Map of Chinese dialects

(2) *Wu* (46 million speakers): dialects spoken in the region adjacent to and in Shanghai itself.

(3) *Hunanese* or *Xiang* (26 million speakers): these dialects are spoken in the larger part of Hunan province.

(4) *Kiangsi* or *Gàn* (13 million speakers): these dialects are spoken in the larger part of Kiansi and also elsewhere.

(5) *Hakka* (20 million speakers): spoken in the mountainous areas in South-western Kwangsi and the northern parts of Kwangtung province.

(6) *Yuè* or *Cantonese* (27 million speakers): a considerable, and sometimes mutually unintelligible, group of dialects spoken in the greater part of Kwangtung (including Canton and Hong Kong).

(7) *Fukienese* or *Min* (22 million speakers): a group of dialects spoken in the south-eastern coastal provinces, as well as in Taiwan and Hainan.

Of these North Chinese, or Mandarin, is by far the most important, not only demographically but also as regards prestige. Mandarin, and especially the Peking dialect, has come to be regarded as the Common Language of China, although this concept is one that has to date not been fully realised; nor is it easy to see clearly what this concept means for those who are accustomed to using only European languages, where a standard is usually not that difficult to locate and refer to. This does not necessarily entail the other dialects dying out, although a policy has existed for many years in Mainland China to promote the Common Language by having it taught universally in Chinese schools. To appreciate what the Chinese language means *to the Chinese* in cultural as well as linguistic terms it has been suggested that we imagine Europe in a different way from what it actually is: to suppose that France, Italy, Spain and Portugal form a single political unit; to suppose further that Latin is still their common form of writing; and finally to imagine, for the sake of argument, that French as spoken in Paris is their proper means of oral communication. (A readable and scholarly discussion of the modern Chinese Language may be found in Paul Kratochvil's *The Chinese Language Today* (London, 1968).)

All the Chinese dialects are tonal: that is, each syllable can be modified in meaning or function by a change of tone. Tones may be of a rising, falling or even variety; or they can be high-pitched, middling-pitched or low-pitched. Mandarin has only four marked tones; Cantonese has seven (officially more than seven).

Chinese is not, as is sometimes believed, a pictorial or even a pictographic language. Even the earliest known characters, dating back as far as 2000 B.C., have evolved well beyond purely natural-istic representation of objects. The Chinese writing system evolved gradually, as one might expect, and the characters assumed their modern shape approximately only about the third century B.C. To be able to read a modern Chinese newspaper with comfort one needs to be able to recognise about 3000 characters; and con-siderably more if one wants to read classical literature. In recent years in Communist China drastic simplifications of the charac-ters have been introduced.

The Chinese character is the equivalent of a word, or part of a word, in Roman script. Its structure is always formal, often intri-cate, being made up usually of two or more elements or 'radicals'. The picture or pictures out of which the character evolved are in most cases no longer apparent. Yet, when we compare some of the modern characters with their ancient prototypes, we can de-tect the pictorial basis. Consider the following:

Modern   Ancient

mang 'high plants, luxurious vegetation'

mang 'a hound frisking about in the thickets'

mo 'the sun fading away at the horizon'

In the first group, the four groups of plants are gathered to form a single character. Two groups would have indicated ordinary plants; four formally indicates luxuriance. In the second group, we see a dog running between the thickets. In the third, we see the sun low down over the tops of the thickets, partly concealed between them.

The foregoing is little more than a sketch of the almost infinite variety of the world's languages. Much might have been said, for instance, of Japanese, with its outlandish habit of meticulously expressing different shades of respect, humility, subservience and kindred social conventions; of Dravidian, the group of pre-Indo-European languages of the Indian sub-continent that distinguish in their genders not sex but *caste*—the distinction is between superior and inferior beings, all women and even goddesses belonging to the latter division. There are as well the numerous languages of quasi-primitive peoples, of which something is said elsewhere.

4 Language in Time

Comparative linguistics is concerned in the main with the linguistic past, and only incidentally with the languages of the present day. In fact, the term *historical* linguistics is often preferred.

As we shall be seeing later, much of the linguistic endeavour of the nineteenth century was historically inclined, and many of the more scholarly 'grammars' produced in the last century were constructed on historical principles. Concern with the history of languages, though, was by no means a nineteenth-century innovation. However far back in time we go, it is always possible to find speculations about the origins of words and other features of language; and especially about writing and written forms. The difference was that during the nineteenth century the historical study of languages became increasingly a rigorous one.

Alongside comparative or historical linguistics and during the same period there had been a growing but largely separate interest in the *structure* of language in its own right. This was a different kind of interest from that of the 'normative' grammarians who, in Europe, can be found as early as the Greeks. The new orientation can be ascribed to a number of factors; and above all to the German Romantic philosophers. Prominent among these was Wilhelm von Humboldt, the 'humanist without portfolio' as he has been described. Among Humboldt's dominant concerns, perhaps his chief concern, was the relationship between speech and thought, culminating in the famous introductory section[1] to his *On the Kawi language of Java*. A further providential fillip had come from the 'discovery' in the previous century not only of Sanskrit but, more important still, of the marvellously sophisticated Sanskrit grammarian Pāṇini, who had flourished in the third or fourth century B.C. Added to this, and especially during the latter half of the nineteenth century, numerous psychologists, anthropologists, ethnologists, and even biologists and physicists lent their weight to a discipline that has become known in our own century variously as *general*, *descriptive*, *theoretical* or *modern* linguistics.

Although there had been some interaction between the two

[1] The full title of this section is: *On the variety of human language structures and their influence on the mental development of mankind.*

parallel streams, and although it would not be strictly accurate to regard them as isolated developments, very few scholars had been able to forge any real synthesis between the historical and 'theoretical' approaches to language. One notable exception was the American linguist William Dwight Whitney.[1] By the end of the nineteenth century, however, the somewhat rampant growth of historical-comparative linguistics and the emergence of both speculative and empirical procedures for investigating the nature and structure of language and languages were threatening not so much to blur as to confuse the two still decidedly separate approaches.

This particular problem was solved, provisionally at any rate, by the Swiss linguist Ferdinand de Saussure at the beginning of the twentieth century. Saussure was himself a distinguished comparatist; but growingly, towards the end of his life, he had become preoccupied with general linguistic issues. It became his contention that there are two distinct, but complementary, ways of looking at language. We can look at it from a historical, or as he put it *diachronic*, point of view; or we can consider a language as a contemporaneous, or *synchronic*, structure or state at a particular moment of time, now or in the past. We can, then, consider language from a *diachronic* or from a *synchronic* point of view. Change is diachronic; state is synchronic. The term diachronic linguistics has become synonymous with historical and comparative linguistics, and is not seldom used.

The diachronic view

Saussure[2] was the first to take a consistent view of language as a series of states threaded along the dimension of time. An analogy that immediately springs to mind is that of a series of frames making up a film strip. The analogy employed by Saussure himself was the chess game. Any game of chess can be regarded as a series of states, each state being independent of all previous states. Take any one of these states, one that, for sake of argument, has been brought about by the move of my opponent's queen. If any-

[1] See especially *Language and the Study of Language* (New York, 1867) and *The Life and Growth of Language* (New York, 1874).
[2] *Course in General Linguistics* (ed. Charles Bally and Albert Sechehaye; and trans. W. Baskin (London, 1960)).

one cares to argue that the present state of the game is dependent on what has gone before, I can reply that the present board can if desired be taken as the beginning of a new game. In chess I can begin a new game anywhere and with any prearrangement of pieces I care to choose. It is partly convention that dictates that

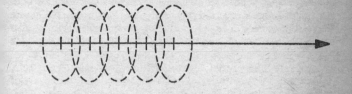

State 2   State 4
State 1   State 3   State 5 etc.

Figure 6

players normally begin with a full board of duly drawn-up pieces. The same is true of a language, which can be viewed as a series of states independent of any future or earlier states. The states are *synchronic*, whereas the transition from one state to the next is *diachronic*. Another, perhaps closer, analogy is the billiard game, when the geometrical arrangement of the balls is never repeated and the situation determining successive possible shots is never the same twice in succession. Language is likewise a series of states which are in equilibrium (synchrony) from an internal point of view but are likely at any moment to have this equilibrium disturbed from outside (diachrony); the period of disequilibrium may be brief or continuous but will sooner or later resolve into another and different state of equilibrium.

I shall be introducing these concepts in what is otherwise a more or less conventional approach to comparative linguistics. My attempt at hybridisation may not be altogether successful, but I feel it to be sometimes a necessary antidote to the kind of comparative linguistics sometimes picked up by students. A student of Old French, for instance, can be fascinated by tie-ups with later French and the Vulgar Latin sources of origin, but is often irritated by other elements that 'do not fit in', especially the syntax or idiom which bears only slight relation to either Modern French or Latin. Anything that does not somehow square with the sequence Latin → Old-French → Middle-French → Modern French seems simply annoying. The error that the student has made is that he has taken the (legitimate) diachronic perspective and ignored the synchronic. As soon as he realises this he finds that he is up against a language in its own right, namely Old French, which has a multitude of distinguishing features that set it apart from any other language before or since. Increasing fascination for the *internal* structure of this language then begins, until the student has discovered the hidden springs and balances that have given the language its equilibrium and resilience.

Inevitably, the present book will be dealing almost exclusively with various features of diachronic linguistics. In the remainder of this chapter, therefore, I want to touch on a number of rather general matters, some of which do not belong to linguistics proper. My remarks are in the nature of tentative reservations— and rather less tentative caveats—which the student or practitioner of comparative linguistics would probably do well to bear in mind. My illustrations, when I need any, will be taken from English.

My first point is that the historical linguist is nearly always working from written texts or inscriptions. I shall have more to say about writing in the next chapter. Suffice it for the time being to recollect that information about how a language was spoken is seldom easy, and usually extremely difficult or impossible, to come by. And the chances of being able to reconstruct the speech of a regional unwritten dialect are usually too remote even to consider. The comparatist mostly has to rely, then, on a type of language that, especially in times past, was restricted in use and available only to a tiny minority of the population. Thus the diachronist is in danger of becoming like the desperately short-sighted train traveller who thought that, wherever he went, everything looked about the same—only telegraph poles, occasional railway stations, tunnels and other trains.

If I might be allowed to mangle this analogy a little, our diachronist—this time normal-sighted—will find the tunnels frequent, long and usually disconcerting. As he emerges from a tunnel he notices that the landscape has changed all right, but he does not always realise, when he *should*, that he is in a different country. Language history is riddled with tunnels, the periods during which cultural as well as linguistic continuity is interrupted. These are, as it were, the missing links of language history. One of the things the historical linguist will usually be adept at is reconstructing the missing links. He will, moreover, often be forced to do this on the flimsiest of evidence; and sometimes on the supposition that some kind of continuity was maintained despite every appearance to the contrary. Imagine for a moment our historical linguist living in the year A.D. 3973, and for the sake of argument that he is using the same linguistic procedures as those current today. Let us also suppose that he is making a special survey of the period 1700 to 2000 of the English language but that by, let us say, some inexplicable set of circumstances all printed material published between 1760 and 1970 has been wiped out. The only works from that period he knows of are post-1970 editions of the nonsense rhymes of Edward Lear, and *Finnegans Wake*, as well as a miraculously (but regrettably) preserved English translation of *Mein Kampf*. The texts he has access to in the period preceding 1760 are, let us suppose: Dr. Johnson's Dictionary, *Tristram Shandy*, parts of Addison's *Spectator*, two anonymous sectarian tracts, and some correspondence of Benjamin Franklin. For the period after 1970 he has a few numbers of *Playboy* magazine, two issues of *The Financial Times*, an English edition of *The People's Daily* and a couple of novels by an as yet unknown novelist. I now leave the reader to imagine what bizarre guesses our tunnel-bound diachronist would be making about the English language during the nineteenth and early twentieth centuries. I am, of course, using a deliberate exaggeration. My purpose was simply to demonstrate the extreme skill, good sense and perspicacity required of the diachronist, even in what might seem to be less unfavourable circumstances. Needless to say, these requirements are multiplied in the case of the comparatist, who is often dealing with several different language traditions at once. I don't think I need labour the point further.

The descriptive linguist, or synchronist, whose purpose is usually to describe a modern language, can ignore the diachronic features altogether. The diachronist, on the other hand, can only wonder at the variegated patchwork the modern language presents to his eyes. In English, for example, there are words and grammatical features that date back to neolithic times, and

possibly earlier. A word like *ox* has 'evolved' not too far apart
from the Sanskrit *ukša*, either in form or in meaning. But the
separation of the Germanic and Indic language communities
probably took place in pre-Agrarian times. The English words for
many objects, numbers, trees, animals and several of the kinship
terms (*mother*, *brother*, etc.) are still recognisably Indo-European.
These words, which for millenia had been in the dialects that the
Anglo-Saxons brought to the British Isles, continued to exist
happily alongside many new elements that came into existence
since, and especially from the time when English was transplanted
to North America and to the remaining parts of the English-
speaking world. The coexistence of these motley elements is
almost too harmonious. A verb like *go down*, a compound verb
antedating the Norman Conquest, gets along so amicably with
godown (= 'a warehouse') that most speakers of English would
not suspect that the latter is a word of Malay origin, introduced
into 'Anglo-Indian' English in the seventeenth century. Again, a
word of venerable scholastic origin like *compound* cheerfully
accommodates another near-relative from Malay: *kampong* >
compound (= 'enclosure'). The French borrowed *riding coat* from
English in the eighteenth century and pronounced it *redingote*.
The more fashionable English borrowed *redingote* back from
French in the nineteenth century, pronouncing it *re-din-gote* in
the English manner. In the Far East *business* came to be pronounced by certain communities to whom English was a second
language as *pidgin*. Since then, of course, *pidgin* has been adopted
as the name of a quasi-English language used widely in Melanesia
and in West Africa. As if this were not enough to distract the
historical linguist, he must also cope with thousands of items that
are brand new, still in the limbo of not-quite-respectability:
words of technical, commercial or slang origin. More than this, he
must also take account of the various dialects. The history of the
English dialects is by no means congruent with that of the
standard. Certain dialects of the north-west of England still
preserve the Anglo-Saxon pronoun *hīo* = 'she' (dialect spelling:
who). The statement *Who does this* means in these dialects *She
does this*. In all the other English dialects *hīo* had been replaced by
she by about the time of Edward the Confessor. Sometimes the
dialect relic gets taken back into the spoken standard for a time,
usually to convey certain connotations. The word *tea* first came

into English as *cha*, and this word was preserved in London colloquial dialects. For a period, and especially during the Second World War and after, non-dialect speakers would often be heard referring to *a cup of cha*. Hundreds of like examples could be given. But I think we have seen enough for the reader to appreciate that the task of the diachronic linguist is no simple one.

Language, history and people

This brings us into the vast and relatively unexplored no-man's-land between language and social mores, between language and ingrained human habits. Here, the linguist is up against the ordinary folk who shape the course of a language. It is because language is a mirror of the way we live, our foibles, excesses and virtues, our sense of play and fun, that it is such a slippery thing to map historically.

Let us begin with children. Much is now known about the ways in which children learn to speak. It was once thought that children acquired their mother tongue by imitating adults; but nowadays many students of child language are inclined to the view that children develop their own language systems, modifying them gradually until they come to resemble the language used by adults. Be that as it may, there are undeniably many features of adult language that resemble the speech forms developed by young children. Whether this is the direct influence of children, an extension into adulthood of children's ways of talking, or simply a by-product of the baby-talk used by adults we cannot be sure. But we can note the similarities, and take account of them. It is, for instance, a well-observed fact that children play about with the adult language, in ways adults do not always approve. Many games played by children make use of language play: puns, rhymes, consonant substitutions, word substitutions. Such features have been observed in the (adult) American Indian languages. Sapir[1] reported that in the Nootka language links have been established between speech defects, 'mocking-forms', and consonantal play. He was of the opinion that consonant substitutions have developed a consciously humorous use and were connected with the tendency to set up myth-character relationships

[1] Mandelbaum, D. G. (ed.), *Selected Writings of Edward Sapir* (Berkeley and Los Angeles, 1958), p. 191.

for particular members of the community. The diachronist, when he encounters Middle English changes like *an naddre* > *an adder* and *a napron* > *an apron*, or conversely *an eke-name* > *a nick-name* and *drink a rouse* > *carouse*, must sometimes wonder to what extent the play habits of children have shaped them. He *can* sometimes explain them on purely linguistic grounds. But *should* he? Even if his conscience is clear as far as these examples go, he must surely feel that the principles of diachronic phonology would be pushed rather too far if they were expected to provide a *complete* explanation for folk-etymological changes like (Fr.) *quel-quechose* > (Eng.) *kickshaws* or *Eleanor Infanta of Castile* > *Elephant and Castle*.

All languages make use to some extent of morphological or syntactic play. Many languages, for instance, have developed in-built features of syllable *reduplication*. In an Indonesian dialect we discover a form *igi* (= 'many') being reduplicated as many as four times: *igi-igi-igi-igi* (= 'more numerous than anything'). The Papuan reduplication of *pinimina* (= 'fragment') to give *pinipinimina* (= 'crumb') is related in form, if not in function, to the tendency of a number of Indo-European languages to re-duplicate the first syllable of the stem to form the perfect tense (e.g. Latin *parco* = 'I spare' > *peperci* = 'I have spared'). Nor is it functionally unrelated to expressions like *teeny-weeny* as used in English 'baby-talk'. Nor, again, is it all that different, either in form or in function, from the Italian *pian-piano* (= 'very soft') and *molto molto* (= 'very much'), or from the Russian *davným-davnó* (= 'long, long ago'). Any explanation of English folk-creations like *mish-mash* or *midge-madge*, or standard forms like *higgledy-piggledy*, *tittle-tattle*, *hugger-mugger* and *willy-nilly* must surely make allowance for the human play element.

A child's early gropings in the direction of the language of its parents are, like many other of its activities, bold, energetic and incautious. An old-style grammarian would regard it as nothing less than miraculous that a child ever mastered language at all. There is no logic or method. Jespersen gives a number of examples he had collected of attempts to build up vocabulary. One child of 1 year 6 months learned the word for *pig* and then used the same word to represent (i) *the drawing of a pig* and (ii) *writing in general*. Another child of about the same age used the word *daisy* (i) correctly, (ii) for *any flower*, (iii) *any conventional flower in a pattern*,

(iv) *any pattern*. There is a mass of such examples to be found in the etymological development of particular languages. The word *treacle* is a stock example, starting its career as a remedy against viper bites as in the biblical 'There is no more triacle at Galaad'. The respectable *Tripos* began its life as a 'three-legged stool', and later its meaning became attached to the 'man who sat on a three-legged stool to dispute with candidates for degrees at Cambridge'. The comic verses provided by Mr. Tripos were called tripos verses. The word *coffin* signified originally a basket or case, as in the compound *custard-coffin* (*Taming of the Shrew*) and *pie-crust*.

The list of parallels between adult and child language is endless, but we shall have to content ourselves with this brief sketch and leave the matter at that.

Fashion, that maker of small-fortunes by the multi-million, cannot be ruled out either. People do tend to copy one another, and especially the smart or trendy set, even to a ludicrous degree. 'Fashionable', 'trendy' words and phrases are never hard to find. They range from the overspill hippy jargon to the rarified locutions of science that easily stray so incongruously outside their natural habitat. *Square, cool, dig, groovy* have all been a 'must'; and some of them after only a few years seem as quaint as the old-boyisms of Bertie Wooster. Terms like *ecological, parameter, motivation, module, computerise, anomie, alienation, algorithm* appear to have a longer life span, but ultimately they too will mostly fall on the scrap-heap of disused vocabulary, or else retreat into their proper sphere.

Imitation is the crux of the matter. 'Man is apt to imitate throughout the whole of his life. . . . What he imitates in this as in other fields, is not always the best; a real valuation of what would be linguistically good or preferable does not of course enter the head of the "man in the street". But he may imitate what he thinks pretty, or funny, and especially what he thinks characteristic of those people whom for some reason or other he looks up to.' Words and phrases rise and fall in value like share prices on Wall Street. One day a word is on everyone's lips, the next finds it dropped or relegated to its former position. Readers will have no difficulty in finding such examples for themselves.

Not a few instances of verbal fashion seem inept or nonsensical, uneconomical or just plain silly. I recall an acquaintance who announced that he had lately met a millionaire who unfortunately 'had a neurosis about spending'. My matter-of-fact rejoinder 'Oh, you mean he's a bit of a miser' was not overwelcome and his reaction was a little dazed. Again, why do people waste their vocal energies on such all-of-a-lump phrases as *to all intents and purposes* when *virtually* or even nothing at all will do just as well? Some abbreviations and acronyms require more effort than the phrases they represent. Why do people say TWA (tee-double-u-ay: five syllables) when Trans-World Airlines contains only four syllables!

Another factor affecting the course of a language in time is *slang*. Wherever you have groups of people, especially minority groups, you have slang. On the one hand, slang exists in its own right in a great diversity of forms and, on the other hand, has intimate relationships with the growth of normal language. Children are perhaps most given to slang, although nearly every group of individuals that considers itself either select or 'superior' (inverted snobs included) has its own argot. Slang must not be confused with vulgar speech or jargon; and, despite any superficial affinities, it is neither of these. 'The ultimate impulse to the creation of slang is a certain feeling of intellectual superiority. We find that some particular word or expression of the normal language has grown trite, it is too well known, we are sick of it, and so we seek for a new word, that will tickle our fancy and satisfy our desire for something amusing, or at least pleasurable, by way of a change. Slang is an outcome of mankind's love of play; it is the playful production of something new, where, properly speaking, nothing new was required . . . Slang is a linguistic luxury, it is a sport.' This is Jespersen's classic description[1] and one that leaves out absolutely nothing.

One important sign of the superiority of the slang-user is that he can mercilessly 'crush' any intruder into his speech who dares put a foot wrong. We see this with children, particularly schoolchildren, all the time. One finds it variously in university commonrooms, sports clubs, specialised hobbies such as fishing, gliding, yachting and in teenager terminology. The military thrives on it. Poets, and men of letters in general, have been variously attracted by slang. But its use is perilous. A writer has to be sure of his readers (e.g. in a locality, common way of life, class, etc.) or else

[1] Jespersen, O., *Mankind, Nation and Individual* (London, 1946), p. 150.

has to be apparently indifferent to them (Joyce's *Finnegans Wake* is a very good example). The use of slang will always raise barriers of obscurity to the general reader.

Many slang words have found their way into official usage either spontaneously or through the influence of writers. It has been described as 'a peculiar kind of vagabond language, always hanging on the outskirts of legitimate speech, but continually straying or forcing its way into the most respectable company'. Useful words with a precise technical meaning such as *boom*, *slump*, *crank*, *fad* have a slang origin. Another example is *joke*.

One class of words in particular is likely to be of slang origin. This class arises from the fact that some things, more than others, have provoked irreverent shafts of slang: the various parts of the body, especially the *head*—not to mention the synonyms that have remained slang: *nut*, *nob*, *loaf*, *bonce*, *block*, *dome*, *onion*, *turnip*, *chump*, *crust*, *top-knot*, *upper storey*, *upper works*, *attic*, *garret*, etc. In some languages slang words have acquired official status. German has *Kopf* (from Lat. *cupa* 'cup'). The French *tête* has been usually taken as the derivative of Vulgar Latin *testa* 'a piece of baked earthenware, an earthen pot' (although this has lately been questioned).[1] The true derivative of Latin *caput* (= 'head') is *chef*, which has since taken on a more abstract meaning. Words for hands and feet, speaking, eating, money and others have constantly been subject to slang encroachments. A comparison of the European verbs 'to speak' will show little equivalence. The Latin *loqui* 'to speak' survives in none of the Romance languages. Instead we find a range of different words: (Spanish) *hablar*, (Port.) *falar*, (Rom.) *a vorbi*, (Ital.) *parlare*, (Fr.) *parler*. Only the last two are counterparts and both are derived from the later Vulgar Latin word o[1] Christian origin *parabolare* 'to speak in parables'.

Jargon or specialist words have a way of infiltrating into language in much the same way as slang. But whereas slang is a luxury, jargon generally fulfils some utilitarian end. The words of the specialist have usually crept into everyday use only because it is more convenient to have them than to be without them. Many of the words of Greek and Latin origin that found their way into English in the sixteenth and seventeenth centuries have remained

[1] Elcock, W. D., *The Romance Languages* (Faber & Faber, 1960), pp. 155–6.

in use after having found for themselves a suitable niche in the general language.

Of all the specialists of the last few centuries, the scientist under his many guises has been responsible for the bulk of such words. A number of them, such as *thermometer*, *symptom*, *electricity*, *meteorology* and hundreds of others have made themselves indispensable to the layman. Others have served for the nefarious purposes of 'blinding with science' or for the casting of professional spells.

When introduced into general usage, some of these words were frowned upon, just as we might nowadays look askance at such innovations as *ergonomics*, *semanticist*, *rodent operator*, *social pathologist* or *educationalist*. Even as late as 1840 *scientist* was branded as an 'ignoble Americanism' or 'a cheap and vulgar product of trans-Atlantic slang'.

It is unfashionable nowadays to lard one's speech with the many specialist terms. It is nevertheless true that words are constantly 'leaking' from the special sciences into popular usage. Thus the man in the street may bandy about such terms as *complex* (the noun), *introvert*, *superego*, *psychosis* without having more than the faintest idea of their true significance. The exact scientific meaning of certain words is eclipsed by an everyday meaning. A good example is *velocity*, which in standard usage is used loosely as a synonym for *speed*, whereas in physics the word carries a special and precise meaning.

Writers and especially critics have introduced innumerable foreign words and phrases, and have often created jargons of a singular kind. As a result, the purist is constantly on guard against precocity. Having myself had such scruples not very long ago about the word *malaise*, I consulted the dictionary. (Later) I asked students in one of my adult classes for their opinions on the subject. Some thought that *malaise* was not English and a few felt that it should therefore not be used; one or two hazarded a guess that the word had been introduced around about the beginning of the present century. One or two felt that it was by now a native English word and could well have been in the language for well over a century. In a sense all of them were right because, although the *Oxford Dictionary* gives 1766 as the date of its introduction, the word has remained 'alien and not naturalised'. English must be unique in this respect.

Languages in history are not only affected but also to a large extent *controlled* by the interplay on a vast scale of people's mores, fads and fashions. A purely linguistic residue remains—one that, as we shall see, can be meaningfully investigated—but the 'extra-linguistic' forces are ever-impinging, and never far over the horizon. Linguists have perforce become increasingly circumspect. And a part of the linguist's traditional operating ground has been conceded to the sociologist, the social historian and the cultural anthropologist, and even the folklorist has come back into his own.

One tendency which happily has by now virtually disappeared is that of treating languages as if they were watertight entities with their own separate historical life-line. Ancient Greek was the natural ancestor of Modern Greek, Old Slavonic the precursor of Russian, Anglo-Saxon the forerunner of English, and that was that. We now know that languages do not develop in anything like isolation, and that even not too closely related languages sometimes develop parallel features. And, because of the tunnels I was talking about farther back, the language scene is subject to change in abrupt and inconsistent ways, not totally explicable on purely diachronistic grounds.

I don't remember who it was who said that if Aristotle were alive today he would find it easier to write in French or English than in Modern Greek (although he might still want to *talk* in Greek). Possibly the Norse saga-tellers of old would find modern Danish or Norwegian quite a let-down after the strength and exuberance of the language they were used to. And although in a very real sense Shakespeare played an important part in shaping modern English, one wonders how he would react to the vastly different 'languages' of Pinter or Beckett.

When we come to a language like English we find ourselves dealing with several languages rolled into one. Ever since the tenth century English has been like a vacuum cleaner-cum-sausage machine, sucking in whole chunks or scattered bits of languages from just about everywhere under the sun and reshaping them in such a way that the speaker of English would seldom guess that they had ever been 'foreign'.

Take Shakespeare, for instance. He takes a new word, a word of learned origin, and handles it with as much ease and grace as if it had been one of the oldest words in the language. Owen

Barfield[1] cites the example of his effective use of the word *propagate*, which appeared for the first time in English in 1570. See how Romeo uses it (and *figuratively* too):

> Griefs of mine own lie heavy in my breast,
> Which thou wilt propagate, to have it prest
> With more of thine.

The English language is such that it has affinities, however indirect, with every major Western European language, ancient, mediaeval or modern.

One of the strangest things of all about English is that it is still possible to construct fairly normal sentences using exclusively vocabulary taken from the separate strata (Old English, Norse, French, 'learned'). The following are given for the record:

Old English:

> The man in the wilderness asked of me
> How many strawberries grow in the sea?
> I answered him as I thought good,
> As many red herrings as grow in the wood.
>   (*Anon.*)

French:

People prefer travelling in groups particularly during certain seasons despite very considerable reasons favouring possible contrary arrangements.

Latin:

Devastating conflagrations, incinerating vast rural areas, inflicted incalculable, irremediable destruction, exceeding prevalent popular expectation.

To write a work of literature in English is like writing in a set of different languages—take Eliot, Joyce or Pound, for example— or else choosing a particular 'dialect', dialect in the sense of a particular way of bringing the English language into focus. Examples of the latter would be D. H. Lawrence, Faulkner, Sillitoe and P. G. Wodehouse.

[1] Barfield, O., *History in English Words* (London, 1926), p. 138.

The virtues and vices of English cannot be dealt with here. The reader will find much discussion elsewhere on the richness, flexibility, special qualities, idiosyncrasies and a great deal else. If I were asked to single out the most individual quality of English—a quality that is perhaps unique—I would point to the comic and nonsense element bound up in the entire fabric of the language. Few other European languages can produce humorous verse out of verbal incongruities such as this:

> The common cormorant or shag
> Lays eggs inside a paper bag.
> The reason you will see no doubt
> It is to keep the lightning out.
> But what these unobservant birds
> Have never noticed is that herds
> Of wandering bears may come with buns
> And steal the bags to hold the crumbs.

The reader may easily find more comic examples in the general anthologies of the comic and nonsense verse type. The sheer just plain fun must be nearly impossible to convey to a foreigner. Why is the word *bun* or, for that matter, *paper bag* so funny? And so to the great comic poets of the English language, a unique race. The closely packed laughter of Edward Lear:

> There was an Old Man with a beard,
> Who sat on a horse when he reared;
> But they said, Never mind!
> You will fall off behind,
> You propitious Old Man with a beard!

Could the Latin scholasts and pedants of the Revived Learning ever have imagined what waggishness their *propitious* would acquire in this poet's hands?

The secret of this linguistic fun is without question the rich source of children's lore, an impressive slice of which has been collected by Iona and Peter Opie in their *Lore and Language of Schoolchildren*. It is only after acquaintance with this seemingly inexhaustible fund that one discovers the childhood merriment that underlies much English speech and undermines solemnity at a stroke.

Linguistic change

When considered over a long period of time, many of the major European languages have been not one, but several; and not always in a clear-cut sequence either. French has been at various times and in various places: Old French, Gallo-Roman, Anglo-Norman, Provençale, Middle French; German embraces Old High German, Old Saxon, Middle High German and Low German; English is an amalgam of Anglo-Saxon, Anglo-Norse, Anglo-Norman and Middle English. Each period of history is associated with a certain language shape, a certain 'style' which sets these languages apart from preceding or later periods. The Anglo-Saxon *Battle of Maldon* has features that liken it to the Old French *Chanson de Roland*; it has something of the Norse sagas, and not a little in common with the *Lay of Igor's Campaign* composed in far-away Ancient Russia. They all belong to the same period of the early Middle Ages. What they do have in common is not so much the actual language structure as the *diction*—the poetic material itself, the mode of expression, the tone, right down to the way the poem is set out on the manuscript page.

The assumption of many nineteenth-century scholars was that a language is an organic, integral thing spread out through time, and that it undergoes a process of evolutionary change. Undoubtedly much of this prejudice can be ascribed to the origin of comparative-historical linguistics in the German Romantic era, certain ingredients being traceable to the fountain-head of organic philosophy, Johann-Gottfried von Herder. The view of perhaps most modern diachronic linguists would be that languages do not change in an organic way—like people change as they grow older —but that they undergo a series of shifts, transpositions, re-alignments, distortions and substitutions. An older feature is replaced or eclipsed by a rival. Moreover, the shifts and displacements are probably of a 'quantum', not a gradual, kind. In the majority of instances, these shifts and displacements will have been brought about by *language contact*, a phenomenon that occurs[1] when a speaker belongs to two or more speech communities (i.e. is bilingual in the sense we discussed in Chapter 2) and when there exists a substantial body of such speakers in one place and over a significant period of time. This language contact

[1] Weinreich, V., *Languages in Contact* (The Hague, 1966).

need not entail two separate national languages or two separate standards; for language contact occurs when a standard language and a dialect of the same 'language' are spoken or used by the same speaker.

The first scholars to have more than an inkling of the importance of bilingualism in language history were the so-called Neogrammarians in the late nineteenth century. One of them, Hermann Paul, insisted that all borrowing from one language to another must assume some minimum of bilingual mastery of the two languages between which borrowing took place. It is now widely recognised that for a language to change in any major way there needs to have been a period of bilingualism during which foreign ways took predominance over indigenous ways. The mother tongue (MT) and another tongue (OT) become fused in a new tongue (NT):

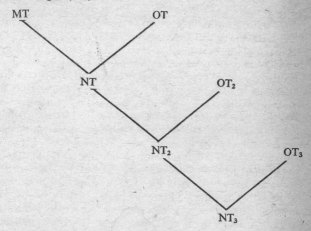

Figure 7

Linguistic change and bilingualism in English

During the time of the Roman Empire a distinctive culture, known as Romano-British, developed in Britain. The language of the towns was probably not too different from that used throughout the rest of the Roman Empire—namely, Latin. Although some of the wealthier and more cultivated people outside the towns probably understood Latin, their first language (mother tongue), along with that of the mass of the people, was British or, more accurately, Brythonic Celtic. It was clearly a highly developed language, containing a fair proportion of borrowings, or 'loan words', from Latin, many of these borrowings being of Christian origin. Like Latin, this Brythonic language died out completely in what is now England and the Scottish Lowlands, being replaced by Anglo-Saxon. In these areas the only surviving relics were the place-names and river-names. At one time it was assumed that the British population was wiped out or driven out. Nowadays, from a combination of archaeological, linguistic and other historical evidence, we know that this was not so. As one recent Celtic scholar has said: 'Taking together all the evidence on the linguistic relations of Britons and Saxons, and though it is impossible to generalise, we do seem to observe the following features: the Britons learned the language of their conquerors, and they acquired its sound-system and vocabulary very completely, their own phonetics having no discernible effect on the new language, and their own vocabulary very little . . . *All this suggests a bilingual stage*, when the Britons knew both Anglo-Saxon and British . . . and it is not probable that the conquerors learned much of the language of the conquered.'[1] (My italics.) The first period of bilingualism in Britain seems to have lasted at least 200 years, from about A.D. 450 to 650, and possibly longer. Figure 8 opposite illustrates this.

At the time of the Anglo-Saxon invasion of Britain there were four possibilities: (i) that Anglo-Saxon would survive in pure form (which, in fact, it did, at least for a few centuries); (ii) that Anglo-Saxon would become dominant but with a Celtic admixture; (iii) that British would remain the dominant language but would become mixed with Anglo-Saxon; and (iv) that only British would survive. Possibilities (iii) and (iv) became ruled out from the start because the British were learning Anglo-Saxon in large numbers; but not the other way round. Already the survival of British in pure form was an extremely remote possibility—except, of course, in Wales, where apparently this tendency for Britons to learn Anglo-Saxon did not occur. All this suggests that

[1] Jackson, K., *Language and History in Early Britain* (Edinburgh, 1953), p. 245.

it was desirable that the British learned to speak Anglo-Saxon, but that the Anglo-Saxons felt no need to learn British. It would be jumping to rather unwarrantable conclusions to suppose that Anglo-Saxon was the prestige language, or that the British were compelled to learn Anglo-Saxon (as the Poles were compelled to

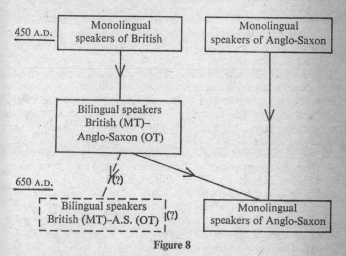

Figure 8

learn Russian in the last century). A number of intriguing explanations, from which the reader may choose, suggest themselves if we are to explain why Anglo-Saxon survived and especially why it remained pure. The first of these hypotheses is that the *language loyalty*[1] of the British was weak or non-existent. But there is no historical evidence for this. On the contrary, the Welsh and the Cornish have been extremely 'loyal' to British. The Welsh still speak it, as do the Breton descendants of Cornish settlers. The second supposition would be that the British were co-ordinate bilinguals, using one language in one set of circumstances and the other in a different, but largely non-overlapping, set of circumstances. This second possibility does not, however, tally too well with the accuracy and completeness with which the British seemed to have learned Anglo-Saxon, and passed it on to their children.

[1] Technical term used in the literature on bilingualism.

A third possibility is that the British did not want to mix their British with their Anglo-Saxon. This could be the sign of a fanatical kind of language loyalty; something akin to that found among persecuted Yiddish-speaking communities in Eastern Europe. At any rate, this third hypothesis has the advantage of squaring satisfyingly with the aura of legend surrounding King Arthur and Camelot. If it is the right one, then British would have gone on being spoken, and possibly even written, until a much later time than is generally thought likely. It is not impossible that British would have been retained for certain religious, poetical, ritualistic and perhaps other specialised purposes. Also, it is far from improbable that those who after many generations still felt strongly about their mother tongue would have gone to live in Wales or, like the Cornishmen, have taken to their fishing boats and settled in Brittany. This theory also goes some way towards explaining the extraordinary vigour and, until modern times, the purity of the Welsh language. And, as many readers are doubtless aware, the Welsh bilingual is as skilled and accurate a bilingual as one will find anywhere.

The second period of bilingualism in Britain coincided with the Viking or Norse incursions and was in marked contrast with the period we have just been discussing. This second 'Anglo-Norse' period began about A.D. 800 and lasted until the Norman Conquest. These Norse speakers came mainly from Denmark and settled chiefly in Lincolnshire and the Midlands. We know this from the rather large number of Scandinavian place-names, including those ending in -by ('township') as in Derby, Wetherby, etc. Settlers also came from Norway; it seems that they (as one might expect) took to Scotland and the far north of England where the topographical aspect is not unlike Norway. At that time, English and Scandinavian dialects were by no means so far apart as they are now in the twentieth century. The theory has been advanced that Old English lost the greater part of its complex flexional system (genders, cases, etc.) during the time of the Scandinavian influx for the very reason that, although their declensional endings were totally different, their words or vocabulary were basically the same. Jespersen puts the matter as follows: 'As the Scandinavians and the English could understand one another without much difficulty it was natural that many niceties of grammar should be sacrificed, the intelligibility of either tongue coming to depend mainly on its mere vocabulary. So when we find that the wearing away and levelling of grammatical forms in the regions in which the Danes chiefly settled was a couple of centuries in advance of the same process in the more southern parts of the country, the conclusion does not seem unwarrantable that this acceleration of the tempo of linguistic simplification is due to the settlers, who did not care to learn English correctly in every minute particular and who certainly needed no such accuracy in order to make themselves understood.'[1]

Many of our intimate everyday words, e.g. *egg*, *skill*, *skin*, *law*, *window*, *gift*, *bread*, *dream*, *take*, *call*, *scrub*, *scrape*, *scream* and a multitude of others, are all taken directly from Norse. Indeed, in some instances, if we did not know from the various texts whence a particular word originated, we should never be able to tell, for in both languages, Old English and Norse, the words were in every respect identical.

The next wave of linguistic influence was quite another matter; a wave that at one stage threatened to become a serious contender with English for supremacy. This was the language of the French nobility who claimed terrains in England from the time of the Norman Conquest onwards. At first, the language of these nobles was Norman (subsequently called Anglo-Norman), a sub-dialect of French, but later French proper. These landowners, soldiers and high churchmen for nearly two centuries made no attempt to learn English, and regarded the English much as more recent British colonialists did the Irish, Hindu or Kikuyu. One important difference emerged. The French nobility who settled in England were eventually cut off from their mother country when the French crown claimed Normandy and other continental Norman territories for itself. The French who remained in England were gradually obliged to learn English, thus bringing all kinds of conflict and social tensions into being.

During the period after the Norman Conquest many English speakers, particularly from the higher social classes, seem to have learned French, whereas only a minority of the Normans acquired any English. However, the miscellaneous facts left behind by history do give some grounds for wariness. Born in England not long after the Norman Conquest, and son of a

[1] Jespersen, O., *Growth and Structure of the English Language* (Basil Blackwell, 1960), pp. 75–6.

Norman priest and an Englishwoman, the writer Orderic Vital first came into contact with the French language when he was sent to school in Normandy. This is reasonable proof that Vital's parents spoke only English in his presence, which in turn rather suggests that they spoke only English to each other at all times. William of Longchamp had minstrels brought from France to sing his praises in the streets, which again suggests that at least a proportion of the populace would know what they were singing about. Even in 1970 the English town-crier calls out: *Oyez, Oyez!*, the Old French imperative *Hear!*

The years 1204–5 mark a turning point in Anglo-French history; for it was from that time onwards that the French lands of Norman nobles whose abode was in England were confiscated by the King of France. Those who remained marooned in England inevitably committed themselves to English ways; and these included the language. But for at least some this adaptation would not have been so painful. Stephen Langton, Archbishop of Canterbury during these difficult years, is known to have preached in English, although he appears to have preferred French or Latin for writing. The year 1300, which ushers in a third period, saw the appearance of manuals for the teaching of French, a sure sign that at least partly French-speaking Englishmen were worried that their children might have difficulty learning the French of France.

Up until 1200, and even later, French remained the language of prestige and influence. Besides having become politically supreme since the Norman Conquest, French acquired an additional and political cultural ascendancy in the thirteenth century, which helped to postpone the inevitable end of the Anglo-French bilingual era and to ensure that English would emerge from this phase with an abnormally heavy dosage of French in its system.

The English and French languages proved strange bedfellows enough, although the matter did not end there. Far more crucial were differences of social class. The Normans had almost without exception been aristocrats and had simply remained so over the generations. All positions of power and prestige, with few exceptions, were occupied by them. Not only this, but the French had developed a civilisation more sophisticated and an economy more complex than anything the English had attained; they were, relatively speaking, 'underdeveloped'. Thus normal class differences were even further exaggerated. One has only to look at the

Norman cathedrals (Durham, for example) and the Norman castles to form some idea of the architectural splendour of conception and of the economic and craft resources needed to make them possible. The social differences are vividly preserved in the English language, which eventually absorbed a sizeable proportion of the French vocabulary. The Old English *stool*, which originally signified any object made for sitting on, even the king's throne, gave way to *chair*, which even today clearly retains the usage it came to have when the crisis between English and French was resolved. It is nearly possible to draw up a hierarchy of types of objects for sitting on, to draw a dividing line across and to classify everything below the line as 'stools' and everything above as 'chairs'. This is no isolated example. *Cottages* were finer than *huts*; *to dress* presupposed a finer garment than *to clothe*. A *tailor* would have been a cut above the *weaver* and so on.

Perhaps the oddest example of all—the French nouns *mutton*, *pork*, *veal*, *beef*, etc., which have indeed become part of the English vocabulary but only in so far as these animals turn up cooked on the table; a fact that indicates (although does not prove) that these words attained their present usage from the French nobleman's exclusive use of these words in their culinary context. Thus the English herdsman would rear a 'pig', and the French baron and his retainers eat it as 'pork'. The cook might well have known both words but would already have been familiar with their separate and proper contexts. The English herdsman would eventually have learnt the French word and used it appropriately for what we nowadays might call snob reasons, or possibly even simply to make himself better understood. It is more than possible that the social origins of a particularly noticeable English trait (to foreigners at any rate) dates back to this time. Jespersen, normally an anglophile, has this to say on the matter: 'We are allowed to connect this adoption of non-technical words with that trait of their character which in its exaggerated form has in modern times been termed snobbism or toadyism, and which has made certain sections of the English people more interested in the births, deaths and especially marriages of dukes and marquises than in anything else outside their own small personal sphere.'

Although the Norse and, later, the Norman-French influence has struck deep roots in the English Language, the same is not true of the next great 'wave'—Latin and Greek. This influence was brought not by invaders but by scholars. This linguistic 'invasion' is very complex, and it would be impossible here to provide even an adequate sketch. A number of pointers may, however, be given. The 'revival of learning' (i.e. classical learning, otherwise termed the Renaissance) began to reach Britain from the late fourteenth century onwards, and had culminated in importance by the sixteenth century. This 'revival' was accompanied by a large influx of new concepts and ideas, which, the scholars felt, could hardly retain their subtlety and nuance in the vulgar tongue (in this case English). Thus the scholars who trafficked in these, and who spoke and read Latin and sometimes read Greek, tended to preserve the original terminology when introducing them into their native tongue. Such words as *propagate, generation, fundamental, phenomenon, anachronism, scientific, economic* and several thousand others, some still insinuating themselves into the English language. The sticking power of such words was reinforced by two further factors: (i) the invention of the printing press in Germany in the middle of the fifteenth century, introduced into this country by Caxton in 1476, and (ii) the spread of education to large sections of the community who were not scholars. Literacy was common among the middle class by the end of the fifteenth century. The demand for books was not confined to this country and by 1500 the number of books printed was as high as 35 000.

One of the arguments frequently put forward for retaining Latin in schools is that it teaches the use of English vocabulary. A farcical situation. Even so, it is probable that the size of one's Graeco-Latin vocabulary is in direct proportion to one's standard of education, and to some extent one's social background. I mention the latter, since colloquial English, the English of the various regions, is still rich in terms that can often render much more vividly the comparatively lifeless Latinism. It is easy for us to be overimpressed by (and thus to *misunderstand*) a language like French, which appears to consist entirely of the upper 'spectrum' (French, Latin, etc.) of English vocabulary. Some time ago I heard a broadcast in which a famous English historian commented upon the poverty of the average Englishman's vocabulary in contrast with the sophistication of that of the average Frenchman. He mentioned the comment of a French taxi-driver, as they were passing over a Rhone bridge, that the river was very 'capricious'.

How many English taxi-drivers, he asked, would have known that word? The comparison is invalid for the very reason that in English the word *capricious* (a word taken from French and ultimately from Italian *capriccioso*) is not a part of the ordinary man's vocabulary, whereas the Frenchman has very little choice but to use *capricieux*; there is very little else he could use. Standard English has a fund of synonyms for *capricious*; among them are *fickle*, *whimsical*, *freakish*, *erratic*, *fanciful*, *fitful*, *wanton*, *wayward*, *contrary*, etc. Colloquialisms and regionalisms such as *chancy*, *faddy*, *giddy*, *you never know when you have him* (*or her*) lengthen the list. where

A study of English synonyms is to be recommended as a way towards understanding the range of the various components of English. I was once illustrating the variety of English synonyms based on the use of the word *courage* to a large lower sixth form. I drew up three columns on the blackboard, asking the class to name all the possible synonyms they could think of. The table emerged somewhat as follows:

Germanic (Old English, Norse)	Norman-French and later French	Latin (and other)
boldness	*courage*	*tenacity*
daring	*bravery*	*audacity*
rashness	*gallantry*	*intrepidity*
manliness	*valour*	*fortitude*
pluck	*heroism*	etc.
steadfastness	etc.	
stoutheartedness		
guts		
etc.		

I was trying to put across possible sociological and cultural differences that these various 'strata' of words indicated, when suddenly a hand shot up. 'Please, sir, aren't all those French words the ones people get medals for?' He had hit the nail on the head! Three of these words were, in fact, introduced by the Norman knights and nobles, and conjure up the virtues that went with the elaborate warfare of the later Middle Ages, where armour-clad warriors, precariously mounted, proceeded into battle according to a well-defined ritual. The words in the first column belong to a more primitive, impetuous, hit-and-run kind of warfare in which sheer physical courage (*manliness*, *pluck*, *guts*) count for more than tactics and strategy. In the third column, all the words are remote from everyday usage, and of these *fortitude* seems to be practically confined to moral or spiritual courage.

In the past few pages I have indulged in asides of a mainly non-linguistic nature. My remarks have been directed towards the earlier phases of the English language, if only because this seemed a less daunting task than coming to grips with more recent English. Distance, even in time, lends homogeneity. The reader may feel that I have said far too little about English in modern times, thus evading the multiplicity of problems created by its having become the world's chief language. But this would have taken us well beyond the scope of the present book and, one ought to add, beyond the competence of present-day diachronic linguistics. My aim was simply to highlight, before heading into the technicalities of diachronic linguistics, the intimate bonds existing between the history of language and the history of the peoples who speak, and have spoken, a language. I wanted to emphasise yet again that language is more than a gratuitous exercising of the vocal cords, more than a set of grammatical puzzles for schoolchildren and foreign learners, more than an idle pastime for lexicographers. Language is yet another of the ways we live.

Linguistic change and sociology

One of the main achievements of the Neo-grammarians was their deflection of focus away from language as 'text' to language as speech behaviour. Hermann Paul was further convinced that what the linguist should concentrate upon is the individual. Language homogeneity was no more than an 'average' diffused among a range of individual speakers with their individual languages. The grouping of speakers into dialects is arbitrarily determined by the linguist, not by the speakers themselves. If speakers do designate themselves speakers of a particular dialect, it is for non-linguistic reasons, such as regional loyalty, community awareness and so forth. Specific language changes, according to Paul, are changes not in the language average but in the totality of the speech habits of the individual (nowadays called *idiolect*). Linguistic change, then, would amount to a summation of shifts in 'idiolects', all moving more or less in the same direction. A summation of this order would in Paul's scheme be the equivalent of dialect.

Among the difficulties created by a theory of this kind is that linguistic geography nowhere reflects any such situation. There is a tendency for certain kinds of isoglosses to form themselves into loosely knit bundles; but others, especially lexical isoglosses, tend to run in every direction. To trace innovations by means of iso-glosses would often be impossible. On the dialect map the kind of shifts expected by Paul seldom appear. And, as Bloomfield later pointed out, it would be futile 'to ask what person or set of persons first favoured variants . . . By the time sound change becomes observable, its effect has been distributed by a levelling process that goes on within each community.'[1]

Rather different, but at the same time complementary to the idiolectal approach to linguistic change, was that developed by linguists of the Prague School between the two world wars. Prague had developed the notion that a speech community was not so much an amalgam of dialects as a layering of speech styles, on which the changes were rung by any speaker in that community. Instead of idiolectal *homogeneity*, therefore, the Prague linguists posited linguistic *heterogeneity*. *Style switching*, they held, is in-dulged in by all speakers of the community. Only the degree and amount of switching will differ from individual to individual. This facet of language is a well-known obstacle in the way of the advanced foreign-language learner; and it can rarely be success-fully overcome except in the country or countries in which the foreign language is spoken.

The sociological approach to language and linguistic change is consequently nothing new. Meillet, more than sixty years ago, had proclaimed a 'diachronic sociolinguistics' when he wrote: 'Since language is a social institution, it follows that linguistics is a social science, and the only variable element to which one may appeal in order to account for a linguistic change is social change, of which language variations are but the consequences.'[2] The

[1] Bloomfield, L., *Language* (New York, 1933), pp. 480–1.
[2] Meillet, A., *Linguistique Historique et Linguistique Générale* (Paris, 1926), p. 17.

achievement of recent 'sociolinguistics' is that an empirical dimension has been added to what previously were purely analytical conjectures. Today, studies of communities at first hand are the rule. One such study,[1] of a small and rapidly changing bilingual community, was carried out at Hemnesberget in Norway. Here, two types of linguistic relationship were observed: a *dialectal* or *inter*-personal variation occurring among socially and geographically distinct groups; and a *superposed* or *intra*-personal variation reflecting shifts in idiolect. These two schemes interrelate in such a way that dialect features reflect an individual's personal history (he may have been brought up on a farm, then become a mechanic and later a successful entrepreneur), whilst the 'superposed' variations mirror the activities in which an individual regularly engages in his daily routine. In these latter, two types of 'switching' was observed to occur: *transactional* switching, in situations where the same person was a customer in a shop, or getting a telephone call put through, or going to the doctor (in these cases, people were found to act according to their status); and *personal* switching, apparent in more relaxed situations, with friends, family, peer groups, etc. The investigator's tentative conclusions were that dialectal variation and superposed variation suggest two simultaneous on-going processes. The study also demonstrated conclusively the ways in which switching operated between the strata that are functionally available to all members of the community.

Another case-history of linguistic change in progress was William Labov's study of the social stratification of English in New York City.[2] Labov investigated the use of the variable [r] among adult native speakers in casual speech. He found as a result that the distance between the upper-middle class and the rest of the population is increasing. The [r] phone has acquired the social significance of a prestige pronunciation. A recent conclusion based on this and other such studies is that linguistic change is not originally idiolectal or dialectal: 'Linguistic change is rarely a movement of one entire system into another. Instead we find a limited set of variables in one system shift their model values

---

[1] Gumperz, J. J., 'On the Ethnology of Linguistic Change' in Bright, W. (ed.), *Sociolinguistics* (The Hague, 1966), pp. 27 ff.
[2] Labov, W., *The Social Stratification of English in New York City* (Washington, D.C., 1966).

gradually from one pole to another.' The same authors further conclude that: 'The generalization of linguistic change throughout linguistic structure is neither uniform nor instantaneous; it involves the covariation of associated changes over substantial periods of time, and is reflected in the diffusion of isoglosses over areas of geographical space . . . Linguistic and social factors are closely interrelated in the development of language change. Explanations which are confined to one or the other aspect . . . will fail to account for the rich body of regularities that can be observed in empirical studies of language behaviour.'[2]

[1] Weinreich, U., Labov, W., and Herzog, M. I., 'A Theory of Language Change' in Lehmann, W. P., and Malkiel, Y., *Directions for Historical Linguistics* (Austin, Texas, 1968), p. 185.
[2] *ibid.*, p. 188. (It is only fair to point out that these quotations are extracted from a set of seven conclusions presented by these authors.)

5 Writing

All that we know about languages before the invention of the phonograph comes through writing. Comparative linguistics could never have come into existence without the densely scattered specimens of writing preserved in almost every part of the world. By far the larger part of these specimens are in printed books; but many date from long before the invention of printing. Only the most recent of the latter are preserved in manuscript. The rest are on stone, clay, pottery, metal, bone, wood, skin and papyrus. The repertoire of ingenious methods developed for 'reconstructing' *proto*-languages and the common ancestors of languages not written down until comparatively recent times, or for determining the way in which languages were spoken in ancient times, or, again, for arriving at assertions about spoken vernaculars or dialects known to have existed but never recorded in writing—all these methods and many others besides were built up at first out of purely written data, and only relatively recently, since the time of the Neo-grammarians, and even then only to a small degree, on spoken data. Writing remains the staple fare of the diachronic and comparative linguist.

This does not mean that our knowledge of a particular language at a particular moment in time is always limited to what is known about the written, or literary, language. Growingly, the diachronist has learned to use the evidence derived from the written language as a means of discovering, or at any rate deducing, facts about the spoken language, or even the various dialects of a language.

The diachronic linguist can seldom operate alone. If he is dealing with ancient languages he will probably depend more or less on the *epigraphist* (one who deciphers inscriptions), and perhaps also the archaeologist or even the physical scientist. He will usually in addition work in close co-operation with the *philologist*, whose interests overlap with his. The philologist is the one who makes sense of texts and inscriptions, who places them in their historical and cultural context. The philologist has been defined as one whose task it is to interpret the literary monuments in which the spiritual life of a given period has found expression.[1]

[1] Pedersen, H., *The Discovery of Language* (Bloomington, Indiana, 1959), p. 79.

In modern times, partly owing to the descriptive linguist's and the anthropologist's almost exclusive concern with speech, a certain fastidiousness has developed, inhibiting and even producing a reaction against the use of written records. How valuable, then, the contribution of the diachronic linguist of today, who has helped to preserve and restore the balance between an earlier overexclusive devotion to the written text and the modern swing in the opposite direction. The diachronist is able to remind us that a language we happen to be observing is not just an abstract mass of structures but the end-product of a subtle, vital and often playful interaction between speaking and writing. Yakov Malkiel tells us that this is especially true of the Romance diachronist: 'Romance linguists stand apart almost *en bloc*: they cherish treating the spoken and the written on a par, delighting in tracing their interactions (including the increasingly frequent surrender of speech habits to the pressure of spelling), and refuse to abjure their active interest in literary analysis . . . In fact, joint concern with spontaneous dialect speech and with stylized, sophisticated discourse, and purposefully developed deftness in examining their complicated interactions have become the hallmark of Romance scholarship at its most satisfying.'[1]

The origin of writing

No doubt writing has a ritual or aesthetic origin. The prehistoric cave paintings and rock paintings to be found in many parts of the world could well be the distant and not so distant ancestors of the various forms of early writing known to us: the picture-writing of the Aztecs; Egyptian and Hittite hieroglyphic writing; Sumerian cuneiform; the ideographic inscriptions of Ancient China; and many others.

Since the invention of printing, in the West at any rate, and especially since the industrialisation of print in the last century, nearly all connection with the artistic function of writing has been lost. In the Chinese tradition, however, the human touch has survived alongside a much earlier tradition of printing than that of the West; and in certain quarters, even today, calligraphy continues to take precedence over painting. Even though the Chinese

[1] Malkiel, Y., 'Distinctive Traits of Romance Linguistics' in Hymes, D. (ed.), *Language in Culture and Society* (New York, 1964), p. 676.

characters have since millenia ceased to be 'pictures' and have become stylised and abstract representations of 'morphemes' (the smallest meaningful parts of a language), calligraphy is still regarded as having an expressive value over and above the conventional symbol. A character drawn with grace, strength and individuality—a 'character' in the true sense of the word—is seen to have greater expressive power than one that is not.

Writing systems

Most people would probably agree that he who manages to 'break' a code is cleverer than the one who has devised it. But, with codes, the inventor of a new cipher has innumerable models from which to start; and in any case he is doing no more than converting from existing alphabets, numeric series, etc., which are themselves codes of a sort. The cryptographer's ingenuity is limited to devising the ultimate cipher. Not so the anonymous inventor of ancient writing systems. He may in some cases have adapted his symbols from already existing systems (which he may have seen carved on rock perhaps), but in every case the system he creates is entirely original. Without in any way wanting to belittle the staggering achievements of generations of epigraphists who have deciphered one script after another for nearly two centuries, I propose turning our attention for a moment to those genial souls, the inventors of writing, both ancient and not so ancient, who do not always receive their fair share of glory.

Let us imagine a language that has not hitherto been written down. And let us, in addition, imagine a speaker of this language who, in common with the rest of the people in his isolated community, has had no contact of any kind with writing. Let us go on to suppose that his tribe already employs certain pictorial representations as charms or ceremonial figures, and that he is something of an artist and something of a linguist too. He will be aware that the flow of speech is interrupted at irregular intervals, and that certain chunks of this speech flow represent objects of various kinds, people's names, species of animals and many other things as well. If he finds himself inclined to 'draw' his language he will probably end up with a *pictographic* form of writing, which will probably contain symbols for such phenomena as 'water', 'fire', 'mountain', 'sun', 'star', etc. If he should happen to want to develop this 'picture-writing' he may add a few abstract symbols to represent features such as the seasons, bravery, storm, hunting and so forth. He will thus have gone on to develop an *ideographic* form of writing. So widespread are systems such as these, among 'primitive' peoples as well as in prehistoric locations, that one is tempted to conjecture that this rudimentary form of writing is as old as language itself.

Now let us suppose that our imaginary speaker belongs to a community that has developed a store of knowledge and a fairly elaborate tribal lore; that he is aware of certain recurrent patterns, especially in the oral literature, such as rhyme and assonance; and lastly that his community is in some sort of contact with another even more highly developed and powerful community, which employs a 'potent' script familiar to the many but understood only by the few. His own people may well be using an ideographic system already, and our would-be scribe sees only too well the shortcomings of the latter. He is particularly unhappy about the large number of signs used in writing by his own tribe, and so he does not want to increase the already cumbersome stock by creating the new symbols for mental and spiritual activity that the script so badly lacks. In any case, all the possibilities, all the permutations of lines and shapes seem to have already been used up. To begin with, then, he will probably take a look at the more prestigious script used by his more powerful neighbours; and he will probably learn economy of symbolism from them, even if he becomes frustrated in the process by not being able to read the script. But he is a highly resourceful individual, having a fair grasp of the way his language works. He already knows something of the phonetic patterning. He notices, though, that the same block of sound can represent a number of different objects and things. So he sets up two series of signs: one set to represent groups of *sounds*, and another set to represent *classes*: deities, names, inanimate objects, birds, fishes, etc. By combining a pair of signs, one from each set, he finds that with a few score of 'combinations' he can represent more than a thousand items. In addition, he will probably take a few of the picture signs from the older script and use them for expressing abstract ideas as well as their established objects. For example, he could use the symbol for 'eye' to represent also 'conscience' or 'perception'. In this way our remarkable tribesman will have developed a fully-fledged *system* of writing; and in many important respects it will resemble the systems of writing developed in Sumeria, Ancient Egypt, the Indus valley, Ancient China and the Maya civilisation of Central America. The following are some examples of pictograms from Sumerian:

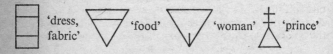

And these are some examples of *determinatives*, used to distinguish between classes of objects:

'divinity'   'birds'   'vegetables'

Additional signs were created by combination or doubling:

'eat'   'princess'   'double; multiply'   'hero'

The origin of these ancient *analytic* systems is understandably the subject of much controversy. Some authorities are prepared to underwrite Kroeber's 'idea-diffusion' theory,[1] which posits the existence of a generic *idea* of systemic writing, which developed separately in the discontinuous areas of Mesopotamia, Egypt, China, etc. That this is more than mere speculation can be borne out by evidence of a unique and remarkable kind. In the 1870s in the Cameroons there was a young Sultan called Njoya. He had a dream in which a stranger handed a tablet to him and bade him write certain signs on it. As a result of this dream, Njoya set about devising a script for his people, the Bamum. He invented seven scripts in all; each is an advance on the one before, and each represents a totally distinct system. Njoya was familiar with both Arabic and Roman scripts, and must have been a born descriptive

[1] Kroeber, A. L., *Anthropology* (New York, 1948), *passim*.

linguist. Over the years between the first and the sixth scripts, Njoya had progressed from a rather crude pictography to a full-blown analytic script using only ninety-two symbols. He composed several works in his later scripts, and these have been kept in use until quite recently.

From the known analytic scripts (Chinese is the only important one still in use) to *syllabic* and *alphabetic* scripts is a very large step. Basically, a syllabic script is an analytic script with all but the 'phonetic' elements removed. The signs used, as in Linear B,

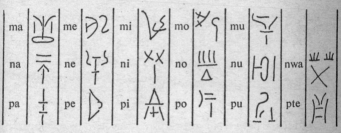

Figure 9 Fragment of the Mycenaean syllabary deciphered by Ventris and Chadwick

may betray their pictorial origin, but the pictures represent only sounds. Apart from Linear B, the script of Ancient Crete and Mycenae, recently deciphered by Ventris and Chadwick (see Figure 9), there are several syllabaries known to have existed. The only important one in use today is the Japanese syllabic script, which is used as a kind of supplement to the Chinese system borrowed by the Japanese.

From the syllabary to the *alphabet* is perhaps the largest step of all. To recognise that two chunks of continuous sound resemble one another is one thing, but to manage to decompose the sound chunk into its constituent 'phonemes' is quite another. Speakers of English, for example, are aware that *ping* and *pig* do not sound the same. Even young children can tell when endings rhyme. As long as we are working with a syllabary the problem does not arise, but in devising an alphabet we need different signs to represent the -*g* and the -*ng* sounds. We also need to distinguish the initial bits of *big* and *pig*. Finally, we need a set of vowel signs (to keep *big* apart from *bag*).

It is not known for certain which people it was that first achieved this linguistic triumph. Some remain convinced that it was the Israelites themselves, but the evidence points rather more generally to a North Semitic origin. The first known alphabet closely resembles Early Hebrew and Phoenician. But it is thought that the North Semitic system came into existence much earlier. Most of the alphabetic systems in use today are descended from the North Semitic script. Those wishing to supplement this rapid survey should consult David Diringer's scholarly but very readable *The Alphabet* (London, 1968).

Writing and culture

It is not difficult to share the enthusiasm of the claim that 'simple as it *now* seems to us, the inventor, or the inventors, are to be ranked among the greatest benefactors of mankind'.[1] And yet, remarkable though the discovery of the alphabet undoubtedly is, it is too easy and too tempting to assume that the alphabet automatically represented progress.

It has often been claimed that if Chinese or Japanese school-children did not have to learn as many as 2000 to 3000 characters, but instead only a couple of dozen letters, they would achieve literacy much quicker and with far less effort. Although many Westernist reformers are convinced that character writing must go, or at any rate—as in Mainland China—be considerably and progressively simplified, I must record my own personal testimony that very few of the writers of Chinese *and* English I have spoken to agreed that learning the Roman alphabet was easier than learning to read Chinese. Not a few claim to have found alphabetic spelling odd and not easy to adapt to. A Chinese colleague of mine described her first experiences of English as 'strings of snakes'. When you come to think of it, the user of alphabets is only at the beginning of literacy when he learns the alphabet. Thereafter, every word has to be learned separately. The Chinese schoolchild, however, becomes more literate with every character memorised. No Chinese I have ever met has been totally illiterate. Even though many have never been to school, they all seem to know more characters than I could master by a

[1] Diringer, D., *The Alphabet* (London, 1968), Vol. I, pp. 163–4.

year or more of sustained effort. And just think of all those peculiar 'ideographs' in English like *yacht, ought, cough* or *pterodactyl*!

I will spare the reader further flights of fancy and restrict myself to a few definite facts:

(1) Almost all languages have some form of writing, and many that do not themselves possess a highly developed system may well have come under the influence of systems more developed than theirs. The latter will be either some 'literary' language spread by cultural diffusion, the language of an imperial power, or a language of commerce.

(2) Whenever there exists a thriving potent culture embracing large numbers of separate smaller peoples or tribes, either through religion as in the Arab countries or through a common ethos as in China, the literary language will usually influence the vernaculars, or spoken dialects, in such a way that they will have undergone uniform changes of various or specific kinds. All the Chinese dialects have a virtually identical syntax and lexical morphology, but they sound entirely different. This is not really surprising. Identity of syntax and lexicon is essential if people are to communicate with one another using Chinese writing, but no such requirement arises in the case of pronunciation. Any language, in fact, whose syntax and lexicon was close to Chinese could adopt Chinese writing. Even Japanese, which is structurally very different from Chinese, was influenced in profound ways from the time when Japan adopted Chinese writing. The fact that scholars in England during the sixteenth and seventeenth centuries mostly used Latin when writing produced some remarkable effects on the English language: the absolute participle, for example (*This being so . . .*). It is probably only ridicule that has prevented the textbook grammarians from finding a whole series of Latin subjunctives and a genitive and dative case in English. Other European languages have been affected in parallel ways.

(3) Writing is not merely a graphic representation of speech, and it is only in modern times that a claim such as this has been made. The written language is a system unto itself, with its own quirks and idiosyncrasies: 'The fully grown literary language, whatever trickling or torrential sources and tributaries may have fed it, tends to fall into a system, or subsystem, of its own . . . In some

respects . . . this stylised language may display a greater abundance of resources or more delicately graded patterning, bordering on the ornamental. As an intricate but ordered whole . . . it invites individuating study at the same levels—sounds, forms, constructions—as any adequate speech specimen and is available in various sizes, ranging from a single passage, stylistically uniform or split, via an extant text, fragmentary or complete, to the collected works of a given author, to a genre, or to the cross-section or even the sum total of writings attributable to a certain period.'[1]

That branch of linguistics which concerns itself with written language is known as *graphemics* or *graphology*. Despite various differences in interpretation and definition, linguists are agreed on one thing: namely, that the written expression of a language is not coincident with its spoken expression. In a language like English, which is so notoriously difficult to 'spell', the gap is obvious. But even a language like Czech, whose script is as near 'phonetic' as could be, retains the spelling of certain words borrowed from other languages and thus acquires purely graphic elements, since not all these borrowings are pronounced according to Czech phonology.

How 'phonetic' should a writing system be? To some the answer is clear and simple: languages must be written as they are spoken. George Bernard Shaw was merely one of the last of a line of fanatical protagonists of this view, who have probably existed ever since alphabetic writing began. We know that the Sanskrit grammarians of antiquity kept a zealous watch over the correctness of sacred words and recorded in script the finest shades of pronunciation, lest the religious sacrifices fail.[2] Their script therefore is delicately discriminating, capable of reproducing in symbols the most minute differences in pronunciation.

Whatever the arguments in favour of phonetic spelling, maintaining a certain distance between the spoken and written languages has its advantages too. Perhaps the main advantage is that a written language can remain 'neutral' among a group of mutually contending regional dialects. In languages like English or French the gap between the written and the spoken system is so wide that this kind of neutrality is achieved, for no one expects

[1] Malkiel, Y., *op. cit.*, p. 677.
[2] Pedersen, H., *op. cit.*, p. 14.

either English or French to be spoken in the way they are written. With a phonetic written language like Czech, on the other hand, trouble can arise, in that speakers of non-standard Czech dialects could (although they do not, so far as I am aware) feel that their own dialect is being discriminated against.

Let us take a somewhat far-fetched illustration. Imagine a fanatically separatist Yorkshire schoolmaster with a marked linguistic bent. He wants, let us suppose, to disengage 'Yorkshire' from standard English as the first step towards a Yorkshire U.D.I. To do this he creates two separate spellings: one for Yorkshire English and another for standard English (a new standard, that is). Adept at phonetics, he observes that the spelling *London bus* conceals two totally different pronunciations. One of these is the Yorkshire pronunciation, which he proceeds to render as *Lunden bus*. The other is the standard South-eastern English pronunciation, which he 'revises' as *Landem bas*. Notice that he writes different vowels in the first and third syllables of the phrase, and records the admittedly marked tendency of the southerner to turn the final *n* preceding a *b* into a kind of *m* (the Yorkshireman does the same thing, but not quite to such an extent). You will now see how spelling can be marshalled towards political ends. Likewise, in accordance with unimpeachable phonetic principles, he is entitled to render *cricket* as *krikit*. But either he will not do this, since the Yorkshire and standard pronunciations are too close, or, if he does, he will probably leave the standard form unrevised. At the end of his labours our Yorkshireman will be able to claim that his language is not English, for the spelling will be there to prove it.

Another advantage of retaining a separate system of writing is that it will tend towards conservatism and resist being reformed, whereas the spoken dialects will constantly shift their pronunciation. Modern English is spelt largely as it was in Chaucer's day. We can then, if we want to, get to grips with Chaucer quite easily. A Chinese schoolchild in Hong Kong, Taiwan or Singapore can read passages written two and a half millenia ago—Confucius, say, or Mencius—with relative ease. If you reform the spelling you run the risk of wiping out the whole of a people's literary culture; or, worse still, leave it in the manipulating hands of an academic élite.

Finally, a language that preserves the autonomy of its writing can, and usually does, develop a distinctive 'profile', the reflection of a homogeneous culture, built up as it is largely from elements taken from other cultures or its own earlier history. Joyce's *Ulysses* is from one point of view a diachronic compendium of the English literary language and culture. Take, for example, an ordinary everyday word like *ocean*. The reformers would have us spell it *otion*. But *ocean* retains its Latin spelling (minus the accidence) and thus, in turn, a fragment of Roman culture. One wonders too how much less 'ghostly' a word like *ghost* would look if it were spelt *gost* or *goast*. This 'eye'-value of English spelling was remarked upon by Otto Jespersen,[1] who recognised that there were words in English such that 'people freely write them and understand them when they see them written, but are more or less puzzled when they have to pronounce them'. Two examples he cites are *hegemony* and *phthisis*, for each of which the dictionaries record no less than nine possible pronunciations.

Written records and the comparatist

Since the corpus of the world's written records is so bewilderingly vast, I am restricting my remarks to the Indo-European languages. The Indo-European family embraces practically every known form of writing, from the cuneiform inscriptions of the Hittites and the syllabic script of Linear B to the very latest in phonetic spelling, and the International Phonetic Alphabet itself. The Indo-European comparatist is confronted with every conceivable type of problem therefore: from epigraphy and interpretation to the conventions of orthography and transliteration. The latter seem almost arbitrary, and the stickler for order will not always be too impressed by the orthographic habits of his forbears. Orthographic accuracy has not always been the fetish that it has become in a world of mass literacy. As long as a century after Caxton, printers in England were still showing, by modern standards, a cavalier lack of consistency; and it is reckoned that mediaeval scribes were sometimes given to padding out words with extra letters to earn more money. Changes in spelling (orthographic) conventions do not necessarily indicate linguistic change,

---

[1] Jespersen, O., *Growth and Structure of the English Language* (Oxford, reprinted 1967), p. 133.

whilst changes in the structure of a language are not always reflected in the orthography.

At the time when 'comparative grammar' came into existence, early in the last century, the most exciting of the then known Indo-European languages was *Sanskrit*. The antecedent of Sanskrit, the language of the Vedic hymns, was in use in the first half of the second millenium B.C., the period during which, it is presumed, the 'Indo-Aryans' settled in the midst of an already highly developed culture in Northern India. Vedic literature remained oral for a very long time and was not written down until historical times. Sanskrit, the language in which this oral tradition was eventually recorded, is a much later development and in some ways an artificial revival by Brahmin priests of a language that was to become the pillar of Hinduism, possibly as a counterforce to the rapid expansion of Buddhism and Jainism in the subcontinent. The earliest Sanskrit inscription dates from about the time of Christ, but the script in which it appears—the Brahmi script—had already been in use for several centuries previously. There is general agreement that Brahmi is a syllabic adaptation of the (alphabetic) Semitic alphabet, having been borrowed thence probably by sea-traders. Brahmi script is by no means the earliest Indian script. It could be no more than one script in a long series of related and unrelated developments, the earliest known of which is the pre-alphabetic Indus valley script. Brahmi rose to a position of pre-eminence along with Sanskrit, which in due time was to become the language of Indian religion—Buddhist, Jain and Hindu alike—standing in a somewhat similar relation to the various Indian languages as Latin formerly did to the European languages. The modern Indian script, the Deva-Nagari, had developed from Brahmi by the eighth century A.D. As one can see from the early inscriptions, the famous Aṣoka inscriptions for example, Brahmi is very much closer in style to the Semitic script than it is to the modern Deva-Nagari scripts.

A group of ancient Indo-European languages closely related to Sanskrit was *Old Persian*, two types of which survive. These survivals have proved not only immensely valuable to the comparatist; but the Achaemenid script, which was cuneiform, led by a series of steps to the decipherment of Assyrian-Babylonian, and ultimately Sumerian. The Achaemenid script is known mainly from a set of inscriptions discovered in and around Persepolis;

but its most dramatic relics are the colossal rock inscriptions at Bisutun. Although cuneiform, this Old Persian script is, in fact, a modification of the Semitic alphabet, supplemented by a few ideograms. Some believe it to be the creation of King Darius himself. The *Avesta*, the name given to the Zoroastrian sacred literature, is written not in the script just mentioned but in a modified form of the Pahlavi, or 'Middle Persian', script. Modern Persian writing has been developed from the Arabic script. This Persian–Arabic script is used to write Urdu and some other languages of the North-western India sub-continent.

Perhaps the earliest known Indo-European language is that of the *Hittites*, a language used from the second half of the second millenium B.C. during the period of the powerful Hittite Empire. The system of writing was hieroglyphic, and numerous specimens of it are preserved on stone and cliff inscriptions in various parts of Asia Minor. It is partly syllabic and partly pictographic. The pictograma bear a remarkable resemblance to Cretan hieroglyphs, but no connection has been proved since the latter remain undeciphered.

The *Greek* language was in recent times given an unexpected lengthening of its time scale by the decipherment of Linear B, which, as we have already seen, was an ideographic syllabary. No one knew for certain before this decipherment whether the language of the Achaeans resembled that of later Attic Greece. Now the uncertainties are largely removed. The Mycenaean–Minoan civilisation, however, was interrupted by the so-called Dorian invasions at the end of the first millenium. When Greek re-emerges it is written in the earliest script that can be definitely called an alphabet, with a fully developed series of vowels as well as consonants. Tradition and scholarship concur in ascribing the origins of the Greek alphabet to the Phoenicians. The advance upon the Phoenician model is generally regarded as a remarkable achievement. The Greeks not only developed a distinct series of vowels and diphthongs—possibly, it is thought, as a result of early Pythagorean concerns with harmony—but the Semitic model had imposed upon it a phonetic and visual symmetry that reflects the proclivities of the Greek mind. A seemingly innocuous discovery like A-E-I-O-U not only became the *graphic* feature par excellence of all the European languages—their scripts are all derived directly or indirectly from Greek—but one also wonders to what extent the *phonetic* shape, and even the entire structure of these languages, has been determined by the creation of these vowels. The Romance languages, Roman-influenced Welsh, the southern and eastern Slavonic languages, not to mention Greek itself, are (in the Western sense of the word) remarkably 'musical', i.e. vocalic or vowel-like. Italian, based as it is on the Tuscan dialect, has maintained not so much a phonetic script as one which lends itself as ideally as could be imagined to singing. Even the less obviously mellifluous Northern European languages like English can become musical when need be. One has only to think of the Elizabethan stage, or Purcell, or the poetry of Keats and Tennyson. The ubiquitous but unassuming teacher of elocution is perhaps, for all she knows, continuing the work begun in the dim and distant past by pre-Socratic phoneticians, philosophers and harmonists. In Figure 10 below, a selection of letters from the Greek alphabet are compared with Early Greek and North

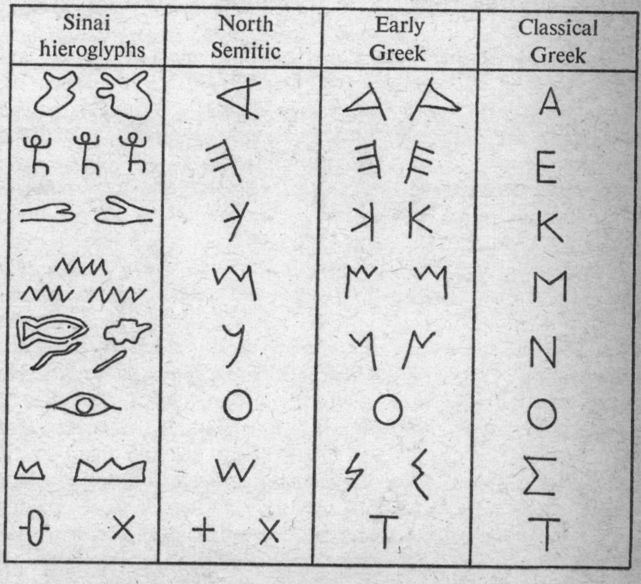

Sinai hieroglyphs	North Semitic	Early Greek	Classical Greek

Figure 10

Semitic symbols, and in turn with hieroglyphs found on inscriptions in Sinai, which some scholars believe to have been the prototypes of North Semitic.

The earliest Italic inscriptions are in Oscan and Umbrian and date from the period 500 to 200 B.C. Some of them are written in Greek script, others in Latin and the rest in a special alphabet derived from Etruscan. Both languages are more archaic than Latin, and certain of their features are recognisable as antecedents of the dialect of Latium (Latin). The Latin alphabet of the Romans is a later development from Etruscan. A curious fact is that the Etruscan alphabet is derived from Greek and is thus not difficult to *read*; but we do not know what the language *means*. It is thought by some to be related to the now distant Caucasian languages.

Irish Ogham script is descended from Roman and probably does not antedate the fourth century A.D. It looks more like a cipher than an alphabet (see Figure 11) and is engraved on stones scattered not only over Ireland but also over Wales, Scotland and the south-west of England. The Ogham alphabet consists of parallel strokes in groups of one to five arranged along an axis of reference.

The Runic alphabets, which some think are based on the Roman alphabet and others directly on Etruscan script, became a form of writing common to all the Germanic peoples. Runic inscriptions are found scattered throughout the length and breadth of Europe: from Sweden to the north of Italy, and from England to the lower Danube plains. The Goths were the first to abandon Runic writing, possibly partly due to their many contacts with Southern Europe but mainly due to Ulfilas adopting the Greek alphabet for his Gothic translation of the Bible in the fourth century (the Gothic script, so-called, has nothing to do with Gothic or the Goths). The last place to give up using runes was England; and not before they had influenced the way in which the Roman alphabet was adapted to Anglo-Saxon. The earliest Runic inscriptions occur in Scandinavia, and may date from as early as the second century A.D. The runes themselves (see Figure 12) were such that they could be quickly carved on wood with a knife. But they could also be carved on stone and metal. Much of our linguistic knowledge of the earlier phases of Germanic are derived from these inscriptions. The runes were thought to possess great magical power by the pre-Christian Germanic peoples, and the god Odin (or Woden), legend had it, hanged himself to gain possession of the meaning of the runes.

r z ng gm q c t j h n s f(v) l b i e u o a

Figure 11 The Irish Ogham alphabet

For the Slavonic languages two scripts, Cyrillic and Glagolitic, were developed from Greek at the time of the conversion of the Slavs to Christianity. The earliest documents date from the tenth and eleventh centuries. The origin of Glagolitic and its relationship to Cyrillic is the subject of much debate. Glagolitic was important in Moravia, and among the Balkan Slavs, but in all regions has given way either to the Roman script or to Cyrillic. Cyrillic has been, and is being, used for the writing of non-Slavonic languages. Until the middle of the last century Romanian was written in Cyrillic, and many Ural-Altaic dialects in the Soviet Union appear in this script.

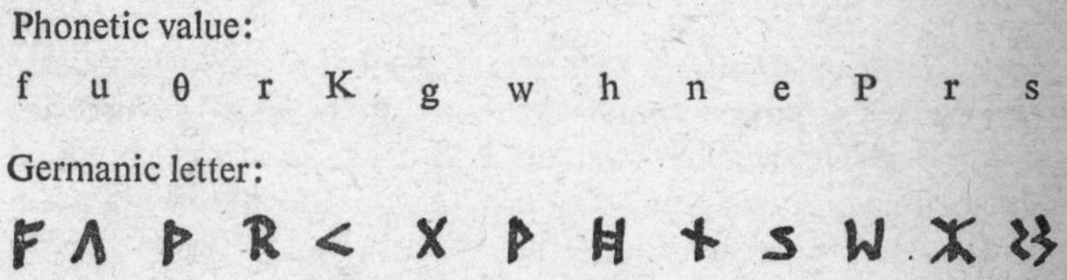

Phonetic value:

f   u   θ   r   K   g   w   h   n   e   P   r   s

Germanic letter:

ᚠ ᚢ ᚦ ᚱ ᚲ ᚷ ᚹ ᚺ ᛏ ᛋ ᚹ ᛉ ᛟ

Figure 12 Germanic runic writing

This hasty survey of the written records of Indo-European will, I hope, at the very least have highlighted the labyrinthine complications that the comparatist faces. The comparatist who shirks his epigraphy may have excellent editions and compilations on which to base his investigations, but he will always be plagued by the awareness that his sources are second-hand.

6 The Comparative Method and the Scope of Comparative Linguistics

There are various possible ways of marking out the scope of comparative linguistics; but the historical approach seems to me the best. I shall assume on the part of my reader none of the knowledge that may yet be gleaned from the remaining sections of this book.

My 'history' begins with the word *philology*, a term with a long ancestry going back to the Alexandrian period of the Greek civilisation. Interest in language, however, as with everything else in Greece, can be traced back to a much earlier period. Plato, Aristotle and their predecessors expended much discussion on this theme. It was Aristotle himself who laid the foundations of 'grammar', as well as the basis from which sprang the mediaeval *trivium* of Liberal Arts: logic, grammar and rhetoric.

And yet, as far as comparative linguistics (or comparative philology) is concerned, it was not the Greeks but the 'Sanskrit grammarians' of ancient India who were the pioneers. Their marvellous capacity for analysing speech sounds found its embodiment in a remarkably precise system of phonetic analysis, together with an astonishingly well-conceived scheme of grammar. Without the impact of the latter on European philologists of the early nineteenth century, the science of comparative linguistics might never have been born. Throughout the Middle Ages and until the end of the eighteenth century, grammar was synonymous with *Latin* grammar. Latin dominated the entire curriculum of schools and universities, and came to be the standard by which all vernaculars, or modern languages, were judged. Few Western European languages escaped unscathed, and the rigid hand of the cut-and-dried, artificial system of categories, tenses and moods was everywhere to be found. School textbooks of English to this day bear the stamp of Latin. 'The mischief consequent on this unfortunate method of measuring all grammar after the pattern of Latin grammar has not even yet completely disappeared, and it is even now difficult to find a single grammar of any language that is not here and there influenced by the Latin bias.'[1] Progress in linguistics remained impossible until the rediscovery by Western philologists of ancient Hindu scholarship.

[1] Jespersen, O., *Language*, p. 23.

The growth and development of comparative linguistics

'Philology' was first used as a scientific discipline by Friedrich Wolf in 1777. To this day the term bears its original connotation, although frequently and erroneously confused with *comparative philology*'. The purpose of philology was, and still is, to correct, interpret and comment upon *written texts*. The philological method found easy rapport in literary history and criticism, social customs, culture and civilisation, and comparative religion. The Romantic Age is to some extent a philological age. Philological motivation is transparent in Coleridge, Shelley, Keats, Goethe, Hugo, Sainte-Beuve and many others. Since then it has become fixed; and the fascination for word origins, etymology, evolution of meaning, sense of linguistic 'period' is to be found in the works of many modern poets and critics.

In another direction, the 'philological movement' led more obviously to the numerous, masterly, although frequently laboured, commentaries of eminent nineteenth-century scholars. Until the latter half of the last century, attention was almost exclusively devoted to Latin or Greek sources. Gradually, more exotic as well as only lately respectable languages were introduced. The middle decades of the nineteenth century witnessed an efflorescence of comparative linguistic studies: Sanskrit, Romance, Germanic, Slavic, Celtic—not to mention non-European 'discoveries'. Philology became an important tool in the decipherment and editing of texts unearthed from antiquity and sometimes of uncertain origin.

At its inception, philology was devoid of a sense of historical perspective. It was only hazily realised that languages are in turn derived from earlier languages. Philologists were too inclined towards a slavish preoccupation with texts from the past, neglecting living languages almost entirely.

The next stage, the stage of 'comparative philology' proper, begins in 1816 with the publication of Franz Bopp's *On the System of Conjugation in Sanskrit*. In this work, a comparative study of Germanic, Greek, Latin, Sanskrit and other European linguistic groups prepared the way for the later Indo-European comparatists.

The new science of comparative philology aimed at no more than *comparing* one language with another, *illuminating* one language through another, *explaining* the forms of the one by the forms of the other, rather in the manner that botanists have compared species of flora, noting and classifying according to similarity or divergence. Not that the approach was wrong in itself; simply that it was unaware of other dimensions which were to lend it purpose and, ultimately, success.

Franz Bopp, although a pioneer, was perhaps the most comprehensive and possibly the most original of the early comparatists. Unlike a number of his successors, he was convinced that Sanskrit is not the ancestor of the rest of the European languages. It is not possible in this space to present a complete account of his work. Perhaps the most significant of his discoveries was the recognition of the Sanskrit verbal roots *as* (** es*) and *bhu* in the integral parts of the European conjugational system. First, he analysed the Indo-European word into three parts: (i) *root*, (ii) *suffix*, (iii) *ending*. It was the suffixal element in which Bopp so frequently detected the two Sanskrit roots. For example, in considering the Latin future tense of the verb 'to go': *ibo* 'I will go', he deduced three parts $i + b + o$, where *i* is the root, *b* is the suffix (from *bhu*) and *o* is the ending. Similarly, with the Latin perfect, he found that *scripsi* 'I have written', the perfect tense of *scribere* 'to write', contained the three elements *scrip* (root) $+ s$ (suffix) [from *as*] $+ i$ (ending).

In one sense it is true to say that Bopp discovered Comparative Philology whilst his ambition had been restricted to a study of the ultimate origin of the flexional elements of verbs. His immediate successors were less cautious than he and allowed themselves to be blinded by the initial success of their science. August Schleicher, another German comparatist, misled by the apparent ancestral position of Sanskrit, set about reconstructing the proto-Aryan (= Indo-European = Indo-Germanic) language. To celebrate his success he composed *A fable in the original Indo-Germanic language!*

To point out the defects of the first generation of comparative philologists is not to belittle their achievements. For instance, etymological dictionaries have undergone no fundamental revision since their days. Their serious error (and they can hardly be blamed for this) is that in their investigations they never asked themselves the *meaning* of their comparisons or the significance of the relations they discovered. Their method was exclusively comparative, not historical. One of their most serious methodological errors arose through their working on the assumption that languages, like animals and plants, have evolved through *identical* stages. This has led to several restrictive blunders, at least one of which will occupy us elsewhere.

Between 1870 and 1880 far-reaching changes took place in the method of comparative philology. To such an extent that the new or renovated science has only a limited connection with the earlier phase.

This new philology was first sketched by the great American scholar Whitney in his *Life and Growth of Language* (1875) and *Language and the Study of Language* (1868). Also, it is from this time that *written* language, which had been the sole interest of the philologists, regains its proper perspective. From now on, texts and inscriptions are used to supplement vernacular material when it is lacking, and vice versa. The roles of written and spoken languages are now complementary. The fashion was established almost overnight of playing down the former to the advantage of the latter. Within a few years came the *Neo-grammarians* (Brugmann, Paul, Osthoff, Sievers, Leskien and others), whose approach was radically different from that of their predecessors. The Swiss comparative linguist Saussure describes the change in these words: 'Their contribution was in placing the results of comparative studies in their historical perspective and thus linking the facts in their natural order. Thanks to them, language is no longer looked upon as an organism that develops independently but as a product of the collective mind of linguistic groups. At the same time scholars realised how erroneous and insufficient were the notions of philology and comparative philology.'[1]

The 'elder statesmen' of comparative philology were naturally reluctant at this new departure. Sanskrit had been unseated from its long-held position of eminence. Curtius wistfully and ironically writes of his regrets and misgivings: 'Sanskrit, once the oracle of the rising science and trusted blindly, is now put on one side; instead of the traditional *ex oriente lux* the saying is now *in oriente tenebrae*.'

The testing of theories became more rigorous. This arose to some extent from pure motives, though not unmixed with 'a desire to keep up with the Jones's', to give comparative linguistics

[1] Saussure, F. de, *Course in General Linguistics*, p. 5.

the status of a *true science*. Whitney says: 'The difference between the old haphazard style of etymologising and the modern scientific method lies in this: that the latter, while allowing everything to be theoretically possible, accepts nothing as actual which is not proved by sufficient evidence; it brings to bear upon each individual case a wide circle of related facts; it imposes upon the student the necessity of extended comparison and cautious deduction; it makes him careful to inform himself as thoroughly as circumstances allow respecting the history of every word he deals with.'[1] As we shall see later, the quest for scientific rigour went to the extreme of a frantic search for scientific uniformity of the kind that the laws of physics were thought to exhibit.

It was left to the Neo-grammarians (Paul, Osthoff and the rest) to banish this illusion for ever. Irregularity was their sole and overnourishing diet. Regularity was to them almost of no interest. A new concept of theirs, which was to have far-reaching effects on both comparative and general linguistics and eventually on the practical study of languages (applied linguistics), was based on *analogy*—a principle that runs directly counter to the notion of rules. The role of association, memory and fancy take the place of rules of *grammar*, which under natural circumstances were of no use to anyone.

A discussion of 'analogy' will be left until the appropriate place in this book. Meanwhile, a personal reminiscence will not be out of place. Like thousands of other secondary schoolchildren, I studied Latin with the machine-like methodicality of the kind advertised formerly by all the best textbooks. Naturally I was not a little impressed by the complexity of Latin and (by extension) the mental capacity of the Romans who spoke it. All seemed so marvellously ordered and so intricate. Later came my introduction to Russian, also by the use of textbooks. Here was a language of rival complexity, a multitude of rules, a galaxy of exceptions, with the result that it took me some time to get over the fact that this language was actually widely spoken by several million living inhabitants of the U.S.S.R. belonging to all walks of life. I suspected that there must be a dodge somewhere, that Russians *cheated* in ordinary conversation, somehow speaking a kind of basic Russian with little or no 'grammar'. My first disenchantment

[1] Whitney, W. D., *Language and the Study of Language* (New York, 1867), p. 386.

came with my first encounter with 'live' Russians. I was the guest of a group of students, children of Russian émigrés, who every year set up camp in the French Alps. Hauling up my rucksack and bags to the camp from the main road below, I was met by a group of children. They had lost the ball they had been playing with and asked me, in apparently flawless Russian, if I had come across it on my way up to the camp. To my utter astonishment there was the complicated instrumental case, verbal aspects, declined numerals and just about everything else. For a time I accepted the fact as little short of miraculous.

But in the light of modern linguistics all this is really not so strange. Grammar is a high *abstraction*, remote from the process of learning or understanding a language. The Neo-grammarians were right after all. People learn to speak in a hit-and-miss manner, and their success is not impaired by ignorance of grammar. As Paul put it: 'While speaking, everyone is incessantly producing analogical forms. *Reproduction by memory* and *new-formation by means of association* are its two indispensable factors. It is a mistake to assume a language as given in grammar and dictionary, that is, the whole body of possible words and forms, as something concrete, and to forget that it is nothing but an abstraction devoid of reality, and that *the actual language exists only in the individual*, from whom it cannot be separated even in scientific investigation.'[1]

The other fillip given to the new direction in comparative linguistics was *phonology*. A number of discoveries made around 1880 led to an understanding of the historical evolution of linguistic sounds, and to a wealth of theories of sound change. The more relevant aspects of this will be outlined in Part II of this book.

The comparative method

Ferdinand de Saussure summed up the purpose of comparative linguistics under two headings:

(1) To describe and trace the history of all observable languages, which amounts to tracing the history of families of

[1] Quoted in Sweet, H., *Collected Papers* (Oxford, 1913), p. 112.

languages and reconstructing as far as possible the mother language of each family.

(2) To determine the forces that are permanently and universally at work in all languages, and to deduce the general laws to which all specific historical phenomena can be reduced.

These were to be part of his scheme for a general linguistic science in which he intended to include comparative linguistics. It is over fifty years since Saussure gave his courses in general linguistics at the University of Geneva. Since then much has been achieved, partly thanks to him, in the spheres of both general and comparative linguistics. There is no doubt that the two spheres can only artificially be separated, and the rest of my book will separate them for entirely practical reasons.

The comparative method is lucidly set forth in Meillet's *Introduction à l'étude comparative des Langues Indo-Européennes* (Paris, 1937) and his scheme is the one I am using here.

Briefly, the science of comparative linguistics is interested in three things: 'phonetic laws', 'analogy' and 'loan words' (i.e. words taken into a given language from another language). It owes its origin to the studies of Romance and Germanic linguistics. In the case of Romance, the mother tongue, at least in its literary form—Classical Latin—was available in abundance. All that had to be done was to reconstruct the stages in between, in particular the 'Vulgar' Latin from which all the Romance languages (French, Spanish, Italian, Portuguese, Romanian) take their origin. This was carried out with great success by Romance specialists. Similarly with the Germanic languages. Although the mother language was not available, from a comparison of Gothic, Old Norse, Old English, Old High German and other elements, a Proto-Germanic (sometimes called Gothonic) was hypothetically established, in much the same way as Vulgar Latin had been established by inferring earlier from given forms in Romance.

In Romance we have the following set of correspondences for the first person singular (*I*) and the second personal singular (*thou*) pronouns:

	1st person sing.	2nd person sing.
Italian	*io*	*tu*
Spanish	*yo*	*tu*
Romanian	*eu*	*tu*
French	*je*	*tu*
Old French	*yo*	*tu*
Portuguese	*eu*	*tu*
Provençal	*eu* (*ieu*)	*tu*
Classical Latin	*ego*	*tu*

There are clearly no insuperable problems here. First, no great ingenuity would be required in either case to reconstruct the parent form for these pronouns. Secondly, the parent forms inferred turn out to be exactly those *found* in Classical Latin. What could be smoother? All the forms given in the columns above the line are called 'correspondences' and can safely be said to be derivatives of the two forms below the line respectively.

With the Germanic languages the data is not so cut-and-dried, for the simple reason that no proto-Germanic language has been recorded. Gothic, although the oldest, is not necessarily in every respect the most archaic (comparatists have sometimes been misled by failure to realise this), and in any case is not the parent language. Thus a reconstruction of the parent forms for these two pronouns, for example, can only be conjecture and never certainty. Thus the seven Romance forms (*tu*) adduced for seven different languages in no way *prove* that the Vulgar Latin form was also *tu*, despite the considerable probability. Nevertheless, as we shall see later, conjecture can become certainty.

The real difficulties arise when we turn to Indo-European. Here we have nothing in the way of records or texts remotely akin to this prehistoric parent of all present and past, living and extinct, European and Indic languages. Not only this, but the separate language families are vastly dissimilar. Indeed, if we had not the ancient languages, Latin, Greek, Sanskrit, etc., but only the contemporary languages, we should have been able to establish no such thing as a proto-Indo-European language.

Suppose for a moment the imaginary and naïve case of a Romance linguist who, spurred on by his success in his own field, turns to Indo-European. What does he find when, for instance, he draws up a list of correspondences for his two pronouns? His list might begin somewhat as follows:

	1st person sing.	2nd person sing.
English	*I*	*thou*
Latin	*ego*	*tu*
Russian	*ya*	*ty*
High German	*ich*	*du*
Welsh	*i(fi)*	*ti*
Old Norse	*ek*	*thu*

There *seem* to be patterns of correspondences but no overall uniformity. And even reconstructing a phonological evolutionary series would by no means yield certainty. It is not outside the bounds of possibility that the similar or corresponding forms are similar only by coincidence. Slightly less unlikely is that they are the product of some non-linguistic cause: psychological, physiological or otherwise.

To escape from all possible ambiguity the comparative method has to base any proof of common linguistic origin and inference of proto-language forms on words that cannot conceivably be the product of coincidence brought about by extralinguistic factors. Fortunately, in the European languages there are such words. There are the so-called 'colourless' verbs 'to be'.

But even this is not enough. We have to increase the improbability of coincidence by finding correspondences for at least *two* parts of the present tense of verbs 'to be'. This can, in fact, be demonstrated for the third person singular and the third person plural of this verb:

	3rd person sing.	3rd person pl.
Latin	*est*	*sunt*
Mod. High German	*ist*	*sind*
Old English	*is*	*sindon*
Greek	*esti*	*(ei)sin*
Sanskrit	*asti*	*santi*
Proto-I-E	*es-ti*	*s-enti (s-onti)*

All these and the rest of the languages that have so far been classified as Indo-European are in strict correspondence and can be deduced from the hypothetical proto-Indo-European forms given below the line.[1] It is fantastically improbable that coincidence should have created these regular correspondences.

This has important consequences, for, if a previously unknown language is brought to light by archaeologists, once the language has been deciphered definite criteria can be applied to establish whether in fact the language is Indo-European or not. This has been done in the case of Hittite, an ancient language of Anatolia, the Tokharian manuscripts found in Central Asia and, more recently, in the decipherment of Linear B. Clearly, starting with the one just given above, there is a hierarchy of criteria, through which the comparative linguist will descend to find more and more support (or possible refutation) for a given hypothesis. He may not in any case be so fortunate as to have the forms of the present tense of the verb 'to be' in the manuscripts he is considering. The hierarchy will proceed through the more 'colourless' forms, such as pronouns, articles, particles, flexional endings, until these have been exhausted.

The comparative method is thus a rigorous method of finding and testing 'a system of correspondences between an initial language and languages arising at a later period'. The method may also lead to an explanation of how and why certain changes took place in a certain order, in turn creating new languages. When it succeeds in this it may define laws governing single or sets of changes, but this activity is really secondary and has so far had comparatively little success. We shall have to postpone illustration of the correspondence method until more has been said about the nature of sounds and sound change.

Internal reconstruction

In comparative linguistics it often happens that the comparative method cannot of itself provide a complete solution, and sometimes fails to provide any solution at all to a particular problem. This is not through any shortcomings of the method itself, but through an insufficiency of comparative data. In such cases, the

[1] Asterisks are used for forms not actually recorded but artificially reconstructed by the comparative linguistic method.

comparatist has to resort to a variety of different methods. And one of the most important of these is the method of *internal reconstruction*.

Examples of applications of this method are included in later sections of this book, but at this point I would like to mention two contrasting situations in which the method has been used.

A particularly fascinating piece of internal reconstruction, and one of the first of its kind, was that carried out in the late 1870s by Saussure. The anomaly Saussure was concerned with was the already well-attested fact that, although the great majority of Indo-European roots were of the structure: consonant + vowel E + consonant, there were a few roots that did not fit into this pattern. Examples of the former and usual ones are: *ped-* ('foot'), *wekᵂ-* ('voice') and *bher-* ('bear'). Examples of the exceptions are: *sta-* ('stand'), *dhe-* ('place') and *es-* ('be'). Saussure proposed that all Indo-European roots originally had the same form but that in all the known Indo-European languages a few roots had, independently or jointly, acquired a different form by the process of linguistic change. Not many were convinced by Saussure's theory. And it was not until the decipherment of Hittite many years later that Saussure's claim was vindicated. Saussure had posited a series of laryngeal consonants—consonants articulated in the region of the throat—which had disappeared in the course of time. It was these very laryngeals that were discovered in Hittite, which was by a few centuries the earliest recorded language of Indo-European. As a result of Saussure's and others' findings, the three exceptions listed above are now reconstructed with laryngeals as: *steh-*, *dheʔ-* and *ʔes-* (ʔ being the phonemic sign for a glottal plosive).

An equally outstanding use of internal construction in combination with the comparative and other methods is Karlgren's reconstruction of Proto-Chinese forms and Archaic Chinese. There is no space here to do more than refer in passing to Karlgren's work, and readers seeking a more detailed picture should consult R. A. D. Forrest's *The Chinese language* (London, 1965).

Chinese, as we have seen, represents a cluster of spoken dialects and a single written language. Nothing is known directly about how these dialects were actually spoken before the present day; and the only indirect clues come from Japanese and various South-east Asian languages which borrowed from Chinese at various periods. The characters of Chinese, however, contain phonetic elements which provide information about which characters rhymed with which in very early times when the characters assumed their permanent forms. Karlgren had begun by examining the modern dialects. By using the comparative method he was able to establish that some dialects contained earlier or more archaic forms than others. For example, Hakka /muk/ 'wood' would be older than Fuchow /mu'/ (ending in a glottal stop), and older still than Peking Mandarin /mu/, in which every trace of the final /k/ had disappeared. Karlgren then used the method of internal reconstruction to attempt to find out why certain characters which nowadays sound totally different from each other were in ancient times known to have rhymed. By this method, and at the same time by making comparisons with Tibetan and early Chinese borrowings in Miao and Thai, Karlgren was able to show that the Chinese syllable in ancient times (during Confucius' day, for example) contained a whole range of initial consonant clusters (two or more consonants not interspersed by a vowel or vocalic feature) which are unknown and completely alien to any modern Chinese speaker. The initial groups Karlgren reconstructed, such as *kl-, *gl-, *sn-, *km- would seem about as strange to the average Chinese as a Russian cluster like mst- (as in the Russian name *Mstislav*) sounds to an English speaker.

A note on modern linguistics and its implications for comparative linguistics

In our own time, and especially since the period between the two world wars, the comparative-historical linguist has increasingly had to take account of the enormous and ever-growing body of theory and observations brought together under the heading of what is variously called *modern, general* or *theoretical* linguistics. Like all new and rapidly developing sciences, modern linguistics is the outcome of a confluence of various streams of thought and enquiry, on occasions ill at ease in each other's company and still bearing the clean trade-marks of their origin.

This is no place, though, to attempt a survey of modern linguistics. I propose therefore to restrict my incursions into this domain, both here and in later sections of this book, to those features which the diachronist can ill-afford to ignore and which have already affected, or seem likely to affect, his methods and conclusions. Those wishing to acquire an all-round view should consult John Lyons' *Theoretical Linguistics* (Cambridge, 1968), a comprehensive, balanced and non-partisan survey.

It was Whitney who first clearly foresaw the shape of modern linguistics. It was in the 1870s that Whitney drew the distinction between comparative linguistics—then more usually known as comparative philology or comparative grammar—and what he called linguistic science.[1] But the true father of modern linguistics is nowadays generally reckoned to be Ferdinand de Saussure. His intention had been to widen the scope of comparative linguistics and to create a science of general linguistics, which would in turn have close links with the social sciences. Nevertheless, Saussure believed that clearer demarcation lines would be needed so that linguistics could be distinguished from ethnography, psychology, sociology or anthropology. Much of what Saussure hoped for has no doubt been to a great extent achieved, and largely thanks to his own efforts. But in an age when compartmentalism is out of fashion, one wonders to what extent Saussure's preoccupation was a bogus one. As Karl Popper has argued, 'studies' or 'disciplines' are not distinguishable by the subject matter that they investigate: 'Subject matter, or kinds of things, do not, I hold, constitute a basis for distinguishing disciplines. Disciplines are distinguished partly for historical reasons and reasons of administrative convenience, and partly because the theories which we construct to solve our problems have a tendency to grow into unified systems . . . *We are not students of some subject matter but students of problems.* And problems may cut right across the borders of any subject matter or discipline.'[2] The case of linguistics is well accounted for by a view like this. Linguistics has its traditional basis in philology and has grown from it. At the same time it has grown into a unified system, but not one that is insulated from the rest of the human sciences. But this, it should be admitted, was not Saussure's sole concern. He above all wanted to extend the cultural influences of linguistics and to lift it out of the narrow confines of the scholar's study: 'That linguistics should continue

[1] Whitney, W. D., *The Life and Growth of Language* (New York, 1874), pp. 315–16.
[2] Popper, K., *Conjectures and Refutations* (London, 1963), pp. 66–7.

to be the prerogative of a few specialists would be unthinkable—
everyone is concerned with it in one way or another.'

From a totally different direction came Franz Boas' *Handbook
of American Indian Languages* (Washington, D.C., 1911–22),
in which we find not only original and invaluable language
descriptions but also a lucid exposition of the new-found principles of *descriptive*, or what Saussure would have called *synchronic*, linguistics itself. In their attempts to come to grips with
the 'exotic' languages and cultures they were investigating, men
like Boas and Sapir were obliged to act as anthropologist and
linguist rolled into one.

From yet another direction came the influence of psychology,
especially that of Wundt, which seemed to provide a bridge from
the older comparative philology to a newer kind of linguistics.
Bloomfield started out from Wundt but later realised that linguistics could make do with its own methodology: 'We have
learned . . . that we can pursue the study of language without
reference to any one psychological doctrine, and that to do so
safeguards our results and makes them more significant to workers
in related fields.'[1] The modern linguist has long ceased to be
anxious about the status of linguistics, and can nowadays usually
work harmoniously in collaboration with the psychologist
(psycholinguistics) and with the sociologist (sociolinguistics),
as also with specialists from a number of other fields. He is
nowadays given to taking his colleagues in adjacent disciplines to
task. I am thinking especially of the Chomsky *et al.* v. Skinner
dispute of recent years over the nature of human behaviour.

One of the central concerns of modern linguistics has been with
structure. Most of the continental and, until lately, many American descriptive linguists have been 'structuralists' more or less.
A key contribution to the structuralist view of linguistics came
from a group of Russian linguists, a number of whom emigrated
after the Revolution to Prague, where they became co-founders
of the Prague School of Linguistics. The Prague structuralist
approach centred especially, though by no means exclusively,
upon the Russians' discovery of the *phoneme* (about which more
will be said later). Those inclined towards the structuralist viewpoint see each language as a system of relations, the elements of

---

[1] Bloomfield, L., *Language* (New York, 1933), p. vii.

which have no validity independently of the relations of equivalence and contrast which hold between them.[1] It will not surprise the reader that structuralism, which was closely associated in Russia with 'formalism', has come in for some ill-deserved criticism.

There are many ways in which modern linguistics, and in particular descriptive (or synchronic) linguistics, has affected the historical linguist. In the first place, the diachronist is now forced to take account of the fact that the techniques of the descriptive linguist can not only apply to languages spoken today but can equally have relevance to languages spoken at different times in the past. One thing the descriptive linguist has demonstrated is that features of a language do not exist in isolation but affect each other, sometimes in surprising ways. A language is a set of interrelated systems. Any readjustment in any one of these systems will affect other elements not only in the same system but in many or all of the other systems too. To return to Saussure's analogy of the chess board: the moving of one piece in the game or the taking of the opponent's piece alters the entire situation on the chess board. If it is only a pawn that is moved or taken, the effect may not be very great; but if it is the queen, anything might happen. Consequently, even when information used about a language of the past is insufficient to construct a *description* of that language, the diachronist has to be extremely wary, lest a change he may have supposed to be due to purely diachronic factors of a historically linear kind (*a* is derived from *b*) turns out, in fact, to have been part of a whole *pattern* of changes, or even some kind of complicated readjustment (*a* is only one feature of *A*, and *b* only one feature of *B*; only *A* as a whole is derived from *B* as a whole). The more traditional account of the history of a language would take a particular vowel, for example, and trace its development from, say, Vulgar Latin to Modern French. Nowadays, the historical linguist would look at the sound system (phonology) as a whole, and from the data available would attempt to reconstruct the total phonological picture for the various 'milestone' languages along the way (e.g. Old French, Middle French). He would also have to reckon with the possibility that even this may not be enough. The sounds of language, as we shall see, do not exist in isolation from the grammar or the vocabulary. For example, in

[1] Lyons, J., *Theoretical Linguistics* (Cambridge, 1969), p. 50.

modern standard English the *long* in *longer* is pronounced differently from the *long* in *longing*. This reflects the tendency of English to keep verbal (and verbally derived) elements apart from adjectival comparison. To take a different example: the stressed *y* in English is as a rule pronounced 'eye' (e.g. cycle, bye, Skye), but in a class of words originally restricted to use by botanists the same stressed *y* can be pronounced as *i* in *kick*. Such as the case with *cyclamen* (a word that has in general usage long replaced the more popular *sowbread*).

The importance of the spoken word *vis à vis* the written word has been recognised ever since the time of the Neo-grammarians. But the historical linguist has continued to rely on written records, since facts about the *spoken* language at a particular period of time can be deduced, directly or indirectly, only from written language sources. Nowadays, it is recognised that a knowledge of a language gathered solely through writing will be very one-sided. The diachronic linguist therefore has been turning more and more to the social historian, the historian of crafts and industrial and agricultural techniques, the folklorist, the ethnologist, the social anthropologist and the archaeologist. The more complete his knowledge of the society speaking a particular language, the more certain his knowledge of that language is likely to become. Reciprocally, the findings of the linguist can be put to very good use by the social historian and many other types of specialist.

A rapidly developing branch of linguistics, variously referred to as *quantitative*, *computational* or *mathematical* linguistics, should also be mentioned. There is no central core or method, but rather a heterogeneous agglomeration of attempts, some successful, others difficult to assess, to apply various mathematical and statistical techniques, as well as information theory, to the solution of linguistic problems or to large-scale linguistic investigations. Comparative linguistics, too, has witnessed in recent years the development of various quantitative methods, known as *lexicostatistics* and *glottochronology*. Useful applications of these methods have been in the classification and typology of languages, and in 'time–depth' computations. In these latter investigations it has been possible to compute the length of time during which two languages have developed independently as separate branches of a common stem. As these computations are based on such nebulous factors as 'cultural universals' and on the assumption that word roots (root morphemes) remain stable for millenia, it is only natural that the conclusions reached should have met with a degree of scepticism. A recent interesting application of glotto-chronology was to the Germanic sub-family of languages. Its aim was to test the current theories of the relationships obtaining between the Germanic dialects. Whereas the traditional division has been into three—West Germanic, North Germanic and East Germanic—statistical analyses using the time–depth formula indicate a fourfold division, with the traditional West Germanic being divided into North-Sea Germanic and Inland Germanic. This tallies, incidentally, with certain findings based on non-statistical and more orthodox methods.

Finally, mention must be made here of an approach to language and languages which is not only fundamentally different from that adopted by historical linguistics but poles apart too from the still comparatively recent procedures developed by descriptive linguistics. During the period between the two world wars there had developed a flourishing structural linguistics in North America, the foundations having been laid by Bloomfield, Sapir and others. The procedure was that a corpus of a given language was collected and then analysed into its component 'utterances'— an utterance being a speech sequence of determinate length, entirely explicable in terms of its own formal components and the environment to which it belongs.[1] After this the utterance was 'segmented', and the segments classified. The utterance would usually be what the traditional grammarians called a sentence. This was further segmented into its 'immediate constituents' (clauses, phrases) and each segment further subdivided into *its* immediate constituents until one arrived at the smallest units of the utterance: the phonemes. The segments were then classified according to their 'distributional' relations. In this way words in English that can have different functions were able to be classified indubitably within the word class to which they belonged, without futile attempts at definition. Thus *book* in *He reads a book* and *They book him* appears as a noun and a verb respectively. In the first sentence *book* cannot be other than a noun because it 'follows' *a*, a particle associated only with nouns and nominal phrases. Likewise, *book* in the second sentence must be a verb because the sentence distribution pattern of English points only to this conclu-

[1] Harris, Z. S., *Structural Linguistics* (Chicago, 1951), pp. 1–28.

sion. Nouns and verbs are no longer definable entities but distributional relations. In the phrase *a poor lover* the second word would be classified as an adjective; but *book* in *a book lover* would not. This is because *a book lover* is 'distributionally equivalent' to *a lover of books* and, secondly, because there does exist a form, *bookish*, which seems by distributional comparison to be the equivalent of *poor* in *a poor lover* and hence a member of the 'adjectival' class.

The structuralist method, like other methods, had its shortcomings; and its exponents were not seldom aware of these. One rather serious shortcoming was that the method could deal only with one set of features at a time, and was unable to generalise to cover other possible or actual sets. The descriptive linguist was not too different from a blind man who with every new or unfamiliar situation has to work out the shape, arrangement and location of everything from scratch. True, the blind man has learned a whole repertoire of skills which makes adjustment easier and quicker; but he lacks the advantage of the sighted person who is able to size up a situation at a glance (except, of course, when it is pitch dark). The latter can, for instance, see a block of flats and say to himself: 'that is a block of flats'; but the blind person, unless he asks someone, has to go into the block, probably up the lift, and complete a tour of one of the floors until he can reach the same conclusion. Another drawback was that the structuralist method had no means of distinguishing between two patently different sentences which had, superficially at any rate, the same structure. *John is eager to please* looked as if it were the same kind of sentence as *John is easy to please*. In the first, however, John is the subject, whereas in the second he obviously is not.

The change came with a completely different approach to descriptive linguistics. I am referring to what is known variously as *transformational* or *generative grammar*, introduced in the 1950s by Noam Chomsky and since adopted by many linguists in all parts of the world. Generative grammar shifts the emphasis away from language as organised data to the *human capacity* that *produces* such data. Instead of analysing the overt structures of individual sentences, comparing and classifying them, generative grammar has attempted to find the underlying system responsible not only for a particular specimen of a sentence but also for many other similar sentences. The term 'generative grammar' was used for the purpose of distinguishing it from those grammars (structural or descriptive) which present merely an inventory. The exponents of generative grammar hold that underlying the superficial structure of a sentence is another and far more *abstract* syntactic structure, related to the superficial or surface structure by a complex chain of rules. Chomsky defines a generative grammar as no more than 'a system of rules that in some explicit and well-defined way assigns structural descriptions to sentences'.[1] This new approach takes into account the very important fact that speakers of a language are constantly uttering as well as hearing things they have never previously said or heard. Generative grammar has set itself the task of discovering the set of *finite* rules underlying the production of an *infinite* range of possible sentences. A sentence such as *He likes caviar* may well have been spoken or heard before, but the sentence *He likes caviar in his porridge on St. Swithin's Day* in all probability has not. Yet no user of English has any difficulty in understanding or producing such a sentence, should the need for it arise. I shall be returning to the generative method later on. Suffice it for the moment to say that the approach is already widely used in diachronic linguistics, and one can reasonably expect that before long comparative and historical linguistics will have been markedly affected by it.

In the remainder of this book I shall be trying to strike a compromise between a more traditional treatment of comparative linguistics and one that I hope will serve a wider purpose, taking some account of recent developments in linguistics as a whole. Part IV 'Meaning', for example, will have much in common with the traditional philological approach to language, but also with the newer approaches to semantics. This fourth part will take us frequently outside linguistics proper, and into literature and the philosophy of culture. In Part III 'Grammar', I have departed somewhat from the more usual treatment of 'accidence', although I have given the latter its due. Rather, I have attempted to explore the formal and syntactical structure of language from the point of view of the whole. Part II 'Sounds' by and large follows a more conventional approach to historical phonology or sound change.

[1] Chomsky, N., *Aspects of the Theory of Syntax* (Cambridge, Mass., 1965), p. 8.

Part II

SOUNDS

7 Sounds in Language

Language has in every time and place relied most heavily, and sometimes exclusively, upon vocal sound as its normal medium of expression. A vocal sound is any kind of sound that can be produced by the speech-organs, and recognised as such, and that can at the same time be distinguished from other types of sound produced by the speech-organs. The sounds are almost invariably real; but they can also be imagined or 'illusioned' (for example, when you think someone is talking to you, but this someone is actually suffering acute indigestion); or, nowadays, they can even be simulated by such technological wonders as 'speech-synthesisers'. The science that makes a special study of vocal sounds is known as *phonetics*.

It is commonly felt to be absurd to describe or classify the vocal sounds produced by parrots, baboons and chimpanzees, even though in practice they are all capable of uttering sounds which are sometimes remarkably like those of humans. This is because phonetics makes little or no sense unless *language* is presupposed. The phonetician may well be intrigued by the mating calls of gibbons or guinea-fowls, but he is rarely given to elaborating descriptions of these creatures' phonetic repertoire. He will usually leave this kind of thing to the zoologist.

The (human) speech-organs themselves sometimes possess a remarkable history of biological evolution (but we cannot go into this here), and all the organs are used for other purposes than speaking—particularly respiration and mastication. In fact, the human 'speech tract' is a set of fixed and movable parts situated all the way back from the lips to the lower part of the throat (see Figure 13). Two of the most interesting and complex 'organs' are the tongue and the larynx. Owing to its endless capacity for altering its shape—flattening, elongating, contracting, swelling—the *tongue* has become the chief mobile resonator, giving rise to a fantastic range of vowels and vocalic sounds. The *larynx* can be described as the uppermost part of the windpipe, which besides incidentally keeping people alive has become adapted to a variety of articulatory functions. At the aperture is a tube of cartilaginous rings connected by membranes which ensure maximum opening or firm closure. The *vocal cords* lie on either side of this aperture, and when the aperture is nearly closed these cords lie adjacent to one another and produce musical vibrations, which are the basis of speaking as well as singing.

But the organs of speech are by no means essential to speech. Surgery has shown that once a particular 'organ' has been removed the speech function of this organ is taken over by residual parts of the speech tract. We must not allow ourselves to forget that the governing factor is not the tongue, the lips or the palate but the motor function of the cerebral cortex. Our brains are what really count. Injury to certain areas of the brain can produce irreversible speech defects in corresponding parts of the speech tract, but not the other way round.

Phonetics

Phonetics is usually divided into three areas: *articulatory*, *auditory* and *acoustic* phonetics. From the point of view of the historical linguist, articulatory phonetics is by far the most important, if only because the International Phonetic Alphabet has been compiled according to articulatory principles, as indeed, but not until recent years, has the phonological description of languages.

Articulatory phonetics

Articulated sounds are described in two ways: firstly, the sounds are classified into groups; then each of these groups is further classified according to the manner in which the group feature is actually articulated.

The first group of articulations are known as *stops* or *plosives*. They are produced by momentary but firm contact between two parts of the speech tract, followed usually by a sudden release. In English /b/ and /p/ are produced by contact between the upper and lower lip; /t/ and /d/ by an instantaneous pressure of the tip of the tongue against the teeth ridge; and /k/ and /g/ by the raising of the rear portion of the tongue until it presses against the soft palate (see Figure 13). Even the larynx itself can produce a 'stop' simply by suddenly releasing air from the windpipe aperture. This kind of sound is known as the 'glottal stop'. It occurs in 'Cockney' pronunciation of phrases like *a bit rotten* [ə biʔ rɔʔən] or *glottal stop* [glɔʔəl stɔʔ], where the symbol resembling a truncated question mark represents the glottal stop.

In some words the vocal cords are vibrating, producing a phenomenon known as *voice* or *voicing*. The phonetician calls them *voiced*, to distinguish them from the *voiceless* variety, which occur when the vocal cords are not vibrating. In English, /b/, /d/ and /g/ are voiced stops. They are not quite so 'voiced' as their

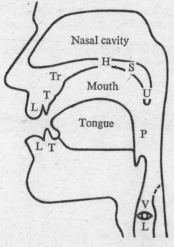

L.	Lips
T.	Teeth
Tr.	Teeth ridge
H.	Hard palate
S.	Soft palate
U.	Uvula
V.	Vocal cords
L.	Larynx
P.	Pharynx

Figure 13

equivalents in French or Spanish, but to about the same degree as in German or Cantonese. The English /p/, /t/ and /k/ are, however, 'voiceless'.

If there is *some* contact, but not a completely firm contact, between two parts of the speech tract, we encounter a group of sounds classified as *fricatives*. The incomplete blockage allows air to pass along the vocal tract, and it is this that gives the fricatives their peculiar qualities. This passage of air can sound like ordinary hard breathing, as in English /h/; or hissing, as in /s/ and /z/; or shushing, as in /ʃ/ 'sh' and /ʒ/ as in 'pleasure'.

When the vocal cords are vibrating but there is nothing like firm contact between any parts of the speech tract, we have two classes of sounds: the *vowels* and the *sonants*. English 'sonants' include /m/, /n/, /ŋ/, /l/ and /r/.

Customarily, speech sounds are divided into two classes: the *consonants* and the *vowels*. Vowels in this context includes diphthongs.

The consonants can be represented on a two-dimensional grid. This grid takes account of three features for each sound: (i) whether the sound is *voiced* or *voiceless*; (ii) the *point of articulation*; and (iii) the *manner of articulation*. In the grid given below (Figure 14) the points of articulation are set out horizontally and the types of manner of articulation are arranged vertically. It comprises only the present-day standard English consonants. The comparatist obviously would work with a much more compre-

		BILABIAL	LABIO-DENTAL	DENTAL	ALVEOLAR	ALVEO-PALATAL	VELAR	GLOTTAL
STOPS	voiceless	p			t		k	
	voiced	b			d		g	
AFFRICATES:	voiceless					tʃ		
	voiced					dʒ		
FRICATIVES:	voiceless		f	θ	s	ʃ		h
	voiced		v	ð	z	ʒ		
LATERAL:	voiced				l			
NASALS:	voiced	m			n		ŋ	
SEMIVOWELS:	voiced	w			r	y		

Figure 14 Table of English consonants

hensive 'grid', which would represent not only the sounds of English but also the sounds of all the languages with which he happened to be dealing. If he is drawing comparisons between various regional dialects, he may even want to draw upon the entire range of the International Phonetic Alphabet (for an updated version of this, see Robins, R. H., *General Linguistics: An Introductory Survey* (London, 1964), pp. 92–3). In the grid, or table, given in Figure 14, the 'sonants' have been subdivided into 'laterals', 'nasals' and 'semivowels'. This is a normal subdivision. *Nasal* consonants are those pronounced through the nasal passage instead of through the mouth. What happens in the case of nasals is that the *uvula* (see Figure 13) is lowered, thus shutting off the flow of sound through the mouth and directing it through the nasal passage instead. The *semivowels* are neither vowels nor consonants but something in between. (Please note that it is only the standard English *r* that is a semivowel. When the *r* is rolled, as in mock-Scottish, or 'burred', as in many dialects, it is usually classified in a different way.) The *affricates* start off by being stops but immediately turn into fricatives. An example of an affricate from a different language is the German /pf/ as in *Pferd* ('horse'). Along the horizontal axis the following explanations should prove helpful. The *Labio-dental* sounds are produced by the contact of the upper teeth with the lower lip. *Alveolar* consonants are those pronounced by the tip of the tongue against the upper teeth ridge. (Note that in many languages—the Romance and Slavonic languages, for example—the /t/ and /d/ are not 'alveolar' but 'dental'; that is, produced by the contact of the tip of the tongue against the teeth.) *Velum* is the Latin word for *palate*. The important *alveo-palatal* articulation occurs in the area between the hard and soft palates (see Figure 13).

Reading off from our grid (Figure 14) we get the following descriptions of the English consonants:

/p/ —voiceless bilabial stop
/b/ —voiced bilabial stop
/m/—voiced bilabial nasal; (or voiced nasal bilabial)
/w/—voiced bilabial semivowel
/f/ —voiceless labio-dental fricative
/v/ —voiced labio-dental fricative
etc., etc.

(*Suggestion:* Continue this list, writing out the descriptions; and at the same time see if you can check the description against your own (English) articulation.)

The *vowels* and *diphthongs* could have been entered on the grid we have just been considering, but as they are all 'voiced sonants' this would not be very useful. Instead, the vowels (and diphthongs) are best represented on a very different kind of grid. This was first developed by the British phonetician Daniel Jones (see Figure 15).

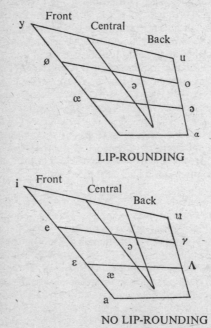

LIP-ROUNDING

NO LIP-ROUNDING

Figure 15 The cardinal vowels

The characteristic features of vowels are: (i) presence or absence of lip-rounding; (ii) the position and shape of the tongue; and (iii) the presence or absence of 'nasalisation'. The Jones Vowel Diagram can represent all three features. The intersections on the grid mark the 'mid-point' of the tongue, and they tell us whether the position of the mid-point, and hence the whole tongue, is towards the front or back of the oral cavity; or whether it is raised or lowered. The uppermost and farthest forward vowel is the Italian or French /i/ (the English /i/ is lower and farther back, relatively speaking); the vowel /ɑ/ as in English *car*, is the farthest retracted and the lowest placed (if the doctor wants a good view of your throat he asks you to say /a/). In English all the 'front' vowels are without lip-rounding; but in French and German, for example, there is a whole series of front vowels *with* lip-rounding. These are /y/ as in (Fr.) *tu*, /ø/ as in (Fr.) *jeu* and /œ/ as in (Fr.) *peur*. The 'central vowel' /ə/ occurs in English *the* and French *le*. Standard English has a single, unrounded back vowel transcribed as /ʌ/. Nasalisation of vowels does not occur in English but is quite important in European languages such as French, Portuguese and Polish. Nasalisation is easily indicated by placing a mark /˜/ above the vowel that is nasalised. French has four nasalised vowels: /ã/ as in *vent* /vã/, /ɛ̃/ as in *rien* /rjɛ̃/, /œ̃/ as in *un* /œ̃/ and /ɔ̃/ as in *son* /sɔ̃/.

Diphthongs consist of a glide from one vowel to another. The direction of the glide can be marked on the vowel grid by an arrow. The arrow starts from the first vowel of the diphthong and points in the direction of the second vowel.

Acoustic phonetics

As phonetics became more scientific, it felt the need for instruments that would objectively and accurately measure or record the sounds of human speech. Instruments of various kinds have been in use for a very long time. But a major breakthrough came with the development of the *sound spectrograph*. This machine can provide a photographic representation of a segment of speech, from which the phonetician can read off various acoustic characteristics. One of the gains is that the phonetician now knows more about the discrepancy between what a speaker hears and what he *thinks* he hears. The aural illusion has become as well established as the optical. Although acoustic phonetics has had a revolutionary effect upon phonetics itself, and an already marked effect on descriptive phonology, it is too early to say what are likely to be its repercussions for the diachronist.

Phonology

The /k/ sounds in *keep* /kiːp/ and *coop* /kuːp/ would be recognised by all English speakers as the same. Speakers of many other languages would not, however, recognise them even as similar.

The Arabic speaker would insist that they are different sounds. In Arabic there are two /k/ sounds where English recognises only one. A speaker of Arabic not only represents them by different symbols, but also if he says *kalb* he means 'a dog' and if he says *qalb* he means 'he cut'. The /k/ in *kalb* is pronounced something like the English /k/ in *keep* and the /q/ in *qalb* not too differently from the /k/ in English *coop*. The difference is that whereas the English speaker hears, or *perceives*, them as one sound the Arabic speaker perceives them as two distinct sounds.

The interesting question is *why* the English speaker pays no attention to and does not even notice the difference, whilst the Arabic speaker would think you were pulling his leg if you told him you even had difficulty in noticing a difference. It would be rather like a speaker of a language that makes no voiced-voiceless distinction between consonants telling you he could not hear the difference between *big* and *pig*. You would be doing him an injustice by telling him to have his ears tested! The Japanese student of English notoriously experiences difficulty in distinguishing between English /l/ and /r/. He cannot *hear* the difference because Japanese makes no distinction between /l/ and /r/. As far as the speaker of Japanese is concerned, they are the *same sound*. Speakers of Cantonese who in English have no problem about distinguishing *nil* for *Lil* or *nip* from *lip* not only happily tolerate but also do not usually notice the fact that *in Cantonese* some speakers use /n/ in initial position, whereas others use /l/. It is only confusing for the foreign learner of Cantonese.

This *why?* is largely what theoretical *phonology* is all about. The phonologist is, of course, interested in phonetic descriptions, but he is primarily concerned with the way in which sounds within a particular language form a *system*. He is interested in those *minimal* sound features of the language which *distinguish meanings*, and which he calls *phonemes*.

I will not bother the reader with the intricacies associated with the problem of defining the phoneme. It will be simpler if we return to our Arabic–English contrast. We can say that in English there is a single /k/-phoneme, which in Arabic would be subdivided into two phonemes: a /k/-phoneme and a /q/-phoneme. And to take the Japanese–English contrast, English has an /l/-phoneme and an /r/-phoneme, but Japanese has a single

/r/-phoneme which straddles both the English sounds. A phoneme, then, is the minimal sound feature of any language which is perceived as different from all other sound features (phonemes) of that language by a speaker of that language. Thus the reader is able to appreciate that the phoneme is highly abstract. It is not really speech sound as such but the *linguistic perception* of speech sound.

I said earlier that, although the native speaker of English does not notice the fact, the /k/ sounds in *keep* and *coop* are considered by the phonetician (as well as the Arab) to be quite different sounds. The phonetician and the phonologist both call them *allophones*. It is usual for each *phoneme* in a language to assume concrete shape in the form of one of *several* allophones. An allophone takes on its quality from its speech environment. 'Initial' consonant allophones are not usually the same as 'final' allophones. A following vowel (as in *keep* and *coop*) will often affect the quality of the consonant, making it into a separate allophone. If you are pernickety enough you can insist that every occurrence of a phoneme in a different environment represents a separate allophone. But phoneticians do not go to such lengths. They tend to keep their basic division to a minimum, and only to subdivide further in cases of need. A very sensible procedure.

The phoneme is generally pegged to the most commonly occurring allophonic feature. Thus, most commonly, English /t/ occurs in the alveolar position (as in *ten* or *table*); the *alveolar* feature is the predominant one. But there are allophones of /t/ that sound nothing like the predominant one. The /t/ in *kettle* is described as a 'laterally exploded' sound; and the /t/ in *mutton* is exploded in the nasal cavity.

This allophone subdivision has its practical uses. For example: a rather peculiar allophone of /t/ occurs before an /r/ (as in *trick* or *treacle*). This allophone is remarkably similar to the basic sound feature of a Hindi /t/-phoneme. So that, if you are learning Hindi and are a speaker of English, you would do well to take a word like *train*, suppress the *-rain* part and pronounce the *t* in isolation. This will give you a tongue position something like the one needed for a common Hindi allophone.

If we look at speech as a continuous flow (interrupted by pauses) the phoneme strikes us as decidedly mysterious. If we take a word and 'segment' it into its phonemes—e.g. *s-t-i-l-t*—we usually do not find this too difficult; but when we consider two *neighbouring phonemes* we may start to wonder how it is we know when we have passed from one to another. The sound did not stop, yet in pronouncing *s-t-i-l-t* we traversed no less than five distinct phonemes. In fact, the phonologist does not concern himself with possible no-man's-land between one phoneme and the next (although the phonetician sometimes does). Instead, he sees the phoneme as a kind of 'quantum': there is either a phoneme or nothing.

We now know, as a result of the distinguished collaboration of three linguists,[1] that the speech continuum is not a simple thing at all. The phoneme itself turns out to be a mere 'stopping place' along this speech continuum. Each phoneme consists of a complex bundle of *distinctive features*. These distinctive features had been posited quite a long time ago by the Prague School, but it is only more recently that an acoustic basis has been given to these features. The distinctive feature is a simple two-way alternative, like an on-off switch or a binary choice. For English phonology there are ten such alternatives operating *simultaneously*, so that every phoneme is a nexus of ten simultaneous choices. A transition from one phoneme to the next is neither more nor less than a rearrangement of these choices. It is something like a kind of formation dance in which the dancers change partners at predetermined intervals. The dancers are always the same people, but they are constantly being rearranged by the rules of the particular dance. But it is high time we turned to historical phonology.

[1] Jakobson, R., Fant, C. G. M., and Halle, M., *Preliminaries to Speech Analysis* (Cambridge, Mass., 1967).

8 Sound Change

For the next stage, the study of sound change or *diachronic phonology*, a grounding in phonetics is a necessary preparation. For some, this is among the most engrossing aspects of comparative linguistics, an entire world of its own.

We should first of all find out what it is we are dealing with, for the heading of the chapter is not, I fear, self-explanatory.

To begin with, sound change is a term employed to describe the passage or historical transition from a given phoneme or group of phonemes to another, e.g. the change of Germanic *sk* into Old English *sh*. Alternatively, the term may cover the creation or disappearance of phonemes. A good example of the latter is the elimination of χ in Old English [liχt], leaving Modern English [lait] *light*. To describe sound changes is one thing, to explain them is quite another. How and when does a sound change begin to occur? It is not true, for instance, that, if I suddenly resolve to alter and perpetuate in my own speech the pronunciation of a particular word or phoneme, I will thereby have brought about a sound change. Even if I subscribed to the idiosyncratic pronunciation of a certain group of people and modified my speech to match theirs, neither my own nor the group's acquired speech habits would constitute sound change. The unlikely converse situation of a group imitating *my* pronunciation of certain sounds would also fail to produce sound change.

Let us take a firmer hold of our original question: how and when? First of all, it is useless to look for the *beginning* of a particular sound change, for, by an old tautology, a sound change can only be said to have occurred *after it has occurred*. Only the most abstract formulation will do. A sound change can be said to have occurred when the pronunciation by a social unit (town, village or nation) of that sound at a time A is different from what it was at an earlier time B.

And as for the question: how? We have already seen that sounds do not change in any organic way. What happens is that the new pronunciations replace earlier ones. But, whatever the true nature of sound change, we are certainly dealing with a *statistical* kind of change, with a group average and not with individual pronunciation. No sound change can ever be brought about deliberately by an individual unless a section of the community of unpredictable size decides to follow suit. *Unpredictable* is the key word here.

It is indeed odd to think of the process of sound change as statistical, yet think of it this way we must. And we are now right at the core of the difficulty. Take a look at contemporary R.P. English. Doubtless certain 'changes' are at this very moment taking place, however subtle. It would be a rash phonetician who dared to predict what these changes would be. Even, say, thirty years hence the same phonetician (were he still alive) priding himself in a correct prediction would not be able to say for certain that John Collins in Camden Town or Mary Adams in Stoke Poges had modified *their* pronunciation. They may still have exactly the same pronunciation in 2000 as they had in 1970. You may object that they are only exceptions; but just how many exceptions is it possible to allow? Where do we draw the line? It is rather like the problem of how many hairs make a beard. A further complication is that John Collins may have two pronunciations, one for home and another for the office. Which is his *real* pronunciation then?

The hardest fact of all remains: that sounds have indubitably changed; otherwise Englishmen would still be pronouncing words in the manner of their Anglo-Saxon predecessors, and Frenchmen and Italians speaking like citizens of the Roman provinces during the time of Cicero. It is a fact that French *chien* in Roman times was pronounced *cane*(*m*), and *oreille* 'ear', *auricula*(*m*). Likewise, English *sister* had the very different appearance of *sweoster* or *swuster*. Our examples could run into tens of thousands. When we turn to Indo-European the divergences are even more alarming. French *cent*, English *hund*(red), Russian *sto*, Sanskrit *satam* are known to be related and must have begun life as something so unlikely as *$k\eta tom$, a word hypothetically reconstructed from historical descendants and described by comparatists as 'Indo-European'.

Before plunging further into the technicalities of sound change, it will be as well to review some of the more important theories attempting an explanation of the phenomenon.

Theories of sound change

We can, I think, pass with irreverent haste over those theories that have long since been discredited. But I am mentioning them, not merely for the record but because they are precisely the ones that suggest themselves to the popular imagination.

The first of these discredited theories is that sound change is brought about by *anatomical changes* within the population. This theory seemed plausible enough to the early comparatists; and later came to have a strong appeal for those inclined towards racialism. The simple observation that the children of immigrants or refugees learn the language of adoption with little, and often no, trace of imperfection is sufficient to put paid to any theory which claims that speech habits have a basis in race.

Equally certain is it that language sounds have nothing to do with *climate* or *geography*. Harsh climates, as Sapir pointed out, do not engender harsh-sounding languages.

It was Wundt, at the turn of the century, who came up with the ingenious theory that the phonetic character of speech is determined by *social conventions*. He cited the case of the Iroquois Indians, who regarded it as improper to close the mouth while speaking and hence had no labial consonants in their language. Although it can be conceded that mores may in some cases have affected speech, it cannot be that their influence has ever been more than marginal. Moreover, with theories of this kind, it is possible to turn them round to argue the direct opposite. The claim that the phonetic peculiarities of language have influenced mores is not less plausible than the claim advanced by Wundt and others.

I now pass on to more plausible theories, none of which can be dismissed as entirely untenable.

Social historical

The kind of theory subsumed under this heading is described by Saussure: 'There have been attempts to relate phonetic changes to turbulent periods in a nation's history and in this way to discover a link between political instability and linguistic instability; this done, some think that they can apply conclusions concerning language in general to phonetic changes. They observe, for example, that the sharpest upheavals of Latin in its development into the Romance languages coincided with the highly disturbed period of invasions.'[1] Jespersen lends firm support to this hypothesis, citing in particular the case of the Black Death, and the

[1] Saussure, F. de, *op. cit.*, p. 150.

wars and social disruption of the later Middle Ages, which in England and France at any rate coincided with the most rapid linguistic change.

Linguistic substratum

Substratum theories are based on the assumption that the absorption of newcomers or immigrants by indigenous populations has brought about certain changes. This has often been brought forward to explain the 'Gallic' characteristics of French, and the divisions particularly marked between the regions of Provençal and French proper which are supposed to correspond with the population and distribution of Celtic tribes in Gaul during the time of the Roman Empire. Similar attempts have been made to assess the possible influence of prehistoric Etruscan and Ligurian on the various Italian dialects. The main flaw in these theories is that it is impossible to know what the indigenous languages were actually like, phonologically or otherwise. In any case, one finds oneself caught in an infinite regress, because there must have been 'pre-indigenous' and 'ante-pre-indigenous' populations in these areas at an even more remote time.

The Ease Theory

I leave the last word on this to Jespersen: 'I am not afraid of hearing the objection that I ascribe too great power to human laziness, indolence, inertia, shirking, easygoingness, sluggishness, or whatever other beautiful synonyms have been invented for "economy of effort" or "following the line of least resistance". The fact remains that there *is* such a tendency in all human beings, and by taking it into account in explaining changes of sound we are doing nothing else than applying here the same principle.' The main objection to the Ease Theory was levelled by Osthoff, one of the Neo-grammarians, who pointed out that 'easy' and 'difficult' are relative terms, and that what is easy to one speaker may be difficult to the speaker of another language. The English /θ/ and /δ/ are not difficult for the English speaker; in fact, they seem to be quite natural, for English people when more than a little drunk tend to affricate their plosives, saying 'puth ith thown' (for 'put it down'). To a foreigner, however, these sounds can present very serious problems.

One positive piece of support for the Ease Theory is that certain

sound changes appear to be irreversible, and that in these cases
the direction of change corresponds with ease of articulation.
Thus there are no cases of breathed /h/ becoming /χ/ (velar fricative) as one might expect; /χ/ requires a great deal more physical
effort than /h/ (although the latter is not necessarily *easier to
learn*). There are a few other examples, one such being that /s/
becomes /h/ in a number of languages.

Imitation

Of all the theories of sound change so far advanced, none seems
particularly plausible, if only because, despite their ingenuity or
partial significance, they all depend on the assumption, so far
unproved, that sounds do in fact *change* or *evolve*.

The Imitation Theory avoids this assumption altogether and
confines itself to stating that whenever a sound changes we can do
no more than deduce that one sound has been *replaced* by
another. Jespersen was an upholder of this, claiming that the
origin of phonetic change, as indeed any other linguistic change,
is due to imitation, whether conscious or unconscious, of the
speech habits of other people. I would also add the corollary that,
just as imitation produces change, so also does *resistance to
imitation*. I believe this to be important, especially in the study of
dialect *vis-à-vis* language. Dialects resist each other's influence
just as much and probably more than they imitate each other's
characteristics. Local pride in football teams, 'talent', crafts
extends to dialect. Not surprisingly, since speech, as we have seen,
cannot be isolated from social activities in general. It is possible,
even probable, that dialect breaks down only when the equilibrium between imitation and resistance to imitation is upset, and
when the latter is reduced. In the case of English, dialects lost their
literary status and all that went with it as long ago as the fifteenth
century. With the spread of literacy towards the end of the last
century, and with growing mobility of population coupled with
mass media, local dialects have lost more and more ground to the
nationally accepted standard. R.P. English will presumably
continue to spread by imitation until within a few decades only
remote and scattered traces of dialect will remain.

Until thoroughgoing studies are made in this direction it will
be impossible to know whether imitation explains all, or even
nearly all, sound change. There does seem to be a layering of

English speech habits with the more archaic characteristics to be found only in the more remote and hilly districts (the Northern Pennines and Exmoor, for instance), followed next in order by the less accessible and less mobile rural areas, and so on until one reaches the most recent speech developments confined to 'London and Home Counties' upper-middle-class speech, and the speech of suburbia. This 'layering', rough as it is, supports the imitation hypothesis. The contours are difficult to follow, however, owing to the fact that they are not only geographical but social-class contours as well. There are still parts of England, particularly in the north, where phonetic characteristics have not changed greatly since the time of the Norman conquest. As far as these areas are concerned, the so-called 'great vowel shift', which affected the English standard during the fifteenth century, might never have occurred.

Speech interference

Perhaps the most potent and widespread cause of linguistic change is the bilingual speaker. In almost any bilingual speaker *speech interference* will exist to some degree. Interference arises when a bilingual identifies a phoneme of his second language or dialect with a phoneme in his mother tongue (or mother dialect), so that when he reproduces a sound in his second language he subjects it to the phonetic strictures of the mother tongue. This phenomenon is not confined to the bilingual but is commonly met with in the foreign-language learner. The English-speaking student of French will, unless he is carefully taught, tend to pronounce French in an English way: that is, he will substitute a convenient allophone of an English phoneme for the correct allophone of the equivalent French phoneme. Instead, for example, of pronouncing French *fini* with the vowels very 'closed' and medium in length, he will say something like *fee-knee* with the vowels too long, not forward or high enough, and too 'open'. The same kind of thing happens in all but exceptional cases with the bilingual (the bilingual who speaks both his 'languages' without a trace of 'accent' is the exception, not the rule). When an entire population is bilingual the same feature will be diffused throughout that population. Studies of Romansch bilingual speakers of Swiss German have shown that this clearly is so.[1] The mechanism of phonemic inter-

[1] Weinreich, U., *Languages in Contact*, p. 14 ff.

ference is an exceedingly complex one, with socio-cultural factors playing a likely, but still not clearly determined, part. Actual sound changes do not, however, seem to be dependent on cultural considerations but on the *structural* conditions of the language itself in which the sound changes occur. It appears that languages undergo sound change only when 'the language contact and the resulting interference could be considered to have, at best, a trigger effect, releasing or accelerating developments which mature independently'.[1]

Before turning to a summary of the various kinds of sound change, it is as well to remind ourselves of the danger of abstracting or isolating sound change from other kinds of linguistic change. As Jespersen said: 'Phonetic changes to be fully understood should not be isolated from other changes, for in actual linguistic life we witness a constant interplay of sound and sense . . . Sounds should never be isolated from the words in which they occur, nor words from sentences. No hard-and-fast boundary can be drawn between phonetic and non-phonetic changes.'

Types of sound change

Sound changes are as many and various as the languages in which they occur. In this section I shall have to restrict myself to the more prominent changes, and also to those which concern the Indo-European area primarily. Further examples will be found in Chapter 10.

Sound shift

One very important feature of language divisions within the Indo-European group is 'sound shift'. This, however, is not completely understood and simply describes a shift that has taken place in a certain direction.

Perhaps the most well-known sound shift is the Germanic (or Gothonic) sound shift. This was originally explained by the equally famous 'Grimm's Law'. Grimm was one of the founders of comparative philology, and it is therefore hardly surprising that his account was considerably wide of the mark.

This shift, as it is now precisely understood, can be stated,

[1] Weinreich, *ibid.*, p. 25.

although in a somewhat oversimplified form, as follows: Provided that other conditions have not intervened, the Indo-European voiced plosives /b/, /d/, /g/ have become voiceless plosives /p/, /t/, /k/ throughout the entire Germanic speaking area (which, it will be remembered, includes Britain and Scandinavia as well as Germany, Switzerland, Austria and the Low Countries); the original Indo-European voiceless plosives /p/, /t/, /k/ shifted to the corresponding fricatives /f/, /θ/, /χ/. The following diagram will help:

Indo-European (I–E)   Germanic

$$voiced\begin{cases} /b/ \rightarrow /p/ \\ /d/ \rightarrow /t/ \\ /g/ \rightarrow /k/ \end{cases}voiceless$$

$$voiceless\begin{cases} /p/ \rightarrow /f/ \\ /t/ \rightarrow /\theta/ \\ /k/ \rightarrow /\chi/ \end{cases}fricative$$

One interesting feature of this shift is that the Germanic languages gained an identical set of phonemes to the ones they lost, viz. /p/, /t/, /k/. A number of examples illustrate this shift. Here are a few:

(i) (Lat.) _pecu_, 'herd'.	(Gothic) _faihu_ 'cattle'; (O.E.)[1] _feoh_ 'fief'.
(ii) (Skr.)[2] _tri_ = (Greek) _tría_ = (Lat.) _tria_ 'three'.	(Goth.) _thrija_ = (Old Icelandic) _thriu_ = (Eng.) _three_.
(iii) (Skr.) _kataraḥ_ = (Lithuanian) _katras_ = 'which of two?'	(Goth.) _hwathar_ 'which of two?' = (Eng.) _whether_.
(iv) (Lith.) _dubus_, 'deep'.	(Goth.) _diups_ = (O.Icel.) _diupr_ = (Eng.) _deep_.
(v) (Skr.) _dantam_ = (Lat.) _dentem_, 'tooth'.	(Goth.) _tunthu_ = (Eng.) _tooth_.
(vi) (Greek) _gonu_ = (Lat.) _genu_ = 'knee'.	(Goth.) _kniu_ = (O.E.)[1] _kneo_ = (Mod. Eng.) _knee_.

---

[1] O.E. = Old English.   [2] Skr. = abbrev. 'Sanskrit'.

This shift is sometimes classified as a 'sound law' and left at that. More recently, some light was thrown upon the Germanic sound shift by M. Grammont, the French phonetician, who demonstrated experimentally that a German pronouncing a /b/ would articulate almost exactly the same sound that a Frenchman would utter when pronouncing /p/. Thus the initial consonants of German *bau* and French *pu* turned out to be phonetically identical. It could also be shown that Germans when articulating /p/ would introduce a fricative or aspirated element, sometimes represented as /pʰ/. All this has important comparative implications, for it may be that the Germanic sound shift may never have been a shift (that is, a change) in the true sense but that speakers of certain regions, namely the Germanic regions, may from earliest times have substituted their own phonetic variant of the Indo-European originals. It is probably safer to describe the shift as a *correspondence* and to stick to that until further insight into the matter has been gained.

Compression or *shortening*
Neither of these terms forms part of the nomenclature of comparative philology, but I am using them to denote a wide range of sound changes that share the common feature of reduction of phonetic length of given words or phrases. *Compression* represents internal shortening of a word and *shortening* the clipping off of affixes or endings. The latter is common in slang and has led to a mass of words such as *cab*, *bike* and, more recently, *telly*. This process has also been responsible for the reduction of grammatical endings, about which more will be said in a later chapter.

A much more complex and perplexing phenomenon is *compression*. This occurs frequently in everyday speech, as, for example, in *good morning*, which is normally pronounced in practically every way but the correct one: /gud mɔːniŋ/. It is, one supposes, the *frequency of repetition* that has caused the individual speaker to find the shortened form that he finds the easiest to say, and that others will still recognise as the standard greeting; so much so that if we happen to be greeted by the full and correctly expanded form we will consider it 'hypercorrect'. But there comes a stage (or stages) in the evolution of any language when such 'compressions' become unrelated to the full expansions, and the latter as a consequence are replaced and eventually disappear. At some stage, and possibly within a few decades, the following compressions took place in the Gallic Romance area and the original forms were forgotten:

     (Lat.) *biberaticu(m)* > *beuvrage* (Eng. *beverage*)

and   (Lat.)   *auricula(m)* > (Fr.) *oreille* 'ear'

The only explanation of such changes that really makes sense is that *oreille* and *beuvrage* were 'local' variants of the original which subsequently 'caught on' on a nation-wide scale.

There is a certain amount of evidence that 'local' words, for instance place-names, are the kind that undergo the most compression; and these compressions will occasionally be in advance of the orthography, which may date from late Saxon times or later. Thus the inhabitants of Cirencester refer to their own town as Sisister; the townsfolk of Barnoldswick on the Lancashire-Yorkshire border say Barlick. In most cases, however, the compressed forms are those that have gone on record *since* the time when local pronunciation had reached its ultimate compression. Compare the Saxon and later official spellings of the following place-names:

Saxon	Present day
Cloppaham	*Clapham*
Gatatune	*Gatton*
Hrofescestre	*Rochester*
Folcanstane	*Folkestone*
Glestinganbyrige	*Glastonbury*
Weoduningas	*Weedon*

The reader may care to look in the place-name dictionaries for some of the hundreds of other examples.

A point I would like to make is that such compressions almost certainly only occur on a local scale (place-name, slang, local variant) and, to influence the language as a whole, must spread either by imitation or by literary perpetuation. The influence of the written word can also override local malformations and distortions (for example, it did not allow Barlick for Barnoldswick). It is incredibly unlikely that Harlow New Town or Welwyn Garden City, in speech at any rate, will ever be pronounced differently (*except* by the local inhabitants) unless some major national catastrophe intervenes. And this brings me to my last point.

An alternative explanation of these 'compressed' forms is offered by the social historical theory of sound change, that in fact disasters did occur which completely obliterated local tradition. Even in our own age, with the threat of nuclear annihilation, it is difficult to imagine such disasters. Yet we must not forget that the population of mediaeval England was much smaller and more scattered; we know also from recent studies based on parish registers that local famines wiping out entire villages occurred even as late as the seventeenth century. If such unrecorded catastrophes were possible in the seventeenth century there is no reason why they should not have been just as frequent in earlier centuries. Breaks in local or regional tradition would be sufficient to explain the compressions that have been observed in local words, and perhaps even of less localised words such as *biberaticum*, *auriculam* and thousands of others.

Assimilation

This is one of the most widespread forms of sound change. Assimilation is a change of sound of a consonant or vowel brought about by the influence of a neighbouring, usually adjacent, consonant or vowel. As we have already seen (in Chapter 7), a phoneme makes its appearance as one of several different allophones, these allophones being given their specific articulation by the sounds coming immediately after and before them. To take an example at random: the word *misshapen* /misʃeipən/ tends to be pronounced [miʃʃeipən] in normal connected speech. The /s/, because of the closeness between its allophone in this particular position to the succeeding /ʃ/, becomes 'assimilated' to the latter. Assimilations of this kind are a normal part of everyday speaking.

But [miʃʃeipən] and the many other assimilations of everyday speech do not constitute sound *change*, for they can easily be 'hypercorrected'. [miʃʃeipən] can very easily be given its 'proper' and full phonetic value if we want it that way. In fact, none of the assimilations we make in our normal speaking can be called sound change.

It is only in the *diachronic* process that assimilation produces

sound *change*. In the case of a synchronic state—our own
mother tongues, for instance—we are always dimly conscious of
the assimilations we make, and can correct them. In the diachronic process there comes a stage at which the speakers of a
language cease to realise, or even forget, that they are actually
changing their pronunciation and not just making sporadic
assimilations. As if to perpetuate this lack of awareness, or
forgetfulness, they eventually begin to *spell* the word differently
from the form in which the assimilation originally occurred. During the period in which modern French emerged, the /s/ that had
been pronounced in Old French *escole* had become assimilated
through a weakening of articulation to the vowel and had ceased
to be pronounced. We still find the *s* retained (in the writings of
Montaigne, for example) for some time; but eventually the
spelling *école* gives full and final acknowledgment to the disappearance of the *s*. Spelling, as we have seen earlier, is conservative. In English *castle* still retains its mediaeval spelling, even
though it has long been pronounced /kɑsl/; and the assimilation
of /d/ to /t/ in /wɔʃt/ is even now not recognised by the spelling
washed.

Examples of diachronic assimilation are many, and we shall be
encountering some of them in later chapters. In the meantime, let
us take a look at two examples from Romance. The historical
relationship between the Italian forms *otto* 'eight' and *sette*
'seven' and Latin *octo* and *septem* (respectively) suggests that
changes occurred some time between Roman times and the period
of the Middle Ages when Italian came into its own. The /k/ of
Latin /ɔkto/ has become a /t/ in /ɔtto/ and the /p/ in /sɛptem/ has
also become /t/ in /sɛtte/. In both cases it can be said that, in
Italian, the Latin consonant cluster, stop+stop, has produced a
different consonant cluster, in which the first stop has become
assimilated to the second stop. Both /k/ and /p/ in Latin have
come assimilated to /t/—that is, they have shifted their point of
articulation—in Italian when they immediately precede a /t/. (We
know, incidentally, that this assimilation was not diffused
throughout the Romance-speaking area. Romanian has *şapte* and
French still retains the /p/ in the spelling *sept*.)

Assimilations of this type are particularly common in place
names. Take, for instance, *North Riding*, which originally was
North Thriding (*Thriding* = 'a third part'); or *Surrey*, which a

one time was *Suthrige* (*Suth* = 'south'); or *Winkelbury*, which had started life as *Winterbury*.

The oddest and most intriguing kind of assimilation is termed *assimilation at a distance*. The most famous example is *ma tante*, where the initial /t/ of *tante* has been created by assimilation with the final /t/. Originally, the phrase was *ma ante* (Eng. *aunt*). Another example of assimilation at a distance is:

(Early Lat.) **pequo* > (Classical Lat.) *coquo* 'I cook'

Assimilations, especially those 'at a distance', have been attributed to 'a certain mental restlessness, which anticipates sounds to come'. Memory and the total mental impression of a word is also responsible. Indeed, the restriction of assimilation to word units is perhaps corroboration that words exist as *units* and have a separate identity.

Two aspects of sound change related to and included within the scope of assimilation, which will be dealt with more fully in Chapter 10, are:

Umlaut or vowel mutation. This is fundamental to the Ural-Altaic languages, where the entire word takes on the root-vowel coloration; e.g. (Hungarian) *ház-ban* 'in the house', *kéz-ben* 'in the hand'. Vowel mutation is also highly important in Germanic comparative studies; cf. Mod. German: (sing.) *Buch*—(pl.) *Bücher*; (sing.) *Apfel*—(pl.) *Äpfel*. Also English: (sing.) *tooth*—(pl.) *teeth*; (sing.) *foot*—(pl.) *feet*. Some consider vowel mutation to be a form of *assimilation at a distance*.

Vocalisation. The absorption of a voiced consonant between two vowels by these vowels. An example of this is the English word *poor*, which derives from Old French *povre* (Mod. Fr. *pauvre*). Vocalisation can be regarded as a special type of *assimilation*.

Dissimilation

In many ways this is the converse of assimilation. This phonetic occurrence creates a difference between like sounds in order to facilitate articulation. Examples are:

(Spanish) *coronel* > (Fr.) *colonel* (Spanish has dissimilated the first *l* substituting an *r*)
(Latin) *flabilis* > (Fr.) *faible* (reduction of first *l*)

(Old. Fr.) *livel* (Eng. *level*) > (Fr.) *nivel* (> *niveau*)
(Old. Fr.) *Amabel* (Eng. *Mabel*) > *Annabel* (dissimilation of labials *m* and *b*)
(Latin) *quinque* > (Ital. & O. Fr.) *cinque*
(Latin) *peregrinum* > (Fr.) *pélérin* 'pilgrim'
(Latin) *grammar* > (Scots dial.) *glamour*

Metathesis (*change of position*)

Despite the fact that in diachronic linguistics this is all-pervading, it is a primitive feature belonging very much to the infancy of language, a time when position of vowels and consonants was not fixed. Consonants /l/ and /r/ are the most frequently 'metathesised' consonants. For examples of /r/ metathesis compare:

> (Latin) *prima*—(Germanic) *furst, first*
> (Mod. High German) *brennen*—(Eng.) *burn*

The same 'root' gives English *verge* and *bridge*. According to Weekley,[1] *wattle* and *wallet* are used indifferently in Middle English for 'a little bag'. An example of another kind of metathesis is *mosquito* and its French relation *moustique* (from an earlier form *mousquite*).

The remainder of this section is devoted to terms that will keep cropping up from time to time.

Nasalisation and denasalisation

Nasalisation is the term used to represent nasalisation of either vowels or consonants, a phonetic process that has occurred most profusely in French. Vulgar Latin *montem* becomes Early Fr. /mont/ > /mũ(t)/ > (Mod. Fr.) /mɔ̃/. Latin *vanum* becomes French /vẽ/ (*vain*).

Denasalisation is the same process reversed. Loss of /n/ is common enough in Old English and is responsible for such doublets as:

> *tenth*—*tithe*
> (High German) *fünf*—(Eng.) *five*
> (Gothic) *tunthus*—(Eng.) *tooth*

Weekley, E., *The Romance of Words* (London, 1913), p. 59.

Palatalisation

This is very important both in Romance and in Germanic. In these groups palatalisation is a unidirectional passage of velar consonants into palatal or palato-alveolar consonants. A diagram will illustrate this movement (Figure 16). Phonetically what

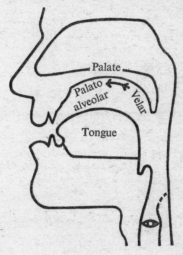

Figure 16

happens is that a velar phoneme /k, g, χ, γ/ becomes frontalised (as in English *Kew* and *keep*), afterwards enters a brief transitional stage of /k′, g′/, etc. (or palatalised velar), and finally is converted into a palatal or palato-alveolar phoneme, i.e. /k/ > /ʃ/ (and then sometimes /s/); similarly /g/ becomes /ʒ/ or /dʒ/ (and sometimes /z/). Compare, for example:

Scottish /kɛrk/—English /tʃəːtʃ/ *church*
Latin /kanɛm/—French /ʃjɛ̃/ *chien*

More will be said about palatalisation in subsequent chapters.

9 Historical Phonology

Phonology holds prime place in diachronic linguistics. Without an understanding of the way in which 'sound laws' or 'phonetic laws' operate, and of the evolution of sounds themselves, it would be impossible to take more than a few tentative steps into the process of language reconstruction. Also, none of the branches of Indo-European comparative linguistics (Romance, Germanic, Slavonic, Indic, etc.) would have progressed very far; and some would never have begun.

Once again restricted by space, I have chosen to single out those general aspects of historical phonology which will be helpful to students, leaving the more particular aspects to the next chapter. First of all, I shall say a little about the *direction* and *sequence* of sound change; then I shall delve to some extent into the more knotty problem of sound laws, partly in preparation for the following chapter and partly because any student of comparative linguistics should have clear in his own mind what sound laws can be said to be and what they are about. I have included exercises here for the first time, since I am convinced that *practice* will give closer familiarity with what can otherwise seem remote, abstract and theoretical. (Answers to the exercises are given in the key on pp. 352–5.)

Direction and sequence of sound change

In my earlier discussion of the scope of comparative linguistics, I explained that the comparative linguist has to content himself with 'formulas of correspondences'. The following Indo-European comparisons:

Sanskrit	Greek	Armenian	Germanic
bharami = *phero*	= *berem*		= (Goth.) *baira* 'I carry'
nabhah = *nephos* 'cloud'			= (Old Saxon) *nebal*

yield the correspondence formula:

$$\text{(Skr.) } bh = \text{(Gr.) } ph = \text{(Arm.) } b = \text{(Germ.) } b$$

But one has to go further than this stage, since the comparatist wants to know whether any one of these correspondences chronologically earlier than the rest and, if so, which and why. Let us begin by trial and error. First let us try:

/b/ → /bh/ is certainly possible *phonologically*, as it would require only the aspiration of /b/ and there are numerous precedents for this. For /b/ to become /ph/ would require two stages, both of which are without precedent in Indo-European. It will be best to leave this combination for the time being and to try to find a better. In the following combination:

$$ph \swarrow \searrow$$
$$bh \qquad b$$

The sequence /ph/ → /bh/ is possible but unprecedented in Indo-European; it would require a single stage only, viz. 'voicing'. The /ph/ → /b/ is much more open to question and would require at least two stages, namely 'voicing' and 'aspiration'. We may as well, then, pass on to the third possible combination:

$$bh \swarrow \searrow$$
$$ph \qquad b$$

This has the advantage of being the one which involves only a single change in each 'leg' of the formula. This is easily the most likely sequence, for the reason that it is at the same time phonetically the simplest (requiring single 'unvoicing' in one leg and 'de-aspiration' in the other); there are also clear precedents for both changes. It would not do, however, to let the matter go at that. To be certain we should have to study the Indo-European labial aspirates /bh/, /ph/ and labial plosives /p/, /b/ as overall classes. If we found consistency here, we should have greater certainty that our proposed sequence was the right one. Not satisfied with this, we then have to look at the behaviour of the entire aspirate and voiced plosive classes as a whole /ph/, /th/, /kh/, /kʷh/;[1] /bh/, /dh/, /gh/, /gʷh/;[1] /b/, /d/, /g/, /gʷ*/; and unless we find consistency, or rather nothing that militates against our hypothesis that cannot be explained on other grounds, we shall be left with serious doubts. In actual fact, we do find the consistency demanded, and we shall be able to take it that the above sequence is beyond reasonable doubt the true one, i.e. the only one that fits and that has no cognate inconsistencies.

Now for a more complicated case:

Skr.	Hittite	Gr.	Lat.	Arm.

hanti 'he hits'
ghnanti 'they hit' } = _kuenzi_;   _theino_ = -_fendo_
                         'I hit'

harah 'heat'
gharmah 'heat' } =   _thermos_ = _formus_ = _jerm_

It is certainly possible to make a start on this, and to sketch a possible scheme of sequences, but it is impossible to find the antecedent phoneme for the entire group. How much, in fact, do we know? The following sequences are the possible ones:

(i) /gh/ ⤳ /h/
          ⤳ /g/ → /j/ (palatalisation of /g/)

(ii) /ph/ → /th/ (there is a special 'law' governing this sound shift in Greek)

but that leaves us with the Hittite _ku_ (= kʷ) unexplained. We are brought squarely up against the necessity of positing a _hypothetical_ antecedent sound in order to solve the puzzle, but at the same time

---

[1] kʷ and gʷ are symbols conventionally used by comparatists to represent /k/ and /g/ with lip-rounding (as in Eng. _queen_ and _Gwen_); /kʷh/ and /gʷh/ are the aspirated equivalents.

one that is internally consistent with the rest of Indo-European phonology. The solution is as follows:

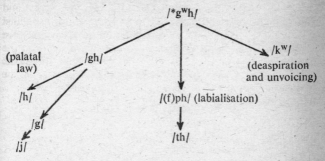

A few caveats are necessary, however, before letting the matter pass:

(1) It is possible for consonants to have *different* formulas of correspondence according to their position in the word, e.g. the 'initial' *bh* in Skr. *bharami* corresponds to Lat. *f* (as in *fero*), whereas the 'intervocalic' *bh* (as in *nabhah*) corresponds to the Lat. *b* (as in *nebula*).

(2) There is always a danger of making a false comparison based on an imperfect series of correspondences. Thus, given:

(Skr.)   *bandhah*   'bond'
(Goth.) *bindan*   'to bind'
(Gr.)   *pentheros* 'father-in-law; ally'

we are tempted to deduce the formula: (Skr.) *b* = (Germ.) *b* = (Gr.) *p*, from a hypothetical antecedent *b*. But this unfortunately conflicts with other known and well-established correspondences:

(Skr.) *bh* = (Germ.) *b* = (Gr.) *ph*
(Skr.) *b* = (Germ.) *p* = (Gr.) *b*

We are safe in concluding therefore that our correspondence *b* = *b* = *p* is false and quite unwarranted. When we look further, it is then that we find the *b* of *bandhah* to be the result of a 'law' peculiar only to Sanskrit; a law which states that when there are two aspirates within the root of a word the first of them is de-aspirated. The original Sanskrit form was *bhandhaḥ*.

(3) It is *never* safe to use etymological coincidence as a means of identifying 'formulas of correspondence'. Word meanings are the worst guides. Etymology is entitled to take over only when the phonological correspondences and sequences have been firmly laid down. And to this end historical phonology is a formidable tool indeed.

(4) Even if it were possible to reconstruct Indo-European in its entirety as far as vocabulary and grammar are concerned, we should still have no certainty as to what Indo-European was like as a language. A hugely impressive system of interlocking phonological correspondences and morphological elements, but still no language. This will strike the reader as odd. But it is not really so odd as it seems. Imagine the analogy of someone who is trying to deduce the physical characteristics and behaviour of a particular male great-great-great-grandparent by studying the offspring of the present generation and other comparative evidence, including photographs, family portraits, letters, diaries and other records. One might, for instance, by a series of ingenious steps arrive at the conclusion that this ancestor ate boiled parsley for breakfast, but there might be absolutely nothing to indicate the fact (which, shall we say, comes to light later from non-comparative sources) that he read the *Morning Post* as well and consequently always suffered from indigestion. The boiled parsley hypothesis might also be only partly true. This great-great-great-grandparent may, for all we know, have given up the habit of eating boiled parsley in middle life. The analogy (as far as analogies go) is good for Indo-European too.

Exercise 1 (For key see p. 352)

(a) Identify the *consonant* correspondences common to the entire group in the following, and (b) suggest the original or antecedent form in each case:

    (i) (Skr.) *madhu* = (Gr.) *methu* = (Old Icelandic) *miodr* = (Old Slav.) *medu* = (Irish) *mid* = (Eng.) *mead*.
    (Skr.) *ádhat* 'he placed'; (Arm.) *ed*; (Gr.) *ēthos* 'custom'; (Goth.) (ga-)*deths* 'action'; (Lith.) *deti* 'to place'.

(ii) (Skr.) *stigh-* 'to stride'; (Gr.) *steikhō* 'I walk'; (Goth.)
steigan 'to mount'.
(Skr.) *meghá-* 'cloud'; (O. Slav.) *migla* 'mist'; (Albanian)
mjegule.

(iii) (Skr.) *ká-* 'who?' = (Lith.) *kás* = (O. Slav.) *ku*(-to) =
(Gr.) *tis* = (Lat.) *quis*.
(Skr.) *kr̥mi-* = (Lith.) *kirmêlê* = (Irish) *cruim* = (Welsh)
pryf = 'worm'.
(*Notes:* (Gr.) *tis* and (Welsh) *pryf* are the result of labialisa-
tions of velar consonants $/k^w/ > /p/ (> /t/$ in Gr. before
$/i/$ and $/e/$). This sound change has occurred in many
different regions owing to the important part the lips play
in articulating $/w/$. The *c* in Irish *cruim* is very far back as
regards point of articulation and can be equated with
Latin *qu*.)

(iv) (Skr.) *rátha-* 'chariot' = (Lat.) *rota* = (Irish) *roth* = (Welsh)
rhod = (Old High German) *rad* = (Lith.) *rātas* 'wheel'.

Law of sound change

In general nowadays, comparative linguists avoid using the term
'law' in their accounts of phonological change. They prefer to
restrict themselves to a statement of phonological correspondences
or to particular phonological phenomena (e.g. palatalisation,
umlaut, etc.). In fact, the use of the term is no longer fashionable.
The student of comparative linguistics will nevertheless come
across references to various sound laws, in particular 'Verner's
Law' and the 'Palatal Law'.

In both these instances, the use of the term 'law' is misleading,
in so far as it implies that sounds have in effect *changed* from one
state to another. As we saw earlier, the evidence for sounds having
changed *in this sense* is, to say the least, rather weak. All we can
say for certain is that an earlier sound has been replaced by a later
one, but this does not imply evolution. As we have also seen, a
German speaker pronouncing a French $/b/$ will articulate a sound
nearer to the Frenchman's $/p/$ (there are well-known instances of
this in Balzac's novels and elsewhere). I hope to show that
phenomena such as assimilation and umlaut are more adaptable
to the concept of law than is either Verner's Law or the Palatal
Law.

The greatest confusion of all arises from the use of the word 'law' in a number of incompatible senses. In physics all had to be explained causally, and every exception had to be accounted for by the counter-operation of other laws. A solid body, according to a well-known law, will fall to the ground at a predictable speed provided that there is no substance, for example air, to resist or set up a counter force. In this case, both the law of gravity and the law of air resistance could be causally determined. Worried by this the comparative philologist Curtius wrote in 1858: 'Only that which is governed by law and reducible to a coherent system can form the object of scientific observation; whatever is due to chance is best guessed at, but will never yield to scientific inference.' A pessimist.

The succeeding generation, known as the Neo-grammarians, took a broader view, introducing the concept of *analogy* into their phonology, as into all else, to explain exceptions which were everywhere to be found. These 'exceptions' had previously been attributed to chance. Readers with even the slightest experience of comparative linguistics will have found analogy a highly indispensable concept, since there are very few exceptions that it will not explain away. Leskien, undaunted by legions of exceptions, claimed that one had only to explain them and then all 'appearances were saved'. For example, the change of /θ/ to /ð/ ((O.E.) /broθar/ to (Mod. E.) /brʌðə/) can be explained by analogy with (≠) *father* /faðə/ and *mother* /mʌðə/. This was a great step forward. The only trouble with such an immensely fruitful concept is that it has been *too* successful, and in certain instances has actually prevented further advance in linguistic science. Analogy is sometimes little more than a way of avoiding arbitrariness and chance by circumventing the necessity of looking further into linguistic processes.

In the present century the earlier concept of 'law' has been gradually and generally abandoned. Even in the natural sciences, causal explanation has lost much of its plausibility. Nowadays, even physicists prefer to frame their logic: 'whenever X, then Y'— and, one might add, 'unless Z'. Unfortunately, the laws of phonology are not of this kind either; and reluctantly the physical analogy has had to be dropped.

It was Whitney who first doubted the universality of particular sound changes and who suggested that not all sounds of a single kind yield to the same change simultaneously: 'phonetic change is not invariable . . . but honeycombed with inconsistency and anomalies'. Later Oertel drew attention to the possibility that a linguistic or phonetic change does not gain currency simply because many individuals of the same generation produce it. A change is propagated only because a large number of individuals are *willing to accept* it and *imitate* it. Linguistic changes are in many respects not unlike social changes (e.g. institutions, beliefs, traditions, customs, dress, etc.).

Phonologists of today are cautious and prefer to talk of models or formulas rather than laws. The advantage of the former is that they do not imply change but stop at evolution, which is a broad and accommodating enough term, serving to indicate that phonetic conditions have changed, whether spontaneously, or by imitation, or otherwise. Grammont was forced to the conclusion that: 'phonetic[1] laws are valid for a single determined place and time. When a law has had its effect on the phonemes on which it has been operating, it ceases to exist in that language altogether.' These laws seem to depend on complex conditions which have a negligible chance of twice recurring in an identical order. They differ from physical laws in that the latter remain invariable from one age to the next as far as one can tell from observation. Phonological laws, however, vary from village to village, and perhaps even from street to street, because the linguistic state and the hereditary conditions are never repeated. Grammont's definition remains the most satisfactory and the one that is most appropriate to the present state of knowledge: 'a phonetic law is the formula which defines the change undergone by an articulation in a determined region and at a fixed time.'[1] The key word here is 'undergone'; a phonological law is really a historical law in that it describes phenomena only retrospectively.

Phonological evolution illustrated

Indo-European languages have long been classified into two groups, called *centum* and *satem*. The distinction is based primarily on phonological peculiarities. The two groups take their names from the way they treat the Indo-European frontal velar

[1] By 'phonetic' Grammont meant, according to the terminology of today, 'phonological'.

/k/ in the word for 'hundred', (I–E.) *kṇtóm. The *centum*-
languages preserve it in its original state; in the *satem*-languages
the phoneme appears as a palato-alveolar fricative /s/, /ʃ/, which
can be tabulated as follows:

(Lat.) *centum*	(Skr.) *śatám*
(Gr.) *ékáton*	(Avestan) *satəm*
(Irish) *cet*	(Lith.) *szimtas*
(Tokharian A) *känt*	(O. Slav.) *suto*

The *satem*-languages form a central group comprising: Indo-
Iranian, Balto-Slavonic, Armenian and Albanian (together with
the extinct languages, Thracian and, probably, Phrygian). A
glance at a linguistic map will show such a geographical contiguity even now. The *centum*-languages are best divided into four
peripheral groups:

(1) Western: Italic, Celtic and Germanic.
(2) Greek, which has nevertheless some shared structural and
    lexical peculiarities with the satem group.
(3) Eastern, surviving only in Tokharian.
(4) Hittite.

The 'law' which first explained the phonological separation of
satem from *centum* is known as the Palatal Law. It is not known
for certain who actually discovered it, and there exists more than
one claimant. The first to mention it was Vilhelm Thomsen in
1875.

The correspondences for this palatal sound shift can be
tabulated as follows:

Indo-European (*centum*)		*satem*
(Labio-velar):		(Velar):
/kʷ/	→	/k/
/gʷ/	→	/g/
/gʷh/	→	/gh/
(Palato-velar):		(Palato-alveolar):
/k̂/	→	/s/, /ʃ/
/ĝ/	→	/z/, /ʒ/, /dʒ/
/ĝh/	→	/z/, /ʒ/, /dʒ/, /h/ (Skr.), /d/ (Alb.)

The reader may already have noticed that the palato-velar → palato-alveolar shift is a clear case of 'palatalisation'.

The basic 'shift' (known as the 'first palatalisation') can be illustrated as follows:

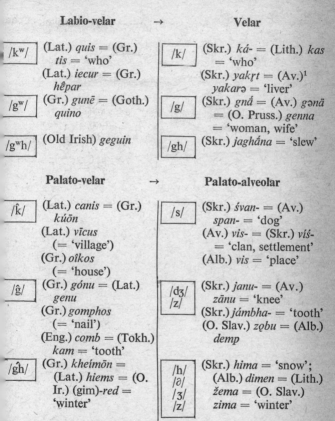

	Labio-velar	→	**Velar**	
/kʷ/	(Lat.) *quis* = (Gr.) *tis* = 'who' (Lat.) *iecur* = (Gr.) *hễpar*		/k/	(Skr.) *ká-* = (Lith.) *kas* = 'who' (Skr.) *yakṛt* = (Av.)[1] *yakarə* = 'liver'
/gʷ/	(Gr.) *gunē* = (Goth.) *quino*		/g/	(Skr.) *gnā́* = (Av.) *gənā* = (O. Pruss.) *genna* = 'woman, wife'
/gʷh/	(Old Irish) *geguin*		/gh/	(Skr.) *jaghā́na* = 'slew'

	Palato-velar	→	**Palato-alveolar**	
/k̂/	(Lat.) *canis* = (Gr.) *kúōn* (Lat.) *vīcus* (= 'village') (Gr.) *oîkos* (= 'house')		/s/	(Skr.) *śvan-* = (Av.) *span-* = 'dog' (Av.) *vis-* = (Skr.) *viś-* = 'clan, settlement' (Alb.) *vis* = 'place'
/ĝ/	(Gr.) *gónu* = (Lat.) *genu* (Gr.) *gomphos* (= 'nail') (Eng.) *comb* = (Tokh.) *kam* = 'tooth'		/dʒ/ /z/	(Skr.) *janu-* = (Av.) *zānu* = 'knee' (Skr.) *jámbha-* = 'tooth' (O. Slav.) *zǫbu* = (Alb.) *demp*
/ĝh/	(Gr.) *kheimōn* = (Lat.) *hiems* = (O. Ir.) (*gim*)-*red* = 'winter'		/h/ /ə/ /ʒ/ /z/	(Skr.) *hima* = 'snow'; (Alb.) *dimen* = (Lith.) *žema* = (O. Slav.) *zima* = 'winter'

The reader should be warned of a few apparent and important exceptions, which are normally treated as the pure velar series

[1] Av = Avestan.

/k/, /g/, /gh/ as opposed to /k̂/, /ĝ/, /ĝh/ or /kʷ/, /gʷ/, /gʷh/. An excellent brief account of these is given in Burrow's *The Sanskrit Language* (London, 1959), pp. 75–6.

The 'second palatalisation' already referred to above may have been simultaneous with or later than the first palatalisation. The latter case is the one usually supported. Briefly, what happened is that the labio-velars /kʷ/, /gʷ/, /gʷh/ which became velars /k/, /g/, /gh/ in the course of the first shift now appear as palato-alveolars (of a different series) but only when preceding the 'front' vowels /e/ and /i/. The comparison is a little difficult to follow because in Indo-Iranian the original *e* had changed into *a*. The shift can be represented as follows:

First palatalisation	Second palatalisation
/k/	→ /tʃ/ (*č* in Slav; *c* in Skr; *k* in Lith.)
/g/	→ /dʒ/ (*ž* in Slav; *j* in Skr; *g* in Lith.)
/gh/	→ /dʒ/ (> *h* in Skr.)

The second palatalisation may be illustrated as follows:

/kʷ/ (Lat.) *quattuor* = 'four'
(Lat.) *quinque* = (Gr.) = *pénte* = 'five'

/gʷ/ (Lat.) *vivus*
(Goth.) *qens* = 'wife'

/k/ (Skr.) *catvắras* = (O. Slav. *četyre* = (Lith.) *keturi* = 'four'
(Skr.) *páñca-* = (Lith.) *penki* = 'five'

/g/ (Skr.) *jīvá-* = (O. Slav.) *živu* = 'alive'
(Skr.) *jāni-*

By the end of the next chapter the reader may begin to wonder where the whole business of palatalisation ends. One thing, however, is certain: an understanding of the general principles of palatalisation and its particular historical features is a major step forward in the study of phonology in comparative linguistics as whole.

Exercise 2 (Key on p. 352)

(a) Identify only the palatal correspondences in the following groups: (b) classify them into *satem* and *centum* groups; and (c) construct rough diagrams of phonological sequence of the kind used in the early part of this chapter:

(i) (Sanskrit) *rajatá-* = (Avestan) *rəzata-* = (Greek) *árguros* = (Latin) *argentum* = (Irish) *argat* = 'silver'.

(ii) (Skr.) *kṛmi-* = (Lithuanian) *kirmêlê* = (Irish) *cruim* = (Welsh) *pryf* = 'worm'.

(iii) (O. Slav.) *slovo* = 'word'; (Lat.) *clueo* = 'I am called by name'; (Skr.) *śrávah* = 'fame'; (Gr.) *kléos* = 'fame'; (Goth.) *hliuma* = 'hearing'.

(iv) (Skr.) *lih-* = (Arm.) *lizum* = (O. Slav.) *lizati* = (Gr.) *leikhō* = (Lat.) *lingo* = (O. Irish) *ligim* = (Goth.) bi-*laigon* = 'lick'.

(v) (Skr.) *cakra-* = (Gr.) *kuklos* = (Tokh. A) *kukäl* = (Old Eng.) *hweohl* = 'wheel'.

10 Further Notes on Historical Phonology

This chapter is intended to be no more than a brief survey, or rather listed brief descriptions of those phonological aspects of comparative linguistics likely to be encountered by the student. The reader who finds this chapter too technical is advised to skip to Chapter 11.

Vowel mutation: umlaut

Vowel mutation, or *umlaut*, occurs in many languages. There are two classes of umlaut: (i) where a subsequent vowel is influenced by the enunciation of a preceding vowel (as in Finno-Ugrian), and (ii) where a subsequent vowel influences a preceding vowel. It is the latter class that is important in Indo-European. Of the 'families' from which I am borrowing illustrations, only Germanic has been widely affected. Here the extent of vowel mutation is considerable; indeed, a thorough grasp of *umlaut* is indispensable for an understanding of the core of Germanic phonology.

Roughly speaking, Germanic vowel mutation is of three types: *front mutation* (variously called *palatal umlaut* or *i-umlaut*), *a-mutation* (or *a-umlaut*) and *back mutation* (sometimes called *guttural umlaut* or *u-umlaut*). In Old Norse there occurs a *w-mutation*, which can, however, be regarded as a variant of back mutation.

In the types of umlaut we are concerned with, the phonological development can be ascribed to conditions in which the vocal organs can be said to have assumed prematurely the aperture they physically require for uttering the next syllable.

Proto-Germanic umlaut

The earliest stage of Germanic umlaut occurred in Primitive or Proto-Germanic, at a time when the Germanic group as a whole was acquiring its general characteristics. There were two forms of umlaut in this prehistoric period:

(1) *i-umlaut*. Initial accented /e/ > /i/, but only before a front vowel /i/, /j/ in the following syllable. The following brief comparison will illustrate this:

Lat.	Gr.	Gothic	Old High German	O.E.
	esti	_ist_	_ist_	_is_
medius		_midjis_	_mitti_	_midd_ 'middle'
sedere		_sitan_	_sizzen_	_sittan_ 'to sit'

It will be noticed that the final _i_ or _j_ has generally disappeared, especially in the case of the Germanic examples cited. In some instances, its earlier existence can be inferred when comparison suggests that this type of umlaut has occurred. This change is thought to date from the first century A.D., for Tacitus, the Roman historian, spells _Segimerus_ (thereby suggesting the lack of mutation) whilst elsewhere indications are that the change had already taken place, as, for example, in _Sigismudus_ (earlier form: _Segismundus_).

(2) A complicated form of umlaut, comprising certain features both of the _u_-mutation and of the _a_-mutation. The most significant effects are that /i/ > /e/ (the reverse of _i_-mutation) before a syllable containing /a/ or /o/. Phonetically, this is a clear case of 'lowering' and retraction:

(I–E) *_wiros_ (= Lat. _vir_)   > (O.H.G. and O.E.) _wer_
(I–E) *_nizdos_ (= Lat. _nidus_) > (O.H.G. and O.E.) _nest_

The vowel /u/ becomes /o/ in similar circumstances. This change (occurring only before syllables containing /a/ or /o/) has produced some curious doublets in Old English:

cnotta 'knot'—cnyttan 'to knit'
coss   'kiss' —cyssan 'to kiss'
corn   'corn'—cyrnel 'kernel'

(The forms in the right-hand column earlier contained root vowel /u/ (_knuttjan_, etc.), but in every case this has moved 'forward' to /y/ by umlaut in Old English.)

Umlaut in Old English
Old English (along with Old Frisian) umlaut, although complicated, is restricted to frontal or _i_-mutation. The particular vowel

mutations observable are peculiar to these dialects of Germanic. What happened can be described briefly as follows. Originally there existed in Early Germanic a range of forms in which the first syllable (or stem) contained a back vowel or an open vowel and the second syllable contained a vowel /i/ or a semivowel /j/. Vowel mutation in Old English caused all the vowels of the first syllable to become partially assimilated to the vowel of the second syllable. As a result, the back vowels became front vowels and the open vowels became closed vowels. In becoming front vowels, the back vowels in all but one case lost their lip-rounding: /ɔ/ > /e/ and /oː/ > /eː/, but /u/ > /y/. In Middle English the latter lost its lip-rounding and became /iː/.

Early Germanic		Old English	
/a/	(Goth.) *andeis* (Goth.) *baddi*	/e/	*ende* 'end' *bedd* 'bed'
/aː/	(Goth.) *dáiljan*	/æː/	*dǣlan* 'divide', 'deal out'
/ɔ/	(Latin loan) *oleum*	/e/	*ele* 'oil'
/oː/	*tanthiz* > */toːθ-/	/eː/	*tēth* 'teeth'
/u/	(O.H.G.) *kuning* *musiz*	/y/	*cyning* 'king' *mȳs* 'mice'

The evidence, drawn mainly from literary sources, is that Old English umlaut developed (or extended its sphere of influence) in the sixth century A.D.

Umlaut in Old Norse

Vowel mutation is widespread in Old Norse phonology, and all the types so far mentioned are to be found there. It is an odd coincidence that individual mutations run closely parallel to those of Old English.

(1) *Frontal mutation.* The main difference between Old Norse and Old English is that the back vowels in Norse retained their lip-rounding. It is this that creates one of the main differences between Old Norse and Old English phonology. In the modern

Scandinavian languages some of the lip-rounded vowels retain their characteristics from that period. Examples of Norse *i*-umlaut are:

Old Norse

/a/	*mann* (sing.)	/e/	*menn* (pl.)
/o/	*høggva* 'to cut'	/ø/	*høggr* 'he cuts'
/ɔ/	*koma* 'to come'		*kømr* 'he comes'
/u/	*brun* (sing.)	/y/	*brynn* (pl.) 'eye-brow'

It may already have been assumed that the front vowels which prompted the umlauted forms in the second column disappeared in the Primitive Norse period. This is, in fact, the case. It will be seen that Norse umlaut plays havoc with the customary regularity of declensional and conjugational paradigms. I would not have introduced the complicated business of Norse umlaut at all had it not been for the fact that students of Old Icelandic can easily be deterred in the early stages by apparent incongruities of this kind.

(2) *u-mutation* (including *w*-mutation). Not only did the earlier presence of front vowels influence stem vowels in Norse but there was another type of umlaut which caused stem vowels to become lip-rounded vowels or back vowels. This again was due to the presence of /u/ or /w/ in the second syllable. The two vowels affected are:

$$/e/ > /ø/$$
$$\text{and } /a/ > /ɔ/$$

As a result of the combination of the effect of the *i*-umlaut and the *u*-umlaut, the declensional and conjugational paradigms look very irregular indeed, with the stem vowel sometimes changing as frequently as the grammatical ending:

(sing.) *land*—(pl.) *lond*
roa 'to row'—*røru* '(he) rows'

The extent of the irregularity produced by Norse umlaut is well illustrated by the paradigm of the noun *tǫnn* 'tooth':

	Sing.	Pl.
Nom.	*tǫnn*	*tennr*
Acc.	*tǫnn*	*tennr*
Gen.	*tannar*	*tanna*
Dat.	*tǫnn*	*tǫnum*

The original Primitive Norse form survives only in the genitive singular and plural. Every other case of the paradigm has been affected by umlaut.

Exercise 3

(1) Identify and describe the types of vowel mutation illustrated by the following series:

(a) (Goth.) *bugjan* = (O.E.) *bycgan*.
(b) (Goth.) *kuni* = (O.H.G.) *kunni* = (O.E.) *cynn* = (Mod. Eng.) *kin*.
(c) (Goth.) *sokjan* = (O.E.) *sēcan* = (O. Norse) *sækja* 'to seek'.
(d) (O.E.) *tōth* (sing.), *tēth* (pl.) = (O.N.) *tonn* (sing.), *tennr* (pl.)

(2) Identify the original root vowel in the following Norse paradigm and describe each of the modifications of this original root vowel in terms of vowel mutation:

vǫllr 'full'

	Sing.	Pl.
N.	*vǫllr*	*vellir*
A.	*vǫll*	*vǫllu*
G.	*vallar*	*valla*
D.	*velli*	*vǫllum*

I have omitted any mention of High German umlaut (*Buch-Bücher*, *Mann-Männer*, etc.) owing to shortage of space. An excellent and detailed account of the historical scheme of the High German mutations may be found in Priebsch and Collinson, *The German Language* (London, 1946), p. 147 ff.

Phonology and Orthography

Immediately upon setting out on a study of a language at a remote period, or of a language that has possessed a literature of its own at some earlier period, we are faced with recurrent discrepancies between orthography and phonology. With the exception of Sanskrit and, to a lesser extent, Attic Greek, it is only in recent times that spelling has become consistent with pronunciation, although so far not in English nor in many other languages.

Ferdinand de Saussure has found two main reasons for the discrepancy:

(1) Spelling in general lags behind pronunciation. He cites the example of French at various periods of its historical development:

	Pronunciation	Orthography
11th century	(a) *rei, lei*	*rei, lei*
13th century	(b) *roi, loi*	*roi, loi*
14th century	(c) *roè, loè*	*roi, loi*
19th century	(d) *rwa, lwa*	*roi, loi*

The changes of pronunciation that have been observed since the thirteenth century have simply not been taken account of by orthography. Much the same is true of English. The orthography of Modern English is almost ideally suited to the late Middle English of Chaucer's day. (I am not one of those, however, who advocate radical spelling reform, and remain unconvinced by statistics produced to show that phonetic orthography is easier to teach to children than our present system. Arbitrarily alter the orthography of Modern English and, in the opinion of some, you alter the language as well.)

(2) When an alphabet is borrowed from another language, its resources may not be appropriate to its new function. When the Germanic runic signs þ and ð came to be represented in Romanic, there was only the symbol *th* to represent both these separate sounds.

Until comparatively recent times, orthographies have fluctuated from period to period. One might even say that mediaeval scribes and renaissance printers seemed to pride themselves in spelling variants. Nowadays, all this is lost in a uniformity from which only the sinful depart—though it needs little imagination to see that such fluctuations are the curse of comparative linguistics. 'Writing obscures language; it is not a guise for language but a disguise.' Certainly language is capable of throwing up the oddest situations. The French word *oiseau*, for example, contains not a single representative of its component phonemes in its orthography—orth: *oiseau*; phon: /wazo/.

Palatalisation

The 'palatal law', discussed in the last chapter, has already to some extent familiarised the reader with the phenomenon of palatalisation. Since this can be an obstacle for the newcomer to phonology, I propose to deal with two further examples—one from Romance, the other from Old English.

Palatalisation in Romance

Let us begin with the example of the Latin word *centum*. The Italian form, as the reader may already know, is *cento* /tʃɛnto/; the French is *cent* /sã/. These exemplify a Romance sound rule that Latin /k/, /g/ have become palatalised in late Vulgar Latin when they precede the front vowels /i/, /e/. As might be expected, the ultimate forms attained in the individual Romance dialects differ. The unusual feature is that the development or evolution of the /k/- and /g/-phonemes is not exactly parallel.

For Latin /k/ the scheme is simple, and roughly divides between transalpine Romance (Spanish, Portuguese, Gallo-Romance) and the rest (Italic, Balkan, etc.), with the sole exception of Sardinian, which has preserved the original /k/ intact. The scheme can be formulated thus:

Latin /k/ (before /i/, /e/)
$$\begin{cases} = (\text{Sard.}) \ /k/ \\ >(\text{Transalp.})/k'/>/t'/>/ts/ \begin{cases} (\text{O. Fr.}) \ /ts/>(\text{Fr.}) \ /s/ \\ (\text{Span.}) \ /\theta/ \end{cases} \\ >(\text{others}) \ /k'/ > /t'/ > /t\int/ \end{cases}$$

The following comparisons (with phonemic transcriptions in brackets) will illustrate the scheme:

V. Latin	Sard.	Fr.	Ital.	Rom.
centum /kɛntum/		cent /sã/	cento /tʃɛnto/	
caelum /kaelum/	kelu	ciel /sjɛl/	cielo /tʃjelo/	cel /tʃɛl/
circare /kirkare/	kirkare	chercher /ʃɛRʃe/ (O. Fr.) cerchier /sɛrtʃje/ (Eng. search)	cercare /tʃɛrkare/	a cerca /tʃɛrka/

The Latin /g/-phoneme, on the other hand, has evolved in a way that geographically cuts across this. Such an anomaly is uncommon in phonology, for as a rule the voiceless (in this instance /k/) and voiced counterparts /g/ undergo parallel transformation. In Old French one would naturally expect /dʒ/, the voiced partner of /ts/, but in effect we find /dʒ/ instead. The development of the Latin form *gentem* will illustrate this:

(Lat.) *gentem* /gɛntɛm/ > (O. Fr.) /dʒɛ̃/ > (Mod. Fr. /ʒã/)

The phonological progression can be formulated as:

/g/ > /g′/ > /d′/ > /dʒ/ > /dʒ/ > /ʒ/

This pattern is confirmed by the pronunciation of French loanwords in Middle English, as, for example, in the pair:

city /siti/ — *gent* /dʒɛ̃nt/

and many others. An attempt at phonetic representation appears in the mediaeval English spelling *budget*

It is thought that the preliminary stages of this complex palatalisation, viz. /k/ > /k′/ > /t/; /g/ > /g′/ > /d′/, began in the later period of the Roman Empire, probably in the third century. The later stages occurred independently from dialect to dialect, owing, it is assumed, to their having separated politically and culturally with the decline of Rome.

Yet another brand of palatalisation can be observed in French at a much later date. This was brought about by a tendency to frontalise and raise the vowel *a* inherited from common Romance stock. Compare:

(V. Lat.) *capum* /kapu(m)/ = (Ital.) *capo* /kapo/ = (O. Fr.) *chief* /tʃjɛf/ = (Mod. Fr.) *chef* /ʃɛf/

The reader may already have noticed that English once again preserves the Old French palato-alveolar phoneme *chief* /tʃiːf/, whereas Modern French pronunciation has moved on to *chef* /ʃɛf/. There is an abundance of other examples: (Fr.) *changer*— (Eng.) *change*; (Fr.) *chaise*—(Eng.) *chair*.

Old English palatalisation

Palatalisation affected both velar /k/ and /g/ in Old English when preceding front vowels or front diphthongs (long and short vowels /ǣ/, ǐ, ě; diphthongs ěa, ěo, ǐo) but *not* before vowels that attained frontal position by the process of umlaut or vowel mutation. The conclusion is that Old English palatalisation had struck roots rather earlier than the time when the vowel mutations occurred, although some scholars are of the opinion that the former did not reach its full extent until later Saxon times. Once again, the distinction between diachronic and synchronic phonology comes to our aid. It is always synchronic conditions set up within a language that work themselves out or resolve themselves diachronically. Thus a given synchronic state will be unconscious of a phonological link between two sets of phonetic series and will *treat* them separately. It is possible, as in the case of Old English, for a language to possess two sets of frontal vowels (of different diachronic origin) and to let them go their separate ways.

The phonological stages in Old English palatalisation were as follows:

$$/k/ > /k'/ > /tʃ/$$
$$/g/ > /g'/ > /j/$$

The consonant grouping /sk/ became /ʃ/ before all vowels, owing to the development of a palatal glide between the /k/ and the succeeding vowel, thus /skʲa/, /skʲu/. This rule does not apply to loan words. A list of Old English words with phonemic transcriptions will help to illustrate this:

Palatalised	Non-palatalised
cinn /tʃinn/ 'chin'	*camb* /kamb/ 'comb'
cealc /tʃalk/ 'chalk'	*cynn* /kynn/ 'race, kin'
ceosan /tʃēosan/ 'to choose'	(/y/ by umlaut)
gear /jear/ 'year'	*coren* /korən/ 'chosen'
geolu /jɛolu/ 'yellow'	*gold* /gɔld/
sceap /ʃeap/ 'sheep'	
fisc /fiʃ/ 'fish'	

This is not the end of the story, for these palatalised consonants have had in turn a disrupting effect on the vowels that originally triggered off palatalisation. Compare, for instance, Latin *castra* with the Old English loan word *ceaster* (Mod. Eng. *-chester*). At first glance, it does not seem at all obvious why the English word should have become *ceaster* /tʃɛastər/ until we learn that it derives from a still earlier form *cæster* /tʃæstər/. Here is no arbitrary interchange of orthographic symbols. What actually happened is complicated. First of all, a 'palatal glide' developed after the already palatalised *c* /tʃ/ phonetically represented as /tʃʲæstər/. The innocent palatal glide subsequently became married to the succeeding vowel to produce a rather curious rising diphthong /tʃeæstər/. Later still, the rising diphthong became a falling diphthong /tʃéæstər/, spelt *ceaster* in West Saxon. This somewhat unusual effect can be seen in the following correspondences:

Old English

> *cieres* = (Lat.) *cerasum* 'cherry'
> *gēafon* = (O.H.G.) *gebun* 'they gave'
> *sceal* = (Goth.) *skal* 'shall'
> *gēar* = (Goth.) *jēr* 'year'

Parallel conditions are to be found in Old Norse and High German. In Modern High German, the proto-Germanic /sk/ has become /ʃ/ (spelt *sch*) in all instances. Norse has shown a similar trend, but only when *sk* precedes *i* or *e*. Compare:

(Goth.) *skip*; (O.N.) *skip* /ʃip/; (O.E.) *scip* /ʃip/; (N.H.G.) *Schiff* /ʃif/.

but:

(Goth.) *skapjan*; (O.N.) *skapa* /skapa/; (O.E.) *scieppan* /ʃeppan/; (N.H.G.) *schöpfen* 'to make'.
(Goth.) *fisks*; (O.N.) *fiskr*; (O.E.) *fisc* /fiʃ/; (N.H.G.) *Fisch* /fiʃ/.

The orthography in these examples is highly misleading, and only the phonetic forms are of value in drawing up comparisons.

Exercise 4

(1) Write out in phonetic transcription the following series of words:

(Lat.) *carum* = (O. Fr.) *chier* = (Mod. Fr.) *cher* = (Ital.) *caro*.
(O. Fr.) *cerchier* = (Eng.) *search* = (Mod. Fr.) *chercher* = (Ital.) *cercare*.
(Goth.) *mikils* = (O.E.) *mycel* 'great'.
(Goth.) *skulds* 'lawful'; (O.E.) *scyldig* = (N.H.G.) *schuldig* 'guilty'; (O.N.) *skyldr* 'obliged'.

(2) Comment on any of the historical sound changes observable in these series that you consider significant.

Vowel fracture and diphthongisation

These two phonological processes have something in common. The latter (diphthongisation) refers to situations in which simple vowels have become compound, or, as we say, 'diphthongised', either directly or indirectly. *Vowel fracture*, on the other hand, denotes rather a process of assimilation of a preceding vowel by a consonant, whereby the vowel develops a glide between itself and the consonant, and eventually merges with the glide into a diphthong proper. This is a feature of both Old English and Old Norse.

Diphthongisation

This is present in nearly all language histories at some period in their diachronic development. I shall restrict my illustrations to diphthongisation in Old English and to the 'Great Vowel Shift' that occurred in early Modern English.

Diphthongisation in Old French. Tonic (or stressed) vowels in Romance are classified as either 'free' or 'blocked', according to whether the syllable in which the vowel occurs is *open* (i.e. ends in a vowel) or *closed* (i.e. ends in a consonant or semivowel). The tonic vowel in *florem* 'flower' (*flo-rem*) is 'free' since the syllable containing it can be regarded as *open*, whereas in *septem* (*sep-tem*) the tonic *e* is 'blocked'. 'Free' vowels in Gallo-Romance, and in Old French in particular, undergo radical diphthongisation, whereas the 'blocked' vowels remain unaffected. Compare:

'Free'	'Blocked'
(Lat.) *pi-lum* > (O. Fr.) *peil* > *poil* > (Mod. Fr.) /pwal/ 'hair'	(Lat.) *sep-tem* > (O. Fr.) *set* > (Mod. Fr.) *sept* /sɛt/
(Lat.) *pedem* > (O. Fr.) *pied* 'foot'	(Lat.) *por-ta(m)* > (O. Fr.) *porte*
(Lat.) *flo-rem* > (O. Fr.) *flour* > (Mod. Fr.) *fleur* /flœːR/	(Lat.) *vil-la(m)* > (O. Fr.) *ville*

Another series of Old French diphthongs arose from the conversion of consonants, particularly the velar variety, into the palatal semivowel *yod* /j/. These changes were brought about in various ways. The following series will illustrate the diversity:

(i) (*k* + *t* > *yod* + *t*): (Lat.) *fructum* > /fruḱtu/ > /frujtu/ (O. Fr.) *fruit*.

(ii) (Intervocalic *k* > *yod*): (Lat.) *voce(m)* > (O. Fr.) *voix* > (Mod. Fr.) /vwa/.

(iii) (Lat. *j* > *yod*): (Lat.) *major* > (Fr.) *maire* 'mayor'.

A third type of diphthongisation arose from a vocalisation (i.e. conversion into a vowel) of /l/ whenever it originally preceded another consonant. In a position of this kind /l/ shows a proneness towards such a change, especially when the consonant has the retracted or 'dark' pronunciation. The following is a random selection of examples from Old French:

/ol/ > /ou/:   (V. Lat.) *colpu* > (O. Fr.) *coup* >
                   (Mod. Fr.) /ku/ 'blow'
/al/ > /au/:   (V. Lat.) *alter* > (O. Fr.) *autre* /autr/ >
                   (Mod. Fr.) /otR/ 'other'
/il/ > /ɛl/ > /ɛu/: (V. Lat.) *illos* > (O. Fr.) *eux* /ɛus/ >
                   (Mod. Fr.) /œ/

(Note the orthography, which in every case is appropriate to Old French and not to Modern French.)

With this far from exhaustive treatment of Old French diphthongisation, we now turn to English.

The 'great vowel shift' in English. This sound shift, which occurred in the fifteenth century, was probably relatively local in origin and spread by imitation throughout the entire English-speaking area of the British Isles. There are still many regional dialect accents unaffected by it. The shift is responsible for the anomalous spelling of the vowels of modern English which are more appropriate to the period *before* the vowel shift occurred. Compare, first of all, the modern English orthography and probable Chaucerian and Shakespearian pronunciation of the following words:

Mod. Eng. orthog.	Chaucerian	Shakespearian	Recent
five	/fiːf/	/faiv/	⟶
seed	/seːd/	/siːd/	⟶
clean	/klɛnə/	/kleːn/	/kliːn/
name	/naːmə/	/neːm/	/neim/
goat	/gɔːtə/	/goːt/	/gout/
root	/roːtə/	/ruːt/	⟶
down	/duːn/	/daun/	⟶

The main shift, complete by Shakespeare's time, can be visualised in Figure 17 opposite.

The progression is not unlike musical chairs. Each vowel has moved up one place, and the raised vowels, having been displaced, make as if to join the end of the queue for another round /i/ > /ai/, /u/ > /au/, but this time *as diphthongs*.

Note that in Elizabethan English *clean* was still pronounced /kleːn/, a fact borne out by Shakespeare's rhyming it with *lane*. The further shift to /kliːn/ happened towards the end of the seventeenth century. The other changes /neːm/ > /neim/ and /goːt/ > /gout/ are less precisely determined but had certainly become fixtures by this time.

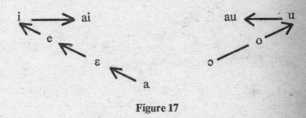

Figure 17

The reader will have noticed that the last column contains only two *pure* vowels, *i* and *u*, whilst the rest are diphthongs, also with *i* and *u* as the second element. This is no more than speculation— but the regular occurrence of the most closed vowels of all, *i* and *u*, may be due to the noticeable Southern English habit of partly closing the jaws whenever a consonant is uttered.

Vowel fracture in Germanic

Vowel fracture, sometimes known as *breaking*, is widespread in Old English phonology. It is the result of the influence of /l/, /r/ or /h/ on a preceding vowel. Assimilation to the consonant has taken place. The vowel has been 'broken' or 'fractured' in the direction of /a/ or /ɔ/ depending on the vowel.

I have introduced Old English vowel fracture for the special reason that its effects on the orthography of that period are sometimes a stumbling-block to students of this language. The orthography was nevertheless based on phonetic fact, and the pronunciations it represents are still to be heard in the West country and elsewhere. Typical are the following:

$\boxed{/e/ > /eo/}$: (O.H.G.) *melkan* = (O.E.) *meolcan* 'to milk'
(O.H.G.) *kneht* = (O.E.) *cneoht* 'boy'
(O.H.G.) *erda* = (O.E.) *eorthe* 'earth'

$\boxed{/i/ > /io/}$: *lirnojan* > (O.E.) *liornian* 'to learn'

$\boxed{/œ/ > /ea/}$: (Goth.) *kalds* = (O.E.) *ceald* 'cold'
(Goth.) *barn* = (O.E.) *bearn* 'child'
(Goth.) *ahtáu* = (O.E.) *eahta* 'eight'

For vowel fracture in Old Norse the reader is referred to Gordon, E. V., *An Introduction to Old Norse* (London, 1957), p. 274.

Germanic diphthongs

I am including this section almost as a postscript without any attempt to treat the matter with the thoroughness it certainly deserves. My remarks are intended mainly as a guide to those readers who may eventually be concerned with Germanic linguistics, and especially for those intending to work outwards from Old English to Norse, Gothic or Old High German (or from any one of these to another).

Proto-Germanic contained a series of four diphthongs, all of which have undergone considerable mutation in the various dialects of Germanic. Only Gothic has preserved the originals. The correspondences may be outlined as follows:

	Goth.	O.N.	O.H.G.	O.E.
*ai:	ái	ei	ei(ē)	ā
*au:	áu	au	ou(ō)	ēa
*eu:	iu	jō(jū)	eo	ēo
*iu:	iu	jū(ȳ)	iu	īo > īe > ī

The following table illustrates these correspondences:

Pr. G.	Goth.	O.N.	O.H.G.	O.E.	
*ai	*áins*	*einn*	*ein*	*ān*	'one'
	háils	*heill*	*heil*	*hāl*	'whole'
*au	*dáuthus*	*dauthe*	*tod*	*dēath*	'death'
	áugō	*auga*	*ouga*	*ēage*	'eye'
*eu	*diups*	*djūpr*	*tiof*	*dēop*	'deep'
	liufs	*ljūfr*	*liob*	*lēof*	'dear'
*iu	*liuhtjan*	—	*liuhten*	*līehtan*	'to give light'

(A fuller treatment of this subject may be found in Wright J. and E. M., *Old English Grammar* (London, 1929), pp. 68–73, as well as in Wright, J., *Grammar of the Gothic Language* (London, 1910), pp. 19–21.)

Exercise 5

(1) (Only for readers with a knowledge of French.) Given the Vulgar Latin form and the phonetic spelling of what is historically the same word in Modern French, attempt to infer the Old French form (orthographic) of the following:

(V. Lat.) *tēla*　 = (Mod. Fr. phonetics) /twal/ 'linen, cloth'
(V. Lat.) *alba*　 = (Mod. Fr. phonetics) /oːb/ 'dawn'
(V. Lat.) *tructa* = (Mod. Fr. phonetics) /tryit/ 'trout'

(2) Deduce the Old English forms of the following 'proto-English' forms, taking into consideration vowel fracture:

sah 'he saw'; *haldan* 'to hold'; *sex* 'six'; *lēht* 'light'; *herte* 'heart'.

(3) Fill in the blanks in the following examples, using the table of Germanic diphthong correspondences given above:

Goth.	O.N.	O.H.G.	O.E.	
háitan = h..ta	= h..za	= h..tan		'to call'
ráuths = r..thr	= r..t	= r..d		'red'
kiusan = k..sa	= k..san	= c..san		'to choose'
w..t = v..t	= w..z	= *wāt*		'he knows'
-b..dan = *bjōda*	= b..tan	= b..dan		'offer'

The Germanic (Gothonic) sound shift

A brief note about this important sound shift is called for at this point. I shall do no more than state the correspondences. The so-called High German sound shift, which has gone one stage further, is given in the last column. (Please note, however, that orthography, not phonemic transcription, is used.)

Table of the Germanic consonant shift

	Indo-European	Pr.-G.	Goth.	O.E.	O.N.	O.H.G.
Voiceless Plosives	$*p$	$*f$	f	f	f	f
	$*t$	$*\theta$	þ	þ	þ	d
	$*k$	$*\chi$	h	h	h	h
	$*k^{w}$	$*\chi^{w}$	ƕ, h	hw, h	hv, h	(h)w, h
Voiced Plosives	$*b$	$*p$	p	p	p	pf, ff[1]
	$*d$	$*t$	t	t	t	z, zz[1]
	$*g$	$*k$	k	c	k	k, hh[1]
	$*g^{w}$	$*kw, k$	q, k	cw, c	kv, k	qu; k, hh[1]
Voiced Fricatives	$*bh$	$*b$	ƀ	b, ƀ	b	b
	$*dh$	$*\eth$	ð	d, ð	d	t
	$*gh$	$*g$	g	g, ȝ	g	g
	$*g^{w}h$	$*g, w$	g, w	g, w	g, w	w

A more complete treatment of this subject is to be found in Wright, J. and E. M., *Old English Grammar*, pp. 111–25. The High German sound shift is described in great detail in Priebsch and Collinson, *The German Language*, pp. 109–21.

[1] Non-initial consonants.

Examples of the Germanic and High German shifts

	I.-E.		Goth.	O.E.	O.N.	O.H.G.	
p > f	(Lat.) piscis	=	fisks	= fisc	= fisk	= fisk	'fish'
t > þ[θ]	(Lat.) tu	=	þu	= þu	= þu	= du	'thou'
k > h[χ]	(Lat.) canis	=	hunds	= hund	= hundr	= hunt	'dog'
kʷ > hʷ[χʷ]	(Lat.) quis	=	hvas	= hwa	= hverr	= hwer	'who'
b > p	(Lith.) trobà 'house'	=	þaúrp 'field'	= þorp	= —	= dorf	'village'
d > t	(Lat.) decem	=	taíhun	= tien	= tio	= zehan	'ten'
g > k	(Lat.) ego	=	ik	= ic	= ek	= ih	'I'
gʷ > kʷ, k	(Lat.) vivus (> *gwiwos)	=	qius	= cwicu	= kvikr	= quec	'quick, alive'
bh, b,	(Skr.) bharami 'I bear'	=	bairan	= beran	= bera	= beran	'to bear'
dh, d,	(Gr.) thura	=		duru		turi	'door'
gh, g,	(Lat.) longus	=	laggs	= lang	= langr	= lang	'long'
gʷh, g, w	(Russ.) sneg 'snow'	=		sniweþ		sniwit	'snows'

Exercise 6

Using the table of consonant correspondences for the Germanic
and High German sound shifts, fill in the blanks in the following
series:

(i) (Lat.) *verto* 'I turn'; (Goth.) *wair..an* = (O.H.G.) *wer..an*
   'to become'.

(ii) (Lat.) *..res* = (O.E.) *..ri* = (O.N.) *..rir* = (O.H.G.) *dri*
   'three'.

(iii) (Lat.) *linquo* 'leave'; (Goth.) *lei..an* = (O.H.G.) *li..an*
   'lend'.

(iv) (Lat.) *..ens* = (Goth.) *tunthus* = (O.E.) *..ōth* = (O.H.G.)
   ..and 'tooth'.

(v) (Lat.) *au..ere* = (Goth.) *áu..an* = (O.N.) *au..a* =
   (O.H.G.) *auhhon* 'add'.

(vi) (Skr.) *bhra..ar* = (Goth.) *..rōthar* = (O.E.) *..rō..or* =
   (O.H.G.) *..ruo..er* 'brother'.

Accent

The type of accent we are familiar with, more appropriately called
stress—the form of accent emphasising a particular syllable—is a
relatively recent arrival in the Indo-European group of languages.
In the historically recorded Indo-European languages of antiquity
there is no suggestion of stress in our sense, only a musical modu-
lation of pitch. The Sanskrit grammarians were quite explicit as
to its nature, and the original 'pitch' accent is preserved in traditional recitation of the Hindu Vedic poems. Pāṇini described this
pitch accent as *udātta* 'raised'. This rising musical pitch was followed in the next syllable by a falling accent. Classical Latin,
Greek, Sanskrit and Old Persian all incorporated this musical
variation of pitch in their poetry and drama. Of the present-day
dialects, Serbo-Croat alone retains this original trait. In all other
dialects of this widespread family, either no trace has remained or
the musical has given way to a stress accent (as in Baltic, Slavonic
and Greek). The Scandinavian languages have developed a
characteristic pitch accent, which has certain features in common
with the ancient variety but is not historically descended from it.

The older musical stress was much less rigidly fixed and could fall on any syllable. Greek and Sanskrit show similar treatment in this respect. There is agreement also with the more primitive forms of Balto-Slavonic, particularly Lithuanian.

The pitch accent in Classical Latin was not inherited by Vulgar Latin, and in the latter a stress accent had taken its place. Germanic had in early times developed a stress accent closely associated with the root syllable of the word, generally the first syllable.

Stress accent, as opposed to pitch accent, is liable to play havoc with the forms of words. In general, the heavier or more accentuated the stress, the more marked the transformation. The reader may be familiar with the way in which English reduces unstressed syllables in such a manner that the original quality of these vowels is lost. This reduced syllable is usually articulated centrally, phonetically represented by /ə/. For instance, the words *necessary* /nesəsri/, *unfortunately* /ʌnfɔːtʃənətli/. No doubt the 'erosions' of the Anglo-Saxon place-names listed in Chapter 8 arose partly from this kind of phonetic distortion. Particularly prone to damage, erosion and subsequent levelling by the process of analogy were the grammatical endings. A glance at the Germanic '*u*-stem declension' of nouns will reveal the stages of this gradual wear and tear:

		Pr.G.	Gothic	O.E.	Mid. Eng.	Mod. Eng.
Sing.:	N.	*sunuz	sunus	sunu	sone	son
	A.	*sunun	sunu	sunu	sone	son
	G.	*sunauz	sunáus	suna	sones	son's
	D.	*sunwai	sunáu	suna	sone	son
Pl.:	N.	*suniwiz	sunjus	suna	sones	sons
	A.	*sununz	sununs	suna	sones	sons
	G.	*sunuwȏn	suniwē	suna	sones	sons'
	D.	*sunumiz	sunum	sunum	sones	sons

Accent in Romance

In Vulgar Latin accent was regularised according to four basic types. A few examples of the types of transformation that can occur may be illustrated by a single feature. A number of Vulgar Latin words with their accent on the ante-penultimate syllable (*proparoxytone*) shifted this accent so that it now fell on the pen-ultimate syllable (*paroxytone*); this was, however, confined to Hispanic and Gallo-Romance areas. Observe the differences created by such an apparently innocuous caprice:

(proparoxytone stress)			(paroxytone stress)		
V. Lat.	Ital.	Rom.	V. Lat.	French.	Span.
hómines 'men'	*uómini*	*oámeni*	*homínes*	*hommes*	*hombres*
dúodecim 'twelve'	*dódici*		*duodécim*	*douze*	*doce*
fráxinum 'ash'	*frássino*	*frásinu*	*fraxínum*	*frêne*	*fresno*
péctinem 'comb'	*péttene*	*péttine*	*pectínem*	*peigne*	*peine*

It will be seen that in the case of the Vulgar Latin *proparoxytones* —those which have, in fact, retained the original stress on the root—the Romance derivatives have preserved the first and second syllable intact (e.g. (It.) *uomini*), whereas the shift of stress to the penultimate syllable (*paroxytone*) has weakened consider-ably both the first and the second syllables, and in each instance a phonetic reduction has taken place, the French and Spanish derivatives terminating with a single syllable in place of two syllables.

Readers will find a detailed account of the development of the Vulgar Latin accent in Elcock, W. D., *The Romance Languages*, pp. 39–55, and are advised to consult this or other accounts before proceeding to a comparative study of the Romance languages.

Verner's Law
The student of Germanic linguistics is bound sooner or later to encounter Verner's Law. Although discovered and described by Karl Verner as early as 1877, this sound law still presents a certain challenge.

This 'law' was the outcome of attempts to reconcile various irregularities inherent in the Germanic consonantal alternations in such pairs as these:

> (O.E.) *teah* 'he drew'—*tugon* 'they drew'
> (O.E.) *seah* 'he saw' —*sawon* 'they saw'
> (Eng.) *was* —*were*
> (O.N.) *ulfr* 'he-wolf' —*ylgr* 'she-wolf'

What Verner had found was that such variations were connected with corresponding alternations of pitch-accent position, all traces of which had long since disappeared in Germanic. In all the earlier Germanic languages the pitch accent had become a stress accent, and its position was now invariably on the initial or root syllable. In a number of comparisons Verner had shown that, whenever the Germanic 'exception' (e.g. *tugon*) involved a voiced plosive, it could be said to coincide with an instance of Indo-European pitch accent falling not on the root but on the suffix or ending. Where the correspondence was normal (e.g. *teah*) Indo-European had its pitch accent on the root. The following is an illustration of this:

	Sanskrit		Proto-Germanic	
accent on root	*vártāmi* 'I turn'	*wérθo	> (O.E.) *wéorþe* 'I become'
	va-várta 'has turned'	*wárθo	> (O.E.) *wearþ* 'he became'
accent not on root	*va-vr̥timá* 'we have turned'	*wúrðumí	> (O.E.) *wúrdon* 'we have become'
	va-vr̥taná	*wurðaná	> (O.E.) *wórden* 'become'

It should be noted that, during a subsequent period, the Proto-Germanic accent was shifted to the first syllable unless it had already been there in the first place.

Verner's correspondences can be stated as follows:

Plosive affected by accent originally on root syllable	Plosive affected by accent elsewhere than on root
/f/	/β/
/θ/	/ð/
/χ/	/γ/
/χʷ/	/γʷ/
/s/	/z/

The Sanskrit 'perfectives' revealed just this tendency to alternate the position of the accent between singular and plural forms, which helped to explain some of the features of consonant alterations in Germanic:

> (Skr.) *véda* 'I know'   *vidmá* 'we know'
>   *véda* 'he knows'   *vidúḥ* 'they know'

Old English shows a parallel correlation—not, of course, by accent but by type of consonant:

> *wæs* 'he was'—*wæron* 'they were'
> *ceas* 'he chose'—*curon* 'they chose'
> *forleas* 'he lost'—*forluron* 'they lost'
> *cwæþ* 'he said'—*cwædon* 'they said'
> *seah* 'he saw'—*sawon* 'they saw'

The Verner's Law discrepancies only exceptionally (e.g. *was*—*were*) survive into Modern English, owing to the operation of the process of analogy in the intervening centuries. The original distinction does, however, survive in such pairs as:

> *death—dead*
> *see—saw*
> *flee—flew*
> *arise—rear*
> *lose—forlorn*

Vocalisation

There exists a phonological tendency for intervocalic voiced plosives or semivowels to become assimilated to the vowels between which they are sandwiched. In some languages this kind of assimilation extends even to voiceless plosives. I include a number of random but useful examples:

Romance

In the Romance languages a very striking feature is the sonorisation of intervocalic voiceless plosives, although as a rule it is confined to the Transalpine or 'Western' dialects (French Provençal, Spanish, Portuguese). A few comparisons will serve to illustrate this:

V.L.	Ital.	Rom.	Span.	Pro-vençal	French	
rīpa	*ripa*	*rîpa*	*riba*	*riba*	*rive*	'bank'
mutare	*mutare*	*a muta*	*mudar*	*mudar*	*muer*	'to change'
amica(m)	*amica*	*amica*	*amiga*	*amiga*	*amie*	'friend'

French, it will be noticed, has proceeded much further than its companion dialects in the direction of vocalisation:

Labial (orig.) /p/ > (Sp. Prov.) /b/ > (Fr.) /v/
Dental (orig.) /t/ > (Sp. Prov.) /d/ > (Fr.) (zero)
Velar (orig.) /k/ > (Sp. Prov.) /g/ > (Fr.) *yod* (or zero)

This series of sound changes is thought to have been a comparatively late development in Western Romance and to have progressed slowly. A curious anomaly is the existence of an area of the Central Pyrenees, extending over both sides of the Franco-Spanish frontier, in which by an odd coincidence Romance words have a closer affinity with Romanian than with any other Romance language.

Norse

Initial semivowels /j/ and /w/ were assimilated to the succeeding vowels, thereby losing their identity. This created a number of apparent discrepancies. Examples of this disappearance of the palatal semivowel are:

(O.N.) *ár* = (Goth.) *jēr* 'year'
(O.N.) *ungr* = (Goth.) *juggs* 'young'

Examples of the disappearance of *w* semivowel are:

(O.N.) *ulfr* = (Goth.) *wulfs* = (O.E.) *wulf*
(O.N.) *orð* = (Goth.) *waúrd* = (O.E.) *word*
(O.N.) *reiðr* = = (O.E.) *wrath*

Old English

Assimilation of the Germanic plosives /k/, /g/ in Old English to the semivowel *yod* has already been discussed under 'Palatalisation'. A further look at this is called for.

We have already seen how /g/ before the front vowels /e/ or /i/ became palatalised to *yod* (a 'y' sound as in *you*), as in *giellan* 'to yell' in *fæger* 'fair' or in *nægel* 'nail'. This is only part of the picture.

In the case of *gg* this double consonant has become /γ/ before a front vowel. The result was a kind of fricative velar to be heard in Modern High German *wiegen* and many other words. In Old English the sound became *yod* in the case of medial consonants:

O.E.		Mod. Eng.
bycgean	>	*buy*
licgean	>	*lie*
lecgean	>	*lay*

In final position *gg* has become /dʒ/:

O.E.		Mod. Eng.
brycg	>	*bridge*
wecg	>	*wedge*
hrycg	>	*ridge*

In instances where Old English medial /g/ originates from a single medial /γ/, /g/, this plosive has become /w/ before back vowels:

O.E.		Mod. Eng.
dragan	>	*draw*
fugol	>	*fowl*
lagu	>	*law*

Final /γ/ generally became assimilated (or palatalised) to *yod* after front vowels:

O.E.		Mod. Eng.
dæg	>	*day*
hālig	>	*holy*
ænig	>	*any*
manig	>	*many*

Exercise 7

Identify and describe any examples of consonantal vocalisation in the following series:

(a) (V.L.) *capra* = (Ital.) *capra* = (Span.) *cabra* = (Fr.) *chèvre* 'goat'.
(b) (V.L.) *fata* = (Rom.) *fata* = (Prov.) *fada* = (Fr.) *fée* 'fairy'.
(c) (V.L.) *apicula* = (Span.) *abeja* = (Fr.) *abeille* 'bee'.
(d) (Goth.) *áugō* = (O.N.) *auga* = (O.E.) *ēage* = (Mod. Eng.) *eye*.
(e) (O.E.) *swelgan* = (M.E.) *swallow*.
(f) (O.E.) *dagas* = (Mod. Eng.) *days*.

Miscellaneous

When using comparative grammars, readers may find the following points of some assistance.

1 Sound change in Indo-Iranian

(a) Indo-European *ŏ*, *ĕ*, *ă* have been reduced to *ă*.
(b) The European short diphthongs *oi*, *ei* appear as *e*.
    The European short diphthongs *ou*, *eu* appear as *o*.
(c) In certain instances, and for complicated reasons, Indo-European *l* has become *r*.

Compare: (Skr.) *cakrá-* = (Gr.) *kuklos* 'wheel'
          (Skr.) *riṇăkti* = (Lat.) *linquit* 'he leaves'

2 Greek labialisation

In Greek the Indo-European labio-velars /kʷ/, /gʷ/, /gʷh/ have become labialised, except after /u/:

/kʷ/ > /p/	(Lat.) *iecur* =	(Gr.) *hēpar* 'liver'
/gʷ/ > /b/	(Lat.) *vivus* =	(Gr.) *bios* 'life'
/gʷh/ > /ph/	(Skr.) *laghu-* =	(Gr.) *elakhus, elaphros*

Before the frontal vowels *i* and *e*, these vowels have in turn become 'dentalised':

$$/k^w/ > /p/ > /t/ \qquad \text{(Lat.) } quis \; = \text{(Gr.) } tis \text{ 'who'}$$
$$/g^w/ > /b/ > /d/$$
$$/g^wh/ > /ph/ > /th/ \qquad \text{(Lat.) } formus = \text{(Gr.) } thermos$$

3 The treatment of Indo-European voiced fricatives /bh/, /dh/, /gh/, /gᵂh/ in Latin

The correspondences are as follows:

$$bh \begin{cases} = f \text{ (initially)} \\ = b \text{ (medially)} \end{cases}$$
$$dh \begin{cases} = f \text{ (initially)} \\ = d \text{ (medially)} \end{cases}$$
$$gh = h$$
$$g^wh \begin{cases} = f \text{ (initially)} \\ = u(v) \text{ (medially)} \end{cases}$$

Illustrations:

		Sanskrit	**Latin**
/bh/	(initial)	*bharami*	= *ferō* 'I carry'
	(medial)	*nabhaḥ*	= *nebula* 'cloud'
/dh/	(initial)	*dhumaḥ*	= *fumus* 'smoke'
	(medial)	*vidhava*	= *vidua* 'widow'
		(Goth.)	
/gh/		-*wigan* 'to move'	= *vehit* 'he carries'
		(Skr.)	
/gᵂh/	(initial)	-*hanti* 'he strikes'	= -*fendo* 'I attack'
	(medial)	*laghu*-	= *levis* 'light'

4 Treatment of Germanic z in West and North Germanic

In Proto-Germanic there were two kinds of sibilant: /s/ (voiceless) and /z/ (voiced). The latter survived only in Gothic; in North and West Germanic this /z/-phoneme has become /r/ by a process which is to some extent the converse of the well-known speech defect, *lisping*.

West Germanic.   Medial   /z/ > /r/
                   Final /z/ is reduced to zero.

Compare:

Goth.		O.E.		O.H.G.
máiza	=	*mára*	=	*méro* 'greater'
batiza	=	*betera*	=	*bezziro* 'better'
huzd	=	*hord*	=	*hort* 'hoard, treasure'
dags	=	*dæg*	=	*tag* 'day'

In a few instances this final *z* appears to have remained as in the O.E. plural *dagas* (from proto-Germ. *dagŏz*).

North Germanic. The main difference between North and West Germanic is that the former preserves final *z* as /R/.
Compare:

(Goth.) *dags*	(O.E.) *dæg*	(O.N.) *dagr*
(Goth.) *dagos*	(O.E.) *dagas*	(O.N.) *dagar*

Exercise 8

(Those readers who feel they would like to revise the foregoing notes on phonology are advised to read through the present and previous chapters, and then to attempt the following exercises.)

Identify and describe any correspondences occurring in the following groups:

(i) (Lat.) *quattuor* = (Gr.) *tessares* = (Goth.) *fidwor* = (Welsh) *pedwar* = (Skr.) *čatvărah* = (Lith.) *keturi* 'four'.

(ii) (Skr.) *panča* = (Lat.) *quinque* = (Gr.) *pente* = (Lith.) *penki* = (Irish) *coic* = (Goth.) *fimf* = (Welsh) *pump* 'five'.

(iii) (Lat.) *tenuis* = (O.E.) *thynne* = (O.N.) *thunnr* = (Mod. Eng.) *thin* = (O.H.G.) *dunni* = (N.H.G. H.G.) *dünn*.

(iv) (Lat.) *cor* (gen. *cordis*) = (Gr.) *kardia* = (O.E.) *heorte* = (O.N.) *hjarta* = (O.H.G.) *herza* 'heart'.

(v) (V.L.) *formaticu(m)* = (Ital.) *formaggio* = (Fr.) *fromage* 'cheese'.

(vi) (V.L.) *parēte* = (Ital.) *parete* = (Span.) *pared* = (Fr.) *paroi* 'wall'.

Note: Confine your descriptions to those aspects of phonology covered so far.

Part III

GRAMMAR

11 Grammatical Analysis

During the past fifty years modern linguistics has developed an impressive, if not always concordant, array of procedures, including some that have become powerful tools in the grammatical analysis of languages. And, more recently, linguistics has seen a renewal of interest in grammar itself, and a rethinking about its nature. What had long since become peripheral to linguistics itself, and been safely relegated to the pedagogue and linguistic historian, has in the past decade or so become a major concern of philosophers, psychologists, logicians, communication theorists and even biologists.

It would not be possible, even in a book devoted entirely to the subject, to give a complete account of this development. But there is fortunately no need. This chapter, therefore, is a selection of features which have already affected, or are likely to affect, the course of historical and comparative linguistics. In the meantime, as we shall see, the historical linguist, with his roots stretching continuously and far back into the last century, has not neglected but has considerably elaborated and reinforced his own methods. I shall be dealing with some of these in later chapters.

A few general preliminaries

Grammar and logic

The legendary Procrustes used to lodge travellers in his own bed. If they were too tall he would chop them down to size; if too short, he took them and stretched them. A 'Procrustean' approach to language was not only predictable but also unavoidable.

Owing to the influence of the Latin grammarians, the illusion arose that somehow language was fundamentally logical; a slight adjustment here and there, and all would be well. The faulty view no doubt arose from the traditional mediaeval association of grammar, logic and rhetoric. The illusion was furthered by the striking regularity of Latin. In this language there is a rule for everything, and the few exceptions can easily be swept under the carpet without anyone noticing. Classical Latin is a wonderfully well-regulated system of tenses, moods, cases, genders, etc. To take the tenses as an example: present, future, imperfect, perfect, future perfect and pluperfect—a truly symmetrical division of the tense spectrum.

Classical Latin must have been to a large extent an artificial, literary language. (Any student of information theory could see immediately that Classical Latin does not contain enough 're-dundancy' to render it usable in ordinary spoken communica-tion.) In Roman times there was a gap, far more marked than in any modern European language, between everyday conversation and the polished language of letters. This no doubt had its advantages. The Roman writers' native dialects were not always 'Latin', and in some cases not even Italic. Seneca and Lucan were from Spain; and Virgil in his northern Italian home setting probably spoke a dialect of Gallic. And so Classical Latin became first the model for Roman writers and grammarians, and subse-quently for mediaeval and early modern writers and grammarians. Even today there are people who throw a fit at the sight of an un-related participle or a split infinitive. The prejudice that somehow language should be 'logical' dies hard.

Influenced by their Latin model, the earlier 'prescriptive' grammarians have left their mark on most modern European languages. Only some of the Baltic, Slavonic and Celtic groups have escaped their influence. French grammarians fought what quickly turned into a losing battle in their attempts to keep French under the thumb of Latin rules. Ridicule was the most effective counter-weapon, from Molière up to the time of the last attempt to legislate on the imperfect subjunctive, when the population of Paris went around hissing this unwieldy and un-necessary tense into its last retreat.

Nowadays, logicians are the first to point out that language is not logical, and at best suitable only for adaptation to purposes of logic. That is why they have gone to such pains to construct 'languages' that suit their purpose better. Symbolic logical lan-guages exclude what are the staple ingredients of natural language.

Grammar and abstraction

As one of the many modern linguists who reacted against the prescriptive, Procrustean approach of the traditional gram-marian, Saussure stressed the precedence of the concrete over grammatical abstraction. The latter, he claimed, becomes pedan-tic or sophistic when divorced from the reality of usage, and loses all justification. Associative relationships, normally expressed as morphological categories, do indeed exist but only as *abstract entities*: 'their study is difficult because we never know exactly whether or not the awareness of speakers goes as far as the analyses of the grammarian. But the important thing is that *abstract entities are always based, in the last analysis on concrete entities.* No grammatical abstraction is possible without a series of material elements as a basis, and in the end we must always come back to these elements.'[1] The same is true of syntax or the wider discourse relationship. Word order exists only as an abstraction. It is only the 'material units', Saussure held, that actually create real value by being arranged in a certain way.

In modern times, prescriptive grammar has given way to *descriptive* grammar. The modern linguist has given up apriorist presuppositions as to what a language *should* be like; and instead of excluding all those features which do not fit into a classical design, the modern linguist allows himself to be guided by his *actual observations* of the language he is in the process of describing. No language is like any other. And the most the modern linguist can do, after completing a description of one or several languages, is to seek out the underlying properties common to languages in general.

Today, the linguist and the logician complement one another. The linguist never ceases to look for ways of bringing order into what would otherwise remain a chaos of haphazard phenomena. It is the logician to whom he most readily turns. But, although he may go far in his quest for 'language universals', he will seldom lose sight of the hard reality of his linguistic data. The Generative Grammarians, for example, in their concern with abstract rules and categories underlying the surface of language, have stressed that, whereas the 'deep' structure of grammar is highly abstract, the superficial structure—what we actually say and hear—remains perfectly real.

The limits of grammar

If any linguist sets out to provide a *complete* descriptive grammar of a language, he is doomed to disappointment. The nearer he seems to be getting to his goal, the more numerous are the features that refuse to comply with his rules or fit into his system.

[1] Saussure, F. de, *op. cit.*, p. 138.

He is forced to create rules and still more rules, until his grammar reaches the point of becoming hopelessly unwieldy and un-economical. The end result would seem like setting up a pile-driver to break a nut.

Perhaps the main difficulty is that it is usually difficult or im-possible for the linguist to decide *which* data is eligible for his analysis. If there existed a 'standard' which all members of a speech community both accepted and followed, the problem would be wonderfully simple. Yet, not only is it impossible to decide in every case what the standard usage actually is, but also speakers are notoriously willing to *accept as grammatical* utter-ances that, on the face of it, seem non-standard and even sub-standard. (This has been demonstrated quite plainly by the results of the experiments carried out at University College, London, by Quirk and Svartik, mentioned earlier.) And who determines what is standard and what is not? The Queen of England or the President of the United States? The universities of Oxford and Harvard? Madison Avenue and Carnaby Street? The writer perhaps?

I take at random two samples of English taken from the work of different writers:

(1) Query. Who's astanding this here do? Proud possessor of damn-all. Declare misery. Bet to the ropes. Me nantee saltee. Not a red at me this week gone. Yours?

(James Joyce, *Ulysses.*)

(2) They had to fill the hole back up of course and besides he had the horse. But even then it was a good while until day-light when he left Highboy with Aleck Sander at the pasture gate and tried remembered to tiptoe into the house . . .

(William Faulkner, *Intruder in the Dust*)

The reader will do right to complain that I have wantonly chosen passages in which writers are trying to express the patterns of *speech*, and that therefore they are not typical. But where is one to draw the line? Neither passage is completely incomprehensible, however, and passage (2) is probably entirely comprehensible.

Should they be ruled out, then, because they break the rules of grammar of standard English? If so, how do we know what these rules are unless we have to some extent 'prescribed' them? Should they be discounted because they are representations of ordinary speech? In this case, are we not being rather snobbish?

It is such problems as these that confront the descriptive grammarian. If he wishes to, he can eliminate all samples of substandard usage. But first he must decide upon criteria for establishing what is sub-standard. There is no doubt, though, that by ruling out sub-standard sentences like *Don't never do that never again, Billy!* he can spare himself the necessity of explaining the use of the triple negative in English. He can with less difficulty rule out dialect and thus save himself the need to justify a local occurrence such as *He likes she*, which runs counter to his most sacred principles.

Even if he decides to restrict his corpus to discursive written English, the grammarian will still be forced to stick to the conventionally straight and narrow. For if he insists on including every piece of descriptive English that falls within his ken, he will find himself in a quandary. If, for example, he includes a sentence on a newspaper vendor's hoarding or a newspaper headline that reads TOPLESS GOODWOOD FAVOURITE, he will probably be strongly tempted to admit that what is *grammatically* (as well as semantically) acceptable depends in the long run on the experience, expectations and tolerance of the reader. He will either recognise or fail to recognise that Goodwood is the name of a race-course, that 'favourite' has a special meaning in horse-racing and that Topless is very probably the name of a horse.

Grammatical categories

The trouble with the traditional grammatical categories, as we have seen, is that they were abstractions hypostatised as real. 'Genitive', 'subjunctive', 'passive', etc., are striking examples. Not one of them is susceptible of general definition, and as categories they behave differently from one language to another. The Danish linguist Louis Hjelmslev[1] claimed that only by taking a pristine *text* could the linguist be sure of finding a truly linguistic structure: 'Our only possible procedure, if we wish to order a system

[1] Hjelmslev, L., *Prolegomena to a Theory of Language* (Bloomington, Indiana, 1953), pp. 7 ff.

to the process of that text, will be an analysis, in which the text is regarded as a class divided into segments, then these segments as classes divided into segments, and so on until the analysis is exhausted.' Even if Hjelmslev's linguistic algebra has not been realised, like a number of modern linguists he was looking forward to a universal linguistics where it would be possible, in Saussure's words, 'to set up a general calculus in which all conceivable cases are foreseen'.

Traditional grammar laid great stress on regularity. Those features which were not regular were deviations or 'exceptions'. The modern grammarian is concerned more with *difference* than sameness, with *variety* more than regularity. The student may find it a nuisance that a particular language uses its cases and prepositions in an apparently chaotic way, but the linguist may find this same proliferation a blessing. The categories are usually easier to locate in a language that offers plenty of signs of their whereabouts than in a language like English where the irregularity is not always so readily apparent. It is the differences—what Saussure called the *linguistic oppositions*—that provide the clues that the grammarian is on the look-out for. Zellig Harris and some other American linguists developed the assumption that it was the proper task of structural linguistics to formulate a technique, or procedure, which could be applied to a corpus of utterances and, using the speaker's (informant's) judgements of 'sameness' and 'difference', could be guaranteed to derive the rules of grammar from the corpus itself. Nowadays, although the notion of linguistic opposition continues to be as important as ever it was, very few linguists would unreservedly accept this procedure. It is no longer supposed that the rules of grammar can be derived from a corpus, or even that an informant's judgement is always reliable. Two sentences like *This book is worth having* and *This book is worth nothing* might on either count be recognised as being similar, whereas in fact they are entirely different.

The traditional divisions of grammar

In the past the domain of linguistics now generally known as grammar was divided into *morphology* and *syntax*. Even recent diachronic studies have made use of this distinction. Morphology dealt with the ways in which words are built up and syntax with the ways in which they combined with each other to form sentences. Sometimes the term *accidence*, a concept borrowed from Aristotelian metaphysics, was used in place of morphology. I am mentioning all this, not simply out of purely historical interest, but because the student of historical and comparative linguistics will frequently refer to authorities who make use of these terms and whose studies are still wholly or partly valid today.

It was Saussure who pointed out that 'morphology' has no distinctly autonomous object. It cannot, he held, be distinguished from syntax. It was Saussure, too, who demonstrated that lexicology cannot be isolated from either syntax or morphology. Not only grammatical forms but differences of words may just as well indicate those oppositions which are generally assigned to syntax or morphology. In Russian the difference between the imperfective and perfective aspects is more often than not expressed by different words, in a few cases quite unrelated. The example usually given is the pair *govorit'—skazat'* (= 'to say, speak'), but there are many others. Many prepositional, adverbial and conjunctional groups are basically lexicological, e.g. *in spite of*, *on condition that*, *in the circumstances*, etc. Expressions that may be expressed syntactically in one language find themselves in other languages expressed by single or compound words, e.g.

'windmill' = (Fr.) *moulin à vent* = (Russ.) *vetryanáya mélnitsa*
'firewood' = (Fr.) *bois de chauffage* = (Russ.) *drová*

'Morphology, syntax and lexicology interpenetrate because every synchronic fact is identical. No line of demarcation can be drawn in advance.'

Although he awarded a separate status to syntax, the traditional diachronist at the same time grossly neglected it. A likely explanation for this state of affairs is that syntax did not usually display the spectacular evolutionary development that had over the centuries reshaped the Indo-European (morphological) nominal declensions and verbal conjugations out of all recognition. To be sure, sentence structure had changed too, but not so remarkably or with such direction; and, more important, it had more often than not changed in ways that were neither easy to discern nor easy to describe. Modern linguistics has reversed this position—so much so that syntax, once the Cinderella of historical-comparative linguistics, has developed its own powerful methods of analysis and promises to transform our view of linguistic change.

Grammatical structure

In our earlier discussion of phonology we saw that the phonemes of a language form a system, and that no one of the phonemes can undergo alteration or substitution without affecting the system as a whole. The same is true of the grammatical units of a language in relation to grammatical systems. Only this time the repercussions of change can be far more extensive, as well as very much more complex. A language has rarely many more than thirty phonemes; but the number of elements and types of structural relations utilised by the grammar runs into the hundreds. For this reason, it is all the more imperative that the diachronist, before embarking upon the history of a grammatical change, should first of all ensure that he possesses as complete a synchronic description as possible of the language states between which the change is reckoned to have occurred. If he happens to be tracing a change which he supposes to have taken place by the time Old English was superseded by Middle English, he must set about gaining as complete a synchronic picture of both these languages or language states as he can.

Let us take the case of a diachronist investigating a change in the tense function of verbs between an earlier state (A) and a later state (B) of a language; for example, where a perfect tense no longer serves as perfect in function but instead has taken on a purely past tense (preterite) function. This change, let us suppose, he represents as: *perfect* tense function X → *past* tense function Y. Now, unless he takes the precaution of establishing synchronic descriptions of (A) and (B) first, he is liable to make any one of the following errors, not to mention the possibility of others besides:

(1) Y may not be the descendant of X at all but the outcome of a syncretic combination or fusion of X and Z. In other words, two functions in the earlier state (A) have combined to produce Y in the later state (B).

(2) Y may not be the sole descendant of X. There may be another (P) which also derives from X. This would make it necessary to investigate the relationship between Y and P in the later state, since they are likely to be related or to contrast in some way.

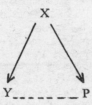

(3) Y may not actually be descended from X at all. What could have happened is that Y represents a fully-fledged development of an embryonic y in the earlier state (A), which could easily have escaped the attention of the linguist, who is ignorant of the synchrony of state (A). Likewise, X may not have changed or disappeared completely in state (B) but may well survive with a completely different function.

In the next few pages a selection of those synchronic features likely to be of special interest and use to the diachronist is given, although in no particular order.

The morpheme

Grammatical structure extends between an 'upper limit'—the *sentence*—and a 'lower limit'—the *morpheme*. In between these limits are the *phrase* and the *clause*. A sentence can be subdivided into clauses, the clauses into phrases, and the phrases into morphemes.

The morpheme has been defined as 'the minimal grammatical unit'. It has also been described as 'the smallest individually meaningful element in the utterances of a language'. A phoneme is not (usually) itself meaningful, and only becomes identical with a morpheme when it does have a meaning. The English phoneme /ɑː/ becomes a morpheme only when it becomes the third person plural form (*are*) of the verb 'to be'.

It is widely agreed that morphemes fall into two classes: those which can stand by themselves, such as *bring*, *catch*, *first*, *fish*, and those which cannot, like the *-ing* in *bringing*, the *-er* in *catcher* or the *de-* and *-ment* in *department* or *deportment*. Bloomfield called the first of these classes *free* morphemes and the others *bound*. Gleason uses the terms *root* and *affix*, which have the advantage of being closer to the diachronist's established terminology.

In a language like English, morphemes are often segmentally identical with words. All the following, and hundreds besides, are both morphemes and words: *bad*, *bright*, *catch*, *take*, *John*, *late*, *Turk*, etc. Sometimes they appear unadorned as 'free' morphemes, but at other times they appear in combination with 'bound' morphemes (affixes). *Give* /giv/ is a 'free' morpheme, but it appears in various combinations as: *giver*, *given*, *to give*, *giving* and *gift*.

There is another type of morpheme that might more suitably be called a 'syntactic' morpheme. Sometimes these morphemes are 'free' (e.g. English *and*, *but*, *whether*), but usually they appear 'bound'. The 'syntactic' morpheme does not have any function but to indicate what a group of words (a phrase, a clause) or another morpheme is doing in a particular environment. In English the segment /s/ in isolation possesses only phonological significance. If, however, /s/ occurs as the final phoneme in *trips* /trips/ it takes on an added *morphemic* significance, in that it distinguishes a plural noun *trips* from the singular form *trip*, or a verb in the third person singular of the present tense from one in any other person or tense (*I trip*, *we trip*, *they trip*, but *he trips*).

These syntactic morphemes are extremely various. Sometimes, for instance, they can become the grammatical equivalent of a question mark, as in Russian *li* (*ne tak li* = 'not so?') or in the numerous particles of Cantonese which are tacked on at the end of the sentence and which indicate not only different forms of question (e.g. 'Is it or isn't it?', 'Is that so?', 'It isn't, is it?', 'And what about (you)?') but also a whole range of statements expressing surprise, familiarity, irony, etc. Sometimes a syntactic morpheme is distributed in two or more positions in the sentence. Examples of these are the French negative adverbs *ne . . . pas*, *ne . . . plus*, *ne . . . jamais*, etc.

Some morphemes are of a peculiar kind. These do not occur as syntagmatic morphemes but as phonemic alternations of a single morpheme. English abounds in examples: *man—men, woman—women, give—gave, sing—sang—sung*. The root or free morpheme of the first group is /m..n/, of the second /w..mən/, and so on. The morpheme inserted into /m..n/ is one of the alternations /æ//e/; into /g..v/ the alternation /i//ei/ is inserted to create *give*, *gave*.

Paradigmatic and syntagmatic

It was originally Saussure's suggestion that any linguistic unit (phoneme, morpheme, phrase, etc.) within a given context enters into relationships of two different kinds. Its relations with all the possible units that can occur in the *same* context are called *paradigmatic*. For instance, in the following sentences:

Every morning he collects his mail from his letterbox
Each day he collects his mail from his letterbox
At nine o'clock he collects his mail from his letterbox

the opening phrases *every morning*, *each day* and *at nine o'clock* are said to be in paradigmatic relationship. But in the sentence:

He has had a long run of bad luck

long run and *bad luck* are in *syntagmatic* relationship with each other. In other words, they precede or follow one another in the same context and are linked by a link-word *of*. Every word in the sentence is 'syntagmatically' linked. If instead of *he* as the first word of the sentence we put *she* or *Tom* or *the gambler*, each stands in *paradigmatic* relation to the other possibilities but enters into *syntagmatic* relations with the other words in the sentence. *Good* stands in paradigmatic relation to *bad*, and both form a 'syntagm' with *luck*, and so on.

One curious consequence of all this is that what is traditionally known as a 'paradigm' is not really paradigmatic at all. There is no paradigmatic connection between *mensa*, *mensam*, *mensae*, etc. (Latin 'table'), since these units will *not* normally occur in the same context, by virtue of their syntactic function, which is different in each case; *mensa* occurs as the subject of the sentence and affects the form of any verb it 'governs', whereas *mensam* is the object, has no such effect on the verb and is sometimes used in connection with prepositions. Even the plural of the noun is not related paradigmatically to the singular, since the form of adjectives qualifying the noun and of verbs governed by the verb will be different for singular and plural. Although *mensa*, *mensam*, etc. do not constitute separate words, in that they share a common stem, they do function very differently within the sentence. Thus we can expect that a diachronic change affecting the accusative case singular (*mensam*, *nautam*, *rotam*, etc.) will not necessarily directly affect the form of the nominative singular (*mansa*, *nauta*, *rota* ,etc.), since these two cases appear in different contexts and set up different syntagmatic links. It is more reasonable to expect that adjectives and nouns in the same *case*, and nouns and verbs of the same *number* would develop similar characteristics but that the different *cases* and different *numbers* and *persons* would go their separate diachronic ways. We shall see examples of this farther on.

Syntactic signposts

If we look at a text in a foreign language we are not too familiar with, the lines of print before us do not fall into any obvious kind of pattern. Certain clues make it possible for us to make limited headway here and there, but sooner or later we have to retrace our steps and return to square one. Even with a language we understand much better, and occasionally even with our mother tongue, we can lose ourselves in the middle of a particularly long and involved sentence or paragraph. Reading or, for that matter, listening to a stretch of language is like following a set of signposts. It is less like watching the unfurling of a film sequence than putting together the clues of a detective plot. Sometimes we don't know who committed the murder until the last page of the story.

A sentence contains a certain number of features which do not have any specific or definite meaning but which convey a great deal of *information* about the structure, or 'plot', of the sentence. These features are known as *syntactic markers*.

Syntactic markers are not unlike a series of traffic signals along a busy main road. Like traffic signals, these markers are of no use unless the rules governing their sequence and function are known in advance. The syntactic markers are the signals scattered along the length of the sentence that guide us to its meaning. Sometimes, when a road is very busy and contains a number of hazards, traffic signs are repeated, or even presented in different ways. The same thing happens with language. We call this extra or 'bonus' element *redundancy*. The brain has to work very fast to decode the meaning of a sentence, and hence the sentence needs a high proportion of redundancy to ensure that if we miss a clue or signpost the first time we don't miss it a second or a third time. Double negatives may seem superfluous, but they do help to get the message across; unless, that is, we heed the logicians, who tell us that a second negative cancels a first. Triple negatives, as used in English sub-standard speech, are particularly effective.

The most evident and, in many languages, the most important kind of syntactic marker is the affix or bound morpheme. Affixes are most often of two kinds: suffixes (attachments following the stem) and prefixes (attachments preceding the stem). Both types of affix occur widely in English, but their form (if not their function) is sometimes ambiguous. The suffix -*ly*, for example, usually indicates the presence of an adverb. *Lovely*, *timely* and *silly*, however, are adjectives, and *reply* and *rely* are verbs. In many languages affixes have one function only. In a language like Turkish, in which a single stem or root is modified by one or more of a large selection of suffixes, we find that the order of the suffixes is determined in a regular and rational way. In the form we discussed earlier *kirilmadilarmi*, the speaker of Turkish knows that *kir* ('break') is the stem, followed immediately and in sequence by a series of signposts: passive voice (*il*)—negative (*ma*)—past tense (*di*)—plural (*lar*)—interrogative (*mi*). An equally unambiguous set of markers—this time *prefixes*—appears in Swahili. In the verbal forms, a series of prefixes attached to a stem or root tells the speaker of Swahili who is the subject, who or what is the object, and the tense. Compare:

ni-ta-m-penda   = (literally) 'I-future tense-him-like' ('I am going to like him')
wa-na-ku-penda = 'They-present tense-you-like' ('They like you')
tu-li-wa-penda   = 'We-past tense-them-like' ('We liked them')

Another important class of syntactic marker is the *function word*. This is particularly evident in English. In many respects an affix and a function word have much in common. Both indicate such functions as tense, voice, relation and so on. The main difference is that function words are separate lexical items. Among the function words are prepositions, conjunctions, articles and pronouns.

In English, Chinese and some other languages, a crucial part is played by *word order*. This is a 'distributive', not a morpheme, marker. In a language like English, word order so overrides in importance all other markers that the meanings of such utterances as *little boys prefer tigers* and *tigers prefer little boys* are distinguished by word order alone. Word order is such a powerful marker that if we come across the sentence *Man bites lion* we shall assume there has been a mistake somewhere!

There have been various theories about the origin of word order. The argument advanced by Jespersen was that there had been a long and slow development of language during which time word order gradually emerged and eventually became formalised. The crux of Jespersen's case is that grammatical simplification accompanies and takes place as a result of the emergence of word order, which in turn renders grammatical inflexions superfluous. 'It follows that a fixed word order must have come in first: it would come quite gradually as a natural consequence of greater mental development and general maturity, when the speaker's ideas no longer come into his mind helter-skelter, but in orderly sequence. If before the establishment of some sort of fixed word order any tendency to slur certain final consonants or vowels of grammatical importance had manifested itself, it could not have become universal, as it would have been constantly checked by the necessity that speech should be intelligible, and that therefore these marks which showed the relation of different words should not be obliterated. But when once each word was placed at the exact spot where it properly belonged, then there was no longer anything to forbid the endings being weakened by assimilation, etc. or being finally dropped altogether.'[1] He uses Cicero as support for his thesis. Cicero had mentioned that there was a tendency to drop the final -*s* (in Latin words), and this is borne out by numerous inscriptions. Jespersen suggested reasons why this practice did not prevail: 'take a page of Latin prose and try the effect of striking out all the final s's, and you will find that it will be extremely difficult to determine the meaning of many passages'.

Invisible structure

In his study and systematisation of Hopi (an American Indian language related to Aztec) the American amateur linguist-anthropologist Benjamin Lee Whorf stumbled upon a means of distinguishing between those languages which have but little or no 'grammar' (e.g. English, Chinese) and those which obviously have (e.g. Sanskrit, Arabic). His discovery, adumbrated over a century earlier by Fabre d'Olivet, a French Romantic 'philosopher' to whom he claims to have been greatly indebted, was that apparently non-grammatical languages do possess covert or hidden categories of a no less systematic kind. Whorf termed the latter *cryptotypes*. A difficult concept, described as 'a submerged, subtle and elusive meaning corresponding to no actual word, yet shown by linguistic analysis to be functionally important in grammar.'[2]

Whorf decided to apply his theory to his own language—English. Here were inconsistencies at every turn, often complacently ignored. One of the most obvious was gender classification. It had long been laid down that English possessed two genders: 'common' and 'neuter', and yet there were three perfectly healthy and thriving personal pronouns, *he*, *she* and *it*. Moreover,

---

[1] Jespersen, O., *Language: Its Nature, Development and Origin* (London, 1922), pp. 361–2.
[2] Whorf, B. L., *Language, Thought and Reality* (Camb., Mass., 1956), p. 70.

the first two of these pronouns were not confined to persons. The following is Whorf's classification:

Most biological classes . . . *it*
Larger animals . . . *he*
Dogs, eagles and turkeys . . . *he* (usually)
Cats and wrens . . . *she* (usually)
Countries and states as fictive persons (but not as localities) . . . *she*
Cities, societies and corporations . . . *it*
Ghosts . . . *it*
Nature . . . *she*
Watercraft with sail or power . . . *she*
Unnamed small craft . . . *it*.

The classification is real enough and entirely *linguistic*. Whorf was at pains to assert the latter, being convinced that psychology was posterior to language. Equally interesting is his theory's relevance to morphemic functions such as prefixes. One of the most fascinating was the harmless prefix *un-*. Most people have the impression that *un-* is simply a negative prefix, and pursue the matter no further. Whorf showed that *un-* was by no means so simple as that. With transitive verbs this prefix was restricted to those verbs which possessed a *covering, enclosing* and *surface-attaching* meaning. In such cases, *un-* simply denotes the opposite, e.g. *uncoil, uncover, undress, unfasten, unfold, unlock, unroll*, but NOT *unbreak, undry, unhang, unmelt*. The exceptions were not important, in that they were semi-archaic, e.g. *unsay, unthink, unmake* (or, as Saussure would have put it, such words do not actively belong to modern English synchrony). The only viable exception appeared to be *undo*, and even this is nowadays almost solely restricted to concrete situations ('he undid his jacket') and in this case lies squarely within Whorf's categories. The difficulty was in finding a means of describing the function of *un-* with transitive verbs in a coherent manner: 'We have no single word in the language which can give us a proper clue to this meaning or into which we can compress this meaning; hence the meaning is subtle, intangible, as is typical of cryptotypic meanings. In the case of a hypothetical form *flimmick*, one could predict that if it includes such meanings as 'tie a can to' then one could say 'he *un*-flimmicked the dog'; if *flimmick* on the other hand means 'assemble', then one could *not* say 'he unflimmicked the radio parts'.

Here is Whorf's view of the structure of English. 'English is indeed almost in a class by itself as regards prosodic complexity, being one of the most complex languages on earth in this respect; on the whole it is as complicated as most polysynthetic languages of America, which fact most of us are blissfully unaware of. The complex structure of English is largely covert, which makes it all the harder to analyse. Foreigners learning English have to absorb it unconsciously—a process requiring years—by dint of constant exposure to bombardment by spoken English in large chunks; there exists at this moment no grammar that can teach it. . . It may turn out that the simpler a language becomes overtly, the more it becomes dependent upon cryptotypes and other covert formations, the more it conceals unconscious presuppositions.'[1]

Surface structure and deep structure

The covert or invisible structure of language has not gone unheeded by a more recent generation of American linguists—even if their approach has been very different from that of Whorf. I am referring to the 'Transformational' or 'Generative Grammarians', who have convincingly brought to light an intricate structure of abstract 'rules' which underlie the sometimes deceptively uncomplicated surface of language.

I shall not attempt in the space available to provide more than an outline sketch of the generative approach, and even then I shall confine myself to the more rudimentary features of the syntactical aspect.

The 'syntactic component' of generative grammar has to do with *sentences* and 'specifies an infinite set of abstract formal objects, each of which incorporates all information relevant to a single interpretation of a particular sentence'.[2] The 'base' of this syntactic component is a system of rules which 'generates' deep

[1] Whorf, B. L., *op. cit.*, p. 82.
[2] Chomsky, N., *Aspects of the Theory of Syntax* (Cambridge, Mass., 1965), p. 16.

structures, represented by a phrase marker. These rules, known as *rewriting rules*, are in the form of a series of 'inputs' and 'outputs' (input → output), and they are applied in a predetermined sequence. (The arrow means: 'rewrite as . . .'.)

Here is a set of rewriting rules:

$$S \rightarrow NP \frown Aux \frown VP$$

$$VP \rightarrow V \frown NP$$

$$NP \rightarrow (Det) \; N$$

$$Det \rightarrow the$$

$$Aux \rightarrow M$$

Applying each rule in turn we can derive a set of 'strings', which lie at the base of a considerable number of possible sentences. (Symbol S represents the sentence; NP and VP the noun and verb phrases respectively; N a noun and V a verb; Aux in this case is represented by an auxiliary verb M.) Our derived progression is as follows:

$$S \rightarrow NP \frown Aux \frown VP$$

$$S \rightarrow (Det \frown N) \frown Aux \frown VP$$

$$S \rightarrow Det \frown N \frown Aux \frown (V \frown NP)$$

$$S \rightarrow Det \frown N \frown Aux \frown V \frown (Det \frown N)$$

$$S \rightarrow Det \frown N \frown M \frown V \frown Det \frown N$$

$$S \rightarrow the \frown N \frown M \frown V \frown the \frown N$$

The last (terminal) string allows for the formation of such sentences as:

The cow can see the moon.

The boy may catch the fish.

The driver will drive the bus.

It can be represented in the form of a tree diagram as a rudimentary phrase marker:

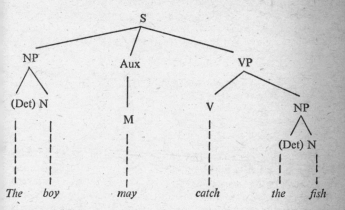

Although the range of sentences supplied by this phrase marker is fairly large, it could not account for the great variety of types of sentence we use. Generative grammar began in a modest way with descriptions such as the ones just given, but it has been in more or less 'permanent revolution' ever since. Its procedures have been more than once radically revised or rejected, and all the time new refinements have been added. Chomsky's *Aspects of the Theory of Syntax*, published in the mid-1960s, does not hesitate to trace the progress of generative grammar since it first started. A set of rules, for example, was needed for deleting particular forms, for allowing for the different categories of noun and verb, for enabling the lexicon to mesh with the syntactic rules, and for taking into account the fact that some forms and structures are sensitive to context.

If we take, for instance, the various classes of noun in English, we can find proper and common nouns, nouns standing for animate beings and inanimate things; we find mass and abstract nouns as opposed to count (or countable) nouns. A set of rules that will permit a sequence of choices between these various categories is therefore necessary. Using a plus sign to indicate the presence and a minus sign to indicate the absence of a particular category, it is possible to draw up a further set of rules, thus:

$$N \rightarrow [\pm \text{Common}]$$
$$[+ \text{Common}] \rightarrow [\pm \text{count}]$$
$$[+ \text{count}] \rightarrow [\pm \text{animate}]$$
$$[+ \text{animate}] \rightarrow [\pm \text{human}]$$
$$[- \text{count}] \rightarrow [\pm \text{abstract}]$$

The first rule indicates that nouns may be common or not. If it is a common noun, there exists a choice between it being a count or a mass noun. If it is a count noun, it must be either animate or inanimate. And so on. By adding this extra set of rules, we can obtain a more adequate phrase marker:

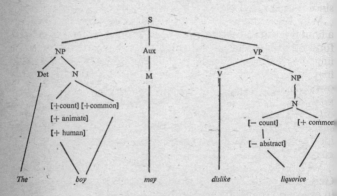

In addition to the base component, there is a very important *transformational* component. It is this component that is responsible for 'mapping' the deep structures into surface structures. Transformational rules take care of such structures as the passive voice, various types of clause, negatives, etc. Theory of transformational rules has been changing so extensively that any attempt to sketch it would probably be out of date before this book appeared in print.

It has been stressed more than once by Chomsky and others that a generative grammar is not a model for the actual construc tion of a sentence by a speaker; 'it can be regarded only as a characterisation of the intrinsic tacit knowledge or competence that underlies actual performance'.

Grammatical categories

The concept of tense

Of all grammatical concepts, that of *tense* is one of the most obscure.

Where 'aspect' is the only verbal pattern of a language, the problem is perhaps smaller than when the situation lies somewhere between. Semitic, for instance, has no means of distinguishing different tenses. It has instead a great variety of ways of translating verbal relatives, e.g. causative, intensive, desiderative, jussive, reciprocal, reflexive. The Arabic imperfect is by no means a tense since it can express the future as well as the present.

With Russian and the other Slav languages, there is more than a faint trace of correlation with tense. There is, in fact, a preterite form of both aspects, and in Russian a composite future in the imperfective aspect. Comparative linguists have sometimes made inappropriate analyses in the case of Indo-European languages owing to the dogged persistence of the concept of tense. Vendryes pointed out how impossible it is to understand the verbal system of Sanskrit or Ancient Greek 'if we do not take these different shades of signification into account, or if we start out with the idea of finding different tenses expressed as they are in our language [French]'.

Where the concept of tense is relevant, as in Romance and Germanic, reclassification and redefinition is sometimes required in order to exorcise the troubled ghost of Latin.

As soon as any attempt is made to reduce tense to what it is supposed to represent, the solid matter dissolves into a sea of perplexities. Even the cut-and-dried Latin tenses are not what they seemed. Of all the tenses the 'future' is the most mysterious, allowing room for a hundred different feelings of expectation, desire, fear and hope. An innocuous statement of the kind *I will do that tomorrow* not only affirms the eventual accomplishment of the action but also conveys a subjective connotation of all manner of shades of meaning, e.g. 'I desire', 'I agree that', 'I am afraid that', 'I intend' and so forth. The logical positivists were inclined to reject the suggestion that the modal auxiliaries and tenses have anything 'occult' about them. Wittgenstein admitted that words have proper jobs to do but that really it is all a matter of 'grammar'. Not only this, languages just do not match up to each other in their *use* of a particular tense. The perfect tense, for instance, can indeed be defined as a retrospective variety of the present, an indication of a present state arising out of past events. Compare: (perfect) *France has had many governments* (implies: 'goes on having'), (preterite) *Rome had many emperors* (= 'now no longer has'). This distinction is true for English but not for French, which uses the perfect as a preterite.

Jespersen has illustrated the purely grammatical difficulty of analysis and description of 'tense'. He proposes breaking it down under three headings: (i) form, (ii) function, (iii) notion. Take as an example the English *function* 'preterite':

Form	Function	Notion
-ed [əd] (*hand*ed) -d [d] (*show*ed) [t] (*fix*ed) -t with root change (*left*) unchanged root (*put*) inner change (*drank*) different word (*was*)	preterite	(1) Past time (2) Unreality in present time (*I wish we* knew) (3) Future time (*It is time you* went *to bed*) (4) All times (*Men* were *deceivers ever*)

One could become reconciled with such complexity were it the same for all languages. But unfortunately no two languages would present the same analysis, except by sheer coincidence. Jespersen described grammatical categories as 'at best symptoms, foreshadowings of natural categories'.

Gender, number and case

These are familiar concepts to anyone who has strayed outside English. Again Latin presents an impressive regularity, with a few exceptions such as *nauta*, a noun of feminine gender but in fact 'a sailor'. The case system is almost perfect, and with the help of a few rules complete mastery can be gained. In German the ground is less certain; one meets oddities more frequently: why, for instance, *das Kind, das Mädchen, das Weib*—neuter gender for animate and even feminine persons? That is only the beginning: for a series of apparently quite arbitrary exceptions; peculiar plurals, exceptions, tier after tier, that have (old style!) to be memorised. Odd uses of cases; why should some prepositions favour the dative, whilst others equally capriciously take the genitive or accusative? If we venture as far as Slavonic (e.g. Russian) we lose all sense of order and begin to suspect that assignment of gender, number and the use of cases is entirely arbitrary and nonsensical.

Linguists and comparatists have long since abandoned any hope of establishing correspondence and regard these concepts as purely grammatical concepts which, like everything else in grammar, are largely the product of analogy. It is only when we have Indo-European (and Semitic) that we find, for example, that the vast majority of languages have no separate forms for 'he' and 'she'. But is it not sometimes a nuisance to have such a distinction? In writing a book such as this I constantly find myself putting: 'if the student . . . he (ought I to put *she*?) will . . .' and then have to use the plural 'students' so that the sexless 'they' and 'their' can get round this difficulty. The poet Coleridge long since regretted the lack of a pronoun of common gender. Those who have used languages with no sex distinction confirm how convenient is!

Some languages make a rough distinction between animate and inanimate, although the dividing line in no way corresponds to ours. Many languages are interested neither in sex nor in the distinction animate/inanimate. Dravidian languages distinguish caste; Japanese, various forms of politeness according to rank. The Masai language of East Africa has one gender for everything big and strong, and another for everything small and weak.

One would expect greater correlation in the use of *number* (plurals and singulars). But nothing of the kind. Russian, an otherwise highly developed language, counts from one to twenty, and then starts again at twenty-one. Twenty-one takes a *singular* noun! The same with thirty-one and all other numbers, with the last element as unity, up to a million and one and beyond. It takes the student bred on Latin some time to recover from the impact of the Russian use of numerals, of which this is only one peculiarity. We do not have to look even as far as Russian for such peculiarities. What of *big fish*, *two fishes*, *fish and chips*? Why *trousers* when

French has *le pantalon* (singular)? Why *a pair of scissors* when we cannot say 'one scissor'? Hungarian says 'my eye is weak' for 'my eyes are weak' (*szemem gyenge*). If singularity is demanded, the Hungarian has to say 'half an eye' (*fél szemmel*).

The use of cases is really too varied to consider. The only thing that one can say, as far as Indo-European is concerned, is that there is a distinct 'dative' or 'indirect object' which is fairly consistent from language to language. An 'instrumental' case survives in some languages, although its use extends beyond instrumentality. Expressions of time, though not regularly, are associated with the accusative case. 'Motion to' is frequently indicated by the accusative case, whereas 'being at a place' is expressed by a locative case or, if there is no locative, by an oblique case other than the genitive. The genitive is used to denote possession.

Case is an obsolescent survival, in many languages sometimes serving as redundancy (e.g. the Russian 'locative' ending is always accompanied by a preposition). The accusative case can be dispensed with when word order is fixed, as in English, French and a number of other European languages. Datives and instrumentals are unnecessary luxuries, the sense of which can be indicated by prepositions (again as in English, French, etc.): *to him, à lui*; *by air, par avion*.

The genitive survives in English (*the boy's book, the boys' books*) but with an acquired and quite incredible versatility. From the sixteenth century and even earlier, the genitive *-s* uprooted itself and became 'mobile', as in *The Duke of Bedford's place* (earlier *The Duke's place of Bedford*). Nowadays, we can get away with *the writer of the book's sense of drama* or *the chief witness for the prosecution's testimony*. Jespersen compares this mobile *s* with the Finno-Ugrian agglutinating languages. The practice, however, has its limits, a fact brought home to me by a story I once heard (attributed to Sir Thomas Beecham). The distinguished wit on this occasion was said to be alone in a non-smoker railway compartment (before nationalisation presumably) when a lady entered and promptly produced a cigarette. Diffidently she asked if he minded her smoking. 'Madam, if you smoke that cigarette, I shall be sick.' (Indignation on part of lady.) 'Sir, do you realise who I am? I am one of the directors' wives!' 'Madam, I do not care if you are the director's *only* wife!'

Word classes

Nouns and adjectives are sometimes difficult to distinguish between. The grammarians had long since decided that the former stood for particular *substances* (hence, 'substantive'), the latter for *qualities* attributed to the substance. In practice, however, adjectives, better called 'modifiers', can often only be distinguished by their location. Thus *yellow* can be a noun or adjective depending on its location. First, *yellow* cannot be a noun if it stands immediately before another noun (and not separated from it by a comma), e.g. *The yellow frock*; also if *yellow* follows an intransitive verb without the intervention of an article (definite or indefinite), e.g. *This frock looks yellow* but not *I like yellow*. In the latter sentence *yellow* is by location (i.e. after a transitive verb) a noun. This, however, is not an infallible rule and has to be further modified; for example, *yellow* in *He paints in yellow* according to an earlier definition would be an adjective, but it is in fact a noun, since prepositions govern nouns. It will be noticed, however, that the distinction is now less clear; one has to think whether the *yellow* in *He paints in yellow* is, in fact, adjectival. In some languages it is not always possible to tell one from the other unless one has a context. In the phrases *un savant aveugle, un aveugle savant*, both could mean either 'a blind scholar' or 'a learned blindman', owing to the fact that (i) *aveugle* and *savant* are adjectival nouns, or nouns from adjectives without any change of form, and (ii) the position of the adjective in French, can either precede or follow a noun according to considerations of style.

The fact remains nevertheless that in the older European languages nouns and adjectives have always had separate paradigms. Even in modern English a noun has plural and genitive -*s* inflexion, but the adjective has no inflexion whatsoever, e.g. *red houses, the tall tree's roots*.

Again, there is no doubt that Indo-European languages have made a morphological distinction between nouns and verbs. Grammarians were quick to assume there was a fundamental difference. English preserves rudimentary traces of the distinction, e.g. *This paper* yellows *at the edges*. In non-Indo-European languages, however, the distinction cannot be maintained and is sometimes irrelevant. In Semitic there is a striking parallel between the three noun cases and the three moods of the imperfective verb. In the Finno-Ugrian 'agglutinating' languages no distinction is made. *Antaa* in Finnish means 'he gives', not the verbal noun 'giving'. In Hungarian the suffix *-ak* serves the purpose of forming noun and verb plurals: *vart-ak* 'they have waited', *hars-ak* 'linden trees'.

In Chinese it is a principle of grammar that there should be *no difference* between nouns and verbs. The Chinese traditional grammarian differentiates only 'living' from 'dead' words (our nouns and adjectives are 'dead' words). Word position alone determines the function of a particular word.

In many ways English is the Western counterpart of Chinese, since morphological function depends very much on word order and scarcely at all on inflexion. There are many words in English that can be used indifferently as noun, verb and adjective. In *He fired the house* and *The wood fired easily* there is no change of inflexion, and yet the one is active the other passive in meaning. The same word *fire* can be used without any inflection in various functions, word order alone indicating the latter:

Put the wood on the fire.
I fire *the wood.*
Fire *the* firewood.
So easy to fire *an open* fire.

English shows no hesitation in using such forms. It seems fairly certain that word order has to become rigid before the *morphological* distortion between noun, verb and adjective can be dispensed with.

12 Grammatical Structure in Evolution

In the last chapter we saw that pitfalls in plenty await the linguist in any analysis of (synchronic) grammatical structure. The traditional categories and methods were found wanting. And yet an end to their current reappraisal is nowhere in sight. Now it is time to turn to the diachronic facets of grammar. In exploring these we shall find that, although in various ways the traditional modes of systematisation are sometimes giving way to ones influenced by trends in modern linguistics, they nevertheless retain a certain validity of their own.

Rather than serve up the usual grammatical classifications, abundantly and admirably presented in the standard works of comparative grammar, I shall confine myself to a treatment of those aspects which will enable readers to consult such works as these with a more lively interest and greater circumspection. Nevertheless, in order that readers should not be completely at a loss when confronted with the morphological sections of the comparative grammars in question, miscellaneous points of guidance will be given in Chapter 13.

Grammatical structure and phonological evolution

Morphemes depend for their physical existence on phonetic combinations of speech sounds. It is no wonder, then, that phonology is of more than marginal significance in bringing about structural re-formations within a language and in determining to some extent the overall structure. Two given words may be morphologically and lexically related; but if phonetic change operates on these words in different directions, the 'grammatical bonds' will sooner or later be broken. The two words will become alien to each other and join up with other classes. English *bitter*, for example, has long since broken its historical connection with the verb *to bite*. French *maison* 'house' is no longer felt to be related to *ménage* 'house keeping', although in Latin the words were morphemically conjoined (Lat. *mansio* and *mansionaticus* respectively).

Sometimes this phonetic change is assimilative in character, producing havoc among even the most harmonious morphemic classes. Latin *berbicarius* 'shepherd' is morphologically one with

berbix 'ewe'. The latter subsequently underwent metathesis of
r- and *e-*phonemes, becoming *brebix* (Mod. Fr. *brébis*). This word
now bears no resemblance to the otherwise parallel form *berger*
from *berbicarius*. The separation in the popular mind means that
they are apart for all time; in local dialects *berger* has succeeded in
taking on the meaning 'herder of oxen'.

The structure of words can be so effaced and eroded by
phonological evolution that the very morphological elements that
helped originally to bring the words into existence become unanalysable and unrecognisable. *Amicus* 'friend' in Latin produced
its own opposite *inimicus* 'not-friend' by the simple device of
employing the negative morpheme *in-*. The Modern French form
ennemi, derived from the latter, now seems totally remote from
ami, except to etymologists.

The easiest victims of this kind of phonetic effacement have
been the grammatical or flexional endings. The loss of dual
number, reduction of cases, confusion of moods, aspects and
genders in Modern Indo-European languages are to be ascribed
in part to it.

Analogy

It is easy to see that, if phonetic wear-and-tear of the sort just
described had been allowed unbridled operation, all language
would long since have disintegrated into a scrap heap of random
fragments. It just happens that this destructive effect is counter-
balanced and even offset by what linguists have called *analogy*.
'To analogy are due all normal, non-phonetic modifications of the
external side of words.' Thus Saussure describes the process.[1]
'Normal' is the key word; there is an implication that *analogy* is
somehow within the limits of human control, whereas phonetic
change (abnormal?) is not.

Analogy operates upon *models* and by *imitation of models*. It
operates in almost the same way as children behave in learning
their mother tongue. The 'instructive' mistakes one is bound to
make in the process of acquiring any language are the very
elements of analogy. One makes such mistakes all the time,
occasionally finds them great fun, but is usually corrected by
parent, teacher or otherwise. Teachers can find students' 'ana-

[1] Saussure, F. de, *op. cit.*, p. 161.

logical' mistakes among the most intriguing sides of language teaching. The difference in the case of language as a whole is that analogical mutations are seldom corrected, and are usually perpetuated.

First, children. Their analogical mistakes are so well known as to be hardly worth mentioning. Analogical verbal paradigms: *I drunked my milk, Grandad comed today, He gived it me* (all strong verbs remodelled on the weak paradigms). Noun paradigms: *tooth* for *teeth, sheeps* for *sheep, gooses* for *geese* (remodelled on the prevailing non-umlauted *s*-plural).

Sturtevant[1] came right to the heart of the matter when he explained this type of analogical re-formation as the direct result of our *learning* words in patterned situations. It is probably untrue that we *learn* weak or strong verbal paradigms, for instance; the only certain fact is that we hear, learn and speak sentences containing *he walked, they talked, she ran,* etc., with relentless frequency. 'We speak and hear vastly more different sentences than different words.'[1] Sturtevant has used this as an argument for leaning more heavily upon syntactical than morphological analogy. From very early childhood we amass a formidable stock of simple sentences: e.g. *What time is it?, I must hurry, Please hurry!, Please pass the marmalade.* On such models are formed: *What time was it?, You must hurry, He mustn't hurry, Please pass the* arsenic, and so on. Larger sentences can be regarded as developments of this, for the various parts of which other parts can be substituted. A simple sentence: *He loaned me his book* consists of five replaceable units: *he* may be replaced by *the man who frequently brings us to town, loaned* might become *recently offered to lend, me* be replaced by *his elderly neighbour* and so forth, until one possesses what looks at first glance a more highly sophisticated statement: *The man who frequently brings us to town [recently offered to lend] his elderly neighbour an interesting and well-known book written about a certain sect.*

It is often easier for a foreigner to create or perpetrate analogical mutations than a native speaker, who, unless somewhat of a poet, wit or punster, will find it difficult to abandon temporarily his own rigidly 'received' patterns. Occasionally, such bastardisations are not deliberate. A German acquaintance of mine had

[1] Sturtevant, E. H., *An Introduction to Linguistic Science* (New Haven, Conn., 1947).

apparently for a long time been using 'writative' (analogy with 'talkative'). The word has been used in English but only in rare cases; he, on the contrary, had taken his own analogical creation to be an ordinary, everyday word.

It is not only foreigners who create deliberate and often diverting analogical formations. A past master at hybrid analogy, for instance, was James Thurber. For him it was a superb game—called 'Ghosts', or as he preferred to call it 'Superghosts'. Given a group of letters in unlikely combination one is supposed to find as many words or compound words as possible containing them. The following are among Thurber's 'super'-analogical hybrids from the cluster *sgra*: *kissgranny*—'a man who seeks the company of older women, especially older women with money . . .'; *blessgravy* 'a minister or cleric; the head of a family; one who says grace'. Not to be confused with *praisegravy*, 'one who extols a woman's cooking, especially the cooking of a friend's wife . . .'; *cussgravy* 'a husband who complains of his wife's cooking . . .'; *dressgrader* 'a woman who stares another woman up and down, a starefrock'; *bassgrave* '(1) cold-eyed unemotional, stolid, troutsolemn; (2) the grave of a bass, obs.'; *blissgrave* 'aged by marriage. Also sometimes, discouraged by wedlock . . .'

To return to the more sober mechanics of everyday analogy. The process can be represented by a simple mathematical equation. Latin, for example, remodelled *honos—honorem* to *honor—honorem* on the model: *amor—amorem; orator—oratorem*. This may be expressed as:

$$oratorem : orator :: honorem : x$$
$$x = honor$$

Generations of schoolchildren, willing and unwilling, have learned that the present tense of the French 'irregular' verb *ouvrir* 'to open' is: *j'ouvre, tu ouvres, il ouvre*, etc. No one had informed them that this irregularity arose because other perfectly 'regular' verbs like *entrer, rentrer, rencontrer* were similarly conjugated (e.g. *j'entre, tu entres, il entre*). The only irregular thing about *ouvrir* in the present tense is the infinitive form itself. How much more fun it is when French verbs are taught not as paradigms but as they are actually used in practice, and to discuss the rules and 'irregularities' retrospectively when the game has been enjoyed and is over with.

'Irregularity' is no more then than a hangover from the age of grammarians when 'analogy' meant 'false analogy'. The earlier philologists had fallen into a trap of their own making, since they had envisaged every deviation from the norm as a distortion of some ideal harmony, whereas in fact they were discounting the vital process of language evolution. *Honor* is no mere de-formation of *honos* but a synchronic rival which ousted it. Saussure argues convincingly that *honos* could have had no part in the production of this rival (*honor*). The two were never related. If they had been, the change would have been resisted. The crucial point is that *honor* is an innovation, not a transformation. 'Whenever we can follow the course of linguistic events, we see that analogical innovation and the elimination of the older form are distinct things, and that nowhere do we come upon a transformation.'[1]

Most of the analogical process is completed *before* the new or innovated form appears. New creations such as *unflappable* are already potentially present in syntagms like: *un-daunted*, *un-moved*, *un-impressible*, *un-scathed*, *imperturb-able*, *immov-able*, etc. 'The final step of realising it in speaking is a small matter in comparison with the build-up of forces that makes it possible . . . That is why I say that analogy is entirely grammatical and synchronic.'

This goes some way towards accounting for the persistence of apparently illogical forms in spite of the bridling restraint of universal literacy. Recent examples are *advance* (the noun), which some speakers insist on replacing by *advancement* (which, of course, means something quite different). And yet the onslaught of *advancement* against *advance* is considerable, and it seems probable that the English language will lose still another useful word, displaced by a vulgar misusage. The forces behind such an almost inevitable change are not hard to find. There are too many comparable syntagms, e.g. *enhancement*, *improvement*, *movement*, and coupled with this the realisation (unconscious) that the corresponding verb forms, *improve*, *move*, *enhance*, have become exclusively verbal syntagms, hence ruling out *advance* as a noun altogether. Even more odd is the attempt to unseat *uninterested* and to replace it by *disinterested*. Perhaps there exists a feeling among speakers of English that not only does *disinterested* sound better but also the occurrence of both *un-* and *in-* (*un-in-terested*)

[1] Saussure, F. de, *op. cit.*, p. 166.

at the beginning of *uninterested* seems unsatisfactory in that both prefixes are rather similar and are used as negatives (e.g. *infallible*, *unbending*, etc.). Although the linguist knows perfectly well that the *in-* of *interested* is not a prefix at all, this does prevent the ordinary speaker from (analogically) feeling that it *is* a prefix and that it gets in the way of *un-* but not of *dis-*.

Analogy, as we saw earlier, is the counterpoise to the phonetic destruction of language. Yet it is fortunate that language digests only a very small proportion of analogical perpetrations. It is almost as if there exists an ecological balance between the two processes: phonetic change and analogical creation. The latter keep their own species within manageable limits. 'Each time a new formation becomes definitely installed and eliminates its rival, something is actually created and something else abandoned, with the result that analogy occupies a preponderant place in the theory of evolution.'[1]

Obsolescent forms are constantly yielding ground to remodellings. The French word *somnolent* 'sleepy' is now popularly analysed as *somnol-ent* and is generally felt to belong to the present participles (e.g. *pouvant, devenant, mourant*, etc.). This is borne out by the existence of a verb *somnol-er* 'to sleep' in colloquial speech. The Latin analysis nevertheless was *somno-lentus*, like *succu-lentus* etc. In even earlier times the word had been analysed as *somnolentus* 'smelling of sleep' and had been associated with *olere*, as in *vinolentus* 'smelling of wine'. The very same word (diachronically) has therefore passed through three distinct synchronic stages, ending up as a present participle.

In one sense, analogy is a reshuffling of the elements within a language. Saussure believed that these 'reshufflings' were more important than sound change in the evolution of language. In the enormous mass of analogical phenomena built up over the centuries, nearly every element is preserved in some shape or form; the only difference lies in the *distribution*. Analogical innovations are perhaps more apparent than real. 'Language is a garment covered with patches cut from its own cloth . . . The vast majority of words are, in one way or another, new combinations of phonetic elements torn from older forms.'

In more recent times, the application of synchronic linguistic principles has led to the discovery of certain patterns or tendencies

[1] Saussure, F. de, *op. cit.*, p. 169.

in analogical development. One such discovery has been that an affix associated with a particular word form becomes extended to all words that function in a similar manner. *Slow* was not originally compounded with the affix *-ly* when used as an adverb; even in present-day English it is sometimes used without, as in *go slow*. *Slow*, when used adverbially, was remodelled as *slowly* by analogy with *wrong*—*wrongly*, *gay*—*gaily*, *hasty*—*hastily*, etc. Where this kind of remodelling has taken place, the overall function of the word set is not always so clear. Take the case of the suffix *-ette*. This affix, which distinguished *cigarette* from *cigar*, *suffragette* from *suffrage* and *pipette* from *pipe*, and which also appeared in words borrowed from French like *serviette*, *vignette*, *brunette*, became the model for more recent forms such as *usherette* and *launderette*. Although the function of this set has obviously something to do with diminutiveness and femininity, it is the speakers themselves who, in producing such analogical remodellings, are unconsciously aware of their common function. Another interesting pattern highlighted is the tendency for replaced forms to take on a subsidiary function. Compare the specialised and restricted use of *brethren* with that of *brothers*; *elder* with *older*; *tide* (as in *Eastertide*) with *time*; or *thrice* with *three times*.

If the historical linguist does succeed in finding a complete set of rules for analogical development, and is able to explain exceptional cases by further rules, it goes without saying that the comparatist will find himself with a powerful tool for linguistic reconstruction.

Agglutination

Syntactic remodelling extends beyond the sphere of analogy proper. Although related to analogy, *agglutination* arises for quite different reasons and under quite other conditions. It consists of the welding together of two or more terms constantly occurring as a syntagmatic group into a single unit, which becomes either difficult or impossible to analyse thereafter.

Agglutination takes various forms. In French, welding becomes complete fusion. Latin *hanc horam* 'at this hour' is the French adverbial unit *encore*; Old French *tous jours* becomes *toujours*; and *dès jà* ('since now') *déjà* ('already'). In English, on the other hand, apart from rare combinations such as *goodbye* from *God be with you*, *walnut* from *Wales nut*, *window* from *wind-eye* (O.N. *vindauga*), the units making up the agglutinated forms retain their identity. Words like *blackbird* and *beefeater*[1] are a different kettle of fish; they retain their units, but their ultimate meaning is not fully deducible from these units. *Blackbird* is no longer any bird that happens to be black, but the name of a particular species. It is not nonsense to speak of an 'off-black blackbird', provided that such exists. Likewise, one may with impunity refer to a *vegetarian beefeater* (for undoubtedly such there have been). In a later section we shall see that French and English compound nouns belong to quite distinct semantic classes.

Saussure preferred to distinguish between *compound* words and truly *synthesised* or agglutinated combinations. The former strictly belong to the broader classification of analogical remodelling. The striking feature of agglutinative combinations is their uniqueness. The Latin form *possum* ('I can'), for example, has no precedent either in that language or elsewhere; it is a synthesised form of *potis sum* 'I am the master'. Likewise, the Romance future tenses resulting from an agglutination of Latin *habere* ('to have') and the verbal present stem is a rare and distinctive occurrence. The syntheses produced are characteristic of Romance alone: (French) *j'aimerai* from *amare-habeo*; *je chanterai* from *cantare-habeo*, etc.

Secretion

Secretion is a term devised by Jespersen to account for the origin or morphological elements not completely explicable either by analogy or by phonological evolution. Saussure and the Neo-grammarians before him seem to have overlooked the phenomenon. Its effects are nonetheless of untold consequence.

We might begin with an example. In Middle English the forms *mine* and *thine* were used as possessive adjectives as well as pronouns, and their former function survived until quite late in quaint terminology (to us) such as *thine eyes, brother mine*. In late Middle English came a stage in which the final *n*-phoneme was dropped, but only when they preceded a noun beginning with a consonant; so that one finds: *my father* but *mine uncle, it is mine*. Eventually the practice of foreshortening was extended to all

---

Please note that *beefeater* is not an original compound but a development from O.E. *hláfæta*, meaning 'loaf-eater'.

instances, leaving *my father*, *my uncle*. Nowadays, *mine* is used exclusively as possessive pronoun (*it is mine*).

An important point is that the distinction was originally purely phonetic, just as in *an apple*, *a pear*, the *n* of *an* being dropped before a consonant. In consequence, a phonetic discrepancy became an important morphemic means of distinguishing possessive pronouns. Jespersen believed that the change to a morphologically significant *n* in this situation is radical and instinctively perceived as such in popular usage; a belief supported by the tendency in certain dialects to tack this morphemic *n* onto pronouns with which it had never had any previous association, as in *hisn, hern, yourn, theirn*. 'He that prigs what isn't *hisn*, when he's cotch'd, is sent to prison. She that prigs what isn't *hern*, at the treadmill takes a turn.'

A far more widely known example is the 'secretion' of *-en* from noun suffixes, eventually becoming available as a means of distinguishing plural from singular. Originally *oxen*—now, of course, the plural of *ox*—kept its *en* throughout both plural and singular in early Indo-European (cf. Skr. *ukṣáṇ*). *En* was of the same class of suffixes found in the Latin paradigm *homo, hom-in-em, hom-in-is*, etc. In Old English, and for that matter in the Germanic languages generally, this *n* suffix provided the so-called 'weak' declension of nouns, with the *n* featuring in all cases except the nominative singular. The suffix is especially important in modern High German (cf. declensions of *Soldat, Knabe*, etc.). The *n* became obsolete in Middle English as far as the singular paradigm was concerned, leaving the suffix in the plural only. By 'secretion' therefore it had managed to become a sign of the plural. The *n* plural was analogically extended to paradigms that had never possessed an *n* suffix, e.g. *treen, synne*. The upshot was a new way of indicating plurality by a morpheme that had never previously served such a function. A parallel development is that High German has found the same morpheme equally productive for a similar purpose. Jespersen's opinion was that all grammatical inflections that could not be traced back to a precise origin should be attributed to secretion.

Another type of 'secretion' includes those instances in which a suffix takes over a chunk of the word of which it was originally merely an adjunct. French throws up many clear instances of this. The suffix *-ier*, which was added to words such as *lait* 'milk' to give *laitier*; the division was later popularly apprehended as *lai-tier* (compare *an umpire, a numpire*). Likewise with words such as *cabaretier*, felt now to be *cabare-tier*. The newly secreted suffix *-tier* adapted itself quickly to other nouns, creating *bijou-tier* 'jeweller', *cafe-tier* 'cafe proprietor'. Rather similar was the situation in which the fruitful Germanic *-ling* suffix arose (as in *gosling, duckling, underling*); the *l* was a borrowing from a chance assortment of nouns and adjectives; (O.H.G.) *ediling* from *edili*; (O.N.) *vesling* from *vesall* 'wretched'; (O.E.) *lytling* 'little one' from *lytel*. The suffix *-ness* is part of the same story. Even in Modern English an analogous interplay of suffixes is very much alive. Suffix *-cism* (from *criticism*) has given *witticism*; *-nist* (originally *-ist*), having been associated with such clusters as *botanist, mechanist*, leads to *tobacconist*. In a few cases, hybrid suffixes of this type have acquired a semantic value of their own. The suffix *-lier*, abstracted from French *chandelier, cheva-lier*, has yielded the secreted forms *gasolier, electrolier*. In English *veget-arian* (originally divided as *vegetar-ian*) has brought into existence its congeners *fruitarian, nutarian*. In an identical manner Romance *septentr*ionalis 'northern' gave rise to its opposite *merid*ionalis 'southern'.

Syntagmatic combinations and paradigmatic contrasts

As we saw earlier, sentences of opposite meaning can in English be distinguished by word order alone. Compare *The big bad wolf caught Jack* with *Jack caught the big bad wolf*.

In Old English this was not so. Being a highly inflected language, like Modern German or Russian, Old English had no need of, nor did it possess, fixed word order. The *forms* of the nouns and adjectives were such that they indicated whether they were the subject of a sentence, the object of a verb, or performed some other function in the sentence. The object could, and often did, precede the verb; and additional elements could be interposed between a preposition and the noun (or noun phrase) it governed, since prepositions were generally linked to particular case forms. The 'endings' of adjectives and nouns in Anglo-Saxon were then distinctively marked to reduce possible ambiguity. *My good wolf* becomes *mīn gōda wulf* if *wolf* is in the nominative case (subject); *mīnne gōdan wulf* if it is in the accusative case (object); *mīnes gōdan wulfes* if it is in the genitive case; and so on.

If we take a closer look at the accusative case form *mīnne gōdan wulf*, we shall see that it is not a complete translation of *my good wolf*. Although the general meaning was the same, the signals for the speaker of Anglo-Saxon were different. *Mīnne gōdan wulf* to the Anglo-Saxon (albeit unconsciously) signified 'my good wolf' *plus* a morpheme marker telling him it was to be interpreted only as the accusative case.

In the (nominative) combination *mīn gōda wulf*, the possessive pronoun (*mīn*) follows the 'strong' declension and the interposed adjective (*gōda*) the 'weak' declension, rather as in Modern German. If we analyse each of the cases in turn, we find that each of them forms a *syntagm* consisting of the pronoun, adjective and noun. The syntagmatic link is very precise. If we change the syntagm by dropping the pronoun we get an entirely different combination, for now the adjective will follow the 'strong' and not the 'weak' declension. An analysis of the nominative plural *mīne gōdan wulfas* reveals the structure:

$$((\text{pron.} + /e/) + (\text{adj.} + /an/)) + (\text{noun} + /as/)$$

whereas the nominative *singular* is of the form:

$$((\text{pron.} + \text{zero}) + (\text{adj.} + /a(n)/)) + (\text{noun} + \text{zero})$$

We are thus dealing with a series of syntagmatically linked morphemes, a separate one for each case, whilst each combination is in paradigmatic contrast with all the other combinations:

Sing.:	Nom.	*mīn gōda wulf*
	Acc.	*mīnne gōdan wulf*
	Gen.	*mīnes gōdan wulfes*
	Dat.	*mīnum gōdan wulfe*
Pl.:	Nom.	*mīne gōdan wulfas*
	Acc.	*mīne gōdan wulfas*
	Gen.	*mīnra gōdena wulfa*
	Dat.	*mīnum gōdum wulfum*

Let us consider this system of cases from the point of view of the information theorist. The latter will take the view that the flow of information is best when the 'bits' or units of information are kept to a minimum. Morse code, using only dots and dashes, is one of the most economical of systems. Although declension systems seldom achieve this simplicity, they rarely make use of more than a handful of features. A comparison with semaphore would be nearer. Declensions make use of a small number of phonemes (including 'zero') and morphemic combinations thereof, with one or two 'loud' signals to help out (something like an S.O.S. in morse). The Old English 'masculine' declension uses only five phonemes, together with 'zero', and one loud signal—the *-um* of the dative, which is the odd-man-out and therefore attracts attention to itself merely by its presence. The feminine declension reduces the number of phonemes to four.

The next thing to consider is that the declensional endings constitute different degrees of signal strength. This difference can be achieved in various ways: (i) by varying the phonemic structure of the affixes; (ii) by reiterating an affix or a phonemic feature of it; (iii) by introducing a 'loud' feature as affix; or (iv) by a combination of these. From these criteria we can see that the most clearly signalled cases are the dative plural, which uses a loud feature *and* reiterates it, and genitive plural, which has three distinct affixes *and* reiterates the terminal *-a*.[1] But signal strengths are relative things. For instance, neither the nominative nor the accusative singular stands out when compared with the genitive and dative plurals. But if we compare the nominative and accusative singulars we will probably be right in regarding the nominative as more clearly signalled than the accusative, because it reiterates 'zero' as two of its endings and reduces the adjectival ending to *-a*. The genitive and dative singulars are probably about the same in strength, the former reiterating *-es* and the latter using the dative 'loud' signal once. The marking suggests that the oblique cases (genitive and dative) are in *contrast* with the other cases, because of their relatively distinctive signals. The nominative and accusative plurals are identical in form, but as a combined pair they contrast separately with the nominative and the accusative

---

[1] The genitive plural is the most differentiated of all. Anglo-Saxon shares this feature with other Indo-European languages. Compare, for instance, the clearly marked genitive plurals in Latin *naut-arum* ('of the sailors'), *domin-orum* ('of the lords') and *rerum* ('of the things'). Compare also the stem modifications in the Russian genitive plural: *sestr-a*, *sestr-u*, *sestr-y*, but (gen. pl.) *sestyor* ('sister').

singulars. The following diagram is an attempt to represent the
signal contrasts between the various cases:

$$
\begin{array}{ll}
\left\{\begin{array}{l}\uparrow\text{Nom. sing.} \\ \downarrow\text{Acc. sing.}\end{array}\right\} & \longleftrightarrow\ \text{Nom./acc. pl.} \\
\left\{\begin{array}{l}\uparrow\text{Gen. sing.}\ \uparrow \\ \downarrow\text{Dat. sing.}\ \downarrow\end{array}\right. & \longleftrightarrow\ \left.\begin{array}{l}\uparrow\text{Gen. pl.} \\ \downarrow\text{Dat. pl.}\end{array}\right\}
\end{array}
$$

As word order in English became more rigid, the need to make
paradigmatic contrasts across the entire combination (syntagm),
as well as the need to have distinctively signalled syntagmetic
morphemes, was substantially reduced. This is the situation we
find in Middle English, and the process had occurred presumably
during the period of the Norse invasions, and in the period following the Norman Conquest. The declension of 'my good wolf' in
Middle English would be as follows:

Sing.:	Nom./acc.	*min gode wolf*
	Gen.	*min gode wolfes*
	Dat.	*min gode wolfe*
All plurals:		*mine gode wolfes*

Note that all differentiation between case forms in the plural has
disappeared but that the distinction between singular and plural
is still maintained throughout. The distinction between nominative and accusative has disappeared, providing good evidence
that the distinction had been made redundant by fixed word
order. Only the genitive and dative singulars are distinctively
marked.

The problem of which came first, word order or the weakening
of inflexions, is yet another version of the dilemma of the chicken
and the egg. But whichever of these processes did actually come
first, it is evident that a speaker or writer during the Middle
English period would have had to pay more than a little attention
to his word order (and possibly was helped in this by his knowledge of French, which had already developed a fairly rigid word
order); otherwise there would be rather too many occasions on
which ambiguity could arise.

It would be incorrect to regard Modern English as yet a

further development of a process well under way in Middle English. *My good wolf* in Modern English is not at all the kind of syntagm it was (although ceasing to be) in Middle English. *My*, *good* and *wolf* function without any real syntagmatic regard for each other's presence. The apostrophe *s* is not a genitive at all but a synchronic feature of Modern English. The quandary of *the director's wives* and *the directors' wives* is, when all is said and done, a modern creation, and one that Chaucer might have had little sympathy with.

The tendency has been for all the languages of Western Europe to develop fixed word order. This happened quite early in the case of the Romance languages and English. But even German, with a fully-fledged system of inflexions, has developed quite definite rules for prescribing word order.

A definite order of words does not rule out the kind of syntagmatic combinations we have examined in Old English. It may even be advantageous, from the point of view of information theory, to have both a fixed word order and declensional morphemes. A language like this (e.g. German) will contain a high level of redundancy and should thus be easier to use. It may breed a certain amount of sloppiness, especially among foreign speakers of the language, but communication is more easily achieved.

I bring this discussion to a close with an example from a language—one of the Bantu languages—that combines regular word order with a morphemic pattern of distribution affecting the entire sentence. Here are some specimens:

Umuntu wetu omuchle uyabonakala, simtanda. (= 'man ours handsome appears, we love')

Abantu betu abachle bayabonakala, sibatanda. (= 'people ours handsome appears, we love')

After a momentary disorientation, we begin to see that, although at first these two sentences looked like entirely different sentences, they are, in fact, the same sentence *phonemically modified*. What happens is that the subject dominates the sentence, and its first segment *umu-* or *aba-* dominates the morpho-phonology of the entire sentence. The whole sentence forms a single syntagm.

Here are a few more sentences paradigmatically modelled on the two just given:

Ilizwe ('country') *letu elichle liyabonakala, silitanda.*
Amazwe ('countries') *etu amachle ayabonakala, siwatanda.*
Intombi ('girl') *yetu enchle iyabonakala, siyitanda.*
Izintombi ('girls') *zetu ezichle ziyabonkala, sizitanda.*

A note on generative grammar and historical linguistics

The reader may feel that I ought to have included a section on the ways in which generative grammar has been applied to the problems of historical linguistics. There are two reasons why I have not. My first reason is that a disproportionate amount of space would have had to be taken up with the technical preliminaries; but a second and more compelling reason is that generative grammar itself is still evolving, with the result that many of the diachronic applications of generative grammar have already been rendered at least partially obsolete by changes in the basic theory.

When the time comes to prepare a later edition of this book, it is to be hoped that the moment will be ripe for this omission to be properly remedied. Suffice it to point out, in the meantime, that the fact that generative grammar has created powerful tools for producing synchronic descriptions of languages, past as well as present, is in itself enough to have already considerably enhanced the possibilities of accurately comparing two or more synchronic states in the history of a language. And this in the long run seems bound to lend greater precision to the diachronist's task of describing language change.

13 Grammar in Comparative Linguistics

The contents of this chapter should be read in the light of what has been discussed earlier. My aim once again is practical, in that I hope to give readers a few signposts to enable them to find their own way around the vast, though negotiable, field of 'comparative grammar'. Space permits only the briefest accounts of the subjects treated. The major part of what follows is strictly 'traditional' comparative philology and takes only slight account of developments since Saussure and Bloomfield, even though I have managed to include a discussion of the validity of the traditional structural analysis of Indo-European. The final part is devoted to syntactical comparisons and commentaries, of a kind not normally found in standard works of comparative grammar.

Indo-European structure

Although our knowledge and hypotheses regarding the structural patterns of Indo-European have been largely coloured by Sanskrit, Latin and Greek, we should remind ourselves that much of the theory was borne out by the discovery of Hittite. The earlier comparatist hypotheses are now susceptible to certain limited verification.

We should not forget, moreover, that the Sanskrit grammarians of antiquity have in their analysis of Sanskrit biased modern comparatists too heavily in favour of *their* kind of analysis.

With these reservations in mind, it should not be impossible to single out the more salient features.

The Sanskrit grammarians had early analysed the word into its three components: *root*, *suffix* and *flexional ending*. The pioneer European comparatists of the early nineteenth century (Franz Bopp, etc.) found that a like analysis was possible with the other ancient Indo-European languages (Latin, Greek, Germanic, etc.) unknown to the Hindu grammarians. The latter had drawn attention to yet another feature: *vowel alternation* occurring in both root and suffix, as well as to the significance and overriding importance of *accentuation*.

Indo-European appears to have subdivided its noun paradigms or use of grammatical number and case into two groups: the one group comprising the nominative and accusative singular as well as the nominative plural, all characterised by accentuation of the *stem* (known as *strong*); the other group (known as *weak*) with the accent on the *flexional ending*. Compare:

| | | (Stem: Skr. *pitar-* Gr. *pater-* | | (Stem: Skr. *pad-* Gr. *pod-*) | |
		Skr.	**Gr.**	**Skr.**	**Gr.**
Sing.:	Nom.	*pitá*	*pátĕr*	*pãt*	*póus*
	Acc.	*pitáram*	*patéra*	*pãdam*	*póda*
	Gen.	(*pitúr*)	*patrós*	*padás*	*podós*
	Dat.	*pitré*	*patrí*	*padé*	*podí*

Roots

'In the beginning was the root.' This dogma first appeared at the time when Franz Bopp had taken over the concept of 'root' from the Hindu Grammarians. Like them, he was convinced that all roots had been originally monosyllabic and were always abstractable from words of whatever kind. There were few dissenters among Bopp's successors until comparatively recent times. This concept of 'root' has been remarkably tenacious and has survived wave after wave of frequently fundamental criticism, and with minor reservations seems to be set fair for the future as far as Indo-European linguistics is concerned.

One of the misconceptions now swept away forever is the notion that Indo-European was a *synthetic* language built up from isolated roots and suffixes, and ultimately from roots alone. It was thought at one time that Chinese, a language of monosyllables, was composed entirely of such roots. It is now known that Chinese lies at the opposite extreme of language evolution; some are of the opinion that its monosyllables are the cores of words from which inflexions (possibly of an Indo-European type, although not necessarily) have been totally 'eroded'; in the same way, English, from a paradigmatic point of view, can be said to be eroded Old English.

Roots, it turned out, are by no means 'aboriginal' and can be created at any time in any language. They are, in fact, *morphemes*. And if one keeps this firmly in mind, false assumptions of the kind that easily arise when one is considering a hypothetical parent-language structure will be avoided. As we have seen earlier, morphemes are pure abstractions and can be regarded as the basic 'atoms' of language structure. English teems with newly created roots or morphemes; take, for example, *pun* together with *punster* and *punning*. In French one might with some justification point to a 'root' *roul-* in *rouler, rouleau, roulage, roulier, roulette, roulement, roulis*. And yet a suggestion such as this would have appeared little short of blasphemous to philologists of the middle of the last century. Outrageous or not, provided that the notion 'root' gives way to 'morpheme', *roul-* is a perfectly legitimate candidate. A few roots can be seen to have been the product of linguistic evolution (diachrony). It is possible to isolate the morpheme *sorr-* from *sorry* and *sorrow* in Modern English, even though these words are derived from different Old English roots: *sorg* 'care', *sārig* 'wounded'.

Jespersen offered the following view of root analysis: 'The proper definition of a root seems to be: that which is common to a certain number of words felt by the popular instinct of the speakers as etymologically belonging together.' The morpheme does not figure in this scheme explicitly, although Jespersen anticipates more recent views: 'the root is something real and important, though not always tangible. And as its form is not always easy to state or pronounce, so must its meaning, as a rule, be somewhat vague and indeterminate, for what is common to several ideas must of course be more general and abstract than either of the more special ideas thus connected . . . But roots thus conceived belong to any and all periods, and we must cease to speak of the earliest period of human speech as *the root period*.'

Duly warned, we are now in a secure enough position to broach the thorny problem of Indo-European roots. Traditional comparative philology has been concerned with the *hypothetical* state of the common language from which the separate 'dialects' of Indo-Iranian, Greek, Italic, Celtic, Slavonic, etc. are descended. In fact, the 'Indo-European' actually under consideration was the synchronic state immediately before the first of the Indo-European dialects became a distinct entity with traits of its own, only partly and variously shared by the rest; for not all the dialects at once, and possibly not more than one at a time, assumed this separate identity. Naturally, the discovery of Hittite caused a certain amount of bewilderment, for the majority of the comparatists had not been clear on this point; the accommodation of

Hittite into the Indo-European scheme entailed among other things choosing another, and hence different, synchronic state, relevant to an earlier period. So many changes seemed necessary that the Hittite scholar and comparatist Sturtevant was in favour of regarding this newcomer as indeed related to Indo-European but derived from a pre-Indo-European state, which he was inclined to term 'Indo-Hittite'. But the name Indo-European has been retained and various modifications made, and the synchronic phase now referred to as Indo-European is as a result somewhat different and relates to a much earlier phase, owing to this discovery of Hittite. It may be that studies of Linear B or Mycenean will provoke further revisions. Nevertheless, wherever one chooses to rule the synchronic line, Indo-European will, however much it may have to be antedated, remain a pseudo-language lacking a true basis in reality.

The Indo-European root (or morpheme) appears to have been in most instances monosyllabic; none contained more than two syllables. Sanskrit terminology is often used to describe the vowel quantity of the root. *Guna* represents normal vowel length, *vṛddhi* the long vowels. I prefer to use the term *zero* when a vowel is totally lacking. Compare the following Sanskrit forms, all from the Sanskrit root *kṛ*, which fit beautifully into this scheme:

(*vṛddhi* or long)	(*guna* or weak)	(zero)
kāra 'doer'	*kárma* 'work'	*kṛta* 'fact'

also:

(*pa*)*prā* 'he has filled'	*párīman* 'abundance'	(*pi*)*prati* 'they fill'

In Indo-European the vowels detectable are *e, o, a*, accompanied by a parallel series of diphthongs *ei, oi, ai* and *eu, ou, au*, all of which were capable of being either long or short. More will be said on this point in due course.

The hypothetically deduced Indo-European root has a quality all its own. Normally, only the disyllabic roots have vowels as their second syllable; monosyllabic roots were generally 'closed', ending in either a plosive or a sonant (the sonants include *l*, *r*, *m*, *n*, *w*, *y*). Examples are:

(root) **tep*:   (Lat.) *tepor* = (Skr.) *tapaḥ* 'heat'
(root) **steigh*: (Gr.) *steikhō* 'I go'; (Goth.) *steiga* 'I climb'
(root) **twois*: (Skr.) *tvesaḥ* 'agitated'
(root) **klew*:   (Skr.) *śrávaḥ* 'fame'; (O. Slav.) *slovo* 'word'; (Gr.) *kleos*

A few roots can be still further subdivided, as they appear to contain what may originally have been a separate suffix. In the different dialects of Indo-European these additional suffixal elements do not always show up. Indeed, they are better regarded not as suffixes at all but rather as a morphemic category, the significance of which, although perhaps real enough in pre-Indo-European, is no longer apparent. An excellent example is provided by the early Greek verbal form *welpo*, *(we)wolpa* and its associated noun *welpis* 'hope', which would clearly point to a root **welp* were it not for the fact that a number of other Indo-European languages share the first three phonemic elements of this root but not the fourth (*p*). The true Indo-European root is **wel*, with no *p* extension, an element apparently confined to Greek. Compare words in other languages from the same root:

(Lat.) *velle* 'to will'
(Goth.) *wiljan* 'to will'
(O. Slav.) *veleti* 'to order'

These inexplicable root extensions occur in a variety of forms, and crop up in a manner that suggests some earlier morphemic function which has since been lost. An instance is the root **ter*, which occurs with at least four different root extensions:

(*p* extension) **tre-p*: (Skr.) *tṛpraḥ*; (Lat.) *trepidus* 'afraid, made to tremble'
(*s* extension) **ter-s*: (Lat.) *terreo* (< **terseo*) 'I frighten'
(*s* extension) **tre-s*: (Skr.) *trasati* = (Gr.) *treō* 'tremble'
(*k* extension) **tre-k*: (Lith.) *trišu* 'I tremble'
(*m* extension) **tre-m*: (Gr.) *tremō* = (Lat.) *tremo* = (Lith.) *trimù* 'I tremble'

Root extensions of this kind have sometimes proved obstacles to satisfactory analysis, as they are naturally inclined to overlap and to become confused with an actual suffix, for at least one of the latter is normally present.

A curious feature of the Indo-European root is its tendency to reduplicate itself. One is reminded of the common speech defect of having to have several goes at beginning a word, as in 'ba-banana' or 'su-sugar'. This propensity has acquired morphemic value in Indo-European, although it is confined to the more ancient representatives: Latin, Greek, Sanskrit, Gothic, etc. With the loss of root identity in more recent times (i.e. the root is no longer felt to have morphemic identity) reduplication no longer operates. This feature has been observed in language families other than Indo-European. In early Indo-European (diachronically speaking) this tendency was used morphemically to indicate intensity of action associated with verbs. For this purpose, English employs an auxiliary verb *he does like*, whereas in Sanskrit the root reduplicates itself as in *var-varti* 'he turns'. The Indo-European perfective verbal forms, now thought to have been originally 'permansive presents' (e.g. *I have been waiting, writing*, etc.) are especially linked with this feature, e.g.

(Skr.) *pi-parmi* 'I fill'

(Lat.) *pe-perci* (from *parcere* 'to spare')

(Lat.) *me-mini* 'I remember' (Vedic *mamnắte* 'they have thought')

(Lat.) *ce-cini* (= (Irish) *ce-chan*) 'I have sung'

(Goth.) *skai-skaith* 'he separated' (from *skaidan* 'to separate')

(Skr.) *śu-śrắva* 'he has heard' (Gr. *ke-kluth i* 'hears')

The Hindu grammarians enumerated some 2000 roots in Sanskrit, although not all are attested in use; hardly more than half, in fact. When allowance is made for excess reckoning, there remain somewhat over 800 roots which form the basis not only of the verbal system but also of the larger part of the inherited nominal stems of the language.

Suffixes

Indo-European suffixes in various ways resemble roots. Like
roots, they may appear either lengthened or 'zeroed'; but they are
not restricted to the root mould, in that they need not be enclosed
by consonants or sonants. Their composition consists only exceptionally of more than three phonemes. Needless to say, their function is almost exclusively morphological, despite the fact that a
number still retain traces of an earlier semantic content. Their
variety may be illustrated in connection with the root **men*:

*men-es: (Skr.) *manaḥ* (gen. *manasaḥ*) 'thought'
             (Gr.) *menos* (gen. *meneos*) 'passion'
*mⁿn-ei: (Skr.) *muniḥ* 'an inspired person'
*mén-men: (Skr.) *manma* (gen. *manmanaḥ*) 'thought, prayer'
             (Irish) *menme* 'spirit'
             (Lettish) *mima* 'enigma'
*men-ter: (Skr.) *mantắr* 'thinker'; (Gr.) *mentor*
*mén-tro: (Skr.) *mantraḥ* 'religious formula'
             (Lith.) *meñklas* (< **mentlo-*) 'monument'

A study of suffixes will of necessity be discursive, and I shall
consequently restrict my remarks to a narrow selection of types
of suffix adaptation in Indo-European:

(1) Suffix **es* (*os/s*) ((Skr.) *sravah*; *manaḥ*; (Gr.) *menos*; (Lat.)
platus). This suffix **es* supplies a very large number of abstract
nouns and, in combination with a further suffix *-ti*, yields the
prevalent compound suffixal element *esti/osti*.
   Examples of the use of the simple suffix are:

   (Skr.) *janaḥ-* 'race' = (Gr.) *genos* = (Lat.) *genus*
   (Skr.) *haraḥ-* 'heat'; (Gr.) *theros* 'summer'
   (Skr.) *sahaḥ-* 'strength'; (Goth.) *sigis* 'victory'
   (Skr.) *vanaḥ-* 'charm'; (Lat.) *Venus*

Examples incorporating the compound suffix (*esti/osti*) are:

   (O. Slav.) *dlugosti* = (Hittite) *dalugasti* 'length'
   (Lat.) *agrestis*; *caelestis* (Eng. *celestial*)

The suffix has also provided both Latin and Sanskrit with their infinitive verbal forms:

> (Skr.) *jivase* = (Lat.) *vivere* ($s > r$) 'to live'
> (Skr.) *ayase* = (Lat.) *īre* ($< $ *iyere*) 'to go'

In instances where the suffix is accentuated, adjectival forms have been created. Compare:

> (Gr.) *pseudēs* 'liar' and *pseudos* 'lie'

It has been suggested that in the mythological era this suffix had acquired in the several Indo-European languages an 'agential' or even 'god-making' function. In such cases, the suffix appeared in its 'alternated' form *os* (see under 'Ablaut') or lengthened alternated form *ōs*. Compare:

> (Skr.) *usåḥ* = (Gr.) *éōs* ($< $ *ausós*)
>   = (Lat.) *aurōra* ($< $ *ausōsa*) 'goddess of dawn'

(2) Suffix *et* (*ot/t*); sometimes known as the *t*-suffix. This has provided a class of nominal neuters exemplified by the primitive Indo-European forms:

> (Hittite) *milit* 'honey'; (Lat.) *caput* 'head'

In later times these originally neuter forms would appear as feminines:

> (Skr.) *nakt-* = (Lat.) *nox, noctis* = (Gr.) *nuks* 'night'
> (Lat.) (acc.) *quietem* 'silence'; *salutem* 'safety'

Meanwhile, the very same suffix had adapted itself to the function of passive past participle, later becoming extensively used in this way as the various Indo-European languages came to depend more and more on a composite past tense (*he has done, they had done*, etc.). In this verbal function the suffix was associated with *-a* and became specialised as *-ta* or *-to*:

> (Skr.) *śrutá-* 'heard'; (Gr.) *klutos*; (Lat.) *-clutus*; (Irish) *cloth*
> (Skr.) *tatá* = (Gr.) *tatos* = (Lat.) *tentus* 'stretched'
> (Skr.) *mistá* 'savoury food'; (Lat.) *mixtus* 'mixed'

Finally, a further class of abstract nouns is marked by the presence of this same suffix. For some reason they are prominent in the satem division of Indo-European, e.g.:

> (Skr.) *devátā-* 'divinity'
> (Skr.) *purnatā-* = (Russian) *polnota* 'fullness'
> (Skr.) *kṛṣṇatā-* = (O. Slav.) *črynota* = (Russ.) *černota* 'blackness'

In Germanic this abstract nominal form appears as *tha* (a shifted form of Indo-European *ta*), e.g.:

$$\text{(Goth.) } diupi\underline{tha} = \text{(Eng.) } dep\underline{th}$$

In the more recent dialects of Germanic the morphemic importance of this suffix shows a regular decline, whilst in Gothic it was highly productive, as in nouns such as *daubitha* 'deafness', *mēritha* 'fame', *milditha* 'mildness', *niujitha* 'newness' and many others.

(3) Suffix *r* and *n*. The *r*- and *n*-phonemes are peculiarly bound up with the ground plan of Indo-European suffix morphology. In the most ancient known stages of Indo-European diachrony, *r* and *n* appear to have become adapted to alternation—a feature clearly marked in Hittite, where we find *n* supplanting *r* in the oblique cases of nouns with quite considerable regularity, as in:

> *ešḫ-ar*   *eš-n-aš*

More often the Hittite suffix is compound and the *n* morpheme resembles an infix, e.g.:

> *ḫanneš-šar*   *ḫanne-šn-as* 'law-suit'
> *papra-tar*   *papra-nn-as* (< **papra-tn-as*) 'uncleanness'

Alternation of this sort is not entirely absent from Sanskrit:

> *áh-ar*   *áh-n-as* 'day'
> *údh-ar*   *údh-n-as* 'udder'

and also provides explanations for otherwise unaccountable alternations in the other Indo-European dialects:

> (Gr.) *dōron* = (O. Slav.) *daru* = (Lat.) *donum*
> = (Skr.) *danam* 'gift'

It is fairly common for *r* and *n* to appear in combination with other suffixes to form the type of compound already illustrated. The following are additional examples:

*wer:

> (Lat.) *cadaver* 'corpse'; (Tocharian) *malkwer* 'milk'

*ter (very common in nouns denoting animate beings):

> (Lat.) *pater* = (Skr.) *pitár-* = (Eng.) *father*
> (Skr.) *duhitār* = (Gr.) *thugatēr* = (Eng.) *daughter*

*men (*mer*):

> (Lat.) *agmen* = (Skr.) *ajma-* 'army'
> (O. Slav.) *vremēn* 'time'

This suffix was especially significant in Vedic and carries the accent when it indicates 'agent' as opposed to action, e.g.:

> *bráhman* 'prayer'—*brahmán* 'priest'
> *sádman* 'sitting'—*sadmán* 'sitter'

Gender

All the known ancient dialects of Indo-European, except Hittite, have exhibited three genders in nominal declensions. The familiar ending -*a*, for example, has served predominantly as an indicator

of both the feminine gender singular and the neuter gender plural.
This trait survives into modern Indo-European languages, where
only English and Persian have completely abolished grammatical
gender. And yet, on the millenial time scale, grammatical gender
is a comparatively recent innovation in Indo-European. Hittite,
the earliest known Indo-European language, is entirely lacking
in a 'feminine' gender or anything approximating to it. Meillet and
others had presupposed this state of affairs even before the matter
of Hittite morphology had been clarified. They had based their
hypotheses on anomalies which in Greek, Latin, Sanskrit and
Balto-Slavonic could not be resolved. In the Greek and Italic
dialects in particular, the bulk of the masculine suffixes occurred
also in association with feminine stems. These anomalies had given
rise to the suspicion that the predominantly feminine (long) $\bar{\imath}$ and
$\bar{a}$ suffixes were not of specifically feminine origin. Readers may be
familiar with the Latin forms *nauta* 'sailor', *agricola* 'farmer' and
others which, although they belong to the feminine first declension, refer, of course, to masculine persons. Even analogical remodelling could not explain these away.

Feminine gender, it seems, springs from an earlier two-gender
system. The change was brought about not in any conceptual way
but *structurally* through morphological specialisation of certain
suffixes, a process in which analogy and secretion have played an
important part. The suffix **ter*, for example, became gradually
restricted to masculine persons, although its earlier masculine-
feminine function still survives in:

(Skr.) *pitár-*	*mātǎr-*
(Gr.) *patēr*	*mētēr*
(Lat.) *patēr*	*mater*
(Eng.) *father*	*mother*

Here we have a convincing instance of *analogical* development of
a system of grammatical gender originally devoid of a conceptual
or psychological basis and arising quite independently in the
various branches of Indo-European. The real puzzle is why such
a system should have arisen at all. If we were, in fact, faced with
systems of different numbers of genders in the various branches of
Indo-European (two, three, four or even six at a time) the whole
phenomenon could have been attributed to chance. There exist

nevertheless a regular recurrence of a ternary system of genders which goes beyond coincidence; and more will be said about this later.

The only formal distinction known to Primitive Indo-European was between 'agent' and 'action', in indicating which accentuation was more important than characteristic suffix. Traces of these two categories are still in evidence as late as Sanskrit. Note the alternations of the following:

> (Gr.) *húdōr* 'water'; (Skr.) *udrá-* 'otter'
> (Skr.) *yáśas-* 'fame'; *yaśás-* 'famous'
> (Skr.) *sthátar* 'stability'; *sthatár* 'stander, standing'

Substantival and adjectival classes

The terms *thematic* and *non-thematic* are part of the jargon of comparative grammar, the former designating those nouns and adjectives with their accent on root or suffix, the latter those with their accent on the ending. Nouns and adjectives are virtually parallel.

A limited class of Indo-European nouns are 'root nouns'; that is, monosyllabic. These were once thought to be the oldest class, but we saw earlier in our discussion of roots that such a conclusion does not necessarily follow. What is certain is that this class was on the decline during quite early times, although it had probably never been large. Meillet was inclined towards the view that this type of noun was a device for bringing to the fore the inner force of the root, and that such nouns probably possessed a religious or ritual value. The class includes such words as:

> (**ped*): (Skr.) *påt* (nom. pl. *pådaḥ*)
> (Lat.) *pés* (gen. sing. *pédis*) } 'foot'
> (Gr.) *pous* (gen. sing. *podós*)
> (**wekʷ*): (Skr.) *våk*
> (Lat.) *vox* (gen. sing. *vocis*) } 'voice'
> (**rēg*): (Skr.) *rāj-*
> (Lat.) *rex* (gen. sing. *regis*) } 'king'
> (Old Irish) *rīg*

The relevant Indo-European stems have been divided into groups according to ending (whether suffixal or otherwise). 'Endings' are not easy to distinguish from suffixes, and the so-called vowel 'stem' of the ending is certainly either purely suffixal or of suffixal derivation. The endings may be grouped as follows:

(1) consonant or sonant ending;
(2) *ā* (sometimes *ē*) ending;
(3) *o* (alternating with *e*) ending.

For convenience, the consonant-sonant endings are divided into two further extensive sub-groups: (i) those incorporating an *s*-phoneme, and (ii) those with strictly *zero* ending in the nominative singular but whose suffix stems show, in the main, final *r* or *n*.

S-endings include: (a) the *root nouns*: (Lat.) *vox*, *rex*, etc., classed as third declension for Latin nouns; (b) *i-stems*: (Lith.) *avis* = (Lat.) *ovis* ('sheep') (Latin fifth declension); (c) *u-stems*: (Goth.) *sunus* = (Lith.) *sunus* 'son' (Latin fourth declension).

Zero-endings include: (Skr.) *mātǎr-* = (Lith.) *móte* = (Gr.) *mētēr* = (Lat.) *matēr* = (O. Irish) *māthir* = (Arm.) *mayer* = (Eng.) *mother*. Also the *n*-stems, e.g. (Lat.) *nomen*, *numen*; (Russian) *vremen-* 'time', *imen-* 'name'.

Ā/(*ē*)-endings include the Latin *ā*-stems (first declension: *mensa*, *nauta*, etc.).

O-endings include: the Latin *o*-stems (second declension: *Brutus*, *dominus*, etc.); in the majority of dialects, e.g. Latin, Greek, Germanic, *s* has been incorporated or added to the stem presumably by analogy with the *s*-endings.

In the light of the earlier discussions on analogy and synchronic morphology in general, readers will expect a great diversity of detail from dialect to dialect of Indo-European. And they will not be disappointed.

Indo-European noun paradigms

In the earlier historical period some affinity between the declensional patterns of the various Indo-European dialects is still apparent. The classifications given below present perhaps an over simplified picture and do not, of course, represent a sequential progression from left to right. The progression is chronological rather than diachronic. I have confined my samples to Sanskrit, Latin, Greek and Germanic. References to comparative grammar

of Celtic, Slavonic, Baltic, etc. will provide any supplement
readers may care to make for themselves. The list of notes and
remarks, although not exhaustive, provides some explanation of
the more obvious deviations. The paradigms selected are intended
to provide no more than a broad outline picture of Indo-European
morphological diachrony; they are confined to the *o*-stem; not all
grammatical cases or numbers are included: the neuter gender is
excluded. Space will not permit further illustration.

O-stems (example: *wlkʷos 'wolf')

Indo-European reconstructed forms

Sing.:	N.	**wl̥kʷ-os*	Pl.:	N.	**wl̥kʷ-ōs*
	A.	**wl̥kʷ-om(-on)*		A.	**wl̥kʷ-ons*
	G.	**wl̥kʷ-osyo(-eso)(-ī)*		G.	**wl̥kʷ-ôm(-ôn)*
	D.	**wl̥kʷ-ei(-oi)*		D.	**wl̥kʷ-ois(-omi)*
	Instr.	**wl̥kʷ-ō(-ē)*		Instr.	*(-obhi)*
	Ab.	**wl̥kʷ-ōd(-ēd)(-ēt/ōt)*			
	Loc.	**wl̥kʷ-ei(-oi)*			

Sanskrit

Sing.:	N.	*vr̥k-aḥ*	Pl.:	N.	*vr̥k-ā́s*
	A.	*vr̥k-ám*		A.	*vr̥k-ā́n*
	G.	*vr̥k-ásya*		G.	*vr̥k-ā́nām*
	D.	*vr̥k-ā́ya*		D./Ab.	*vr̥k-ébhyas*
	Instr.	*vr̥k-éna*		Instr.	*vr̥k-áis*
	Ab.	*vr̥k-ā́t*			
	Loc.	*vr̥k-é*			

Greek

Sing.:	N.	*lúk-os*	Pl.:	N. *lúk-oi*
	A.	*lúk-on*		A. *lúk-os* (dial.) *-ons*
	G.	*lúk-ou*		G. *lúk-ôn*
	D.	*lúk-oi*		D. *lúk-ois*

O-stems (continued)

		Latin	Romance (Old French)
Sing.:	N.	lup-us	loup-s
	A.	lup-um	loup
	G.	lup-ī	
	D./Ab./Instr.	lup-o	
Pl.:	N.	lup-ī	loup
	A.	lup-os	loup-s
	G.	lup-orum	
	D./Ab./Instr.	lup-is	

		Gothic	O. Norse	O.E.	M.E.
Sing.:	N.	wulf-s	ulf-r	wulf	wolf
	A.	wulf	ulf	wulf	wolf
	G.	wulf-is	ulf-s	wulf-es	wolf-es
	D.	wulf-a	ulf-i	wulf-e	wolf(e)
Pl.:	N.	wulf-ōs	ulf-ar	wulf-as	wolf-es
	A.	wulf-ans	ulf-a	wulf-as	wolf-es
	G.	wulf-ō	ulf-a	wulf-a	wolf-es
	D.	wulf-ums	ulf-um	wolf-um	wolf-es

Notes and remarks

(a) The reconstructed Indo-European paradigm shows, as one might expect, some variation in the case forms. Indeed, such reconstructions would be severely suspect if they were regular and lacking in variation. Nowadays, few comparatists would subscribe to a uniform Indo-European. The accusative singular and genitive plural may always have exhibited *m/n* alternation of the kind illustrated, according to dialect. The vowel alternation *e/o* and diphthong *ei/oi* pervades the entire system. (See under 'Ablaut', pp. 253 ff.)

(b) Both Sanskrit and Germanic, but for quite different phonological reasons, have *a* instead of *o* in the stem. Compare: (Skr.)

vṛkas; (Pr. Germ.) *wulfaz*; (Gr.) *lukos*. The Latin *u* appearing in the stem is simply a raised variety of an earlier *o*-phoneme still evident in early Latin.

(c) The Indo-European genitive singular exhibits disparity of form. **osyo* appears in Sanskrit *vṛkasya* and in Hom. Greek *lukoio*; **eso* in Germanic only (Pr. Germ. **wulfesa*); **ī* appears in both Italic and Celtic, and is explained as the specialisation and analogical extension of an adjectival suffix.

(d) Throughout the entire paradigm there is a marked influence of the pronominal forms. The Sanskrit *-ena* is from such a source. The instrumental case shows no unity of form in Indo-European.

(e) The Sanskrit ablative singular derives directly from Indo-European. The Latin ablative *-o* derives from an earlier Italic form **lupod*. Relevant to this is the ancient Latin form *magistratud*.

(f) The nominative plurals of Greek and Latin (*lukoi, lupī*), as in a number of other dialects, are an 'analogically' borrowed pronominal form.

(g) Only the Latin third declension genitive plural (*homin-um*) corresponds with the Indo-European. The forms in *-orum* are of 'analogical' origin.

Verbal system

Owing to the diversity and range of verbal forms and functions in the recorded languages of Indo-European, it is much less possible than in the case of the nominal forms to build up a clear picture of any prototype verbal system beyond the most general framework. A number of features are, however, discernible.

In the first place, it is obvious that tense could not have been an important factor in early Indo-European. Reconstruction informs us that:

(1) The *present stem* originally indicated *action in the process of developing*, and thus includes the imperfective forms in addition.

(2) The *aorist*, important in the early phases, denoted not so much action completed in the past but rather *action pure and simple*, or action envisaged as complete within itself.

(3) The *perfect* served to indicate a state or *permansive present*; a *state* as opposed to a *process*.

(4) A *nasal phoneme n* served a now extinct function of representing a special kind of *becoming*. There are fossilised remnants of this in Latin (*relinquo- reliqui*), Sanskrit and Lithuanian.

(5) The *causative* aspect was far from negligible, although it has since played only a vestigial part in the Western dialects.

As far as tense is concerned, only in the indicative mood did early Indo-European distinguish between past and present. This state is exemplified by Hittite, which has no aorist of any kind. It must have been some time later when a gemination arose by which a dual set of preterite forms was produced; the one possessing a corresponding present (the Indo-Eur. imperfect), the other taking on a special aorist function:

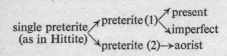

The history of the perfective forms is more obscure, but they are thought to have some relation to certain Hittite conjugational forms. Even in Greek and Sanskrit the perfective is still very much a present tense. In Sanskrit the present *bhayate* means 'he grows afraid', whereas the reduplicated perfect *bibhaya* corresponds to 'he is afraid'. Likewise, *tasthau* means 'he takes his stand', the expression of a completed action in the present, whilst the perfective *tiṣṭhati* definitely signifies 'he stands (permanently)'. The preterite sense must have been acquired only later by the perfect. A *state* is normally the result of an earlier action or process, and it is only natural that the perfect should come to be used eventually to suggest that an action had already taken place but that its effects were still palpable (as in the English perfect *I have been telling him to do such-and-such for a long time*).

Voice. Only Sanskrit exhibits the original division into voices of Indo-European: *active* and *middle*; although Old Norse has preserved a very strong flavour in its passive of the earlier Indo-European middle voice. In Greek there is a well-developed *passive* alongside the middle voice; both have become specialised in historical times. In Latin the middle voice was of purely literary importance and appears to have had no place in popular usage.

The Sanskrit grammarians were fully aware of their own middle and active voices, analysing them as:

(active) *parasmai padam* 'a word for another'
(middle) *ātmane padam* 'a word for oneself'

It is in the middle voice that the subject is in some way or other especially implicated in the *result* of the action of the verb:

katam karoti 'he makes a mat'
katam kurute 'he makes a mat for his own use'
yajati 'he sacrifices for another *or* on behalf of another'
yajate 'he sacrifices for himself'

Conjugational endings. The notion that the endings of the various 'persons' of the Indo-European tense paradigms were originally agglutinated (suffixal) personal pronouns has long since been abandoned. Closer inspection has revealed that these endings are more nearly connected with those of the nominal inflexions. This latter thesis was suggested by the existence in Sanskrit of so-called 'primary' and 'secondary' terminations. The former are confined to the future and present tenses of the indicative, and to some extent distinctly resemble personal pronouns: *-mi, -si, -ti*. These 'primary' endings occur vestigially throughout Indo-European, but they had entirely declined in importance before the historical period in all dialects except Indo-Iranian: (Skr.) *asmi* = (Gr.) *eimi* = (Hitt.) *ešmi* = (Lith.) *esmi* 'I am'.

From the historical point of view, 'primary' and 'secondary' terminations are incorrectly named, for it turns out that the secondary endings were in effect 'primary' (*-m, -s, -t*, etc.), and the so-called primaries can only be explained as a later extension by means of the additional suffix *-i*, perhaps indicating present time. Furthermore, there is little evidence that a morphological distinction between 'primary' and 'secondary' in Indo-European was ever fully worked out.

Ablaut (apophony, or vowel gradation)

'Ablaut', variously also called 'apophony' or 'vowel gradation', is frequently included in the phonological sections of comparative grammars, although in most respects this phenomenon belongs rather to morphology. Strictly speaking, it belongs neither to morphology nor to phonology, and brings into question once again the traditional compartments of comparative linguistics which Hjelmslev and others have been compelled to re-examine.

In the ancient Indo-European languages, and in scientifically reconstructed Indo-European itself, roots and suffixes were capable of acquiring different functions (noun, verb, tense, case, mood, etc.) according to vowel grade. Each individual group of languages within Indo-European has made use of this capacity in different ways, and some have made far greater use of it than others.

To give a slightly oversimplified description, the vowel grades of the reconstructed Indo-European roots and suffixes were: *e* (long or short); *o* (long or short); *a* (long or short); *zero* (either no vowel at all or a short central vowel ə).

Within these grades certain alternations arose, the most prevalent and productive of which is the vowel alternation:

$$\bar{e} \mid \bar{o} \mid zero$$

The Greek verbal system provides the clearest, 'classical' illustrations:

e	*o*	*zero*
petomai (present)	*potaomai* (iterative)	*e-pt-omen* (2nd aorist) 'fly'
pelomai (present)	*polos* 'a pivot'	*e-pl-omen* (2nd aorist) 'be in motion'

Alternation *ē* / *ĕ* / *zero* may be found in certain noun paradigms, e.g. Greek (nom. sing.) *patēr*, (nom. pl.) *patéres*, (gen. pl.) *patrôn*.

Ablaut is actually far more complicated than this, owing to the behaviour of the Indo-European diphthongs which exhibit a parallel alternation. These diphthongs are not confined to combinations of purely vocalic elements but also include vowel + sonant diphthongs of four basic types: The complete series of six diphthongs is as follows:

$$ei \quad eu \quad el \quad er \quad en \quad em$$

These diphthongs do not appear in every Indo-European dialect in their original form. They may, for example, be metathesised, as in Slavonic (*re, le*); or nasalised, also in Slavonic (*ě, ǒ*); or with vowel raised (*ul, un* instead of *ol, on*, and *il, im* instead of *el, em*), as in Germanic, Italic and Armenian. Only Sanskrit has preserved the 'zeroed' forms of the sonantal diphthongs as vocalic *ḷ, ṛ, ṃ, ṇ*, whilst other dialects have substituted a pure vocalic element to fill out these zeroed forms, e.g. *ul, il, en, on*, etc. The diphthong alternations may be set out as follows:

$$
\begin{array}{lll}
ei & / oi & / i \\
eu & / ou & / u \\
el & / ol & / \ḷ \\
er & / or & / ṛ \\
en & / on & / ṇ \\
em & / om & / ṃ
\end{array}
$$

The following are illustrations:

ei / oi / i: (Gr.) *peíthomai*; *pé-poitha*; *epé-pithmen* 'persuade', 'prevail upon'
(Gr.) *leípō*; *lé-loipa*; *é-lipon* 'leave'

eu / ou / u: (Gr.) *keúthein*; *é-kuthon* 'hide'
(Goth.) *kiusan*; *kaus*; *kusum* 'choose'

er / or / ṛ: (Gr.) *dérkomai*; *dé-dorka*; *é-drakon* 'look, see'

el / ol / ḷ: (Lith.) *telpù*; *talpá*; *tilpti* 'have a place for'
(O.E.) *helpan*; *healp*; *hulpen* 'help'

en / on / ṇ: (Gr.) *penthos* 'grief'; *pé-pontha*; *é-pathon* (< *e-*pṇthon*) 'suffer'

em / om / ṃ: (Lith.) *kemšu*; *kamšau*; *kimšti* 'fill, stuff'
(Gr.) *pémpein*; *pé-pompha*; *e-pémpsa* (< *epṃpsa*) 'send'

Ablaut in Indo-Iranian

The reader will have noticed that, in the illustrations given above, not a single example from Sanskrit appears. The reason for this is very simple: neither Sanskrit nor, for that matter, any other of the Indo-Iranian languages show any such alternation, owing to the sole fact that the Indo-European vowels /e/ and /o/ had been lowered to /a/.

Notwithstanding the absence of the simple vowel alternation in their own language, the Sanskrit grammarians did not fail to detect and classify vowel gradation within Vedic and Sanskrit. Naturally enough, this is very different from what one might expect, owing to their complete ignorance of the true Indo-European vowel system of which theirs was only a reduction. It is worth noting that the rising and falling purely vocalic diphthongs do occur as *ai* and *au*. In their lengthened or *vṛddhi* form, they appear as *āi* and *āu*; in their weak or short form, as *e* and *o* respectively. The Sanskrit vowel gradation system can be represented as follows:

	(1)	(2)	(3)	(4)	(5)
zero grade	(-), *a*	*i*	*u*	*ṛ*	*ḷ*
guṇa grade	*a*	*e*	*o*	*ar*	*al*
vṛddhi grade	*ā*	*āi*	*āu*	*ār*	*āl*

Column (1) corresponds to the fundamental alternation *ĕ—ŏ—zero*. Columns (2) and (3) to the diphthong alternations: *ēi/ōi—ei/oi—i* and *ēu/ōu—eu/ou—u* respectively.

Vowel gradation played a major role in Sanskrit synchrony and was capable of influencing the total form a word might assume. Here are a few roots given in Sanskrit *zero* grade, with a number of lexical derivations from them:

	zero	guna	vṛddhi
*budh 'understanding'	*buddhá* 'seeing'	*boddhum* 'understanding'	*báuddha*
*kṛ 'doing'	*kṛta* 'fact'	*kárma* 'work'	*kāra* 'doer'
*bhu 'being'	*bhuti* 'existence'		*bhautika* 'relating to beings'
*viś 'entering'	*viś-* 'village'	*veśa* 'house'	*vāiśya* 'man of the people'

Ablaut in Germanic

In the older Germanic languages, and presumably *a fortiori* in Proto-Germanic, Ablaut had become especially adapted to shaping verbal morphology, although its influence is to be found in almost every structural feature of Germanic.

Gothic, Old English, Old Norse and Old High German share a regular pattern in their strong verbs, the parts of which are differentiated by the familiar alternation *e / o / zero*; with the qualification that short *e* has already become *i* and short *o* appears as *a* in all Germanic dialects. The alternated diphthongs play an equally important part; the *zero*-grade sonantal diphthongs always appear in combination with a preceding vowel (**bn̥den* appears as *bunden*, for example).

(1) *e*-grade has become specialised in the present stem.

(2) *o*-grade has become specialised in the preterite stem, but in the singular only.

(3) *Zero*-grade appears regularly in the stems of past participles, which only gradually evolved the function in combination with auxiliary verbs of the composite perfect and pluperfect, etc. The zero-grade also appears in the plural of the preterite.

(4) Lengthened *ē*-grade occasionally appears in the preterite stem plural (in place of the *zero* grade).

(5) *a*-grade also figures in the Germanic system of strong verbs.

The 'ablaut series' generally appear in the comparative grammars of the Germanic languages in a certain order. I give them diagrammatically so that in the light of what has gone before they may be read off more easily. Only the briefest and most cursory explanations are given.

Complex ablaut patterns in Indo-European

The foregoing introduces no more than the elements of Indo-European Ablaut. So far, we have not seen the effect of vowel alternation upon suffixes. Unfortunately, restriction of space will not allow treatment of this important aspect of Ablaut; nor will it permit development of other kinds of vowel-grade alternation,

Ablaut series	Indo-Eur. alteration	Pr. Germ. alteration	Illustrations			
			Pres.	Pret. sing.	Pret. pl.	Past pt.
I	ei | oi | i | i	i | ai | i	(Goth.) steigan (O.N.) stíga (O.E.) stígan	stáig steig stág[1]	stigum stigu stigon	stigans 'ascend' stiginn 'step' stigen 'ascend'
II	eu | ou | u | u	eu | au | u(o)	(Goth.) biudan (O.N.) bjóða (O.E.) beodan	baud bauð bead	budum buðu budon	budan boðinn $\}$ 'offer' boden
III	$\begin{cases} el \mid ol \mid \underset{.}{l} \mid \bar{e}l \\ er \mid or \mid \underset{.}{r} \mid \bar{e}r \\ en \mid on \mid \underset{.}{n} \mid \bar{e} \end{cases}$	$\left. \begin{array}{l} e(il) \mid al \mid ul(ol) \\ er \mid ar \mid or \\ en(in) \mid an \mid un(on) \end{array} \right\}$ when followed by consonant	(Goth.) hilpan (O.N.) hjálpa[2] (O.E.) helpan	halp halp healp[2]	hulpum halpu hulpon	hulpans holpinn $\}$ 'help' holpen
IV	$\begin{cases} el \mid ol \mid \underset{.}{l} \mid \bar{e}l \\ er \mid or \mid \underset{.}{r} \mid \bar{e}r \\ en \mid on \mid \underset{.}{n} \mid \bar{e} \\ em \mid om \mid \underset{.}{m} \mid \bar{e}m \end{cases}$	$el \mid al \mid \bar{a}l \mid ul(ol)$ $er \mid ar \mid \bar{a}r \mid or$ $en(in) \mid an \mid \bar{a}n \mid on(un)$ $im \mid am \mid \bar{a}m \mid um(om)$	(Goth.) niman (O.N.) nema (O.E.) niman	nam nam nōm[4]	nēmum námu[3] nōmon[4]	numans numinn $\}$ 'take' numen

V	$e/o/\bar{e}$	$e/a/\bar{æ}$	(Goth.) *giban* (O.N.) *gefa* (O.E.) *giefan*[5]	*gaf* *gaf* *geaf*[5]	*gēbum* *gǣfu*[3] *gēofon*[6]	*gibans* *gefinn* *giefen*[5] } 'give'
VI	(uncertain or mixed)	$a/\bar{o}$	(Goth.) *faran* (O.N.) *fara* (O.E.) *faran*	*fōr* *fōr*[7] *fōr*	*fōrum* *fōru*[7] *fōron*	*farans* *farinn* *faren* } 'go'
VII	$\bar{e}/\bar{o}/\vartheta$	$æ/o/a$	(Goth.) *lētan* (O.N.) *láta*[3]	*lōt* *lét*[4]	*lōtum* *létu*[4]	*lētans* *latinn* } 'let'

[1] Pr. Germanic diphthong *ai* becomes *ā* in Old English.
[2] The result of breaking or vowel fracture (see pp. 174–80).
[3] Old Norse has reduced Pr. Germ *æ* to short *a*.
[4] Analogical formations.
[5] Influence of initial palatal consonants.
[6] West Saxon development of Pr. Germ. *æ*.
[7] Pr. Germanic long *ō* foreshortened in Old Norse.

or of another interesting feature, consonant alternation, which in many ways runs closely parallel.

It would be a pity nevertheless not to mention ablaut in so far as it affects disyllabic roots; that is, roots extended by an extra syllable, usually consisting of a single vowel or diphthong. Such roots exhibit permutations of a complex order. The permutations possible, all of which are seldom realised in any one root, are seven in number:

1st syllable		2nd syllable
ĕ	/	zero
ŏ	/	zero
zero	/	ē
zero	/	o
zero	/	zero

We shall take as an illustration the root *genə / *gnē 'knowing', which exhibits six of these possibilities:

ĕ/zero: (Lith.) žen-klas 'sign'; (Skr.) jani-tǎ = (Gr.) gene-tōr = (Lat.) geni-tor 'parent'

ŏ-zero: (Goth.) kann 'he knows'; (Gr.) ge-gon-a = (Skr.) ja-jan-a 'I have given birth'; (Gr.) gon-os = (Skr.) jan-aḥ 'race'

ō/zero: (Gr.) ge-gōn-a 'I let know'; (O.H.G.) kuon-i 'brave'

zero/ē: (Skr.) jñǎ-tum 'to know'; (Gr.) gnē-sios 'parent'; (O.H.G.) knā-an 'to know'

zero/ō: (Gr.) é-gnō-n; (Lat.) -gnō-sco 'I know'; (O. Slav.) zna-ti 'to know'; (Gr.) gnō-tós 'brother'; (Goth.) kno-ths 'race'

zero/zero: (Lat.) -gn-ārus 'knowing'; (Gr.) gi-gn-ō = (Skr.) ja-jñ-é 'I was born'; (Goth.) kun-ths 'known'

Exercise 9

(1) The following items are grouped according to the scheme of a comparative dictionary. Rearrange them according to vowel gradation in three columns (headed e, o and zero). (Sanskrit

examples, unless for other reasons, will belong to both *e* and *o* columns.)

(a) Root **kleu* (alternation: *eu* / *ou* / *u*):
  (Greek) *kle(w)os* 'glory'; *klutos* 'heard'
  (Skr.) *śrāuṣit* 'he heard'; *śuśrotha* 'you have heard'; *śrutaḥ* 'heard'
  (Lat.) *-clutus* 'heard'
  (Goth.) *hliuma* 'heard'; (Old Norse) *hljóð* 'hearing'.

(b) Root **bher* (alternation: *er* / *or* / *r̥*):
  (Skr.) *bhárvati* 'eaten up with passion'; *bhr̥nati* 'injured'
  (Greek) *phárō* 'crease'; *phorkos* 'wrinkle'
  (Lat.) *ferīre* 'to strike'; *forāmen* 'hole'
  (Irish) *bern* 'fissure'
  (Old Norse) *berja* 'to smite'; *bardagi* 'battle'; *bora* 'loch'
  (O.E.) *borian* 'to bore'; (O.H.G.) *bora* 'borer'.

(2) Identify the ablaut series (Germanic and Indo-European) in the following Old English parts of verbs; and explain in note form any apparent deviations in the Old English series:

(a)	*drincan*	*dranc*	*druncon*	*druncen*	'drink'
(b)	*sweltan*	*swealt*	*swulton*	*swulten*	'die'
(c)	*bindan*	*band*	*bundon*	*bunden*	'bind'
(d)	*cwethan*	*cwǣth*	*cwǣdon*	*cweden*	'say'
(e)	*ceosan*	*ceas*	*curon*	*coren*	'choose'

(3) This exercise is arranged as Exercise 1 and concerns the disyllabic root of Indo-European *pelə/plē*, which has five of the seven possible alternations. Rearrange the items given under five columns headed by the relevant alternations.

(Greek) *pol-us* 'full'; (Homeric) *é-plē-to* 'he has filled'
(Lat.) *plē-nus* 'full'
(Skr.) *pári-man* 'abundance'; *a-prāt* 'he has filled'; *pa-prā* 'he filled'; *pi-pr-a-ti* 'they fill'; *pur-naḥ* 'full'
(O. Slav.) *plu-nu* = (Mod. Russ.) *pol-nyy* 'full'
(Gothic) *fil-u* 'much'; *ful-ls* 'full'
Old Irish) *il* 'much'
(Armenian) *(p)li* 'full'

Parallel development

A very remarkable feature of language structure is that, unless historical accidents of a rather serious nature intervene, then the different dialects of a given language group will evolve in parallel fashion *even though there has been no interaction between them.* This same principle applies on a wider scale to the evolution of entire language groups as compared with one another, although in a much less easily discernible way.

This parallel development is best exemplified in the Slavonic group. In these languages (Russian, Czech, Polish, Bulgarian, Serbo-Croat, etc.) there were, for instance, originally two forms of the adjective: the one with a similar paradigm to the noun, the other a composite of simple adjective and demonstrative pronoun suffix. In all the Slav languages the second of these forms has taken over at the expense of the first type, for the very apparent reason that the former could more easily serve to distinguish noun from adjective. The obsolescent adjectival form had been too nearly like the noun. In modern times only traces of the noun-type adjectival paradigm remain.

Slav dialects possessed in addition a number of instrumental forms in both singular and plural for the various genders. Gradually, in the plural, the feminine ending *-ami* was extended to all genders. The striking feature of all this is that these parallel changes have occurred long after the various dialects separated from the parent stock and became isolated geographically and politically. This is especially true of the southern Slav group (Bulgarian, Serbo-Croat, Macedonian), which became entirely separated by Magyar and non-Slav-speaking races.

One of the lessons of phenomena such as these is that similarities occurring within related languages are not necessarily the result of the influence of one upon another, or even of mutual interaction.

Turning to the wider field of Indo-European we discover similar, albeit more general and less distinct, parallel evolution.

In the earliest languages of Indo-European the morphological unit comprised: (i) root, suffix and ending; (ii) a vowel grade, one or more; (iii) a tone or pitch accent. The earliest Hindu texts, the Vedic poems, show exactly this composition. In the last 3000 years these well-defined characteristics have become obscured and have dwindled in significance. In the first place, the root has ceased to be perceptible and has been replaced by equally important morphemic elements in the separate dialects. Suffixes became confused with endings, largely through the introduction of liaison vowels. Secondly, vowel gradation ceased to be observed and gradually ceased to have any importance. Moreover, the vowel coloration was further obscured by contagion of associated sonants: $/y/, /w/, /r/, /l/, /n/, /m/$. Finally, the pitch accent, having been displaced, eventually disappeared, in nearly all dialects being replaced by a stress accent.

A further feature of the parallel development of the Indo-European dialects is a tendency towards simplification, and elimination of structurally obsolescent elements. *Concept* gradually replaces *form*. A curious, if somewhat recondite, example is the disappearance of the so-called *n*-infix. This infix is not, strictly speaking, suffixal but belongs intimately to the root core of the word in which it occurs. In turns up in the present stem of the Latin verb *relinquere* 'to leave' but not in the perfect stem *reliqui*. The Latin is no isolated instance, for the same infix is to be found in the corresponding Sanskrit verb *riṇákti* (where Skr. *r* corresponds to Lat. *l*) = (Lat.) *linquit*. This infixal structural feature occurs in a number of Sanskrit verbs, including *pṛṇắti* 'fill', *vṛṇóti* 'covers' and *stṛṇóti* 'strews'. In some dialects there is no trace of this infix even in the earliest records. Gothic is one of these (compare: (Gr.) *stórnūmi* = (Goth.) *straujan* 'strew').

Pedersen explained that this nasal infix retained its morphological utility only in the Baltic group, where it had become assimilated to the verbal concept of 'becoming', e.g. *bālù* 'written' (note that the *n* has been completely nasalised). In earlier times this infix may have served as a means of aspect differentiation but this is by no means certain.

In some Indo-European languages the infix can, as it were, be observed in the act of eliminating itself. Its means of doing this was to 'squeeze' itself out of the core towards the end of the word. Armenian illustrates this quite graphically. Compare:

(Skr.) *riṇákti* = (Arm.) *lkhanem*

(Skr.) *vinasti* = (Arm.) *gtanem*

The existence of this kind of evolution in Indo-European prompted Meillet to question whether, in fact, Indo-European ever had the kind of initial identity it was usually supposed to have. Could it not rather have been from all time an assemblage of dialects with a related or parallel development? Perhaps this is hardly the time to pose such questions. This nasal infix does nevertheless suggest that the Indo-European dialects had evolved in parallel fashion from a *very* early date, vastly earlier than had been previously reckoned as the period of divergence from the parent stock. In addition, the utility of positing proto-Slavonic, proto-Germanic, etc. was brought into question.

Not only do we find parallel development, but striking convergences as well. In all the early Indo-European languages the present tense had two alternative endings for the first person singular: -ō and -mi. (Compare: Greek *legō* 'I lie down'; *didōmi* 'I give'.) In nearly all Indo-European dialects the tendency has been for the second type (-mi) to gain ground at the expense of the first (-o):

(1) Armenian has generalised -mi as m.
(2) Irish, with few exceptions, has -m (*scaraim* 'I separate').
(3) Old High German had *salbom*, whilst Gothic had the alternative *salbō* 'I anoint'.
(4) Only Latin and Romance derivatives have kept the -o (or descendants of it): (V. Lat.) *canto* = (Fr.) *chante* = (Ital.) *canto*, etc.
(5) Slavonic is particularly interesting because originally there had been no more than five or six verbs with the -mi ending. The rest showed nasal õ. By chance, the commonly used verb 'to have' was one of the few, and caused the -mi ending to spread to other verbs by analogical remodelling. Russian is the exception in generalising the original nasal õ, allowing the -mi alternative to lapse into obsolescence.

Structural changes in Romance

The contents of this section are intended to be no more than a brief summary of a few of the more outstanding structural changes in Romance diachrony. To supplement this oversimplified picture readers should consult one or more of the standard works on

Romance Linguistics listed in the Appendix. I have omitted all reference to the morphology of verbs owing to the complexity of its ramifications, which I could not do justice to in so short a space.

Changes in the Latin gender system

Classical Latin possessed three clearly defined genders: masculine, feminine and neuter. None of the Romance languages has more than two: masculine and feminine. Reduction of the Classical or Early Latin triple gender to the Vulgar Latin two is entirely the outcome of analogical remodelling. The patterns of development are complicated and I shall single out one aspect only.

In Classical Latin the suffixal ending *-a* appears (a) in the singular feminine declension of first declension nouns (e.g. *mensa*, *agricola*, *terra*) and (b) in the nominative, vocative and accusative plurals of neuter nouns (e.g. *bella* (pl. of *bellum* 'war'); *genua* (pl. of *genu* 'knee')).

The feminine singulars of declensions other than the *a*-stem declension underwent a straightforward assimilation to form the basis of the Romance-type feminine ending, on which many other Latin forms were likewise remodelled in relatively early times: (Lat.) *terra(m)* > (Fr.) *terre*; (Lat.) *filia(m)* > (Fr.) *fille*. There is nothing unusual about this. What really is odd is the way in which the Latin neuter plurals (in *-a* always) were not only assimilated to the feminine singular in form but even became *singular in meaning*. A potent instance of the effect of analogy. Thus the Spanish words *arma* (Fr. *arme*), *hoja* (Fr. *feuille*), *obra* (Fr. *oeuvre*) are all straightforwardly derived from neuter plurals: *arma, folia, opera* (sing. *opus*). These examples are far from exceptional. In a few cases, the direct survival of the neuter does occur (e.g. Fr. *vaisseau* (< *vascellum*) beside *vaisselle* (< *vascella*)), but there is no evidence that these were ever used in the Classical Latin way—that is, as singular and plural respectively. On the contrary, the earliest evidence of Vulgar Latin usage from the second and third centuries A.D. shows that neuter plurals (such as *vascella*) had become assimilated to the feminine singular from the period *before* the various Romance dialects had asserted their autonomy.

By a further analogical step, these newly created feminine singulars from neuter plurals (e.g. Fr. *vaisselle, oeuvre, feuille*) formed their own plurals in the normally accepted way, by the addition of -s (*vaisselles*, *oeuvres*, etc.). This progression may be depicted as:

OLD PLURAL (*opera*)→NEW SINGULAR (*oeuvre*)
                                    →NEW PLURAL (*oeuvres*)

Italian and Romanian are exceptional in retaining the plural *meaning* for these older Latin neuters, whilst nonetheless concurring in allowing them *feminine gender*. An even odder situation, when one thinks about it.

Sing.		Pl.	
V.L.	**Ital. (masc.)**	**V.L.**	**Ital. (fem.)**
genuculum	*il ginocchio*	*genucula*	*le ginocchia*
digitum	*il dito*	*digita*	*le dita*
ovum	*l'uovo*	*ova*	*le uova*, etc.

Disappearance and reduction of the Latin case system
Of the Latin system of six cases (nominative, vocative, accusative, genitive, dative, ablative) only one has remained in the modern Romance dialects—the accusative case. In all but rare instances, nouns in these languages have inherited their flexional endings directly from the Latin accusative case, with occasional (analogical) nominative admixture. No more subtle reason can be given for this state of affairs other than the already familiar process of analogical reformation, which does its work willy-nilly as well as highly effectively, and every step of whose workings is traceable in the various Romance languages.

Reduction of the case system of early Latin undoubtedly had its beginnings in popular usage at a time when Classical Latin was at the peak of its literary achievement. The contrast between literary usage and ordinary parlance must have been remarkable; to use six cases in the forum and only two in the market-place! Yet it is pretty certain that not more than two cases survived the fall of the Roman Empire as far as 'living' Latin was concerned.[1]

The earliest case to disappear was the ablative. The genitive, on the other hand, has disappeared not without leaving traces of

[1] Except in the case of Romanian.

its former importance: in the names of the weekdays, (Fr.) *lundi*, (Ital.) *lunedi* from *lunae diem* 'the day of the moon'; in place-names, (Fr.) *Ville favreux* from *villa fabrorum*. The most notable survival is the French *leur* from *illorum* 'of them'.

The reduction of the Latin case system coincided with an over-all analogical reshaping of the Latin nominal paradigms (originally five, together with the imparisyllabic declension) in the general direction of uniformity. It can be said that Vulgar Latin nominal morphology was, with few irregularities, as follows:

		Sing.	Pl.
Declension I:	Nom.	*terra*	*terre* (< *terrae*)
	Acc.	*terra*(m)	*terras*
Declension II:	Nom.	*lupus*	*lupi*
	Acc.	*lupu*(m)	*lupos*
Declension III:	Nom.	*montis*	*montes*
	Acc.	*monte*(m)	*montes*

Within each of the Romance dialects individually, analogy has done its work in reducing the double case system inherited from Vulgar Latin to a single case or 'caseless' system. Spanish (Castilian literary standard) has preserved the Vulgar Latin accusative pure and simple:

	Spanish	
	Sing.	Pl.
(V.L.) I:	*tierra*	*tierras*
II:	*muro*	*muros*
III:	*monte*	*montes*

whereas Italian and Romanian, which treated final *s* in a phonologically different manner, leaving it weak, exhibit hybrid paradigms based partly on the Vulgar Latin nominative and partly on the accusative. Here is the Italian paradigm for comparison:

	Italian	
	Sing.	Pl.
(V.L.) I:	*terra*	*terre*
II:	*muro*	*muri*
III:	*monte*	*monti* (remodelled on II)

Old French preserved the Vulgar Latin dual case system intact. The corresponding forms in Old French are given as follows:

Old French

		Sing.	Pl.
(V.L.) I:	N.⎫ A.⎭	*terre*	*terres*
II:	N.	*loups*	*loup*
	A.	*loup*	*loups*
III:	N.	*monz* (< *monts*)	*mont* (remodelled on II)
	A.	*mont*	*monz*

The nouns descended from the Latin imparisyllabic group (*imperator—imperatoris*; *latro—latronis*; *homo—hominis*) preserved a likely duality of cases in Old French:

N. *homo*   > *uem, on*   N. *traditor*   > *traitre*
A. *hominem* > *ome* (> *homme*)   A. *traditorem* > *traitor*

N. *comes*   > *cuens*   N. *soror*   > *suer*
A. *comitem* > *conte* (*comte*)   A. *sororem* > *seror*

N. *pastor*   > *pastre*
A. *pastorem* > *pastor*

Occasionally, both forms have survived with lexically different functions, as in *on* (indefinite personal pronoun) and *homme* (noun 'man').

It is not difficult to see why the two-case system in Old French should have broken down. In the first place, the French paradigms corresponding to Vulgar Latin II and III (*loups; monz*) offer a confusion of forms, with the singular flexional endings the exact reverse of the plural endings. The 'tension' thus arising within the synchronic phase (Old French) could find its resolution only in a more rational system; a resolution especially aided by the fact that word order was becoming fixed and already making obsolescent the need for case-ending differentiation. We appear to have here a clear corroboration of Jespersen's principle that rationalisation of word order *precedes* reduction and simplification of inflexions. In the light of this, one is not surprised to find that the nominative case had already taken on an 'agential' function; for what other useful purpose could it serve if the accusative was not to become redundant?

There remained only one further step: the disappearance of the nominative, for it had all the time been a linguistic luxury to set aside a grammatical case especially for 'persons' or 'agents'. This disappearance was already well under way in the later Old French period. Modern French preserves only the Latin accusative forms:

French

(V.L.) I:	*terre*	*terres*
II:	*loup*	*loups*
III:	*mont*	*monts*

The progeny of the Latin demonstrative ILLE

In Classical Latin, *ille* was used as a demonstrative adjective or pronoun, but it eventually grew to be accepted as a personal pronoun, having been recognised as such even by Latin grammarians. In popular speech *ille*, which was paradigmatically akin to the adjectives, evolved in two directions: as the Romance personal pronoun for the third person and as the Romance definite article. The two functions were separated and kept apart by means of accentuation; when the stress fell on the root ('tonic') the word could be recognised as a pronoun, but when stressed on the ending the word acquired the force of a definite article. Each of these developments will be looked at separately.

(1) *ILLE as personal pronoun.* In Vulgar Latin the declension of *illi* had been remodelled to a large extent on that of the relative pronoun. The nominative singular masculine was almost certainly *illī*. In addition, there arose two forms for the dative in place of the Classical single form: *illui* ($\neq$ *cui* rel. pron.) and *illaei* (fem.). Old French has one dative corresponding to *illui* (Fr. *lui*) and a second, *li*, corresponding to the Classical Latin *illi*. Italian has masculine *lui* and feminine *lei*, Romanian masculine *lui* and feminine *ei*.

The innovated nominative singular masculine *illī* gives French *il* and Italian *egli*.

The feminine nominative singular *illa* yields French *elle*, Spanish *ella*, Italian *ella* and Romanian *ea*.

Accusative forms were accentuated differently, showing a change of stress position: (m.) *illu(m)* (f.) *illa(m)* become *lo* (Fr. *le*, Port. *o*) and *la* (Port. *a*) respectively.

The neuter forms have, generally speaking, disappeared without trace. The nominative plural *illi* became Old French *il* (although this was remodelled as *ils* in later French) and Italian *egli*.

As with the singular, the accusative plural shows parallel change of stress position *illós*, *illás*, both becoming *les* in French but *los* and *las* in Spanish. The Italian forms *li* and *le* are extensions of the 'tonic' form of the nominative.

A couple of sentences from Modern French will illustrate the essential structural purposes to which this (Classical) Latin 'luxury' word *ille* has been put:

Il le lui donne = 'he gives it to him'
Elle quitte la maison malgré eux = 'She leaves the house despite them'

(2) *ILLE as definite article*. The use of *ille* as definite article, alongside *ipse*, a rival form, belonged to Vulgar and Late Latin. Classical Latin had, of course, no articles of any kind, and both *ille* and *ipse* possessed an emphatic or demonstrative function. This development is in parallel with the Germanic languages, all modern dialects of which have created definite articles out of what were originally demonstrative adjectives or pronouns.

The Romance article generally arose from the 'atonic' (stressed on ending) forms of *ille*. In mediaeval times Provençal retained these atonically derived forms in their original purity:

		Sing.		Pl.	
Masc.:	N.	*illé*	*le*	*illí*	*li*
	A.	*illu(m)*	*lo*	*illós*	*los*
Fem.:	N.	*illá*	*la*	*illáe*	*las*
	A.	*illā(m)*		*illas*	

Old French closely approximates to this system, the exception being that the nominative singular masculine again derives from the Vulgar Latin remodelling *illī*:

		Sing.	Pl.
Masc.:	N.	*li*	*li*
	A.	*lo, le*	*les*
Fem.:	N. & A.	*la*	*les*

Italian and Spanish differ from French and Provençal in deriving their masculine nominative singular from the tonic form of *ille* (*illī*):

	Spanish		Italian	
	Sing.	Pl.	Sing.	Pl.
Masc.:	*el*	*los*	*il (lo)*	*i (gli)*
Fem.:	*la*	*las*	*la*	*le*

Romanian stands singularly apart from the rest in having its article *suffixed* to the noun. This no doubt arose from the congenital Latin practice of sometimes placing *ille* after its noun in accordance with the freedom of word order available to all well-inflected languages. It happens that Romanian has perpetuated the second of the two possible positions. In addition, Romanian preserves the Vulgar Latin forms of the genitive and dative as distinct from the rest of the Romance dialects. The article is agglutinated both in orthography and in pronunciation, but the examples given introduce hyphens to indicate the boundary between the noun and its article:

e.g. (Rom.) *domnu* (< V.L. *dominum*)

	Sing.	Pl.
N. & A.	*domnu-l*	*domni-i*
G. & D.	*domnu-lui*	*domni-lor*

Adverbial suffixes

The Classical Latin suffix formation for adverbs was in the main either *-e* or *-iter*, e.g. *longe, male, bene, fortiter*, etc. Vulgar Latin had, it seems, no place for either of these suffixes but instead seized upon and made wholesale use of *mente* 'in mind' (the ablative case of *mens* 'mind'). A curious development, but foreshadowed in the Latin authors, e.g. Quintilian: *bona mente factum* 'fashioned with a good disposition'. Occasional occurrences in literary usage cannot, however, account for the widespread popularity of *mente* in ordinary speech. This innocent ablative has become perpetuated in Romance: (Fr.) *bonnement*; (Span.) *buenamente*; (Ital.) *buonamente*. There still exists nevertheless in Portuguese and Spanish a 'feeling' that the suffix *mente* is really syntactically distinct, since in constructions involving two adverbs *mente* will be suffixed only to the second, e.g. *clara y distintamente*.

Other quite fortuitous Latin endings have become by analogical transference a separate class of adverbial suffix, although only in Western Romance. Thus the Latin adverbs *plus, magis, satis*, etc. had derived their final *-s* from a variety of morphemic sources; this did not prevent the Romance dialects from abstracting this *-s* and extending its use to adverbs that had been previously without a final *-s*. Examples from French are *volontiers, alors, certes*, etc. Italian, which never employs final *s*, not surprisingly has developed *i* for similar purposes, providing an entire new class of adverbs such as *oggi, domani, avanti, volontieri, fuori*, etc.

Vulgar Latin synchrony seems to have had no taste for the precise and expressive adverbs of Classical Latin, and instead offers a range of compound adverbs which must have made Roman orators and men of letters wince. Examples are:

> *ad satis* > (Fr. *assez*; Ital. *assai*)
> *in simul* > (Fr. *ensemble*; Ital. *insieme*)
> *subinde* (which replaced *saepe* 'often') > (Fr. *souvent*)
> *de ubi* > (Ital. *dove*)
> *dum interim* (Ital. (*do*)*mentre*; Span. (*de*)*mientras*)

These 'barbarisms' remind us of the kind of modern English that prefers *prior to* to *before*, *during the interim period* to *meanwhile*, *obligated* to *obliged*, and the rest. What is more important, comparison compels the conclusion that Vulgar and Classical Latin were virtually different languages, and the former not merely a travesty of the latter. The same is true of each of the Romance languages separately. They are immeasurably more than mere descendants of the popular speech of the Roman Empire. Like natural descendants, they are 'creatures' in their own right, with characteristics, features and co-ordination of parts peculiarly their own.

Part IV

MEANING

14 The Study of Meaning

Our review of historical and comparative linguistics has so far taken in only phonology and grammar. There remains an ill-defined, notoriously controversial and still largely unexplored region which has to do with language *meaning*, and with those elements of language so intimately bound up with meaning—*words*.

The most widely accepted label for this area is *semantics*, although a somewhat similar term *semasiology* is still preferred by some. Semantics (*semantick*) started life in English as the name of a science for predicting the future, particularly the weather. But for its modern use the *Shorter Oxford Dictionary* provides the gloss: 'relating to signification or meaning'. The main difficulty with 'semantics' is that it means different things to different people. The linguist means by it something rather different from Carnap's symbolic processes, and something worlds apart from the 'therapeutic' semantics of Korzybski or Hayakawa. But, even within the boundaries of linguistics, semantics is used in a disturbing variety of ways. Some linguists avoid using the term altogether. Some British linguists prefer to divide the area into *lexis*—the study of vocabulary—and *context*. Whatever the term chosen, it must embrace lexical as well as purely semantic issues. And in treating of words it inevitably has to reckon with overlapping grammatical, and even phonological, features. To the diachronist semantics means *lexical* semantics: the study of the meanings, functions and vagaries of words. Needless to say, his purview will include the more traditional *etymology*.

The problem of meaning

Meaning is a term fraught with ambiguity, controversy and contradiction. Ogden and Richards in their *Meaning of Meaning* counted no less than sixteen different definitions. For the linguist and the philosopher alike, meaning has too often become a dirty word. Even among those who have been reluctant to let go of the concept altogether, there has sometimes been a certain coyness, a tendency to fight shy of it.

In philosophy, Ludwig Wittgenstein appeared to have undermined entirely the concept of meaning, and much of his work (particularly *Philosophical Investigations* and *The Blue & Brown Books*) is devoted to pointing out the superfluousness and often seriously misleading notion of underlying meaning. His dictum, reiterated in many variations, is that the meaning of a word or expression is neither more nor less than its *use*. Usage, not meaning, is the right basis. 'The meaning of a word is its use in the language.' It is only fair to remind the reader that Wittgenstein was far from cocksure about all this. Yet, despite this, language seemed ultimately reducible to a system of signs, and when the mysterious entity *meaning* raised its enigmatic head the whole question turned out to be simply one of 'grammar'. Wittgenstein's feeling was that structural analysis of a given language would banish all ghosts of this kind.

The unfortunate part of all this is that linguists have taken Wittgenstein to task on this very point and, as it were, passed the baby back to him. The sentiment 'Would that the philosophers were more aware of the methods of linguistics' recoils with a vengeance on the philosopher. As W. S. Allen has pointed out, when Wittgenstein really believed he was on to a linguistic equivalence in equating 'bring me a slab' with the exclamation 'Slab!' he was actually remaining squarely within the realms of logic, since no linguist could accept an equivalence of this kind. Language is composed of, and even depends for its very existence on, those very differences that Wittgenstein wanted to rule out.[1]

As for sign symbolism, Hjelmslev has long since demonstrated that in absolute isolation no sign has any meaning. Language *qua* language could not be described as a pure system of signs. It was only with the 'external functions of a language' (for example, description, statement, proposition, imperative) that sign systems began to operate; in other words, in just those directions that a linguist preferred to demarcate outside his own territory, as, for example, logic and epistemology, those very fields that Wittgenstein was hoping the linguists would illuminate.[2]

The most formidable opponents of the concept of meaning within linguistics itself are the behaviourists or 'structuralists', prominent among whom was the American linguist L. Bloomfield, who, starting from purely linguistic premises, arrived at the definition of meaning of a linguistic form as 'the situation in

[1] Allen, W. S., *On the Linguistic Study of Language* (Cambridge, 1957).
[2] Hjelmslev, L., *op. cit.*, pp. 27–9.

which the speaker utters it and the response which it calls forth in the hearer'.[1] Human utterances were supposed to be connected with certain situations and accompanied by certain responses, so that a visitor from another planet would soon get the hang of language, learning to recognise 'recurrent parts of utterances, and to see that words like *shut*, *door*, *apple* occurred in speeches that were connected with acts of shutting something and objects of certain definite types.'[2]

More recently, the Bloomfieldian approach has reappeared, in an even starker form, in the work of Harris. Harris is thoroughly sceptical about the value of linguistic descriptions of meaning. 'It is often impossible,' he claims, 'to state a common feature of meaning.' Harris concludes that, 'the meaning of an element in each linguistic environment is the difference between the meaning of its linguistic environment and the meaning of the whole utterance'. He goes on to give an example: 'Thus the meaning of *blue* in *blueberry* might be said to be the meaning of *blueberry* minus the meaning of berry . . . *blue* here therefore does not mean simply a colour, but the observable differentia of blueberries against other berries.'[3] To my mind, any approach that relegates meaning to limbo is not even as serviceable as the unaided intuitions of common sense. There must somehow be *linguistic* reasons why a sentence like *There are no unicorns on Mars* is unobjectionable if obvious; why *Unicorns detest bananas* seems more questionable and more of a provocation; whilst *Unicorns smell black* we totally reject. And yet we are in none of the three cases talking about anything real. If linguistics cannot come to grips with problems of this kind it is a poor kind of science. More than that, it is an illusory science. Vendryes put the matter in a nutshell when he said: 'A modern descriptive linguist who claims that the analysis of linguistic structure is, in the first instance, undertaken without reference to meaning is deceiving himself.'

When a linguist is working on a corpus of some previously unrecorded language, he must have some guarantee that every part of his sample *means* something. Sneezes, coughs, grunts and other extraneous noises do not count as language, precisely because they do not stand for anything other than themselves. It is

[1] Bloomfield, L., *op. cit.*, p. 139.
[2] Bloomfield, *ibid.*, p. 101.
[3] Harris, Z. S., *op. cit.*, p. 347.

only when a sound of this kind has a definite conventional meaning in a particular social group that it can acquire a sort of marginal status in the language of the community.

Often meaning has to be called in when setting up analogical comparisons in morphology. Faced with the four English words *prince*, *boy*, *princeling*, *boiling*, a linguist would have to scrutinise the contexts in which these words occurred in order to arrive at their meaning and status, otherwise he would be prone to make the false analogy *prince*:*princeling*::*boy*:*boiling*. With 'isolating' languages like English, one could not distinguish between such phrases as *fresh milk*, *hot milk*, *sour milk* on the one hand, and *drink milk*, *fetch milk*, *heat milk* on the other, unless we knew something of the *meaning* of the individual units as well as their usage.

Influenced by Malinowski's refusal to consider the linguistic behaviour of tribal communities in isolation from the general context of that behaviour, and more particularly the real-life situation in which it occurred, Firth contended that contextual meaning was just as important as formal grammar. According to Firth, meaning is a group of 'situational relations in a context of situation and in that kind of language which disturbs the air and other people's ears . . . modes of behaviour in relation to other elements in the context of situation.'[1]

Although no really systematic means of investigating contextual meaning has yet been evolved, it is nonetheless apparent that many locutions do depend entirely on the situation in which they occur. *What tripe!* could be no more than a sharp outburst of derision over something just said or read; but equally it could be an expression of disgust at a real piece of tripe. Without the context we cannot tell. The example given by Firth himself is the expression *Say when!* 'Quite a number of readers will have lively recollections of the very practical use of these two words. Many Englishmen will at once place themselves in a pleasant situation with good glass, good drink, and good company. The two words fit into the situation. They have their "psychological" and practical moment in what is going on between two people, whose eyes, hands, and goodness knows what else, are sharing a common interest in a bit of life.'[2]

[1] Firth, J. R., *Papers in Linguistics* (London, 1957), pp. 12 and 15.
[2] Firth, J. R., *The Tongues of Men*, p. 110.

Speech and thought

Edward Sapir, writing in the early 1920s, turned his attention to the perennial problem besetting philosophers and psychologists alike: the relationship between speech and thought. What, he asked, was the evidence for such a relationship? His salient point was that the use of language in no way entails thought. When we say *I had a good breakfast this morning* we are not necessarily in the throes of laborious thought. It is true that each *element* of the sentence defines a separate concept or conceptual relations, or both, but the sentence has no conceptual significance whatever. This is followed by Sapir's vivid analogy: 'It is somewhat as though a dynamo capable of generating enough power to run an elevator were operated almost exclusively to feed an electric doorbell. The parallel is more suggestive that at first sight appears. Language may be looked upon as an instrument capable of running a gamut of psychic uses. Its flow not only parallels that of the inner content of consciousness, but parallels it on different levels . . . Thus the outward form only of language is constant; its inner meaning, its psychic value or intensity, varies freely with attention or the selective interest of the mind, also, needless to say, with the mind's general development. *From the point of view of language*, thought may be defined as the highest intent or potential content of speech . . . From this it follows that language and thought are not strictly co-terminous. At best language can but be the outward facet of thought on the highest, most generalised, level of symbolic expression. To put our viewpoint somewhat differently, language is primarily a pre-rational function. It humbly works up to the thought that is latent in, that may eventually be read into, its classifications and its forms; it is not, as is generally or naïvely assumed, the final label put upon the finished thought' (my italics).[1]

Sapir regarded the opinion that thought can exist without speech as illusory. Several reasons are given. To begin with, whenever we try to relate the mental image consciously with another, we find ourselves slipping into a silent flow of words. Besides, language is not co-terminous with auditory articulation. The visual symbolism of the printed word can serve equally well.

Sapir, E., *Language*, pp. 14–15.

'The contention that one thinks without language merely because one is not aware of a coexisting auditory image is very far indeed from being a valid one.' Finally, Sapir traces the intimate interdependence between the growth of new concepts and linguistic expression of them: 'The birth of a new concept is invariably foreshadowed by a more or less strained or extended use of old linguistic material; the concept does not attain to individual and independent life until it has found a distinctive linguistic embodiment. In most cases the new symbol is but a thing wrought from linguistic material already in existence in ways mapped out by crushingly despotic precedents. As soon as the word is at hand, we instinctively feel, with something of a sigh of relief, that the concept is ours for the handling . . . Would we be so ready to die for "liberty", to struggle for "ideals" if the words themselves were not ringing within us?'

Meanwhile, Lev Vygotsky, a Russian contemporary of Sapir, had taken a similar view several stages further. Impressed by the intimate bond existing between word and meaning, between speaking and thinking, Vygotsky and others in the Soviet Union performed a series of experiments which, among other things, not only provided confirmation but also led to a sharpening of this view: 'The meaning of a word represents such a close amalgam of thought and language that it is hard to tell whether it is a phenomenon of speech or a phenomenon of thought.'[1] The fallacy of treating words as mere counters in a game called thinking was demolished for ever: 'Thought is not merely expressed in words; it comes into existence through them. The relation of thought to word is not a thing but a *process*.'[2]

The views of Sapir and Vygotsky are borne out by medical science. Kurt Goldstein[3] in America and Alexander Luria[4] in the Soviet Union, in their investigations of language disturbances produced by cerebral concussion and other factors, have pro-

[1] Vygotsky, L. S., *Thought and Language* (trans. Hanfmann, E., and Vakar, G.) (Camb., Mass., 1962), p. 120.
[2] *ibid.*, p. 125.
[3] Goldstein, K., *Language and Language Disturbances* (New York 1948).
[4] Luria, A. R., *Traumatic Aphasia* (trans. Bowden, D.) (The Hague, 1970). See also *Disorders of Language* (ed. De Reuck, A. V. S., and O'Connor, M.). (Proceedings of the C.I.B.A. Foundation Symposium (London, 1964.)

vided clear proof that mental processes do, in fact, depend on verbal processes. What was originally an experiment has since become a standard part of clinical diagnosis. Presented with a pile of skeins of many different shades of colour, patients (who had been pre-tested and shown not to be colour-blind) were asked to select skeins of a particular colour but were found to pick out skeins of quite opposite colour and lump them together as the same colour. Patients were unable to recognise colours because they had forgotten the names for the colours. Goldstein's conclusion was as follows: 'The fact that naming becomes impossible with this change in the character of language reveals the nature of meaning. It is not based on a simple association between an object and a sound, but presupposes a special attitude towards the object. The name is an expression of the conceptual attitude. Words used as names are not simply tools which may be handled like concrete objects but a means to detach man from an external world and to help him to organise it in a conceptual way.' Patients were unable to use a word capable of bearing several meanings (e.g. *head*, *light*, etc.) and were unable to comprehend shifts of meaning. Metaphorical expression was quite out of the question. Goldstein refers us back to Humboldt: 'Language does not represent objects themselves but the concept which the mind has formed of them in that autonomous activity by which it creates language.'

Patients suffering from language disturbances often showed much greater capacity for thought than for power of expression, and supplemented damage to their vocabulary by gestures and inflexions of the voice. They were unable to keep word classes apart. For one patient *doctor* and *lawyer* would be all one. Another patient used the phrase *a pretty girl* when he meant *a nice man*. Aphasia is consequently described by Sir Russell Brain as 'a disorder of schemas'. 'I believe that all patients who have any degree of expressive aphasia are hampered in thought. . . This effort of expressive aphasia upon thinking is not surprising if we realise the essential part played by words in the acquisition of abstract ideas.' He retells the story of the little girl who, when told to think before she spoke, retorted 'But how can I know what I think till I hear what I say?'

Linguistic approaches to meaning

In linguistics the main difficulty has been that of determining the connections and interrelationships between language structure and extralinguistic reality. This has proved a treacherous undertaking; and not least because language (for reasons we have just examined) affects the way in which we perceive and comprehend reality. Indeed, some have held that language is an integral part of this reality and cannot be considered in isolation from it.

The 'contextual' approach to meaning in language, such as the one advocated by Malinowski and Firth, has a refreshing appeal, and does demand a live and first-hand 'field' knowledge of languages as they are actually used; but to date it has produced little to rival the various 'analytical' approaches.

An important analytical approach is the one begun by Saussure. In his concern lest linguistics become confused with psychology and philosophy, Saussure devoted much attention to demarcating linguistic categories and linguistic boundaries. In particular, he wanted a semantics that would keep within these boundaries and categories and leave the extralinguistic province alone.

Saussure's theory of meaning—speech–word relationship—uses the analogy of a sheet of paper whose two sides are two facets of an indissoluble whole, such that it would be impossible to cut one side of the paper without at the same time cutting the other. All words and verbal expressions have a dual structure. 'In language, one can neither divide sound from thought nor thought from sound; the division could be accomplished only in the abstract and the result would be either pure psychology or pure phonetics. Linguistics, then, operates in the borderland where the elements of sound and thought combine; *their combination produces a form, not a substance.*'[1]

The *formal* relationship referred to by Saussure is achieved in the *sign*, and the transfer between 'sound' and 'thought' is between the *signifier* and the *signification*, the dual aspect of the sign. However, the transfer takes place not between two separate domains but within a single continuum. This is not an easy idea to grasp, and it is one that I shall return to in a later chapter. The sheet of paper, though, is a helpful analogy to keep in mind. We

[1] Saussure, F. de, *op. cit.*, p. 113.

cannot do anything to one side (the signifier) without affecting the other side (the signification). (Even if I draw on it I can see this drawing from the other side of the paper if I hold it up to the light, and there will usually be marks of indentation on the reverse side. The same with language.) It is not possible to change the function or meaning of one word without affecting both the meanings and the forms of other words. To return for a moment to an earlier example: if people begin to use *disinterested* instead of *uninterested* (change of 'signifier') they have to start using words like *impartial* more often; and they may even start using forms like *disintentional* for *unintentional*. It is rather like running a needle-and-thread through our piece of paper. It goes in at one side but immediately appears at the other, and so on indefinitely. If a change occurs in the signifier, this automatically affects in some way the signification.

These forms—sound forms and meaning forms—relate in some way to actuality. It is this actuality that is Saussure's *substance*:

(Substance)	(Form)	(Substance)
ACTUAL SOUNDS $\longleftrightarrow$	[SIGNIFIER $\longleftrightarrow$ SIGNIFICATION] $\longleftrightarrow$	CORRESPONDING ACTUALITY

Linguistic semantics restricts its investigations to the formal relationship sandwiched somewhere between the substance of the extralinguistic domain.

Saussure's terminology, signifier and signification, is translated by Stephen Ullmann[1] into *name* and *sense*. The relationship he represents diagrammatically as follows:

$$name \text{ (n)}$$
$$\updownarrow$$
$$sense \text{ (s)}$$

This diagram has the advantage of not restricting the sense-name connection to a one-to-one or to an atomistic relationship, where each sound represents one unit of meaning and vice versa.

Ullmann, S., *Semantics: An Introduction to the Science of Meaning* Oxford, 1962), pp. 62–3.

On the contrary, several senses may be attached to a single name (e.g. *head—head of a company*, *head of a cabbage*, *head of a coin*, etc.) and vice versa (e.g. *car*, *automobile*, *coupé*, *motor-car* 'four-wheeled vehicle for private transport driven by internal combustion engine'). These may be represented respectively by the following diagrams:

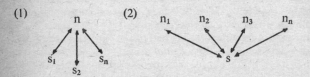

With more complex semantic relationships, the diagram can stand the added complexity. To take the example of *light*, it is easy to classify a number of relationships as follows:

(a) *Homonymic* (or coincident form) relationship: adjective *light* (= 'bright') is a homonym of another adjective signifying 'not heavy'.
(b) *Sense association*. The noun *light* conjures up associations with *sunlight*, *day*, *brightness*, etc.
(c) *Formal and semantic*. The noun *light*, as well as having a direct formal and semantic relationship with its adjective 'light', has similar relationships with the verb *to light* and *to lighten* or the noun *lightning*, etc.

All these cross-connections can be diagrammatically represented as follows:

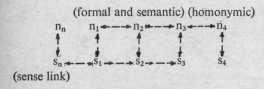

One objection to a description of this kind is that it takes no account of the perpetual variability of context. No two contexts are absolutely identical. If this is the case, should we insist that a word has an indefinite number of 'senses' to match an equally indefinite number of contexts; for, after all, it was just these minute differences that proved so problematic for the patients suffering from language disturbance? Take, for instance, the word *red*. As we know, two reds are only ever alike by sheer coincidence or in patterned situations (e.g. all red telephone kiosks are presumably of the same colour exactly when they are freshly painted). The problem is, however, not completely insoluble, provided that we keep strictly to the *formal* aspect of language. One suggestion[1] is that 'sense' or 'semantic content' is not actualised but only *potential* meaning. It becomes actualised only when a context requires it. That every context is slightly different from the next need not worry us, since contexts belong to actuality, whereas sense only becomes actualised at the moment it is 'applied' to context. Each time a word is used the extraneous, non-relevant areas of the semantic content are filtered out. Thus, for example, if I am referring to a red telephone kiosk, all other possible reds are momentarily blotted out, except the red actualised in this context. The actualisation is not at all simple, and is such that if someone tells me the kiosk is actually brown, and not red, I will assume he is either deceiving me or colour-blind. Moreover, it does not prevent me from believing that kiosks go on being red when I do not see them, after dark, and even when I imagine or dream about them. The epistemological repercussions of all this will be apparent to the philosophically inclined reader, and I do not propose going into them. There is already too much Aristotle hereabouts anyway. It will perhaps be obvious by now to the reader that a strictly 'formal' approach to semantics and meaning can never be entirely satisfactory. But woe betide the linguist who tries to grapple with *actuality*.

[1] Glinz, H., *The Proceedings of the Ninth International Congress of Linguistics* (Camb., Mass., 1962), pp. 1059 ff.

15 Words

Those Modern Europeans who think about words at all usually envisage the printed or written word, a series of syllables or letters, or both. The word has through overfamiliarity, in the press, books, advertisement posters, in whatever direction one turns, lost much of the awe and prestige that surrounded it until quite recent times. The only thing left is its power; one still talks, albeit in cliché at times, of the power of words. The Scottish–English word *glamour*, originally carrying overtones of magic and witchcraft, derives by direct dissimilation from *grammar*, a highly charged word in the popular mind until well into the Renaissance.

The Greek for 'word' was *logos*, which also meant simultaneously 'meaning' and 'reason'. In effect, our own concept of the word did not exist in the ancient world, as it always carried with it a wider sense. The Chinese have a similar concept *tao*. In Alexandria, where Greek, Judaic, Egyptian and other cultures met, the Logos assumed mystical significance, and was to have important repercussions right through the later period of the Graeco-Roman civilisation and into the Middle Ages. This, however, was no innovation, and it may surprise many readers to learn that the oldest civilisations we know, the Chinese, Hindu and Egyptian, all featured the word prominently in their myths of the origin of the world. The earliest Egyptian text, believed to be from the fourth millenium B.C. and known as the Memphite Drama, gives the following account of the origin of the universe:

> [Ptah, acting on behalf of all the other gods] pronounced the names of all things, created the sight of the eyes, the hearing of the ears, the breathing of the nose, that they may transmit to the heart. It is the heart that causes that every conclusion should come forth, it is the tongue which announces the thought of the heart . . . Every divine word came into being through that which the heart thought and the tongue commanded . . .

Ptah was the Egyptian deity who revealed his power in the heart (we should nowadays say 'mind') and tongue. Ptah was greater than all the other Gods for he was the creator. And like the God of the Hebrews in Genesis he 'rested after he had made everything'.[1] One is too easily deterred by the incantatory style; and yet, on closer examination, the theory is hardly any different from Saussure's. If one substitutes '*sign*' for '*divine word*', '*concept*' for '*thought of the heart*' and '*sound-image*' for '*tongue*', then hardly any distance remains from Saussure's scheme, given earlier.

Egyptian cosmology is echoed millenia later in the opening words of St. John's Gospel: 'In the beginning was Word, the Word was with God, the Word was God.' In more recent times Humboldt preferred his own momentous thesis: *no words, no world*.

Comparative studies of non-European languages, of many varied and exotic kinds, have inclined more than one linguist to the view that language as an evolutionary phenomenon must have originated aeons ago, long before the time generally supposed. As Sapir puts it, 'The universality and diversity of speech lead to a significant inference. We are forced to believe that language (any status) is an immensely ancient heritage of the human race, *whether or not forms of speech are the historical outgrowth of a single pristine form*. It is doubtful if any other cultural asset of man, be it the art of drilling for fire or of chipping stone, may lay claim to a greater age. I am inclined to believe that it antedated even the lowliest developments of material culture, that these developments, in fact, were not strictly possible until language, the tool of significant expression, had itself taken shape.'[2] This is supported by the experimental findings of neurologists in the mental impairment of aphasia, discussed earlier.

Much has been written since the age of Darwin on humans' affinities with the higher mammals, notably the anthropoid apes. Among the most outstanding is that of Köhler, the psychologist, who spent a substantial part of his life observing the habits of chimpanzees in captivity, as well as other animals. It would not be fitting to try to summarise the scope of his work. His conclusions are guarded and tentative, and hardly go further than suggesting the complexity of the conceptual and methodological problems facing those who venture into this hazardous domain. Köhler was nevertheless struck by the similarity of human and chimpanzee behaviour. The limiting factors which brought about

[1] Frankfort, H., *et al.*, *Before Philosophy* (London, 1949), p. 68.
[2] Sapir, E., *Language*, p. 23.

the separation of anthropoids from humans were three: (i) lack of a time scale (which he thought responsible for chimpanzees' lapses in ability to reproduce solutions to identical situations); (ii) lack of speech; and (iii) inability to build up 'components of thought', 'images' or concepts.

Köhler regarded language as no more than a 'technical aid', but it seems to me that speech, or rather language, is one basis of the lack of time scale and of concepts as well. Take, for instance, the case of an anthropoid ape in a cage with a relatively simple problem to solve. A banana is placed outside the cage but beyond the animal's reach. A stick is lying on the floor of the cage, and if the stick is protruded it can be used as an implement to draw the banana towards the cage. Not unnaturally, this problem presents scarcely any difficulty whatever to any of Köhler's chimpanzees. The solution was interpreted as insight into the visual situation. I am neither competent nor have I any desire to challenge this view. There is, however, another interpretation which Köhler altogether ignores—the *linguistic* interpretation. If you think of the word *stick* you will soon discover, though perhaps not to your amazement, that the word triggers off a number of verbal functions, e.g. waving, standing, hitting, poking, bending and many others. The word *stick* is, in fact, a *functional* word, for I may use anything with a certain length and rigidity for the purpose ascribed to sticks, from an umbrella to a snake frozen rigid.

This 'verbal' explanation of the way in which humans very largely solve situations had scarcely passed through my mind when I had an experience, which can justly be described as 'traumatic'.

A friend of mine, a research scientist, was in the habit of working late, and one evening, when I called for him to lure him off to the local, things in his laboratory were clearly going wrong. He was on his own and endeavouring to carry out several operations at once associated with a large machine, which conveys no more to me now than it did then. At one end of the lab. and along the entire length of the room ran a bench covered, not to say heaped, with apparatus of all kinds. He beckoned me in this direction asking me to fetch him an ?X?YXX!?—the word—whatever it was—may have ended in 'meter', in fact I suspect that it did, but my memory fails me. I asked him to repeat the word, which he did, but not without showing signs of angry irritation. I made for the bench, tentatively handled a few bits and pieces, but replaced them in despair and crept away bewildered, showing every symptom of loss of face. Speechless at my stupidity, my friend dropped everything, stormed over to the bench and returned without a word with the required apparatus. It was a long time before our relations were normal again!

A little reflection showed me that this laboratory was an alien world—precisely because it was *unnamed*. I knew the name of hardly anything. Even 'knobs' were not knobs and press-buttons bore a multiplicity of mathematical signs with a whole battery of significations. And then—I recalled the chimpanzees. They too were in alien situations and environments, and we were alike in *nameless* situations, for none of Köhler's observations revealed even the most rudimentary language. Otherwise, we had not much in common; a laboratory is not the least like a cage—or is it? If someone had locked me in a laboratory of this kind and devised even the simplest visual problem for me to solve thereby getting my dinner, I should almost certainly long ago have died of starvation. The cage is no less unfamiliar to the chimpanzee than the laboratory is to me.

The upshot of all this was that for several weeks I laboured under a decided feeling of inferiority *vis-à-vis* chimpanzees. If *they* could solve problems of every kind of order involving all kinds of tools *without language*, then they must have far more intelligence and aptitude than Köhler had given them credit for. How immeasurably easier and simpler life is for human beings by virtue of the possession of language. Words surround us at every turn like a cosmic nervous system, a network of links and associations and functions of an intricacy beyond comprehension.

Linguistic definitions of the word

Aristotle's definition of the word as the *smallest significant unit of speech* served adequately until quite recent times. It was found wanting only by modern linguistics.

The word was redefined by Bloomfield as the *minimum free form*. This cleared up a number of anomalies but created several more. The redefinition, for instance, admits *to* in *to swim* or *to climb*, even though the 'word' *to* in these contexts does not have any real meaning, being a purely syntactic marker; and it rules out *-ish* in *bluish* and *greenish* since, despite its semantic value, it cannot appear as a 'free' form (it is a 'bound 'morpheme). On the other hand, Bloomfield's criterion does not make any distinction between the totally different structures of *ran up* in *he ran up the hill* and *he ran up a bill*. In the former case, *ran up* is both two free forms and two words, whereas in the latter it is two free forms but only *one* word.

A more adequate, but quite elegant, formula was subsequently proposed by Meillet: 'A word is defined by the association of a given *sense* with a given group of *sounds* capable of a given *grammatical* use ' (my italics). This formula takes care of many of the anomalies left over by Bloomfield. For example, it would admit both *windmill* and (French) *moulin à vent* as single words since, although they have different forms, they do have the same sense and both function as compound nouns.

This inevitable phase of redefinition and reformulation, of which I have given only two samples, was rapidly matched by a renewed awareness of the real nature of the word. Something that had been treated like more of a commodity by dictionary-makers, etymologists, comparatists and others now began to cast its own shadow and to reveal something of its arcane and impenetrable character, albeit in modern guise.

Sapir, working with American Indian informants, was struck by their intuitive awareness of words in their own (hitherto unrecorded) speech. The words that these informants recognised as words turned out, however, to be very different from the ones familiar to speakers of 'standard average European'. An example of a single word from the Paiute language Sapir gives as *wii-to-kuchum-punku-rügani-yugwi-va-ntü-m(ü)*, literally translated as 'knife-black-buffalo-pet-cut up-sit (pl.) future-participle-animate plural', more freely glossed as 'they who are going to sit and cut up with a knife a black bull or cow'. Sapir suggested defining the word in terms of the aesthetic intuition: 'The best we can do is to say that the word is one of the smallest, completely satisfying bits of "meaning" into which the sentence resolves itself.'

A formidable critic of a 'semantics that persisted in treating word meaning as an association between a word's sound and its content' was Vygotsky. The linguist, he complained, treated words in a much too trivial and uniform way: 'linguistics did not realise that in the historical evolution of language the *very structure of meaning* and its psychological nature *also* change . . . It is not merely the content of a word that changes but the way in which reality is generalized and reflected in a word.' (My italics.)[1] Vygotsky's views are no mere conjecture. Experimentally they have been borne out time and again. Luria describes an experiment carried out in Leningrad in which children between one and two-and-a-half years old were presented with small red and green boxes. The green ones were empty, but the red ones contained sweets. In the event it proved difficult for the children to select the right boxes. Even if progress was made, the correct choice had to be worked out afresh the following day (as with Köhler's chimpanzees). The picture changed completely, however, when speech was introduced. Learning proved not only quicker and more permanent but was also more readily transferred to situations in which different objects were used.[2] Vygotsky was so impressed by his observations that he produced what may be the ultimate in definition: 'A word is a microcosm of human consciousness.'

Is there any definition of the word, then, that is both large enough and yet not too vast for the linguist to work with? I believe there is. It is a definition produced by Michael Halliday. Halliday concedes that the word has many features which make it a unit of the sentence: it may be a noun, it could be marked by gender or plurality, and it may contain one or more affixes. But this is only the beginning of the story. The word, Halliday claims, enters into relationships that lie beyond and even have little or nothing to do with grammar. It is 'distinguished from other grammatical units in that, after it has been exhaustively treated in the grammar, there always remains much to be said about it.'[3]

We shall return to this definition in a later chapter. For the present, I simply want to outline some of the less high-flown features of words as these have been described in semantics.

Full words and form words

Ullmann provides a useful demarcation between what Henry Sweet called 'full' words, or words with an independent sense or

[1] Vygotsky, L. S., *op. cit.*, pp. 121–2.
[2] Luria, A. R., *The Role of Speech in the Regulation of Normal and Abnormal Behaviour* (London, 1961), pp. 10–11.
[3] Halliday, M. A. K., 'General Linguistics and Its Application to Language Teaching' in *Patterns of Language* (London, 1966), p. 18.

meaning, and 'form' words, which are really of a structural function only. This distinction can be traced back to Aristotle. The criterion is purely semantic. A list of words is given as follows:

tree	*if*
sing	*it*
blue	*of*
gently	*and*

The words in the first column have meaning even if they appear in isolation, whereas those listed in the second column have no independent meaning proper: 'They are grammatical elements which will contribute to the meaning of the phrase or the sentence when used in conjunction with other words.' This class of words includes all articles, prepositions conjunctions, pronouns and certain adverbs. They have been called 'synsemantic', that is they are meaningful only when they occur in the company of other words.

Ullmann attempts to base this demarcation on both phonological and grammatical grounds. The latter are the more convincing. He is able to show that certain form words have the same function as grammatical inflexions, in some cases interchangeable with them. The genitive *-s* in English, e.g. *the dog's dinner*, can be replaced by the more clumsy *the dinner of the dog*. Comparatives and superlatives, e.g. *hungrier, hungriest*, can be replaced by *more hungry, most hungry*; *stupider* or *stupidest* by *more stupid* and *most stupid*. He also shows that in French the unstressed personal pronoun may be separated from the verb by one or more form words but never by full words, e.g. *je le crois, je ne le crois pas, je n'y crois pas* but *je le vois rarement*. Form words in French can be shown to be exactly parallel to Latin declensional forms:

soror-i	à la *sœur*	'to the sister'
soror-is	de la *sœur*	'of the sister'
dic-o	je *dis*	'I say'
dic-is	tu *dis*	'you say'

If the distinction is valid, then the field of the lexicologist becomes clearer. He is concerned not with prepositions, pronouns and other 'form words' but with 'full words' or words of independent meaning only. The 'form words' will fall into the category of syntax and syntagmatics. The Modern French isolating constructions which have replaced Latin inflexions have been called by Vendryes *'flexion par l'avant'* (inflexion by prefix). There is nevertheless the important difference that Latin inflexions could not be separated from the stem of the word, whereas the French prepositions and articles etc. are.

Certain of these words can so easily assume full semantic status—e.g. *down*, the preposition, can without change of form be used as a full word: *they down thumbs, tools*; *down train*; *to have a down on someone*; *to down a pint in three seconds*, etc. Even used in complete isolation 'form' or 'pseudo'-words can be highly charged semantically. For instance, the title of Kipling's poem *If*, or Kierkegaard's *Either Or*, or the French magazine *Elle*.

Transparent and opaque words

An important distinction is made in semantics between *transparent*, sometimes called 'motivated', and *opaque*, otherwise termed 'conventional', words. The distinction is not hard to grasp and goes back, like most other things, to the Greeks. Although, as we shall see, the classification is not always cut-and-dried, transparent (or motivated) words are those which show some intrinsic correspondence between sound and sense, the most obvious examples of which are the purely onomatopoeic words such as *cuckoo, coo, buzz, hiss*, etc. Very few words show a perfect or universal correspondence. The remainder, words that have no such correspondence, are opaque (or conventional) words.

A way is suggested of objectively testing for opaqueness or transparency. Three criteria are adopted for establishing one or the other: descriptive, historical and comparative. The example Ullmann takes is the English word *meat*. On *descriptive* grounds *meat* is opaque and unanalysable since, if there were a necessary connection between name and sense, one might expect the same sounds to mean always the same thing. Yet the word has several homophones: *meet*, (to) *meet*, (to) *mete out*. The word has also a synonym *flesh*, which although very close in meaning has not a single sound in common with *meat*. The *historical* test likewise proves negative in that, if the connection between sound and sense were a necessary one, both elements would have shown no historical change or evolution. Yet they have changed independently of each other since Saxon times. Old English *mete* stood for food and drink in general, as it still does in the phrase *meat and drink*. Very few words stand up to the *comparative* test, and my own opinion is that it is not only too rigorous but also goes beyond the confines of any given language (synchronic). The word *bow-wow* is certainly transparent so far as modern English is concerned, but no other language uses the same term; French, for example, has *ouâ-ouâ*. The word *meat* passes none of the three tests and thus can be safely designated 'opaque'.

In their passage from one period or synchronic state of a language to another, words can lose or acquire 'motivation'. Examples of loss of motivation are to be found universally. Latin had motivated words which turn up opaque in French owing entirely to phonological erosion and transformation. Vulgar Latin *pipio*—(gen.) *pipionis*, from *pipire* 'to chirp, peep', a transparent enough word in Latin, appears in French as *pigeon*. Latin *mūgire* 'to low, bellow' lost its onomatopoeic effect by passage of the Latin *ū* to French /ȳ/.

This loss of motivation can often be compensated for in new directions. The best example is the Latin word *murmur* (pron. moormoor), which could convey the effect of rumbling, roaring and kindred sounds. When it passed into French as *murmure* /myRmyR/ the motivation changed with the sound, and the word became expressive of softer and lighter sounds. When the word was borrowed by English from French the vowel quality altered yet again to /məːmə/ at the same time taking on the distant, indistinct, even confused sound one associates with the word. Ullmann gives three first-rate examples from these languages to illustrate the different effects:

Latin: (1) *Magno misceri* murmure *caelum* (= 'the sky is confused with a great rumbling')
                                                    (Virgil, *Aeneid* IV, 1.160)

French: (2) *Ou l'onde qui* murmure *en caressant ces rives*
                                                    (Lamartine, *Chant d'Amour*)

English: (3) The surgy *murmurs* of the lonely sea
                                                    (Keats, *Endymion*, Bk. 1)

Loss of *semantic* motivation can break the metaphorical bond between name and thing referred to. French *pavillon* (Eng.

pavilion) is derived by normal phonological change from Latin *papilionem* ('butterfly'). The French word *papillon* is, of course, felt to have no connection and came to French from the same Latin word by an alternative phonological channel. It could be that the phonologically different histories arose from an unconscious desire within the language to set apart the two unconnected meanings *pavillon* and *papillon*. After all, the English words *person* and *parson* were driven apart by an analogous process.

Poets who have a weakness for etymology can often deliberately *revitalise* words by bringing them back to their etymological origins. It was true of Chaucer and Spenser; it is true in our time of Joyce and Eliot whose poetry abounds in, and even depends for some of its more superb effect on, such revitalisations.

Owen Barfield shows that revitalisation need not be merely etymological but semantic in the profoundest sense, almost as though a word was a seed-kernel which in the hands of a great poet could shoot forth life. A word that has lost one or more of its senses in the course of its history, or which has fallen apart in separate word senses, can be wholly recharged or restored. He takes but one example, the English word *ruin*.

In classical times the verbal idea contained in the Latin verb *ruo* signified 'swift, disastrous movement'—a composite of 'rush–fall–collapse' difficult to render in modern English by any single word. It was only subsequently, argues Barfield, that the three separate meanings fell apart. The noun *ruina* by the time it came into being contained only the last of the three meanings 'collapse' or 'that which has collapsed'. The 'soul' of the word was still unmistakably there, a suggestion of vigorous movement, and in the intervening centuries of the Middle Ages the word retained its potentiality. Its reattainment of full power had to await Shakespeare's magic touch. Salisbury in *King John* is confronted by Arthur's body lying on the stones after falling from the walls to his death:

> It is the shameful work of Hubert's hand,
> The practice and purpose of the King;
> From whose obedience I forbid my soul,
> Kneeling before this *ruin* of sweet life.

Again we encounter an even more striking use in *Antony and Cleopatra*:

> The noble *ruin* of her magic, Antony.

'The word *ruin* . . . has grown with Shakespeare's help into a warm and living thing, a rich piece of imaginative material ready at hand for anyone who has the skill to evoke its power.'[1]

[1] Barfield, O., *Poetic Diction*, p. 120.

16 Semantic Structure

Name–sense relationships

In Chapter 14 the interrelationship between name and sense was discussed in outline. More detail is now called for.

Name–sense relationships can be divided into four categories:

(1) *Sense likeness* but *name difference*. These are the *synonymic* relationships Synonyms are words of identical or similar meaning: e.g. *bad, wicked, evil*, etc.

(2) *Opposite sense* and *name difference*. These are the *antonyms* of language; the words of opposite meaning. Examples are: *bad–good, false–true*, etc.

(3) *Related sense* and *identical name*. This association is technically known as *polysemy*, and the relations as *polysemantic*. Examples of polysemy are: *head* = (a) 'chief', (b) 'part of body', (c) 'one side of a coin', etc.

(4) *Different sense* but *identical name*. These relations are called *homonymic*. Homonyms include such examples as *bear* = (a) the animal, (b) 'to support'.

Synonyms

A synonym may be defined as a word of similar or identical meaning to one or more words in the same language. All languages contain synonyms, but in a few languages, like English, they exist in superabundance. A group of synonyms—that is, a group of words with common fundamental sense—can be called a synonym cluster. A synonym dictionary such as *Roget's Thesaurus* arranges its entries by synonym cluster. Of course, there is much overlapping between the different clusters. An adjective like *sick*, for instance, belongs not only to the cluster *ill, ailing, diseased*, etc., but also to one that includes words like *tired, fed up*, etc., and to one that would bring it alongside *morbid* (as in *sick humour*).

To prevent their meanings or uses from becoming confused, synonyms are 'marked', either semantically or syntactically. Syntactic marking is always easily visible (or audible) and it is achieved by syntagmatic linkage. The various synonyms for *fast*

can occur in a range of syntagmatic compounds, and the association in each particular compound is permanent: *quick*-witted,
fast-moving, *fleet* of foot, etc. Semantic marking, on the other
hand, is covert but achieved in a variety of ways. The first of
these is by *milieu* or *setting*. A *gathering*, for example, is generally
neutral, i.e. 'unmarked' semantically, whereas *audience, congrega-
tion* and *rally* are marked by the different milieus in which they
occur. A second means is by *level of style*. When compared with
gathering, a *throng* sounds high-flown and 'literary', whilst *get-
together* sounds positively colloquial. A third means is *emotive
connotation*. In contrast to *gathering*, the words *plot* or *conspiracy*
have a sinister ring, although, of course, only for those who are
not inside the plot or conspiracy. It all depends on one's viewpoint. *Firm* is more neutral than *obstinate*, and *pig-headed* is
outright condemnation by comparison.[1]

The different milieus, levels of style and even the connotations
can be conveniently brought together under *register*. Register is
the whole gamut of milieus and of stylistic and connotative contrasts. Milieus not unnaturally differ from one speech community
to another. In English the milieus reflected in semantic marking
by register include: military, legal, business, ecclesiastical, nauti-
cal, political, recreation and others. There are three basic levels of
style: elevated or formal, neutral, and informal or colloquial.
These can be subdivided by further semantic requirements.

It will be apparent, then, that synonym clusters can very readily
reflect social conventions. *Clever* is neutral by comparison with
bright, which is generally used only of younger people by older
people. It does not seem quite right to refer to an older person as
'bright', perhaps because it inevitably carries a connotation of
precociousness. A term like *competent* can be used neutrally, but
if we use it as a synonym of *clever* there is usually a hint of reser-
vation, sometimes as if *competent* carried with it the modifier
merely. Even *clever* can become non-neutral (or 'marked') in
phrases like *clever-clever* or *too clever*. Conventions change, of
course, and this change affects semantic marking. A word that
carries very positive and desirable connotations at the present
time is *intelligent*.

In British English especially, socio-cultural stratification can be

---

[1] Robert Thouless in his *Straight and Crooked Thinking* (London, 1930)
suggested the paradigm: *I am firm*; *you are obstinate*; *he is pig-headed*.

vindicated. *Brainy*, the popular synonym of *clever*, is not used by the higher educated to describe themselves or anyone else. A person who uses *brainy* is in some danger of being regarded as someone of inferior breeding.

Antonyms

Like synonyms, *antonyms*—words of opposite meaning—are of some importance in semantic structure. In an antonym pair only one of the members is (semantically) marked. This semantic marking, as with synonyms, occurs on that member of the pair whose use is the more restricted. We can ask: *How big is it?* but not *How small is it?*; and can say *This bed is too big for my room*, but we might sound eccentric if we put it in the form *This bed is not sufficiently small for my room* (although the latter seems more 'logical'). For these and other like reasons, *small* is said to be the marked member of the pair: *small–big*.

Polysemy

Learning a foreign language would be a far easier task than it actually is, were it not for the fact that the words one learns usually have more than one meaning. And the very commonly used words often have scores of meanings. Verbs in English like *make* and *go* run to several columns of entries each in the *Shorter Oxford Dictionary*. A comparatively seldom-used word like *hippopotamus*, however, has only one meaning listed against it in the dictionary.[1]

The most prevalent type of polysemy is that resulting from ordinary contextual *shifts in application*. Adjectives are particularly prone to this kind of shift. Compare, for instance, the different meanings of *red* in: *red ink*, *red hair*, *red deer*, *red cabbage* and *Red Indian*. Only the first item in the list (*red ink*) is really 'red'. Red hair is more usually reddish to ginger; red cabbage is purple, whilst the complexion of a North American Indian is anything from burnished copper to 'pale'.

Specialisation by milieu is another common cause of polysemy.

[1] George K. Zipf discovered a mathematical relationship between polysemy and word frequency. The number of different meanings of a word was found to be equal to the square root of the frequency of that word. See, for example, his *The Psycho-biology of Language* (Camb., Mass., 1965).

Partner contains the basic meaning of a type of relationship between two (or more) people. But a *business partner* is not at all the same thing as a *marriage partner*; and neither would want to be associated with a *partner in crime*.

Another, and very frequent, type of polysemy is that created by *metaphor*. In language metaphorical meanings abound. Metaphorical associations are not always as simple as *leaf* (of a *tree*) → *leaf* (of a *book*), or *hands* → *hands* (of a *clock*). In fact, metaphorical extension is so fundamental a feature of language that it is not by any means always possible to be sure that a 'literal' meaning antedates a metaphorical one. Consider the following example of multiple metaphorical polysemy: *human body*, *heavenly body*, *body politic*, *body* (of a *liquid*), etc.

Finally, polysemy has been complicated still further by the tendency of words to pick up meanings from other dialects, from slang and from foreign languages. As examples of 'semantic borrowings' from slang we could cite *square*, *chicken* and *high* (on narcotics). There has always been semantic borrowing between dialects. Compare the use in British English of the American meaning of *executive* (a manager, director or entrepreneur) with the British meaning (one who acts under the direction of a superior in implementing policy). The American sense has virtually ousted the British one because of the irreconcilability of the two meanings. We shall be reviewing semantic borrowing between languages in a later section.

To bring this discussion of polysemy to a close let us take a single complex example and examine the various uses. The word *mate* has one basic or neutral sense. In referring to a partner of the opposite sex, it can be used of 'mating' in the case of animals and of matrimony in the case of human beings. In British lower-class usage *mate* means an habitual companion, usually of the same sex, and is used as a synonym of *friend*. It is also used as a term of address by working-class people and sailors; and has recently been adopted by some middle-class people with rather interesting connotations of cheeky disrespect (could it be Spike Milligan's doing?). In syntagmatic compounds like *shipmate* the word suggests only that the 'mate' is a member of a ship's crew. In *plumber's mate* he is an assistant. But in *soulmate* he appears elevated in style but, at the same time, because elevated, subject to mockery.

Homonymy

Homonyms are of two kinds: homonyms proper, in the case of which the sound and the spelling are identical (e.g. *bat* = 'cricket bat' = 'flying mammal'); and *homophones*, which are words having the same sound but not the same spelling necessarily (e.g. *pear*, *pair*, *pare*).

Homonymy differs from polysemy only to the extent that the semantic bond has been severed or does not exist at all in the case of the former. Most languages contain homonyms, and languages like English, Chinese and French are teeming with them.

It is perhaps no coincidence that languages with a high degree of homonymy frequently use spelling to distinguish homophones. In Chinese this is easily done, since each word is written with a different character; although even Chinese has some homonyms proper (words sounding the same and spelt the same). In English and French the possibility of permuting orthography is more limited. In English homophones occur most often in pairs: *soul–sole*, *flower–flour*, etc. French has the additional advantage of being able to use gender to differentiate (e.g. *le foie* 'liver', *la foi* 'faith' and *la fois* 'time, occasion'). It is very seldom that three or more spellings are created for the same sound: (Eng.) *pair–pear–pare* and (Fr.) *eau–os–haut*.

Homonyms are the result of two different diachronic factors:

(1) The *phonetic convergence* of two words of dissimilar sound and sense. The English homonym pair *race* derives separately from Old Norse *ras* ('running') and French *race* ('people').

(2) The *semantic divergence*, or loss of semantic bond, between two words once polysemantically related. Examples include *humour* and (*aqueous*)*humour* ('the fluid inside the eye'), and *pupil* (= 'scholar') and *pupil* ('apple of the eye').

The dividing line between homonymy and polysemy is not always too clear, and for this reason some linguists have preferred to use the single term homonymy to embrace both categories.

Semantic fields

Saussure demonstrated that each word in a language is surrounded by a network of associations which connect with still other terms. Some of these connections arise between the five senses (synaesthetic); others between the form or shape of words; whilst others involve formal and semantic connections. 'A given term is like the centre of a constellation, the point where other co-ordinated terms converge, and their sum is indefinite.' To illustrate his thesis Saussure drew up the following diagram:

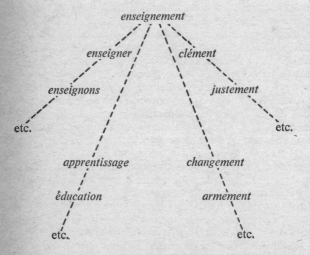

In the first 'leg' of this scheme are the terms *enseigner* 'to teach' and *enseignons* 'we teach', linked by similarity of grammatical form. Those of the second 'leg' (*apprentissage*, *éducation*) are linked to the noun *enseignement* by synonymity or semantic relationship. The words in the third and fourth 'legs' are linked by no more than the suffix *-ment*, which they all share. The 'legs' are kept separate for the simple reason that *changement* and *armement* are nouns, whereas the words of the fourth 'leg' are a miscellaneous, accidental grouping, comprising nouns, adjectives and adverbs, sharing only the element *-ment*.

This semantic theory, never more than an embryo in the work of Saussure, was worked up by his successors into the concept of the 'associative field'. As one of Saussure's pupils expressed it, 'the associative field is a halo which surrounds the sign and whose exterior fringes become merged'. This field is formed by an intricate network of associations: *similarity*, *contiguity*, *sensation*, *name*. The associative field is by any definition *open*; that is, no finite limits can be assigned to any given field. Hence the aptness of the concept 'field', which serves an analogous purpose in physics. The difference between the physical and semantic field is nevertheless important: namely, that no associative field is the same for any particular word from one speaker to the next. One is peculiarly reminded of the dialect 'field' discussed in Chapter 3, which also depended to a considerable extent on the location and point of view of the individual. Guiraud has collected a 'morpho-semantic field' of no less than 2000 terms for the word *cat*, related on either formal or semantic grounds, or both. He eventually managed to reduce this to an absolute minimum of 300 words.

All the foregoing contains immense and far-reaching implications for the future of comparative linguistics. But before discussing this, it is as well to look for a moment at the more immediate and obvious consequences for historical semantics.

To take an example of a word that has traditionally been regarded as an ordinary case of 'restriction of meaning', the French word *viande*. The word now means 'meat', whereas originally it possessed the much wider connotation of 'food'. Etymologists remained puzzled by the fact that in other Romance languages (Ital. *vivanda*, Span. *vianda*, and in the Norman French loan word into English *viands*) no such restriction had occurred.

A little rethinking suggested that the French word had narrowed in meaning because it was needed to take over from its neighbour *chair* 'flesh', which was rapidly falling into disuse. But why this demise? The answer seems to be that *chair* had a homophone *chère* 'face' (surviving in the English loan word *cheer*). Eventually, *chère* developed meanings very close to those of its homonym: 'cheer, fare, living', as in the phrase *faire bonne chère*. Confusion of the two senses would have been particularly embarrassing during Lent, with its strict rules on fasting and abstinence. It fell to *viande* to meet the need thus created. Other words, such as *nourriture*, remained to fulfil the function previously served by *viande*. The restriction of *viande* = 'food' to *viande* = 'meat' is no simple case of semantic restriction but the outcome of a complex of factors, with associative field adjustments in all directions; for it will be obvious that the displacement will have had reverberations in ever-diminishing significance throughout the French language (and others?). Again, one is reminded of the ripple on the surface of a pool.

In the semantic change affecting *viande*, the crucial factor was homonymic clash in words originally unconnected with it. Sometimes, homonymic association will combine with popular etymology and synonymic interference to produce unexpected kinks. For a long time, the French word *maroufle*, with its multiple sense 'cat, scoundrel, strong paste for mounting pictures', had baffled etymologists, until the associative field theory arrived to open up new perspectives. The story of *maroufle* is this. At one time, it was a synonym of *chas*, and both words signified a 'starch paste'. Later, with the phonetic tendency of the final consonant to cease to be pronounced altogether, a homonymic clash developed between *chas* and *chat* 'cat'. At this stage, popular etymology took over and related the two words *chat* and *chas* in meaning as well as sound, and, of course, along with it the synonym *maroufle*. In this way *maroufle* acquired the sense of 'cat'.

The relevance of all this to comparative linguistics is not difficult to see. Whenever one is dealing with synchronic phases of a given language other than that of the present day, there can always be doubts as to the general, let alone precise, meaning of any given word. Only awareness of associative field theory can correct the mistakes or distortions of earlier etymologists. No word can now be viewed in isolation. Diachronic or historical accounts of individual words are bound to go wrong at some stage. The greatest hazard of all is that a word may undergo a significant change of meaning from one period to another without revealing any apparent trace of this. It is just in such cases that the etymologist has to take account of the 'halo' of the word; and this 'halo' may overlap into areas of human activity right outside language.

Although one of the more recent developments in linguistics, field theory of meaning has its beginnings in early nineteenth-century Romantic philosophy. European linguistics, in a sense, began with the idea of language as an organic something, language as an internally co-ordinated 'speech-form'. But European philology was not yet ripe for the pregnant notions of Humboldt, Herder, Coleridge and others of the late eighteenth and early nineteenth centuries. It is only in the last thirty or forty years that these premature theories have been worked up into the concept of linguistic field, under influences from many quarters, linguistic and extralinguistic. The extralinguistic influences include gestalt psychology, neurology (in particular, the study of language disturbance mentioned earlier), post-Wittgensteinian philosophy, field theory of physics. Within linguistics itself, certain scholars, including Weisberger and Trier, have been forced to the conclusion from studies of various synchronic 'periods' of languages that lexical units could not be viewed in isolation; instead, they formed a closely knit and articulated lexical sphere, where the significance of each unit was determined by its neighbours, their semantic areas reciprocally limiting one another. These units were found in all cases to be indissolubly bound up with the social or cultural context.

Weisberger concluded that language is a *supra-individual* cultural product, the heritage of past generations. He went on to envisage what he called a *sprachliche Zwischenwelt*, or linguistic 'screen', interposed between individual speakers and the non-linguistic world.

Once firmly erected, this 'screen' has become the source of unlimited speculation. In the first place, words begin to be conceived of as concentrations within a linguistic field, with direction and momentum but with no isolated identity other than that capable of dictionary definition. Words belong in never-ending chain-sequences to phrases, sentences, contexts, to the fabric of the entire language. The analogy is a limited one, but they are crudely similar to what is known about the individual atoms of a complex molecule, displacement of a single one of which will affect the nature of the entire complex to a greater or lesser degree.

And then, strange to relate, the Sanskrit Grammarians it appears had guessed all this long ago. They had held the well worked-out and sophisticated theory that individual words expressed no meaning until they became joined together in a linguistic whole. It was understood that a child acquired the concept of 'fetching' only by being earlier acquainted with such

sentences as *fetch the cow* and *fetch the horse*. A sentence such as
fetch a cuckoo from the woods leaves the hearer nonplussed not
because he is unfamiliar with the individual words but because (as
Wittgenstein would have put it) words are being *used* in a queer
way. According to these ancient Hindu linguists, the identifica-
tion of any two given units as the same word was for the mere
practical convenience of lexicographers.

All this is not so fanciful as it might appear. It does seem that
individual words do have context—haloes of infinite extent—and
coexist with every other word in the language, *provided that there
is no clash of context*. It does not matter if words coincide as
homonyms, so long as their contexts do not suffer interference.
These 'interference phenomena', as they are sometimes glibly
called, take many forms. It is not that language abhors homonyms, but that it will tolerate them only so long as *contexts* are
left intact. Thus *bat* (cricket) and *bat* (animal) coexist because
there is at most an infinitesimal chance of their clashing in any
conceivable context. Where there is possible confusion through
sense relationship, a critical struggle takes place. In a northern
French dialect the word *vaisseau* 'hive, swarm of bees' was in
direct conflict with the French standard meaning: 'vessel, recep-
tacle'. It was almost as awkward as trying to keep the like poles of
two magnets together. The homonyms could not live happily
together. Attempts were made to alter the spelling of the dialect
usage to *faisseau* or *maisseau* (*m* from *mouche*). A different but
related confusion has arisen in English. One is often asked: 'Do
you mean *funny* ha-ha or *funny* peculiar?'

In more recent times, William Empson developed the notion of
'complex words'. He has been able to show that a play like
Othello revolves, for example, round a single word 'honest', and
that the whole play is a kind of elaborate pun on this concept.
But this idea is apparently nothing new. In Sanskrit the concept
artha 'meaning' had been enlarged to contain all that could be
conveyed by a single poem. The so-called *dhvani* theory operates
in terms of large units and is usually unconcerned with particular
words, although occasionally a single word or phrase may sometimes be sufficient to suggest the whole of its implied meaning. In
the example 'How can you expect us to have elephant tusks or
tigerskins, so long as my daughter-in-law wanders about the
house with dishevelled hair', the *dhvani* arises not from the sen-

tence as a whole but from 'dishevelled hair' alone, which indicates that the hunter's son, who ought to be out hunting, is in fact dallying with his newly wedded wife. In any good poem one can find an intricate overlapping of such *dhvani* units, intertwined 'fields of tension' each resolving only in the totality of all the other fields therein. I have met more than one French student of English who, although highly trained and experienced in the technique of *explication de texte*, has come up with a nil result when faced with a Shakespeare sonnet. These sonnets appear to possess a diamond-like hardness which resists all but the most pedantic analysis. A close look at any one of them may convince the reader of the truth of this. They are supreme examples of closed-field systems which can exist in poetry no less than in the physical world.

Lexical collocation

An approach to semantic structure that is poles apart from the one just discussed has emerged in British linguistics during the past decade or so. This approach eschews the dizzy reaches but also avoids most of the excesses and pitfalls of field theory metaphysics. And at the same time it accounts rather more successfully for the human and social controls exerted constantly upon language use. Language appears as the contingent thing it really is—as none other than an analogue of the living speech community.

The starting point is the notion that words (lexical units) enter into different relations with each other *in addition to* their relations in grammar. These relations are called *collocations*. Moreover, words fall into *lexical sets*. A lexical set is defined rather broadly as a group of words that have approximately the same range of collocations.

Lexical sets in themselves are *extralinguistic*, in that they do not depend on language structure, or grammar, for their composition. The members of these sets 'collocate' with one other either by extralinguistic association or through the sentence (or both). Collocations become *linguistic* only in the latter case, when the structure of the sentence acts as a 'filter' for the various extralinguistic associations. On the other hand, since it is the nature of linguistic structure (grammar) to be sensitive to what takes place outside language, the same structure can as a result of this sensitivity undergo *change*. Language structure behaves therefore rather like a living cell or organism, rejecting some connections and combinations, but accepting, absorbing and even adapting to others.

An example of a lexical set is:

$$\begin{bmatrix} apple \\ pear \\ orange \\ peach \\ \ldots\ldots \end{bmatrix} \quad (1)$$

The members of this set collocate variously with members of other sets, which might include:

$$\begin{bmatrix} sweet \\ tasty \\ juicy \\ delicious \\ \ldots\ldots\ldots \end{bmatrix} \quad (2) \qquad \begin{bmatrix} ripe \\ unripe \end{bmatrix} \quad (3) \qquad \begin{bmatrix} eat \\ like \\ digest \\ \ldots\ldots \end{bmatrix} \quad (4)$$

Although, as we have seen, collocational relations may be established outside language (i.e. extralinguistically) their actual realisation can take place only through the medium of the sentence. A series of sentences will then test the linguistic collocations between these sets:

(Set 1–set 2): *Apples are tasty*; *Which is juicier, a pear or a peach?*; *Don't you think peaches are delicious?* etc.
(Set 1–set 3): *I don't like unripe peaches*, etc.
(Set 1–set 4): *Pears are nice to eat but not always easy to digest*; *Jean likes oranges*, etc.

So far so good. But, you may feel, there is nothing particularly remarkable about all this. Let us look, then, at a few of the more pregnant implications.

First, let us imagine that the point I have just been labouring was being put across to a group of students with little or no English. In this case it is quite possible that, when I came to match set 1 with set 3, I would be asked why I had not enlarged the first set to include *people* along with the varieties of fruit. I might need to be reminded that, in their language at least, not only apples and pears but people too could be 'ripe' or 'unripe'. So I have to explain further to my foreign audience that *people* does not in English collocate with *ripe* or *unripe* but with quite a different 'set' containing the words *mature* and *immature*. I shall not, alas, be able to bring much logic to my aid; and shall be forced to admit, if only to myself, that it is, in fact, quite usual in other languages for 'people' to be 'ripe' or 'unripe' and that English in this instance really is the odd-man-out.

Now let us take a different situation. I am talking to speakers of English this time; not in England, however, but in the Caribbean. I have just explained lexical collocation, using sets 1 and 2 as illustrations. Someone asks why, if I have included *orange*, I did not also include *lemon*. But, I protest, lemons are not sweet but very sour! And just at that point I remember what a friend had told me: lemons do, in fact, get ripe in the tropics and can taste quite sweet when eaten.

Lastly, I am discussing my point with a group of British university students. One of the students suggests adding *cheese* to set 1 when this set is being collocated with *ripe/unripe*. I see no objection. Just then another rather angry young student snaps: 'It's only snobs who would think of something like that! Where I come from they don't go in for all that delicatessen rubbish.' Cheese, as far as he was concerned, did not get ripe but only mouldy or dry if you left it long enough. He had a point though— if only a chauvinistic one. Acceptability of word usage and association (collocation) does depend on a person's background, his experience, his acquaintance with and tolerance of other ways than his, even his social and class prejudices. The typical English cheese does not ripen; and possibly only a minority of British speakers of English would have a clear grasp of the collocation of 'ripe' and 'cheese' even if their prejudices did not get in their way.

Lexical collocation, then, does have many advantages over semantic field theory, and over some other approaches that have not been discussed. It enables us to *contrast* semantic structure in languages in present-day use; to allow for natural geographical diversity within a single world language like English; and makes it possible to trace the variety and variance of speech habits within the larger speech community, as well as the interlocking at certain points of two or more distinct speech communities. (How different, for example, is the purist Frenchman's revulsion to *manger un cheeseburger* from that of our angry young student?)

A further important point, and one that has hardly been explored, is that the lexical collocation scheme furnishes us with an explanation of how word associations can first be established extralinguistically and then realised within the linguistic structure, and vice versa. For example, words like *ulterior* and *interior* are related within the sentence because of their word-class affinities (they both serve as nouns and as adjectives), but they are related outside the framework of the sentence as well. In the imagination of Dylan Thomas *ulterior motive* and *interior decoration* (and, for all we know, other things besides) became associated and eventually found their way into the English language as *ulterior decorator*, creating an entirely new semantic precedent. Perhaps, if properly developed, lexical collocation might lead to explanations of at least some facets of the relationships between language structure and poetic diction.

Some features of this semantic theory have been followed through in some detail by Angus McIntosh.[1] All words and phrases he sees as having a certain *potential of collocability*. In comparing the two sentences: *The molten postage feather scored a weather* and *The flaming waste-paper basket snored violently*, McIntosh has suggested that the difference between them is that the second is more acceptable than the first, even if neither is readily acceptable. The first sentence seems to have no possible application, whereas the second might suggest that it is simply awaiting a use: 'Words have only a certain degree of tolerance or compatibility, only a certain potential of collocability, quite apart from any considerations of pattern in the grammatical sense. It need hardly be said that the edges of this range of tolerance are vague and unstable, and that the question of what we mean by compatibility is a complicated one.' The sentence *The molten postage feather* etc. is rejected *not* because it violates a grammatical pattern, *nor* because it awaits a possible application, but because of its *departure from tolerated ranges of collocability*.

[1] McIntosh, A., 'Patterns and Ranges' in Halliday, M. A. K., and McIntosh, A., *Patterns of Language* (London, 1966), pp. 183 ff.

17 Semantic Change

Causes of semantic change

Numerous causes of semantic change have been described. The ones given here are but a selection. Their range extends well beyond the bounds of linguistics pure and simple—into psychology, anthropology, science, ideas and history.

A number of 'causes' can be grouped together under the broad historical principle that social institutions, cultural outlook and ideas change, and that the words which contain or have become associated with them also change. They may be called *historical* causes. The most obvious example is the word *car*, which ultimately goes back to Latin *carrus* 'a four-wheeled wagon'. Despite the lack of resemblance, the technological development was so continuous as to allow the label an uninterrupted history all its own. Other obvious examples are *nucleus* (German *Kern*; Russ. *yadro*), originally 'the kernel of a nut'; *electron*, the direct descendant of the Greek word for 'amber'; and *calculus*, the Latin for 'a small stone or pebble', almost comically remote from the sophistication of the differential calculus.

A further group may be brought under the vague category of *psychological* causes. Many of these can be further traced to taboo of various kinds. For reasons of taboo, whether from fear, prudery, delicacy or otherwise, words are liable to be replaced by others or they change their signification. Certain parts of the anatomy and functions of the body are never mentioned directly by the native name, and are replaced either by words of Latin origin or by circumlocutions. Extreme mirth or acute embarrassment according to circumstances are invariably the result of directness. At certain periods, this prudery extends itself to absurd limits. Molière's *précieuses* took this practice of euphemism to its extreme in their abhorrence of calling even a literal chair a chair. Language is so ridden with taboo that people often do not realise they are using euphemisms. They may try to sound provocative by saying: 'You mean the lavatory?' when someone asks for the 'powder-room', without realising that the word *lavatory* itself is a euphemism. It is impossible to find a word in this semantic group that is not a euphemism, unless one indulges in deliberate vulgarity.

Semantic histories are sometimes histories of euphemistic substitutions. French ones had a feminine form of *garçon*, namely *garce* 'a girl'. *Garce* acquired the sense of a girl of loose character and was replaced by *fille*, which in time came to develop its own undesirable associations and was replaced by *jeune fille*. In the present century the French word *baiser* is no longer used for 'kiss', having acquired obscene nuances, and has been replaced by *embrasser*, originally 'to embrace'. (The former nevertheless continues to be taught in isolated British schools and a few unfortunate schoolchildren have found to their distress that the word is now taboo.)

Euphemism plays a much wider part in everyday life, commerce and politics. Certain diseases are only rarely alluded to directly, and in some cases elaborate substitutions are necessary. Advertisers and public relations experts could not do without euphemism, and will never give a dog a bad name. Recruiting probably became much brisker in the R.A.F. when garbage removers were glorified with the title of 'administrative orderly'. Readers can probably give a much larger list than ever I could of the 'rodent operator' type. The upgraded absolutely need euphemisms. Some words even become euphemisms in some inexplicable way. We are all familiar with the status-seeking overtones of *executive, postgraduate, studies* (when affixed to a new university course). Politics nowadays includes euphemism as an important part of its diet. Politicians have cultivated great sensitivity in discerning the moment in time when a certain term becomes no longer tolerable. Thus *hydrogen bomb* is replaced variously by *thermo-nuclear device* and *megaton bomb*, eventually by *thermo-nuclear deterrent* and finally by *the deterrent*.

It is not easy to find a cause of semantic change of a purely linguistic kind. There is, however, a facet of semantic change that at any rate seems parallel to that of lexical borrowing or loan words, although in a highly subtle manner. This is the tendency of one language to borrow a particular metaphorical development from another. The example of *nucleus* given earlier is a fairly good example. German and Russian scientists took their own words for 'kernel of a nut' and developed them metaphorically to represent the nucleus of an atom, but were doubtless influenced by the internal development of the English word *nucleus* itself which began its metaphorical blossoming in the eighteenth century.

Unquestionably, languages such as German and Russian have been much enriched by 'borrowing' in this often uncanny way from other European languages—English and French in the main—which in turn drew heavily on the metaphorical resources of Latin and Greek.

The nature of semantic change

Historical semantics grew up on the ground of classical rhetoric. It has even now only partly outgrown these categories.

The most important of these categories is *metaphor*, which accounts for a very considerable proportion of semantic changes . Language teems with fossilised metaphors, which no longer call up the image of the object or objects from which they were borrowed. The *leaf* of a book is not a bad example; better ones are: *hands* of a clock, a clock-*face*, a shoe-*tree*, the *head* of a cabbage. For ages, hidden metaphorical origins of words have caused etymological errors to be made. The Roman orator, Cicero, was astonished by the peasants of a district in which he was staying who had apparently thought of calling the buds on trees by the word *gemma*, which to him meant 'pearl'. Cicero remained enchanted by their poetic imagination and was not to know that *gemma* itself in early Latin (and rustic Latin) meant 'bud'.

Abstract words from one European language to another tend to derive from the same metaphors. *Goodness* is frequently derived from a straight line; *badness* from a crooked line. Indeed, English preserves the opposition in its figurative use of *crooked* ('perverse') and *straight* ('with integrity'). *Intelligence* may take its origin in 'a penetrating point'; *folly* in 'bluntness' or 'blunt instruments'. *Simple* is from a garment with a single fold, and has been taken into more than one European language by literal translation of the Latin word of origin. Many of our indispensable words, *auspicious*, *sinister*, *propitious*, even bear faint traces of their pagan-religious origins. *Influence* we owe to astrologers of old who believed in a fluid emanating from the stars and reacting upon men and things alike; *influenza* is from the same superstition.

Another critical factor in semantic change is the tendency of certain words to occur in near proximity and hence mutually to influence one another. This is called *metonymy*, or change of name. Metonymy occurs in various ways and is responsible for such phrases as *he drinks two cups every morning* (with either coffee or tea understood); in this phrase *cup* is an ellipsis of *cup of tea* (*coffee*, etc.). More recently, creations such as *drink a pinta* have a similar origin. Ellipsis has produced some of the more fantastic histories. *Bureau* began life with the meaning a 'stuff of baize, or thick green cloth', which, however, eventually became associated exclusively with writing-table, and other table-tops. It was only a matter of time before *bureau* came to mean 'a writing-table' (not necessarily covered with baize). In American English the word has proceeded through two further stages: 'an office furnished with writing-tables' and subsequently 'an office'.

To deal fully here with metonymy would be out of the question. The queerest of this species is , I think, worth a passing mention. The type has been classified as the substitution of cause for effect, and brings about such marvellous transferences as *engine*, 'a thing invented' from *ingenium* 'an inventor'. Contrariwise, *sleeping sickness*, as everyone knows, is a disease causing sleep and not, as one might grammatically expect, a disease caused *by* sleep.

The remaining, and not insubstantial, class of semantic change is nearly impossible to define. It is called *catachresis*. One can say with certainty that a historical break in linguistic memory must have occurred. These are, of course, not sudden breaks or total amnesia, but a gradual supplanting of one sense by another for a larger or shorter transitional period. Good examples abound. One of the classics is *spice*, which in the Middle Ages became detached from the parent word *species*, via a transitional stage the *aromatic species*, and ultimately arrived at *spices* pure and simple. Analogously, *sermon* was in earlier times not only a 'religious conversation' but '*any* conversation'. Many such changes are still in a process of transition; *advertisement*, for example, nowadays nearly always signifies 'a commercial ad'. *Charity* is most commonly 'donation to a good cause' and more rarely 'almsgiving'; it has become so difficult to use the word in its original sense that more than one religious writer has found it preferable to dig up the Greek word *agapē*.

One of the chief consequences of semantic change takes the form of change in 'area of meaning'. Each word in a language can be said to have an 'area' or a semantic range within more or less distinct limits. This change appears either as *restriction* or as *expansion* of meaning, and often accompanies changes in outlook or social structure.

First, expansion of meaning. The Latin word *pecunia* designated in particular 'wealth in cattle' (Lat. *pecus* 'a herd'). With the sophistication of the Roman economy, *pecunia* develops the meaning of 'wealth of every kind, especially money'. There is some evidence that the Latin word *tempus*, from which the French *temps* is derived, originally signified only 'heat' (Sanskrit *tapas* 'heat'). With expansion of outlook, the word acquired the special and more abstract meaning of 'time', losing its original sense altogether.

It is equally true that many 'expansions' of meaning are the outcome of chance situations. Thus the English word *Vauxhall* was adopted in Russian as the general name for *all* main railway stations, the noun for the latter being *voksal*. Foreign loan words are prone to adventitious changes of this kind.

Restriction of meaning is no more than the contrary and complementary shift one might expect. Names for classes of animals have a special tendency to become restricted in area. The English word *deer* (German *Tier*) originally included the whole range of wild animals until it acquired its present meaning. Likewise, *fowl*, now used only for wild fowl and large poultry birds, signified birds in general. The word *bird* has undergone a compensatory 'expansion' from the original diminutive sense. There is no scarcity of further examples both in English and in other languages.

A number of Anglo-Saxon words shrunk under the impact of their Anglo-Norman counterparts. *Pond*, partly owing to its confrontation with *lake*, is now reduced to a mere puddle, whereas it still retains its etymological connection with Greek *pontos*, Latin *pontus* 'the sea' or other large stretch of water. So much so that respectable expanses of water which happen to retain their original Saxon nomenclature seem slightly ridiculous. The history of the word *stool* has been mentioned earlier, and clearly belongs to the same class of downgraded words.

A further important consequence of semantic change, not unrelated to 'expansion' and 'restriction' of meaning, remains to be discussed. This is a popular tendency to bring down the lofty standing of certain words, sometimes called the pejorative trend in language.

Sometimes these downgradings retain traces of popular irreverence and derision. The French *prude* was in the Middle Ages simply the feminine of *preux*, both used to indicate the possession of noble qualities and courage. The Middle High German *minne* began its life as an exalted noun, which embraced courtly love, love of God, affection, 'mercy', friendship. By the fifteenth century the word had to be banished from polite usage on account of its, by then, indecent overtones. Analogous influences are now at work on words like *pure*, *art* (already corrupted by *arty*), *holy* (as in phrases like *holy Joe*), *intellectual*, *earnest*, *idealist* and hundreds of others. In a few instances, the pejorative decline has been swift and almost inexplicable; such is the case with *dunce*, which at the close of the Middle Ages and in a little over a hundred years had acquired its modern meaning, a word so recently corrupted from Duns Scotus, one of the great philosopher-theologians of the Middle Ages.

The lexical resources of language

There are, roughly speaking, two ways in which a language can enrich its own resources: by native invention or adaptation, and by the use of foreign lexical elements, called *loan words*. Any enrichment of this kind will lead to a new synchronic phase; the new phase behaves differently from the old. It also seems that, if contact arises between two linguistically separate cultures, the synchrony of the languages of at least one of these cultures will be modified. These points can be illustrated by the history of the English language.

In its earliest Anglo-Saxon stage, English made considerable use of its own native resources, what might be termed a *native-resource oriented* language. But over a period of six or seven hundred years, there was a gradual shift to the opposite extreme. Modern English uses foreign elements (generally Latin and Greek) whenever new word concepts are required, and has become *loan-word oriented*.

The first cultural contact with English to have a transforming effect came in the years around A.D. 600. This cultural entity was not another nation but Christianity, and in particular the Roman Church. Loan words are not entirely absent during this cultural phase, but they are, with a few doubtful exceptions, mainly short words that harmonised well with the native words, nearly all of this character; examples are: *apostol*, *biscop* (from Lat. *episcopus* 'bishop'), *mæsse* 'mass', *munuc* 'monk'.

Such borrowings, however, were the exception, not the rule. The interest of this period lies precisely in the words that were not borrowed.

Before the coming of Christianity, England shared its heathen gods, and many of its customs and institutions as well, with the continental Germans and with the Scandinavians. In a few cases, heathen concepts, rituals or feast-day names were semantically, but not lexically, 'translated' into suitable Christian equivalents. The English word *Easter* is derived directly from the name of an old pagan spring festival, named after *Eastro*, a goddess of spring. Anglo-Saxon used its native word *husl* (modern *housel*), a pagan sacrifice or offering, for the newly acquired Eucharist, and another word *weofod* 'altar' was permitted to remain as a Christian technical term, but transparently compounded of *wig* and *beod* 'idol-table'. *Godspell*, or the 'spell of God', was preferred to *Evaggelion*.

The early English reacted to Christianity not unlike other peoples in Central America, Africa and elsewhere in more recent times. Their interpretation of Christian dogma and paraphernalia was often touching in its naïvety. They preferred, for example, their own word *cristnian* (lit. 'to Christ (someone)') to the less comprehensible 'baptise', and naturally represented 'confirmation' as the act of 'bishop-ing' or *biscepung* (*biscopian* 'to confirm'; lit. 'to bishop').

Although a few of the names of the ecclesiastical hierarchy and institutions percolated as loan words into Old English, Graeco-Roman theological terms were generally rejected outright and replaced by native substitutes. *Trinity* became *thrines* or 'three-ness'; the *three Magi* were designated the *tungolwitegan* from *tungol* 'star' and *witega* 'wise man'; *religious* was rendered by the more homely *godcund*; *service* by *thegnung*; *novice* by *niwcumen mann* ('a new-come man'). Associated 'learned' terms were similarly substituted; *astronomy* finds its equivalent *tungol-ae* 'star-law'; *medicine* was *laece-craft* 'leech-craft'.

Jespersen regarded it as the natural thing for a language to utilise its own resources before drawing on other languages. Few linguists of the present day would agree, however. It is no longer

possible to use the terms 'natural' or 'unnatural' to describe a
given language's predisposition or resistance to loan words.

The next period of the English language—the period during
which Scandinavian dialects were spoken over a large part of the
country—might be crudely termed a 'softening-up period',
during which time Scandinavian loan words began to enter the
English language in the most insidious way possible. They
appeared *as* native words owing to their close similarity and even
identicality. The English language during this period may have
suffered a kind of linguistic neurosis. The Danish loan words were
so close that when language mixture took place around A.D. 1000
bewilderment must often have arisen. The Anglo-Saxon word
shirt existed alongside the Scandinavian exact synonym *skirt*.
When the languages fell together, and owing to the law that exact
synonyms cannot be tolerated in a language, the two words took
on male and female functions respectively. In some cases, mixture
did not occur, and the result was sometimes confusion. Even as
late as the fifteenth century, the Scandinavian *egg* had not yet
ousted its Saxon counterpart *ey*. Caxton mentions an incident,
during his travels, when a merchant visiting an inn asked for eggs
and was told by the hostess that she could not speak French: 'And
the merchant was angry, for he also could speak no French, but
wanted eggs and she could not understand him. And then someone
else asked for *eyren*. And the good wife said that she understood
him well. Lo, what should a man now write these days, *eggs* or
eyren. Certainly it is hard to please every man, by cause of diversity and change of language.' It was only after Caxton's death that
ey (pl. *eyren*) went out of usage.

This casting-a-glance-over-one's-shoulder phase of English ties
up with Sapir's 'drift' theory. The drift is towards effacement of
nuances and grammatical distinctions; 'the drift towards the
invariable word' and towards the word set apart from its neighbours. 'English words crave spaces between them, they do not like
to huddle in clusters of slightly divergent centres of meaning, each
edging a little away from the rest.' Words like *able* and *unable*
hold their own, because they are as unlike as *clever* and *stupid*.
But with the adverbial ending -*ly* the case is different. Sapir held
that statements such as *Do it quickly!* drag psychologically. 'The
nuance expressed by *quickly* is too close to that of *quick*, their
circles of concreteness are too nearly the same, for the two words

to feel comfortable together. The adverbs in -*ly* are likely to go to the wall in the not too distant future for this very reason and in face of their obvious usefulness.' The same conflict applies to the group *whence*, *whither*, *hence*, *hither*, etc. 'In saying *whither* we feel too keenly that we repeat all of *where*. That we add to *where* an important nuance of direction irritates rather than satisfies.' Sapir sums up the linguistic position thus: 'The English vocabulary is a rich medley because each English word wants its own castle. Has English long been peculiarly receptive to foreign words because it craves the staking out of as many word areas as possible or, conversely, has the mechanical imposition of a flood of French and Latin loan words, unrooted in our earlier tradition, so dulled our feeling for the possibilities of our native resources that we are allowing these to shrink by default? I suspect that both propositions are true. Each feeds on the other.'[1]

Sapir's theory is abundantly borne out by the Norman-French and subsequent periods of the English language, in which the language seems to have developed a kind of special digestive organ for the purpose of taking in the most unlikely words: *hegemony*, *chthonic*, *mnemonic*, *psephology* among a thousand others.

So far we have seen what happens linguistically when two cultures with different languages come into contact. But what happens when a highly sophisticated culture encounters one that is scarcely above the primitive level? The answer in general is as one might expect: that the phenomena of internal adaptation and word borrowing are even more acute, and in a few cases bizarre.

Among the most curious of all are the so-called Pidgins and Creoles spoken in various parts of the world.[2] Pidgin languages are especially interesting, in that they can be found at all social levels and in all kinds of situations, but they have arisen most frequently in short contacts between persons desiring to do other things in which detailed exchange of information or complicated activity is not required. Astonishingly, the language from which many of these makeshift languages are compounded is often *English*—not literary or cultivated English, but the distinctly unrefined argot of the ordinary seaman.

---

[1] Sapir, E., *Language*, p. 170.
[2] A recent and comprehensive study is to be found in Hall, R. A., *Pidgin and Creole Languages* (London, 1966).

The grammar of these languages is simple to the point of absurdity, and fundamentally of the English structural pattern. The entire vocabulary is made up of loan words, of predominantly English origin, although very often sailors' slang. Phonetic distortions vary from place to place; but nowhere are words easily intelligible.

The vocabulary is extremely small, and many words have to serve a wide semantic purpose. For example, *nusipepa* (newspaper) represents 'any letter, written, or printed document'. *Mary* is not a christian name but 'any woman'. *Pisupo* is 'any foreign food preserved in tins'; *bullamacow* (rhyming slang 'bull-and-cow') more specifically 'canned beef'. Modern English itself has not a few loan words from these languages, including *pickaninny*, *savvy*, *tiffin* and *taboo* (exceptionally, however, of Maori origin).

Sometimes the result is nothing short of poetic. A three-masted steamer with two funnels can become: *Three-piecee bamboo, two-piecee puff-puff, walk-along inside, no-can-see*. At other times the lexical creations strike the outsider as comic.

Piano has the prize circumlocution: *big fella box, you fight him, he cry*. Perfume is dismissed as *water belong stink*. And the picture of a bald man—*you no savvy that fella white man, coconut belong him no grass*. Sea-sickness might turn up as *belly belong me walk about too much*.

But all this is no linguistic joke in Melanesia, where Pidgin has taken firm root as a 'lingua franca' between mutually incomprehensible tribal languages. In New Guinea, Pidgin is a written language of enormous social (and political) importance. It is reported[1] that the *Nu Gini Tok Tok* ('New Guinea talk-talk') is a serious newspaper dealing with interracial problems, and all the technical, administrative and especially linguistic problems of present-day government. Even its advertisements are in Pidgin. Attempts in the past to eradicate this language have failed, but the Australian government of today has evolved a more sensible policy. Pigdin has as a result been given due recognition and has ceased to be regarded as bowdlerised English.

An important contribution to the linguistic status of Pidgin came from missionaries whose powers of translation were tested

[1] Quirk, R., *The English Language and Images of Matter* (London, 1972), pp. 52 ff.

to the full when they came to translate the Bible into Pidgin. The following are extracts from the story in Genesis.

> So God big fella marster he make Adam go sleep, he take'm one fella bone belong him, and he make'm one fella mary along bone. He call'm this fella mary Eve . . . Eve he talk, talk, talk allee time, allee time mary he talk . . . So these two fella (i.e. Adam and Eve) go eat'm. When they finish eat'm, my word, they bright like hell, and they go hide along scrub . . . (God then expresses his anger). You two fella finish along me altogether. You go catch'm boks belong you, and get to hell along scrub.

I hope the reader will not think that I have included these remarks and excerpts from Pidgin merely for the sake of diversion. My aim was to illustrate the incredible adaptability of language. Given any imaginable (or unimaginable) situation, language is capable of coping with it, like a boa constrictor digesting a pig.

Popular etymology

Whilst a large proportion of the words of a language may 'lose motivation' and become 'opaque' as a result of sound change and erosion, a few words actually acquire motivation as a result of pure chance. Both the French words *gémir* 'to groan', 'to moan' and *geindre* 'to whimper', 'to whine' are expressive in the sense that there is some onomatopoeic relationship between these words and the situations they represent; yet they are phonologically derived from Latin *gemere*, which has scarcely any transparency. This acquisition of motivation has to be put down to popular etymology. Put plainly, this means that ordinary people *feel* etymological connections, which, if they looked them up in the dictionary, might turn out to be non-existent. Ullmann puts it like this: 'the driving force behind popular etymology is the desire to motivate what is, or has become, opaque in language.'

The earlier 'old-curiosity-shop etymologists' relied on this as a major part of their stock in trade. There are many colourful examples of popular etymology, antique and modern. The selection given here are among the classic instances. *Press-gang*

had originally nothing to do with 'pressing'. *Press* in this phrase
was originally *prest*; army and navy recruits received *prest-money*,
a perfectly respectable form of payment for their services. It was
only when the method of enlistment become more 'pressing' that
the popular corruption took place. German *Abenteuer* derives
from the earlier form which is a normal phonetic adaptation of
the Old French loan word *aventure*. It was only in the eighteenth
century that *Abenteuer* took on the suggestion of 'a story related
in the evening (Abend)'. The French word *choucroute* looks to the
average Frenchman as if it is compounded of *chou* (cabbage) and
croûte (crust), whereas in fact it is derived straightforwardly from
Alsatian *sûrkrût* (= German *Sauerkraut*). There are hundreds
more that readers may no doubt be prompted to find out for
themselves.

'Popular etymology' is now taken very seriously by linguists.
Failure to take it into account has led to several otherwise
apparently valid etymologies. The Sanskrit grammarians of
ancient times were aware of the phenomenon, but it is only in
recent times that the possible extent of this factor has been
grasped. The tendency towards popular etymology is latent in
many words, ready to upset the best scientist's calculations. The
linguist's awareness that there is no etymological connection
between *noise* and *noisome*, between *scare* and *scarify* or between
nigger and *niggard* has not prevented the popular mind from
inventing connections. 'The contrast between scientific and popular etymology is another reminder of the necessity to distinguish
between historical and descriptive viewpoints in linguistics. The
ordinary speaker's ideas about the derivation of words are a
linguistic fact worthy of the philologist's attention even if they
contradict his own knowledge of etymologies.'[1]

Lexical borrowing

Languages have always shown a tendency to borrow from other
languages. We have seen that English in particular is packed with
foreign words, a few of them still imperfectly assimilated; the
same is true to a lesser extent of French, Swedish, Polish and other
European languages. Persian, although distinctly Indo-European

[1] Ullman, S., *Semantics*, p. 103.

in structure, has taken the greater part of its vocabulary from Arabic, a semitic language.

'Loan words', whilst sometimes of invaluable help, are just as often the bane of the comparatist. In drawing up a native etymology for any word, he can rarely be absolutely sure that the word is not ultimately a borrowing from another language. He has to be particularly careful in delineating language relationships, since it is always a temptation to establish relationships on the basis of words alone. In English, as we have seen, it is possible to construct sentences entirely of Latin or French words, but we know that no direct linguistic connection exists. Likewise, Hungarian, despite its large number of Turkish words, is not on that account linguistically related to Turkish.

Particularly treacherous is chance similarity or orthography. The amateur etymologist can easily be tempted to draw a connection between French *feu* and German *feuer*. Closer inspection of the available linguistic evidence reveals that the French word is related to Latin *focus* 'a hearth', whereas the German equivalent is kindred only to Greek *pyr* and Armenian *hur*. The phenomenon of convergence is a particularly acute hazard; for example, the coincidence of the English and modern Persian words *bad*, whose identity is entirely coincidental. Hence the unwisdom of Schuchardt's attempt to demonstrate a relationship between Basque and the Hamitic group based on nothing more than word resemblances. As Meillet warned: 'It may be easy to notice resemblances between words, but one has to be an expert to know just how tricky it is to establish the validity of an etymological connection.'[1]

Loan words have, despite all, an important use. The Frankish loan words in Romance are important as a means of dating sound changes, owing to the fact that we know the historical dates for the Frankish and other Germanic invasions. Yet even this is clogged by the uncertainty as to how many of these Germanic words were already present in Vulgar Latin *before* it disintegrated into the different Romance idioms. By various intricate counterchecks nevertheless it is reasonably certain that the Germanic element in Romance is due exclusively to the various invasions that took place from the fifth century onwards. Many common verbs in Romance are of Germanic origin and probably entered

Meillet, A., *Linguistique Historique et Linguistique Générale*, p. 33.

Romance before the breaking up into dialects had become significant—that is, during the fifth and sixth centuries. The following
are a few examples:

Germanic	French	Provençal	Old Ital.	Spanish
Sparanjan				
(Eng. *to spare*)	*épargner*	*esparnhar*	*sparagnare*	—
Warnjan				
(Eng. *to warn*)	*garnir*	*garnir*	*guarnire*	*guarnir*
Waidanjan				
(Eng. *weed*,				
Germ. *weide*				
'meadow')	*gagner*	*guadanhar*	*guadagnare*	*guadañar*

(Old Fr. *gaaignier* still meant 'to till the soil';
Mod. Span. *guadañar* 'to mow'; whereas
both the Mod. Fr. and Ital. mean 'to earn'.)

Hraustjan				
(Eng. *roast*)	*rôtir*	*raustir*	(*ar*)*rostire*	—

This Germanic influx into Romance has created certain difficulties for English etymologists, since in a few instances it is impossible to be certain whether a particular word has come directly
from Germanic through Old English or indirectly via Old French.
Recent linguists have abandoned the attempt and have concen-
trated on the phenomena of convergence resulting in enrichment
of the language. Thus English *rich* could be either from Old
English *rice* 'powerful, rich' or from French *riche*. The truth is
that the Middle English *rich*(*e*) is undoubtedly influenced by both
words. Synchronic theory not only allows for, but positively
demands, such linguistic concurrences. The native English *choose*
(O.E. *ceosan*) was reinforced by the French noun *choix*. Old
English *hergian* and Old French *herier* fall together in Modern
English *harry*. In rare instances, the convergence is almost incredible, and verging on the truly fantastic. Jespersen gives the example
of the English noun and verb *gain*. This was borrowed in the
fifteenth century from Middle French *gain*, *gaain* with its modern
sense. But the word is prefigured by an earlier borrowing from
Old French, spelt variously *gain*, *geyn*, *gayne*, signifying 'advantage, use, avail, benefit', which appears to be from Old Norse
although ultimately both words are from the same Germanic root

Which all goes to show just how little use 'root linguistics' is. Finally, a few French words were borrowed doubtless for the very reason that they *reminded* the English speaker of words that were in the language but already obsolete. French *lake* must have been reminiscent of the Old English *lacu* 'stream, river'.

Occasionally, loan-word infiltrations from one linguistic family to another are useful in acting as counterchecks for hypothetically adduced forms. Thus (hypothetical) primitive Germanic forms are corroborated by Finnish borrowings of certain Germanic words during the time of the late Roman Empire and until the seventh century, when Finns and Livonians were in contact with Gothic tribes in East Prussia. Examples of such borrowings in Finnish are *kuningas*, which happens to be identical with hypothetical form **kuningaz* 'king'; *rengas* < **hrengaz* 'ring'; *kaunis* < **skauniz* 'beautiful' (note: Finnish abhors the consonant cluster $s + k$) and others.

Similarly, Indo-Iranian loan words in the Finno-Ugrian group attest the unity of Indo-Iranian at a period which it is unfortunately not possible to determine; all we can be certain of is that at this period Indo-Iranian was a distinct unit and that this linguistic group was in contact with another linguistic group of Finno-Ugrian speakers, and it is probable that the contact took place in what is now Southern Russia. This supports the evidence from other sources of subsequent migration through Persia and into Northern India of Indo-Iranian speaking groups.

A language like modern English contains literally thousands of lexical loans. Page 719 of the *Shorter Oxford Dictionary*—entries *floppy* to *flounce*—opened at random, reveals a typical distribution: Latin and Latin hybrids, 15; Old French, 4; French, 7; Spanish, 3; German, 2; Old Norse, 3. Only five entries are of pedigree English stock.

Lexical borrowing in English is sometimes of such complexity that a word may be derived simultaneously from two or more different sources. *Typhoon*, for example, is derived possibly from as many as three different sources: Urdu *tūfān* ('turning round'); Greek *Typhon*; and Cantonese *daai fung* ('big wind').

Typhoon, incidentally, has been borrowed back into Cantonese, although with a different pronunciation and a distinctly separate meaning, referring only to tropical cyclones. The Cantonese speaker is incredulous if you suggest to him that *typhoon* and *daai fung* are etymologically one and the same. This process of reborrowing is a widespread phenomenon. American Italian, to take but one example, has readopted *pizza* through the American favourite *pizza pie* and recast the latter as *la pizza paia*.

Semantic borrowing

More elusive, and more difficult to trace, is *semantic* borrowing.

Like lexical borrowing, semantic borrowing is no new phenomenon and has occurred whenever one culture gains ascendancy over others to which it becomes related. The historical linguist can, for instance, observe the semantic influence of Judaeo-Christianity on Greek. The lexical form of *angel* (Fr. *ange*, Ger. *Engel*, Russ. *angel*) is derived from Greek *aggelos*, but the concept itself we owe to Hebrew.

Semantic borrowings constitute the invisible imports and exports of language. It is a process virtually impossible to forestall. Usually it occurs in one of two forms: either the meaning of an existing word is changed and the new meaning replaces the old one completely, or the old meaning continues to exist alongside the new meaning. As an example of the second type, we can take the word *red*. International working-class movements in the last century became associated with the red flag. Since the Russian Revolution especially, *red* has become synonymous with *socialist* and especially *communist*. The new meaning of *red* thus becomes added to the polysemy of that adjective in many languages. Another, and rather different, example would be the Freudian influence on the meaning of *unconscious*. The old adjectival use continues unchanged, but whenever we use *unconscious* as a noun we are mostly using it in the way Freud and his successors have used it. As examples of the first type of semantic borrowing, we could take *dialectic*, which can nowadays only with difficulty be used in its original sense of 'logical disputation'. The newer meaning taken from Hegelian and Marxist thought is now the exclusive one. *Traumatic* used to refer to physical wounding or shock; but this meaning has been superseded by 'a disturbing experience affecting the mind'.

Across the Atlantic there has been much semantic exchange between the English-speaking communities, especially in the direction of British borrowings from American. The use of *academic* as a noun and in its present-day sense is but one of the more recent American additions to British semantics. Many of the borrowings are more than a century old, and a few can be traced as far back as the eighteenth century. In British English *snag* meant 'a trunk or large branch of a tree imbedded in the bottom of a river' until the meaning 'obstacle' was borrowed from American English, which eventually eclipsed the earlier meaning altogether. Similarly, *barbecue* once signified 'a rude framework for sleeping on'; *cocktail* a 'cock-tailed horse' or 'a poorly bred person'; and *liquor* merely a 'liquid'.

In the last twenty years or so this cross-Atlantic influence of American English has affected many European languages; and French more disturbingly than any. French has long been in an exposed position, owing partly to its linguistic proximity to English and partly to its geographical susceptibility in Quebec. Disfigurements in Canadian French such as *grand plancher* 'ground floor' (Fr. *rez-de-chaussée*) are nothing new. But in France itself, French has of late been tending towards 'Franglais'. In his Parkinsonianly funny *Parlezvous Franglais?* (Paris, 1964) Etiemble, writing in a provocatively Franglais prose, exposes the malady and calls for drastic remedy. The worst hit areas of the language are commerce, sport and technology. Etiemble cites such monstrosities as *L'engineering francais apporte une large contribution au développement international.* Note that not only *large* is used in the English sense but *développement* too. The jargon of the American social sciences finds itself being swallowed whole by French. *Specific development*, for example—a piece of jargon used in social anthropology—turns up in French as *développement spécifique*. What Etiemble finds especially inexplicable is that a writer who must be familiar with the *poissons chantants* in Rimbaud's poem *Le Bateau Ivre* yet manages to render *talking fish* as *poissons qui parlent*.

Examples of semantic borrowings from English as Franglais are illustrated in the table overleaf.

Very recently in France official directives have been published in the form of two lists: one of terms that are from now on mandatory for civil servants, and one that is more a glossary of recommended substitutions for Franglais items. Whether 'legislation' of this kind will be effective in stemming the tide remains to be seen.

Semantic borrowing (and lexical borrowing too) occurs

naturally within any cultural orbit. Take, for instance, Europe.
Until the eighteenth century Europe was a relatively confined
cultural area. But the focal points that had successively generated
new ways of thought, political organisation, trade, technical
innovation, and movements in literature and art have all left their

Original French meaning		Franglais meaning
contrôler	'to verify'	→ 'to direct'
éducation	'intellectual and moral formation'	→ 'instruction'
monnaie	'small coins'	→ 'money in general'
suite	'guard of honour'	→ 'apartment; hotel suite'
vice	'opposite of virtue'	→ 'debauchery, prostitution'

mark to a greater or lesser extent on all the languages within the
European cultural area. First Greece, later Rome and Judaeo-
Christianity; after that, Ireland, Anglo-Saxon England, the
Normans, Islam; later, in the Middle Ages, France and Italy;
then sixteenth-century Spain, England and Holland; and eventually France once again. The problem in modern times is that the
old limits have vanished. Europe is now everywhere, and very few
cultures remain intact. The military, technical and economic
might of America, together with the special position of English
(created mainly during the era of the British Empire), have made
American English ways of thinking, and hence American terms
and meanings, very difficult, if not impossible, for most cultures
to resist.

Further examples and implications of borrowing will be discussed in the last section of this chapter.

Field theory in comparative linguistics

A number of perspectives have been opened up to the comparatist
by semantic field theory. The traditional view is that all abstract
meaning has arisen by straightforward metaphorical progression
from earlier concrete meanings. Thus the 'abstract' notion of *right*
would have arisen from the concrete *straight line*, and so forth.
Theory of associative field renders such an hypothesis superfluous. It is, of course, true that metaphors have been and are still

onstantly being created, but it is surprising how few of these
erve the narrow purpose of yielding abstract ideas. Synchronic
eadjustment and re-creation of the semantic associative field is
nough to explain such *apparently* metaphorical transfigurations.

It is, for instance, known, on purely etymological grounds, that
nany Classical Latin words of sophisticated meaning had begun
fe in more humble fashion. *Delirium* is from a Latin verb *delirare*,
vhich must originally have meant 'to stray from the furrow';
kewise *praevaricari* (Eng. *prevaricate*) would have signified 'to
•lough in a crooked line'. Roman military terms were often
·orrowed from the farmyard: *cornu* 'the wing of an army' from
he horn of a cow'; *cohort* 'a division' from 'a farm enclosure';
ianipulus 'a company' from 'a blade of grass'. A *rival* (Lat.
·valis) was originally someone who lived on a *rivus* ('river') and
ended to quarrel with other 'rivals' (presumably over fishing,
avigation, irrigation or other rights). It is, however, a different
hing altogether to suggest that these indubitable semantic exten-
ions were the conscious creation of individuals. The probability
· that such words gradually acquired new shades at the same
me as relinquishing earlier ones until the complete semantic
·ansition was effected. This transition, however, would have been
xactly parallel to the transformation of the Roman society and
·conomy.

The Greek word *pneuma* (Lat. *spiritus*) clearly meant originally
·pirit', 'breath' and 'wind' at the same time. The positivist
·rgument was that 'spirit' was a latecomer, and when the need for
·ıch an 'advanced' concept arose the word 'breath' was naturally
·ansformed by metaphor. One argument is that no such stage
·ver arose. 'Such an hypothesis is contrary to every indication
·resented by the study of the history of meaning; which assures us
·efinitely that such a purely material content as 'wind', on the one
·and, and, on the other, such a purely abstract content as 'the
·rinciple of life within man or animal' are both *late* arrivals in
·uman consciousness. Their abstractness and their simplicity are
·like evidence of long ages of intellectual evolution. So far from
·ıe psychic meaning of 'spiritus' having arisen because someone
·ad the abstract idea 'principle of life' and wanted a word for it,
·ıe abstract idea 'principle of life' is itself a *product* of the old
·ıncrete *meaning* 'spiritus' which contained within itself the
·erms of both later significations. We must, therefore, imagine a

time when 'spiritus' or 'pneuma', or older words from whic
these had descended, meant neither *breath*, nor *wind*, nor *spiri*
nor yet all three of these things, but when they simply had *thei*
own peculiar meaning, which has since, in the course of the evolu
tion of consciousness, crystallised into the three meaning
specified.'[1] The 'associative field' of the word 'spirit' ha
undergone a parallel change with the corresponding trend c
civilisation. The modern Western European 'common sense' car
not tolerate concepts that include 'wind', 'breath' and 'spiri'
within the same circumference; although, with only a sligh
stretch of imagination, it is possible to envisage states of min
alien to us, that could.

It is now realised that the facile 'curiosity-shop' etymology c
half a century ago conceals complex layers of social and cultura
developments. Meillet was among the first to argue that on
cannot know the exact shade of meaning of a word of even
century ago in one's own language without a close study of th
period concerned. An etymologist thus has to be steeped in soci
history and history of ideas, as well as in the literature of th
period under consideration. It is no longer enough to know wh
first used the word in an apparently novel way, but precisely *i*
what sense.

Meillet showed how easily mistaken the pure etymologis
could be. The French word *père* is indeed a morphologic
descendant of Latin *pater*. A simple etymology of this kind, how
ever, covers up the much more important *semantic* change; for i
Roman Latin *pater* was never other than the *pater familias* c
'deity'. The procreator was represented by *genitor*. In the Midd
Ages, *pater* became a term of respect for the clergy, which sen
the word still formally retains.

Much more subtle semantic transformations are concealed i
the well-known etymology of *lady*, which can be traced to th
Anglo-Saxon *hlæfdige* 'loaf-kneader'. A glib explanation woul
impute such a change to advances in social sophistication, accord
ing to which the lady of the house would no longer occupy herse
witp menial chores such as bread-baking. This is unfortunately n
more than a part of the total explanation, and perhaps not eve
that. *Lady* is not merely a new word but a new concept, and t
study its history and origin would be to review the social an

[1] Barfield, O., *Poetic Diction*, pp. 80–1.

cultural history of the entire Middle Ages. The word first appears in the mediaeval lyric after its transition from ecclesiastical liturgical verse, and in keeping with the tone of its context the word 'lady' still bears traces of its non-secular origin. Owen Barfield finds her in a fifteenth-century carol:

> Mother and maiden
> Was never none but she;
> Well may such a lady
> Goddes mother be.

There is no space to quote the entire lyric, but he finds in such a poem 'a kind of cross-section of the growth of European outlook . . . It is so graceful that for the moment it seems as though all these things, with all the pillages and massacres and crucifixions and vast imperial achievements of Rome, had been conspiring together merely to load the homely Teutonic word 'loaf-kneader' with new semantic significance, to transform it into that mystery and symbol in the imaginations of men, a *lady*.'[1] Imagination? I prefer to call it sensitive awareness, a necessary equipment for exploring the new dimension that has been added to comparative linguistics—field semantics.

Semantics and prehistory

For some considerable time, comparative linguists and others have attempted to make use of the vocabulary of the older Indo-European dialects for the purpose of reconstructing the habitat and mores of the (hypothetical) prehistorical Indo-European speech-community. As we have already seen, it is not always too easy to determine the way a particular lexical item was used, in the context of all the other lexical items; and this problem is magnified by the paucity of items of vocabulary which was common to the various ancient dialects.

Nevertheless, a few tentative conclusions are possible. In the first place, the Indo-European kinship terms—mother, father, brother, sister, son-in-law, etc.—and the ways in which these words were used, suggest that the Indo-European community or

[1] Barfield, O., *History in English Words*, p. 111.

communities were patriarchal rather than matriarchal in kinship organisation. This feature is further corroborated by the Indo-European deities, which are for the most part masculine. *Juppiter*, *Zeus* and *Dyaus-pitar* were all 'fathers of the gods'; and the lesser gods were mainly martial, thunder-wielding or performed some other predominantly masculine function. This is in marked contrast to the gods of the Mediterranean peoples with which the Indo-European gods eventually mixed: *Demeter*, *Persephone*, *Diana*, etc.

The lack of common terms for cereals and other crops suggests a pastoral rather than an agricultural way of life. The shared terms include *dog*, *horse*, *sheep*, *goat*, *pig*, *herd*. But the wide-spread appearance of terms like *bee*, *honey*, *duck* and a few others leads one to suppose that they were settled rather than nomadic.

Sanskrit and Lithuanian both have the term for village elder, or more precisely 'head of the households' (Lith. *viẽšpats*; Skr. *viśpatis*), and Sanskrit and Greek a very similar term 'head of the house' (Skr. *dámpatis*; Gr. *despótēs*). This, other evidence and the absence of shared terms for higher sorts of rulers indicates a village organisation rather than a larger feudal organisation. This presupposition is further borne out by the existence until comparatively recent times (and in some areas still existing) of a similar village organisation in Russia, Eastern Europe, the Balkans and India. Words for king and emperor are, with few exceptions all from different sources. Some are historical modifications of Caesar (Ger. *Kaiser*; Russ. *tsar*) and even of Charlemagne (Russ. *korol*, from *Carolus*).

No doubt the techniques of reconstruction developed more recently will throw still further light on this intriguing form of palaeontology.

Is a comparative semantics possible?

Let me say at the outset that it is still too early to reach definite answers to this question. I refer only to a paper containing some highly convincing pointers. The author[1] took his stand on Vendryes' prophecy that a universal comparative semantic

[1] Reifler, E., 'Linguistic Analysis, Meaning and Comparative Semantics' in *Lingua* iii (1952–3).

method would be evolved, wherein a precise knowledge of the universal requirements of the human mind and the general laws which govern its activity would be formed. The same author has made Chinese one of his special fields of study and began by re-examining certain identically pronounced monosyllables which had long since been consigned to the realm of chance homophones. One curious feature that aroused the author's suspicion was their being expressed in the written language by the same character or ideogram. Could the coincidence really be fortuitous?

In Chinese the words 'child' and 'pupil of the eye' are the same in sign and sound. Yet an examination of other language groups showed a similar recurrence. In English *pupil* (< Lat. *pupilla*) is used, as we all know, both for the 'pupil of the eye' and 'schoolchild'. In Greek, *kore* stands both for 'girl' and 'pupil of the eye'. Hebrew *'iyshön* means 'a little man' or 'manikin' as well as the optical one. Most interesting of all, Japanese has two words for the pupil: *manako* 'a child of the eye' and *hitomi* 'a human being's appearance'. A moment's consideration provides the explanation: when we look into other people's eyes, we invariably see there our own reflection in miniature.

To take yet another illustration: the Chinese homophones sheep, goat' and 'to flow with much water, a great expanse of water, ocean' share certain pictographic elements. The following comparisons were adduced: Greek *aiges* = 'goats' = 'strong waves'. Compare: *Aigaios*, 'Aegean'; French *moutons* = 'sheep' = 'foamy waves'. The verb *moutonner* describes the act of covering oneself with small foamy waves. Russian *barashki* = 'sheep' = 'foamy waves'; and *volna* meaning either 'wool' or 'wave', according to whichever syllable is stressed. (Not to mention English *white horses*.) The coincidence of meaning is explained by the fact that waves or white caps on the surf remind sea-gazers of a herd of moving sheep, goats, horses and the wool on a sheep.

This discovery, a mere drop in the ocean and based on at least one unconvincing sample, is nevertheless another small beginning to a comparative undertaking that seems inevitable, even if the results turn out to be negative. Yet who knows what semantic denizens may emerge from a really extensive comparative survey?

Cultural translation

'Language makes it possible for man to *be* historically'
—*Hölderlin.*

'Translation' I often think of as a term that belongs to the same
category as 'cooking' or 'playing the piano'. I shall try to explain
what I mean. Nearly everyone, I suppose, is capable of boiling an
egg or playing *chopsticks* on the piano, and these actions can
justifiably be called 'cooking' and 'piano playing' respectively.
Likewise, anyone can look up a French dictionary for the French
equivalent of the English phrase *car-park* and find what he wants
with the minimum of experience. This act I am obliged to consider 'translation'. Yet, as we are all well aware, there is 'cookery'
and 'cookery', 'piano playing' and 'piano playing'. Just so,
'translation' covers a staggeringly wide range of (admittedly)
related activities. At the one extreme we find the 'beginner'
translating *the pen of my aunt* into French, Spanish or any other
language; at the other, Boris Pasternak translating Shakespeare
into Russian.

One of the more obvious reasons why translation from one
language to another is so precarious is that each language, like the
nation with which it is associated, is a separate culture. I mean
culture almost literally, as a growth, a unique growth. Words of
common origin can grow so far apart in only a few decades that it
is always a wonder that translation is actually possible. When it
first came into English after the Norman Conquest, the word
gentle (Fr. *gentil*) signified 'well-bred, of high birth', but subsequently during the course of the sixteenth century it acquired the
sense of 'mildness' or the opposite of 'harshness'. By the end of
the sixteenth century there remained so little trace of the original
meaning that *gentil* was reborrowed (the French itself having
changed but slightly) as *genteel*. No sooner did this word find its
niche in the English language than a distinct whiff of sarcasm
became associated with its use. By 1650 this note of irony, subtly
tuned by Shakespeare and his generation, had given such a double
edge to the word that Englishmen were unconsciously already
casting around for a substitute. This turned up hardly a decade
later as *jaunty*—this too from Fr. *gentil*, but given a special
refinement and lustre by the manner of the already well-established

French court. It seems that the English language (culture?) has no mind for an undilutedly solemn concept such as 'gentlemanly, well bred', although the language will tolerate 'gentleman'; the being and yet not the attribute! Any attribute taking on the burden of this connotation is bound to undergo rapid and irreverent transformation. Within scarcely a decade of its appearance, *jaunty* already assumed overtones of affectation or, alternatively, sprightliness. A solitary example? Hardly. English teems with words that have behaved in almost parallel fashion.

The history of a particular word runs like a seam through the 'geological strata' of a national culture. Almost any word that has been in the English language since mediaeval times will have its own minute contribution to make to an understanding of any period of history since that time. C. S. Lewis has left us admirable accounts of several in his *Studies in Words*. I shall cite a single example: the history of the word *humour*. Mediaeval philosophers, psychologists and medical men, accustomed to treating body and soul together, found in their 'temperaments' neither an exclusive physical nor a psychic aspect. There were four cardinal humours' (blood, phlegm, choler and melancholy) whose relative proportions determined the individual mixture of physical and mental qualities and disposition in every man. With the arrival of Renaissance humanism in the late fifteenth century, 'humour' tended more and more to be used in an exclusively psychological sense, and the mental–physical cleavage had begun. The word still continued to be used to describe vapours (*the humour of a dark morning*) but not later than 1697. The only 'physical' sense to have survived to the present day is in the special biological usage: the *aqueous humour* of the eye. By the middle of the sixteenth century, 'humour' in ordinary parlance had an almost exclusively psychological usage: mood, temperament, frame of mind. The Elizabethans gave the word an extra twist in their orgy of human comedy; 'humour' now begins to mean a whimsical or capricious turn of mind, as indeed it does to this day. (*I wonder what kind of humour she is in today.*) The witty age of the Restoration, culminating in Pope's *Essay on Man*, brought the word to its final stage. A capricious temperament appears to this excessively sophisticated and detached age as an 'oddity', something provoking a smile and general amusement. By a unique metonymy, this finally gives way to the cult of oddity, or the 'faculty of perceiving what is ludicrous, or of expressing it'. And yet a 'sense of humour' does not convey solely the latter most prevalent and recent sense, but if you think about it you will find that it carries echoes of all the earlier meanings (strata)—even the mediaeval total meaning. A simple statement *he has no sense of humour* is capable of summing up a long slice of English culture. And, of course, it is sentences of just this kind that are so difficult or impossible to translate.

In his remarkable collected papers *Words and Sounds in English and French*, Orr has illuminated the perennial issue of the extent of the impact of French upon English. Although this impact has never been underrated, its nature was on the whole confined to the question of loan words. Orr has much convincing evidence that the impact went far beyond this into the deeper fabric of the English language where 'hidden strands of French modes of speech which affect not only its use of words but its very structure, and consequently condition in a measure the processes of our thoughts, and determine to some extent at least, our attitude of mind.'[1]

The merging of the English verb *fare* (Germ. *fahren* 'to travel') and French *faire* is analysed in great detail. The gist of the matter is that the Chaucerian English verb *fare* is something quite new, a hybridisation, in fact. It still contains a shade of 'travelling' or peregrination but has moved decidedly in the direction of 'behaving', 'acting' and—well—faring as in *How did he fare?* 'Ye fare as folk that drunken be of ale' (*The Wife of Bath*). The contagion has spread to the verb 'to do', which became a synonym of *fare* (*How is he doing?*). Expressions such as *much ado about nothing* would never have come into being without the marriage of English and French in the couple of centuries following the Norman Conquest.

The English language of 1350 is quite a new language, no merely renovated or enhanced. Orr gives numerous examples more than sufficient to drive home his thesis. His conclusion mus have given comparatists much food for thought: 'The fact that we and the French share to a peculiar degree a common linguistic tradition, the fact that in language, as in many other matters, law institutions, manners and outlook even, England is for the French something of a museum of national antiquities, the constant inter

[1] Orr, J., *Words and Sounds in English and French*, p. 28.

change, borrowing, and re-borrowing of words and ideas that has gone on for close on nine centuries between our two countries, all this has inevitably created similarities of mind processes, of methods of thought and presentation of ideas, that link us together in close spiritual affinity.' But, he asks, why are English and French attitudes so different from this common fund of thought and cultural experience? 'While we remain aloof and detached from our formulae, theories and abstractions—when we do not actually mistrust and disdain them—the French take theirs readily to themselves, live and thrive upon them, integrate them, so to speak, more fully into their being.' Linguistic conditions are, he suggests, possibly at the root of this dichotomy. For 200 years, things intellectual and spiritual were symbolised by re-mote, abstract, 'courtly' words, 'redolent of the school rather than the home', whereas the words of everyday usage, the Saxon ones, were closer to the hearts of the man-in-the-street. 'If there is one thing typical in our national psychology, it surely is this ready dissociation of theory from practice, of the abstractions of the mind from the facts of life. I believe that the reasons for this are in great part linguistic, and that the peculiar conditions of bilingualism we have been considering prevailed long enough for an attitude of mind not merely to be created but to become an ingrained habit and tradition and permanent characteristic of our kind.'[1]

A marked contrast with the kind of cultural influence just discussed occurs not where two cultures merge but where there is direct and sometimes literal translation from one language to the other. We have seen that the Anglo-Saxon translation of Roman Christian concepts was of this kind. A much more significant instance, historically, was the wholesale 'translation' of the con-cepts of Greek civilisation into the Latin of the Roman Empire. The dangers here are fairly obvious; distortion occurs at the boundaries, or, rather, in the no-man's land of peripheral contact between the two languages, and thus easily goes unnoticed, especially by the borrowers. The Greeks had an especially original culture, and its building bricks implied a background taken for granted by most citizens of the Greek states. This exclusive vocabulary of concepts led to endless theological diffi-culties in the earlier centuries of Christianity, and ultimately to

[1] Orr, *ibid.*, p. 42.

schism. Since the Renaissance wisdom has prevailed and no attempts were made by Western European scholars to translate Greek terminology, and it is no exaggeration that modern Europe could hardly dispense with it, to be deprived of words like *energy*, *analysis*, *ethics*, *physics*, *organic*, *method*, *theory*, *democracy*, *economic*, *politics*, *mathematical* would be like losing teeth.

Whenever the Romans borrowed a Greek idea they not only gave it a suitable Latin equivalent but, in so doing, imprinted it with the stamp of their own outlook. The Romans were practical men, soldiers, lawyers, technologists, interested (first and foremost) in externals. For Romans 'learning' was synonymous with 'learning to be a soldier'. Consequently, the Greek word *mathematics* from the verb *mathein* 'to learn, to learn by inquiry, to ascertain', and its congener *mathematikos* 'fond of learning, a mathematician', appears in Latin as *disciplina*. For the Greeks 'learning' was always accompanied by pleasure, and it is a pity that one of the few words the Romans took straight from Greek, the word *scola* (Gr. *scholē*), was twisted out of all recognition from its true meaning 'leisure'. How much less painful schooling might have been for generation upon generation of schoolchildren if only the concept schola-leisure had come down to us untainted from Greece. How unnecessary would have been Rousseau's *Emile*, Matthew Arnold's *Culture and Anarchy* and all their progeny of educational enlightenment down to our own day.

To move from one culture or civilisation to another involves a change of consciousness of a kind that puts one's powers of imagination to a severe test. In the economically developed and already developing modern world, the difficulties are obscured by growing convergence of thinking; terms such as *disarmament*, *democracy*, *power politics*, *mass media* translate with ease from one language to the next. Differences take on a sharp definition only when we turn to the more remote communities or to the historical past of our own cultures. To illustrate, I shall take an example remote both culturally and historically. Those readers who have any acquaintance with the Hindu scriptures in translation may have wondered at the sinuous prose and involved thought confronting them. It was only after I had discovered for myself the originals that it became obvious that Sanskrit and Vedic had sentences quite as simple as English, often of a beautiful and laconic simplicity. The stumbling-block was the *concepts*.

These were undoubtedly conceptual and semantic wholes for the scholars and poets of ancient India, but they make no sense to us unless translated by some cumbrous circumlocution, each of whose words point by virtue of their own associations in a hopeless confusion of directions. A Sanskrit-English dictionary offers for the most part only a bewildering array of multiple-meaning words. In at least a number of cases, these concepts are not the contrivances of the Sanskrit literary language but derive from the period of Indo-European when words bore what are to us irreconcilable meanings, e.g. *roka* = 'light' = 'open place' (related to Eng. *lea* and Latin *lucus* 'grove'). The root verb 'to be' in Sanskrit serves a baffling variety of purposes and derivations. *Bhuta*, grammatically a harmless past participle, offers the following profusion of meanings, an entire spectrum of semantic nuance: 'having become', 'existing', 'actually happened', 'being', 'creature', 'uncanny thing', 'fact', 'occurrence', 'element'. A related part of the same verb, this time a causative participle, covers a series of potentialities: 'effecting', 'producing', 'conceiving', 'determining', 'the power of concentration'. Turning to nouns, the complexity in no way diminishes. A commonly used noun *purusah* carries such meanings as 'man', 'person', 'highest personal principle', 'universal soul', 'supreme spirit'. Another concept *buddhi* runs the entire gamut of the vocabulary of European psychology: 'intelligence', 'reason', 'intellect', 'mind', 'wit', 'perception', 'opinion', 'feelings', 'intention', 'will'. The word itself derives from the verbal idea a 'being awake, awakening'. It is clear that sentences composed of bulk units such as these will not go easily into English or, for that matter, into any other modern European language.

Retreating to less unfamiliar territory, we could trace the interconnection of language and conceptional development in Western Europe through the Middle Ages, then through the Renaissance and the 'scientific revolution' of the early seventeenth century, and finally to modern times. Suffice it to say that comparative linguistics has as yet hardly broken through into this rich sphere.

In case the reader remains unconvinced, I suggest an attempt at 'translating' a passage of earlier English, say Elizabethan, into Modern English. An attempt of this kind will quickly show that translation involves a translation of modes of thought, and all this *despite* the fact that the passage we have chosen may be entirely comprehensible. The purpose of the exercise was not to enable us to understand the original fully (although more intimate and more accurate understanding is frequently its by-product) but to discover the unsuspected framework of expression, linguistic habit and attitude that separates us from the Elizabethans.

Half jokingly, I once suggested to a class (who had been whiling away their idle hours in exercises of the kind I have been describing) the task of translating a passage from George Orwell into Elizabethan prose. I did not expect any response, of course. But to my surprise one piece was produced. I am quoting from it because it well exemplifies the kind of conceptual tussle one is bound to enter into in an undertaking such as this:

Orwell:

Every kind of horror is blowing up over the horizon, but somehow it will all come out right in the end. This outlook is probably gaining ground among thinking people; it results from the very great difficulty, once one has abandoned orthodox religious belief, of accepting life on earth as inherently miserable and on the other hand, from the realisation that to make life liveable is a much bigger problem than it recently seemed. Since 1930 the world has given no reason for optimism whatever. Nothing is in sight except a welter of lies, hatred, cruelty and ignorance, and beyond our present troubles loom vaster ones which are only now entering into the European consciousness.

'Elizabethan' version:

Even though the clouds are big with all manner of evil, yet shall we have a happy issue. This mind, that doth increase, among thinkers of the weightier sort, cometh about inasmuch as it is hard, the old faith being cast off, to conceive that his mortal life is by its very nature inclining to melancholy, yet is it realised that to banish ill humours is vastly more difficult than it hath seemed ere now. Since 1534 there hath not been in the condition of the world any cause for sanguine expectation: we can nothing see save a naughty confusion of deceits and hatred, cruelty and ignorance, while beyond our present troubles loom vaster ones of which Christendom is only now becoming sensible.

The first reaction of the reader may be that the 'translation' seems somehow too naïve, disparaging the conceptual wealth of an age that produced giants. And yet, when you think about it, the contemporaries of Shakespeare would have found the entire quotation from Orwell, except for the first half of the last sentence, almost meaningless; for they just did not possess those very concepts on which the whole *point* of the passage rests. Neither *outlook* nor *optimism* had yet entered the English language; and the words *consciousness, orthodox, world, religious* and possibly others had well over a century to wait before they acquired the present-day meanings illustrated by their Orwell contexts.

By the way, this chapter, together with the rest of this book and, of course, many thousands of books on kindred or quite unrelated topics, could not have been written but for the conceptual vocabulary store built up in comparatively recent times and constantly being added to. To think and to exist in the way one does is to have access to a certain fund of concepts and cultural elements, which in turn derive from and depend upon language and words.

I should like to conclude this book with a personal view. At one time, I used to become impatient with the 'layman' who, with his cavalier disregard of the 'expert', comes up with totally 'unscientific' explanations as to how a particular usage came about, why people say this rather than that, why this language is more 'logical' or more easy to learn than another, why one language behaves like this and another language like that. But I now think that not only is the layman entitled to do as much of this kind of popular theorising as he likes but also that he positively *should* do so. In the twentieth century there is a danger of our linguistic blood running too thin. Gone are the linguistic orgies of the past, or even the memories of the romps of our own early schooldays. Instead, writers like Joyce, Pasternak, Quenaud and Grass have been doing our work for us. Few realise that people can make and remake languages in their own image. Languages can bubble with the exuberance of Rabelais or Tolkien, or they can take on a laconic look, like the prose of Cicero or Sartre; they can lapse into the commonplaces of today's popular press, or even wither in the pages of *Pravda* or in the lifeless prefabrications of bureaucrats and technocrats everywhere. In the long run, the kind of language we create, or let be, will become a direct reflection of the kind of people we were in our time.

APPENDICES

Suggestions for Further Reading

Language and Linguistics

The following are some of the recent and more comprehensive surveys of general linguistics:

Fries, C. C., *Linguistics: The Study of Language* (New York, 1964).

Gleason, H. A., *An Introduction to Descriptive Linguistics* (New York, 1955).

Lyons, J., *Theoretical Linguistics* (Cambridge, England, 1968).

Lyons, J. (ed.), *New Horizons in Linguistics* (London, 1970).

Martinet, A., *Elements of General Linguistics* (trans. E. Palmer) (London, 1964).

Malmberg, B., *Structural Linguistics and Human Communication* (1963).

A few of the recent but rather more specialised works on linguistics are:

Chomsky, N., *Aspects of the Theory of Syntax* (Cambridge, Mass., 1965).

Chomsky, N., *Selected Readings* (ed. J. P. B. Allen and P. Van Buren) (London, 1971).

Greenberg, J. H. (ed.), *Universals of Language* (Cambridge, Mass., 1963).

Jakobson, R., *Selected Writings, Volume II: Word and Language* (The Hague, 1971).

Malkiel, Y., *Essays on Linguistic Themes* (1968).

Ullmann, S., *Semantics: An Introduction to the Science of Meaning* (Oxford, 1962).

Earlier studies which have since become classics of modern linguistics, and all of which are reprinted, include:

Bloomfield, L., *Language* (London, 1969: paperback edition).

Firth, J. R., *The Tongues of Men*, and *Speech* (reprinted in paperback: London, 1966).

Jespersen, O., *Language: Its Nature, Development and Origin* (London, 1954).

Sapir, E., *Language* (London, 1949).

Saussure, F. de, *Course in General Linguistics* (trans. W. Baskin) (London, 1960).

Studies embracing language, culture, society, communication and psychology are very numerous, and of great variety. Here is a selection:

Boas, F., *Race, Language and Culture* (reprinted New York, 1966).

Bright, W. (ed.), *Sociolinguistics* (The Hague, 1966).

Cherry, C., *On Human Communication* (Cambridge, Mass., 1957).

Fishman, J. A. (ed.), *Readings in the Sociology of Language* (The Hague, 1968).

Haugen, E., *The Ecology of Language* (1972).

Henle, P. (ed.), *Language, Thought and Culture* (Ann Arbor, Michigan, 1965).

Hymes, D. (ed.), *Language in Culture and Society* (New York, 1966).

Jespersen, O., *Mankind, Nation and Individual* (London, 1946, but since reprinted).

Mandlebaum, D. G. (ed.), *Selected Writings of Edward Sapir* (Los Angeles, 1949).

Miller, G. A., *Language and Communication* (New York, 1951).

Smith, F., and Miller, G. A. (eds.), *The Genesis of Language: A Psycholinguistic Approach* (Cambridge, Mass., 1966).

Vygotsky, L. S., *Thought and Language* (trans. and ed. E. Hanfmann and G. Vakar) (Cambridge, Mass., 1962).

Whorf, B. L., *Language, Thought and Reality* (Cambridge, Mass., 1956).

Historical and Comparative Linguistics

Works of a more general nature on historical and comparative linguistics are still not too numerous in English. They include:

Hoenigswald, H. M., *Language Change and Linguistic Reconstruction* (London, 1960).

Lehmann, W. P., *Historical Linguistics: An Introduction* (New York, 1962).

Lehmann, W. P., and Malkiel, Y., *Directions for Historical Linguistics* (Austin, Texas, 1968).

Meillet, A., *Introduction à l'Etude Comparative des Langues* (reprinted, Paris, 1966).

Pedersen, H., *The Discovery of Language* (trans. J. W. Spargo) (Bloomington, Indiana, 1959).

Ross, A. S. C., *Etymology* (London, 1958).

Spitzer, L., *Essays in Historical Semantics* (New York, 1948).

Indo-European

Birnbaum, H., and Puhvel, J. (eds.), *Ancient Indo-European Dialects* (Berkeley and Los Angeles, 1966).

Cardona, G., Hoenigswald, H. M., and Senn, A. (eds.), *Indo-European and Indo-Europeans* (1971).

Meillet, A., *The Indo-European Dialects* (trans. S. W. Rosenberg) (1968).

None of these three works is too difficult for the general reader; and no extensive knowledge of the standard Indo-European (older) languages is required in order to derive benefit from them. For the student of comparative Indo-European linguistics they are essential companions. More specialised works relating to particular groups of languages are as follows:

Romance linguistics

Not many studies in Romance linguistics are available in English, though this situation is likely to be remedied with various forthcoming publications and reprints. The student of Romance languages will find the following useful:

Posner, R. R., *The Romance Languages: A Linguistic Introduction* (1966).

Menger, L. E., *The Anglo-Norman Dialect* (with illustrative texts) (New York, 1904; reprinted).

Pope, M. K., *From Latin to Modern French* (London, 1952).

Price, G., *The French Language: Past and Present* (London, 1971).

Migliorini, B., *The Italian Language* (1966).

Entwistle, W. J., *The Spanish Language together with Portuguese Catalan and Basque* (London , 1962).

Williams, E. B., *From Latin to Portuguese* (London, 1962).

A well-chosen selection of Romance mediaeval poetry is to be found in:

Brittain, F., *The Medieval Latin and Romance Lyric* (Cambridge, England, 1951).

English Linguistics

There is, not surprisingly, a fairly extensive literature in English on the historical aspects of the English language. The following is but a small selection:

Baugh, A. C., *History of the English Language* (London, 1951).

Clark, J. W., *Early English: An Introduction to Old and Middle English* (London, 1967).

Jespersen, O., *Growth and Structure of the English Language* (Oxford, 1960).

Peters, R. A., *A Linguistic History of English* (London, 1968).

Quirk, R., *The English Language and Images of Matter* (London, 1972).

Rigg, A. G., *The English Language: An Historical Reader* (London, 1968).

Wyld, H. C., *A History of Modern Colloquial English* (London 1956, recently reprinted).

Wright, J. and E. M., *Old English Grammar* (London, 1925).

Wright, J. and E. M., *An Elementary Middle English Grammar* (London, 1928).

Germanic Linguistics

Gothic:

Wright, J., *Grammar of the Gothic Language* (London, 1930). (Includes textual selections with helpful notes and a glossary.)

Scandinavian:

Walshe, M., O'C., *An Introduction to the Scandinavian Languages* (London, 1965).

Gordon, E. V., *An Introduction to Old Norse* (London, 1957). (Includes a wide selection of texts of moderate difficulty.)

German:

Priebsch, R., and Collinson, W. E., *The German Language* (London, 1958).

Chambers, W. W., and Wilkie, J. R., *A Short History of the German Language* (London, 1970).

Lockwood, W. B., *An Informal History of the German Language* (with chapters on Dutch and Afrikaans, Frisian and Yiddish) (1965).

Wright, J., *A Middle High German Primer* (London, 1917). (Includes texts, notes and a glossary.)

Other Indo-European Linguistics

Western European:

Wolff, P., *Western Languages, A.D. 100–1500* (trans. E. Partridge) (London, 1971).

Celtic:

Lewis, H., and Pedersen, H., *A Concise Comparative Celtic Grammar* (Gottingen, 1961).

Whatmough, J., *The Dialects of Ancient Gaul* (1970).

Latin:

Palmer, L. R., *The Latin Language* (London, 1954).

Grandgent, C. H., *Introduction to Vulgar Latin* (1934, recently reprinted).

Greek:

Thomson, G., *The Greek Language* (London, 1972).

Sanskrit:

Burrow, T., *The Sanskrit Language* (London, 1965).

Key to the Exercises

Exercise 1

(i) (a) (Skr.) *dh* = (Gr.) *th* = (O. Icel.) *ð* = (O. Slav.) *d* = (Ir.)
  d = (Eng.) *d* = (Lith.) *d* = (Arm.) *d*.
  (b) *dh*.
(ii) (a) (Skr.) *gh* = (Gr.) *kh* = (Goth.) *g* = (O. Slav.) *g* =
  (Alb.) *g*.
  (b) *gh*.
(iii) (a) (Skr.) *k* = (Lith.) *k* = (O. Slav.) *k* = (Gr.) *t* = (Lat.)
  k^w = (Ir.) $k^{(w)}$ = (Welsh) *p*.
  (b) k^w (*qu*).
(iv) *r* common to all as initial phoneme; therefore antecedent.
  (a) (Skr.) *th* = (Lat.) *t* = (Ir.) *th* = (Welsh) *d* = (O.H.G.)
  d = (Lith.) *t*.
  (b) *th*.

Exercise 2

(i) (Skr.) *j* = (Av.) *z* (satem) = (Lat.) *g* = (Ir.) *g* = (Gr.) *g*
  (centum).

  (I.-E.) *g* → (satem) (ʤ) ⟨ (Av.) *z*
                 (Skr.) *j*

(ii) (Skr.) *k* = (Lith.) *k* (satem) = (Ir.) *c* = (Welsh) *p* (centum).

  (I.-E.) k^w (⟨ (Welsh) *p* (by labialisation)
              (satem) *k*

(iii) (O. Slav.) *s* = (Skr.) *ś* (satem) = (Lat.) *c* = (Gr.) *k* =
  (Goth.) *h* (centum).

  (I.-E.) *k* ⟨ (Goth.) *h* (Germanic sound shift)
             (satem) *s* (Skr. *ś*)

(iv) (Skr.) *h* = (Arm.) *z* = (O. Slav.) *z* (satem) = (Lat.) *g* =
  (Gr.) *kh* = (Ir.) *g* = (Goth.) *g* (centum).

              ↗ (Gr.) *kh*
  (I.-E.) **gh* → (Goth. & Lat. & Ir.) *g*
          ↘ (satem) [ʤ] ⟨ (Skr.) *h*
                      (Slav. & Arm.) *z*

(v) (Skr.) *č* (satem) = (Gr.) $k^{(u)}$ = (Toch.) $k^{(u)}$ = (O.E.) *hw*
  (centum).

  (I.-E.) **k^w* ⟨ (Germanic) h^w
               (satem) **k* → (Skr.) *č*

Exercise 3

(1) (a) (*i*-mutation) /u/ → /y/ (influence of semi-vowel *j*).
   (b) (*i*-mutation) /u/ → /y/ (*i* (influence of *i*)).
   (c) (*i*-mutation) /ō/ → /ē/ (influence of *j*).
                 /o/ → /œ/ (influence of *j*).
   (d) (*i*-mutation) /ō/ → /ē/ (influence of *i*).
      (O.N.) /a/ → /e/ (influence of *i*).

(2) Original root vowel *a* appears only in the genitive sing. and pl.

In the nominative and accusative singular and in the accusative and dative plurals /a/ has become /o/ by process of *u*-mutation.

i-mutation is responsible for the front vowels *e* in the dative singular and nominative plural.

Exercise 4

(1) [kaːrum] = [tʃier] = [ʃɛːR] = [kaːro].
[sɛrtʃjer] = [səːtʃ] = [ʃɛRʃe] = [tʃerkaːre].
[mikils] = [mytʃel].
[skulds] = [ʃyldi(j)] = [ʃuldiɣ] = [ʃyldR].

Exercise 5

(1) *toile; aube; truit.*
(2) *seah; healdan; siex; lēoht; heorte.*
(3)

Goth.	O.N.	O.H.G.	O.E.
háitan	*heita*	*heiza*	*hātan*
ráuths	*rauthr*	*rot*	*rēad*
kiusan	*kjósa*	*kiosan*	*cēosan*
wáit	*veit*	*weiz*	*wāt*
-biudan	*bjōda*	*biotan*	*bēodan*

Exercise 6

(i) *waírthan; werdan.*
(ii) *tres; thri; thrir.*
(iii) *levian; līhan.*
(iv) *dens; tōth; zand.*

(v) *augere; åukan; auka.*
(vi) *bhrátar; brōthar;*
    brōthor; bruoder.

Exercise 7

(a) *b* in *cabra* represents an example of 'Western' Romance vocalisation. In French *chèvre* this vocalisation has proceeded one stage further.

(b) *Fada* as for (a). In French *fée* the Western Romance *d* has become completely vocalised and assimilated to the surrounding vowels.

(c) The V.L. *p* has become *b* in Western Romance dialects, the V.L. *c* having been entirely assimilated to the tonic vowel.

(d) O.E. *g* in *eage* pronounced as *yod* on account of palatalisation.

(e) Medial *g* assimilated to *w* through influence of back vowel.

(f) Final *g* [ɣ] assimilated to *yod* after *æ*, subsequently by analogical development also after *a*.

Exercise 8

(i) For *t* of *tessares*, see p. 190.
 F of *fidwor* by Germanic sound shift.
 Welsh *p* by labialisation of *kʷ*.
 Original stem vowel as in *keturi*; known through second palatalisation in the Sanskrit *čatvǎrah*, which occurs only before what were in pre-Sanskrit front vowels.

(ii) Initial *qu* in *quinque* due to assimilation at a distance (to the second *qu*).
 č in *panča*, and *k* in *penki* as a result of two-stage palatalisation of **qu*.
 Second *f* of *fimf* the result of assimilation to initial *f* (from I.-E. *p*).
 Second *p* of *pump* through labialisation of *qu*.

(iii) *i* of Eng. *thin* as the result of *i* -umlaut. Also *ü* of Mod. High Germanic *dünn*.

(iv) *eo* of *heorte* and *ja* of *hjarta* have arisen through vowel fracture (see pp. 174).
 Other consonant correspondences accounted for by Germanic sound shift.

(v) Transposition of /or/ to /ro/ in *fromage* is the result of metathesis.

Exercise 9

(1) (a)

	eu	*ou*	*u*
	kle(w)os	——	*klutos*
	——————*śrāusit* ————————		*śrutaḥ*
	——————*śuśrotha*————————		*-clutus*
	hliuma		
	hljóð		

(b)

	er	*or*	*ṛ*
	——————*bharvati* ————		*bhṛnati*
		phorkos	*pharō*
	ferīre	*forāmen*	
	bern		
	berja	*bardagi*	*bora*
			borian

(2) (a) III. (b) III. (c) III. (d) V. (e) II.

(3) e/zero: *pariman; filu; il.*
o/zero: *polus.*
zero/ē: *eplēto; aprāt; li; plēnus.*
zero/ō: *paprā.*
zero/zero (*pl̥): *purnáḥ; plunu; pilnas; fulls.*
            (*pl̥°): *piprati.*
            (*pºl): *puruḥ.*

INDEX

INDEX

ablaut (apophony, or vowel gradation), 205, 236, 243, 250, 253 ff.

accent, accentuation, 182 ff., 236, 243

affix, 227

affricate, 131

Afghan language, 51

African languages, 41–2, 217, 234–5

Afrikaans, 41–2, 48

agglutination, 55, 220, 227–8, 271

Ainu language, 47

Albanian language, 53

allophone, 135, 142, 147

Altaic languages (See under *Ural-Altaic*)

American Indian languages, 41, 45, 67, 209, 211, 292

analogy, 110, 112, 158, 222 ff., 265–6, 271, 280

Anglo-Norman, 76, 81

Anglo-Saxon (See under *English: Old English*)

anthropology, 91, 121

antonym, 301

aphasia (See under *language disturbances*)

Arabic, 30, 53–4, 97, 134, 215
  script (See under *writing*)

Aramaic, 54

Armenian language, 53, 255, 263–4

aspect, 51, 201, 215, 222

aspirate, aspiration, 156

assimilation, 147 ff., 186, 188

association, associative, 197, 304–6, 330–1

Australian aboriginal languages, 47

Balochi language, 51

Baltic languages, 50, 182–3, 196, 263

Balto-Slavonic, 50

Basque language, 45, 325

Bantu languages, 234–5

Bengali language, 51

bilingualism, 30, 37–9, 77

bilingual interference, 38, 142–3

biology (See under *language and biology*)

Breton language, 52

Brythonic, 78

Bulgarian language, 50–1

Cantonese, 58, 134, 205, 327

case, 216–18, 222, 230–1, 232–3, 236, 249, 266, 270–1

Catalan dialect, 26, 50

Caucasian languages, 46, 104

Celtic languages, 51–2, 78, 107, 140, 196

'centum' languages, 159 ff.

child language (See under *language*)

Chinese language, 26, 29, 42–3, 56–60, 91–2, 97, 99, 220, 237, 288, 303, 335

collocation, 309 ff.

communication (See under *language*)

comparative method, 111 ff.

compression, and shortening, 145–7

context, 277, 280, 286–7, 291, 301, 307
  of situation, 280, 284

convergence, 325–6

Cornish language, 52, 79–80

correspondence, 115, 152, 155–6, 160, 179

Cretan, 95, 102
cryptotypes, 209–11
culture (See under *language*)
Czech language, 50, 98–9

Danish language, 29, 48, 73
declension, 231–2, 245
denasalisation, 150
dentalisation, 190
diachrony, diachronic, 62–3, 202–3, 221, 244, 248, 264, 277, 303
dialect, 26 ff., 28, 31 ff., 40–1, 66, 77, 86–7, 130, 141, 238, 248, 264, 302, 305
  atlas, 34
  dialectal variation, 88
  dialectology, 34
  isogloss, 33–4, 36–7, 40
  local dialect, 32–3, 37
  switching, 88
diphthong, 131, 133, 178–9, 254–6
diphthongisation (See under *vowel fracture*)
dissimilation, 149
distinctive features, 136
Dravidian languages, 41–3, 60, 217
Dutch language, 42, 48

Ease theory, 140–1
Egyptian, Ancient, 54, 91, 288
English language, 26–7, 30–1, 38–9, 40–1, 47–8, 52, 65–7, 73–5, 77 ff., 97, 99–100, 121, 130, 133–4, 136–7, 140–1, 148, 150, 158, 169, 176, 183, 186, 188, 204, 210–11, 216, 218–19, 220, 225, 227, 230, 233–4, 237–8, 241, 246, 272, 280, 288, 296–7, 300–3, 315, 317, 318 ff., 326–7, 336
  Anglo-Norse, 80, 320
  American English, 328–9, 330

learned influence in English, 83 ff.
Middle English, 68, 76, 150, 166, 169, 171, 176, 202, 228–9, 233–4, 250, 326
Old English, 73, 76, 78, 81, 104, 112, 137, 165 ff., 172–4, 175–6, 177–8, 183, 186–8, 202, 230–2, 250, 257, 296, 318–19, 332
Shakespearian English, 73–4, 176–7, 297–8, 336, 343
synonyms in English, 85
epigraphy, 90, 92
ethnography (See under *language*)
Etruscan language, 45, 104
etymology, 156, 277, 305, 324, 332
  in English, 72, 81, 83–4
  popular, folk etymology, 68–9, 306, 323 ff.
euphemism, 313–14
Ewe language, 42
extralanguage, extralinguistic (See under *language*)

Finnish language, 43, 55, 327
Finno-Ugrian, 164, 218, 220, 327
Flemish language, 42, 48
flexional ending (See under *inflexion*)
'Franglais', 329
French language, 30, 40–2, 50, 63–4, 66, 76, 81–3, 98–9, 120, 133, 148–50, 157, 169–70, 187, 205, 216, 218, 221–2, 224, 226–7, 229–30, 238, 267, 269–72, 294–7, 303, 305–6, 308, 314, 318, 323, 325, 332, 338
  Middle French, 64, 76, 120
  Old French, 63–4, 76, 82, 120, 148–9, 171, 175–6, 227, 268, 270–1, 326

fricative, 129, 188, 190
Fukienese, Min, 58

Gaelic, Scots and Irish, 52, 264
Gallo-Romance, 175, 184
Gan (dialect of Chinese), 58
gender, 216–17, 222, 243, 245 ff.,
    249, 262, 265
German language, 30, 47, 76,
    133, 145, 149, 157, 231, 234,
    315, 324–5
  High German, 37, 48, 76, 173,
    180–1, 188, 229, 318
  Low German, 48, 76
  Old High German, 112, 178,
    257, 264
  Swiss German, 37, 48, 142
Germanic (languages), 48, 104,
    107, 112–13, 122, 137, 144–5,
    150, 164 ff., 169, 177 ff.,
    183–5, 187, 190–1, 215, 229–
    30, 244, 250, 257, 270,
    325–6, 327–8
  Proto-Germanic, 112–13, 164,
    174, 178, 185, 190, 257, 264
glottochronology, 121–2
Gothic language, 104, 112, 178,
    250, 257, 263
grammar, 110–11, 195 ff., 278,
    293
  and abstraction, 196–7
  'comparative grammar', 118,
    221, 236, 249
  descriptive grammar, 197, 199
  grammatical categories, 199–
    200, 215 ff.
  grammaticality, 198–9
  grammatical structure, 202 ff.
  limits of grammar, 197–9
  logic and grammar, 195–6
  transformational and genera-
    tive grammar, 123–4, 197,
    211 ff., 235
grammarians, normative and

    traditional, 61, 122, 196,
      200–2
    Latin grammarians, 106, 195–6,
      269
    Sanskrit grammarians, 61, 98,
      106, 182, 236, 237, 241, 253,
      256, 307, 326
graphology, graphemics, 98
'great vowel shift', 175, 177
Greek, Modern, 47, 52, 73
  Classical and Ancient, 52–3,
    73, 102–3, 106–7, 182–3,
    189–90, 215, 240, 249, 251–5,
    288 334–5, 340,
'Grimm's Law', 143
Gujarati, 51

Hakka (dialect of Chinese), 58
Hamitic languages, 41, 43, 53–4,
    325
Hausa language, 42
Hebrew language, 43, 53–4, 96,
    335
Hindi, 51, 135
Hittite language, 47, 91, 100, 102,
    115–16, 236, 238–9, 244–6,
    252
homonym, homonymic, 286, 299,
    303 ff.
homophone, 303, 305
Hopi language, 209
Hunanese, 58
Hungarian language, 43, 44–5,
    55–6, 149, 218, 325

Ibo language, 42
Icelandic language, 48
idiolect, 87
imitation, 69, 141–2
Indo-Aryan, 101
Indian, Indic languages and
    dialects, 37–8, 41, 51, 60, 66,
    101–2, 113
Indo-European, 41, 43, 47 ff.,

53–4, 66, 100–2, 105, 108, 113–16, 138, 143–4, 152 ff., 164, 182, 185, 190, 201, 215, 218–19, 222, 229, 236–9, 240–2, 244, 246–9, 251–4, 257–60, 262, 264, 333 ff.

Proto-Indo-European, 113, 115

Indo-Iranian, 51, 189, 255, 327

infix, 263

inflexion, 230 ff., 236–7, 253, 266, 272, 294

information, 207, 234

information theory, 231–2

interference (See under *bilingualism*)

International Phonetic Alphabet (IPA), 100, 128, 130

intervocalic, 186

irregularity in verbs, 224–5

Italian language, 29–30, 50, 148, 266–7, 270–1, 328

Japanese language, 41–2, 60, 95, 97, 116, 134, 217

jargon, 71–2

Korean language, 41–2

Kurdish language, 51

Kushitic, 53

labialisation, 189–90

labio-dental, 131

language
    and anthropology, 73
    area, 30
    behaviour, 89
    and bilingualism (See under *bilingualism*)
    and biology, 16
    boundaries, 30
    change, 73, 87–9, 115, 157–9, 202, 222
    child language, 67 ff., 223
    choice, 38

and communication, 17, 34, 234

contact, 76–7, 143

and culture, 18, 30, 40, 73, 313

definition of language, 15–16

disturbances, 282–3, 287, 289

diversity, 41 ff.

and ethnography, 31, 73, 118

extralanguage, extralinguistic, 38

families, 41 ff.

function, 22–3

history, 33, 65, 73, 292, 313

and languages, 25–6, 37, 40, 197, 262

literary language, 28, 30, 90, 97, 109, 196

loyalty, 79–80

nature of language, 15 ff., 21–2, 26, 226, 278, 281, 284, 289, 306–7, 309

and politics, 26–7, 30

and psychology, 118

and society, 17–18, 27, 30, 40, 67 ff., 73, 118, 313

and speech community (See under *speech community*)

spoken language, 121, 198, 273

standard, 25, 28, 31, 37, 77, 141, 199

and style (See under *stylistics*)

and thought, 281 ff.

universals, 197

Lapp language, 55

lateral articulation, 131

Latin, Classical Latin, 40, 50, 58, 64, 75, 77–8, 100, 107–8, 112–13, 148, 170–1, 182, 190, 195–6, 206, 209, 215, 222, 224, 226, 228–9, 246, 250–1, 253, 263, 265–6, 269, 271–2, 294, 315, 317, 331, 340

Latin (*contd.*)
Vulgar Latin, 50, 63, 112–13, 120, 170–1, 183–4, 265, 267–9, 271–2, 325
Lettish, 50
lexical set, 309 ff.
lexical borrowing, 324 ff.
lexicology, 201, 294
lexicostatistics, 121
lexis, 277
Libyco-Berber, 53
Linear B (See under *Writing*)
linguistic geography, 41 ff., 87
linguistic opposition, 200
linguistics, 117–20, 195, 200–1, 226, 278–9, 284
applied linguistics, 110
comparative linguistics, 61–2, 76, 106 ff., 121, 124, 137, 152, 195, 201, 215, 254, 305
descriptive linguistics, 61, 65, 120, 122–3
general linguistics, 61, 112, 117–18
historical, diachronic linguistics, 61–4, 67, 76, 86, 87, 90–1, 120–2, 124, 195, 201, 227, 235, 328
psycholinguistics, 119
quantitative linguistics, 121
sociolinguistics, 119
theoretical linguistics, 61–2, 112–13
Lithuanian language, 50, 183, 334

Macedonian dialect, 50
Malay language, 66
Malayo-Polynesian, 41, 43
Manchurian, 43, 55
Mandarin, 56–8
Manx, 52
marking, 232
Marathi, 51

meaning (See under *semantics*)
restriction and expansion of, 316–17
metaphor, 315 ff.
metathesis, 150
metonymy, 315–16
Mon-Khmer, 46
Mongolian language, 43, 55
morpheme, morphemic, 122, 204–5, 207, 221, 229, 231–2, 234, 237–8, 241, 272
morphology, 200–1, 219–20, 222, 228–9, 242, 244, 249, 254, 262
morphophonology, 234
Mycenae, 95, 239

nasal, nasalisation, 131, 133, 150
Neo-grammarians, 86, 90, 109, 111, 121, 140, 158, 228
Norse, 80–1, 83, 187
Old Norse, 112, 164, 166–8, 173–4, 178, 187, 250, 252, 257, 326
Norwegian language, 29, 48, 73

Old Saxon, 76
orthography, 99–100, 169–70, 178
Oscan, 104
Ostyak, 55

palatal articulation, 151
palatal glide, 172–3
'Palatal Law', 157, 160, 170
palatalisation, 151, 161–2, 170 ff., 187–8
Panjabi, 51
Papuan languages, 47, 68
paradigm, paradigmatic, 205–6, 219, 223–4, 229–30, 233, 235–6, 248–9, 250, 262
parallel development, 262 ff.

Persian (Modern), 41, 51, 102, 246, 325
  Middle Persian (Pahlavi), 102
  Old Persian and Avestan, 51, 101–2, 182
philology, 90, 106–9, 118, 324
phoneme, phonemic, 119, 134–6, 142, 147, 202, 232, 234
'phonetic laws', 112, 152, 157–9
phonetics, 31, 98–9, 102–3, 106, 127 ff., 135
  acoustic phonetics, 128, 133
  articulatory phonetics, 128–31
  auditory phonetics, 128
phonology, 111, 120, 128, 133 ff., 136, 147, 172, 180, 186, 221, 253, 294
  diachronic phonology, 68, 114, 137, 139, 148, 152 ff., 162, 164 ff., 172, 221–2, 226, 228
Pidgin, 66, 321–3
pitch, pitch accent, 182–3, 185
place-names, 80, 146, 148, 183
Polish language, 50–1, 133
polysemy, polysemantic, 299, 301–3
Portuguese language, 41–2, 50, 133, 270, 272
Prague School, 87, 119, 136
prefix, 207, 210, 226
pronunciation, 137–8, 148, 178
proto-language, 90, 114
Provençal language, 50, 76, 270–1
psychology (See under language and psycholinguistics)

Rajasthani, 51
reconstruction, 151 ff., 227, 250–1, 254
redundancy, 207
reduplication, 68, 241
register, 38, 300
Romance languages, 48–50, 71, 91, 103, 112–13, 139, 146, 148, 170–2, 183–4, 186–7, 215, 228, 234, 250, 264–7, 269, 271–3, 305, 315, 325–6
Romanian, 28, 50, 148, 266–7, 269, 271
Romansch, 28, 142
root, 122, 185, 205, 207, 237 ff., 247, 254, 260, 262, 269
Russian language, 29, 41–2, 43, 47, 50, 53, 73, 76, 201, 205, 215, 217

Samoyed, 55
Sanskrit, 30, 51, 61, 66, 98, 101, 107–9, 182–3, 185–6, 215, 236, 239, 241, 245, 247, 249–52, 255–6, 263, 308, 334, 340–1
'satem' languages, 159 ff.
Sardinian language, 170–1
Scandinavian languages (See also under separate languages), 182
secretion, 228–30
segment, segmentation, 122, 200, 234
semantics, 228, 230, 277 ff., 293–4, 295, 299 ff., 305
  comparative semantics, 334 ff.
  historical semantics, 315 ff.
  semantic borrowing, 302, 314, 328 ff.
  semantic change, 313, 332
  semantic content, 19
  semantic divergence, 303
  semantic field, 304 ff., 330 ff.
  semantic motivation, 295–6
semasiology, 277
Semitic languages, 41, 43, 53–4, 96, 215, 219–20
Semito-Hamitic, 41, 43, 53–4
semivowel, 131, 175, 186–7
Serbo-Croat, 50, 182

sign, linguistic; semiotics, semiology, 18–20, 232, 278, 282, 289, 305
signifier, signification, 19, 284–5
Sinhalese, 43, 51
Sino-Tibetan, 41–2, 56–60
slang, 70–1
Slavonic, Slavic, 29, 50–1, 103, 105, 107, 182–3, 196, 215, 255, 262, 264
   Old Slavonic, 73
Slovak, 50
Slovene, 50
sociology, sociolinguistics, 27, 87–8
sonant, 129–31, 240
sound change (See under *diachronic phonology*)
sound shift, 143
   Germanic, 143, 180–1
   palatal, 160–1
Spanish language, 26, 30, 41–2, 50, 149, 267, 271–2
speech communication, 18
   community, 28, 37, 76, 87, 309
   organs, 127, 129
stem, 249–50
stress, 183–4, 263, 270
structuralism, structural linguistics, 119–20, 122–3, 200, 278
stylistics, style, 38, 87
sub-standard, 199
substratum, substratum theory, 140
Sudanese-Guinean, 42–3
suffix, 207, 227, 229, 230, 236, 241, 242 ff., 246–8, 254, 257, 263, 271–2, 304
Swahili, 207–8
Swedish language, 48
synchrony, sychronic, 62–3, 65, 148, 172, 202–3, 210, 225, 234–5, 268, 272, 306, 326, 331

synonym, 85, 299–300, 301, 304
syntagm, syntagmatic, 205–6, 225, 230–1, 233–4, 295, 299
syntax, 200–1, 206 ff., 272, 295
   syntactic marker, 207, 291, 299

Tamil, 43
tense, 202, 215–16, 243, 251–3
Thai language, 42
'thematic', 247
Tibeto-Burman, 42, 56
Tokharian, 47, 115
tonality, tonal languages, 58–60
Turkish language, 53, 55–6, 207
typology, 121

Ukrainian, 26, 50
Umbrian, 104
umlaut, vowel mutation, 149, 164 ff., 223
Uralic languages, 55
Ural-Altaic, 41, 43, 55–6, 105, 149
Urdu, 51, 102

Vedic, 101, 182, 245, 262
velar articulation, 151
'Verner's Law', 157, 184–6
vocalisation, 149, 175, 186 ff.
voice (active, middle, passive), 252–3
voicing, 129, 186, 190
vowel, 95, 130–2, 135, 147, 175, 254
   alternation (See under *ablaut*)
   fracture, 174 ff.
   gradation, 254, 256–7, 263
   harmony, 55
   mutation (See under *umlaut*)

Welsh language, 52, 79–80, 103
White Russian (language), 50
word, 21, 277, 285, 288 ff., 304
   class, 219–20, 247, 283

word (*contd.*)
  compound word, 228
  function word, 208
  loan word, 39, 112, 171, 324 ff.
  order, 208–9, 220, 233, 269
  structure of the word, 222
writing, 90 ff., 121
  alphabetic, 95–6, 103

  ideographic, 93, 97
  pictographic, 92–3
  syllabic, 95
Wu (dialect of Chinese), 58

Yiddish, 80
Yoruba language, 42

'zero', 232, 248, 255, 257

TEACH YOURSELF BOOKS

GENERAL LINGUISTICS

Jean Aitchison

Designed to complement *Comparative Linguistics* in the Teach Yourself series, this book offers a lucid introduction to those approaching the fascinating field of linguistics for the first time. It outlines the scope and history of the discipline, explaining basic concepts and essential terminology with examples drawn mainly from English. Concise discussions of sound patterning, grammar and meaning—the bread and butter of linguistics— are followed by a guide to the means of analysing language and the ways in which languages change.

The book also includes an up-to-date survey of recent developments in this controversial and fast-expanding subject.

UNITED KINGDOM 50p
AUSTRALIA $1.50*
NEW ZEALAND $1.45

ISBN 0 340 12467 9   *recommended but not obligatory

Available wherever Teach Yourself Books are sold.

TEACH YOURSELF BOOKS

SEMANTICS

F. H. George

Semantics is concerned with the analysis of meaning in language. It remains a flourishing subject, for language often obscures facts rather than revealing them.

This general introduction is in ten individual chapters, each dealing with separate aspects of semantics. A certain amount of automony has been accorded to the topics dealt with: the chapters may be studied separately for the subject-matter they contain, while the complete set offers a self-explanatory description of semantics.

'The style of the book is readable; its expositions clear; and its information solid.'

Linguistics

UNITED KINGDOM 40p
AUSTRALIA $1.25*
NEW ZEALAND $1.10

ISBN 0 340 05714 9   *recommended but not obligatory

Available wherever Teach Yourself Books are sold.